THEATER: THEORY/TEXT/PERFORMANCE

Series Editors: David Krasner, Rebecca Schneider, and Harvey Young

Founding Editor: Enoch Brater

MOVING ISLANDS

Moving Islands

CONTEMPORARY PERFORMANCE

AND THE GLOBAL PACIFIC

Diana Looser

UNIVERSITY OF MICHIGAN PRESS

Ann Arbor

Copyright © 2021 by Diana Looser
All rights reserved

For questions or permissions, please contact um.press.perms@umich.edu

Published in the United States of America by the
University of Michigan Press
Manufactured in the United States of America
Printed on acid-free paper
First published September 2021

A CIP catalog record for this book is available from the British Library.

Library of Congress Cataloging-in-Publication data has been applied for.

ISBN 978-0-472-13238-6 (hardcover: alk. paper)
ISBN 978-0-472-12860-0 (e-book)

Contents

Digital materials related to this title can be found on the Fulcrum platform
via the following citable URL: https://doi.org/10.3998/mpub.11522475

Acknowledgments

I owe a deep debt of gratitude to a large number of people who have guided and supported me during the many years it has taken to produce this book. I'd like to extend a special acknowledgment to Elizabeth DeLoughrey, who has been an inspiring example and encouragement since I was her graduate student, and her influence runs through this volume. In Australia, where I began this project, I thank my dear colleagues at The University of Queensland, Joanne Tompkins and Stephen Carleton, for their sage advice, generative dialogues, and valued friendship. Kathryn Kelly's research assistance was invaluable, and I feel very fortunate to have been part of the UQ Drama community. I remain grateful to Gay Hawkins and Graeme Turner for the semester's fellowship at the university's Centre for Critical and Cultural Studies, which provided vital time and space for foundational thinking about this project.

The book changed markedly in the course of its own transpacific journey from Brisbane to California. Deepest appreciation to Harry J. Elam, Jr. for his wise mentorship, and for patiently reading my writing and encouraging me to persevere. Thank you to my academic and administrative colleagues in the Stanford TAPS Department, especially Chairs Branislav Jakovljević and Matthew Smith for creating a cordial and supportive environment for my work. I benefited greatly from Rebecca Wingfield's expert library skills, and from the help of staff at Green Library Special Collections and the David Rumsey Map Center. It's been my privilege to work with a stellar group of graduate student research assistants: my sincere gratitude to Matt Stone, Thao Nguyen, and Doug Eacho; to Suhaila Meera for helping to format the manuscript; and to Anna Kimmel for her wonderful work on the index.

I have been honored to be part of an incredible network of scholars and interlocutors from Oceania and around the world who have helped to guide and shape this work over the past decade. Our conversations in archives, at theaters and galleries, and at festivals, invited lectures, conferences and symposia (and, more recently, online), have been instrumental in developing the book's content, structure, and arguments. Kia ora to Sharon Mazer for putting me up and putting up with me; and special recognition to David O'Donnell, Tammy Haili'ōpua Baker, Charlotte McIvor, and Chantal Adam-Blosse. Particular thanks are due to Helen Gilbert and Margaret Werry for their responses to and suggestions for the manuscript that sharpened my thinking; to Ric Knowles for his judicious counsel; and to Caroline Sinavaiana Gabbard for corresponding about the chapter on transnational Samoa. A warm thank you to Katerina Teaiwa for her kind permission to reproduce Teresia Teaiwa's poem "AmneSia." At the University of Michigan Press, I salute the incomparable LeAnn Fields for believing in this project and helping to bring it into being. I also want to acknowledge Melissa Scholke, Flannery Wise and the editorial, design, and marketing teams for their admirable efforts in producing the volume, especially during the challenges of the pandemic.

My most heartfelt thanks to the many artists and activists, woven throughout this book, who so generously spoke with me about their work, supplied images, and often took the time to comment on my drafts. I'm constantly inspired by your creative energies and by the performing bodies in motion that unfold beautifully and urgently across the moving islands of Oceania, and I hope that this book, in some way, gives something back. Aroha nui to Mum, and to my beloved fellow travelers Andrei and Sam (and, of course, Toby). Words really can't do justice to what you mean to me.

Earlier, partial versions of some chapters were previously published as journal articles. Initial parts of chapter 2 appeared as "Oceanic Imaginaries and Waterworlds: *Vaka Moana* on the Sea and Stage," *Theatre Journal*, special issue on "Trans-Indigenous Performance," 67, no. 3 (October 2015): 465–86, reproduced here with permission of *Theatre Journal*. An earlier section of chapter 3 appeared as "Symbolic Vaka, Sustainable Futures: Climate-Induced Migration and Oceanic Performance," *Performance Research*, special issue "On/At Sea," 21, no. 2 (April 2016): 46–49. Reprinted by permission of the publisher, Taylor & Francis Ltd, http://www.tandfonline.com. The anchor essay for chapter 4 was published as "Moving Islands: Mapping the Samoan Diaspora in Contemporary Transnational Theatre from the South Pacific," *Contemporary Theatre Review*, special issue "South," 22, no. 4 (November 2012): 451–66. Reprinted by permission of the publisher, Taylor & Francis Ltd, http://www.tandfonline.com. The research protocols for this project were approved by The University of Queensland Ethics Review Board and the Stanford University Institutional Review Board.

An island always pleases my imagination, even the smallest,
as a small continent and integral portion of the globe.
 —Henry David Thoreau

The Mediterranean is the ocean of the past, the Atlantic the
ocean of the present, and the Pacific the ocean of the future.
 —John Hay, US secretary of state, 1898

it's easy to forget
that there's life and love and learning
between
asia and america
between
asia and america
there's an ocean
and in this ocean
the stepping stones
are
getting real
 —Teresia Teaiwa, "AmneSia"

on my journey through the remainder of the chapter. I start with the challenge of adumbrating the geocultural parameters of the Pacific commons and interrogate the ways that the Pacific has been represented and produced, analyzing the disciplinary legacies that have precluded more holistic understandings of the region (with corollaries for theater and performance studies). I explore what critical paradigms might help us to look differently at the networked aspects of the Pacific, and what new paradigms might be needed. The chapter then develops these implications for performance, advancing transpasifika as a mediating paradigm to elucidate the intercultural performances I treat, and outlines a method of "constellated reading" for organizing the case studies in the chapters.

CARTOGRAPHIC IMAGINARIES: PICTURING THE PACIFIC

Looking at performance from the Pacific requires different paradigms from those commonly used to comprehend the Atlantic world. Inspired by Paul Gilroy's foundational suggestion that "cultural historians could take the Atlantic as one single, complex unit of analysis in their discussions of the modern world and use it to produce an explicitly transnational and intercultural perspective,"[11] Joseph Roach's landmark study *Cities of the Dead* introduces the concept of "circum-Atlantic performance" to describe the intercultural circulation of performance traditions of the Atlantic Rim arising from the triangulated economic relationship of slave labor, raw materials, and manufactured goods that brought Africans, Native Americans (North and South), and Europeans into correlation.[12] While circum-Atlantic linkages (or the more comparative, international transatlantic analyses that circum-Atlantic relationships enable) are certainly not the only models for tracking Atlantic movements,[13] this dominant commercial circuit undergirds Roach's genealogy of performance-as-surrogation, providing a cohering logic that enables him to refer to "the Atlantic system," "the circum-Atlantic vortex," and "the Atlantic interculture"[14] as comprising a distinct and unitary oceanic formation, albeit one linking many varied identifications and representations. Hence, Roach can claim that beyond his particular case studies (a braided confluence of diachronic cultural transmissions and replications coursing through the entrepôts of London and New Orleans from the seventeenth to the late twentieth centuries), "another body of evidence, drawn from different sites or from the same sites at different times, would have yielded other priorities—very different ones, perhaps, but I suspect not wholly different."[15] This is because, he argues, of certain recurring, characteristic patterns created by that macrostructure, whereby "the mutually interdependent performances of circum-Atlantic memory remain visible, audible, and kinesthetically palpable to those who walk in the cities along its historic rim."[16]

The Pacific defies this kind of organization. Its magnitude and its complex, indeterminate borders mean that the region is far more difficult to conceptualize than the Atlantic, which is one of the reasons it remains undertheorized in comparison.[17] The Pacific's meshwork produces it as the world's largest oceanic interculture with a distinctive sphere of regional interaction. Although studies of seaways or maritime activities in the Pacific have revealed some sense of circuitry,[18] unlike the Atlantic, the Pacific lacks the systematic linking of its subzones into a single scheme that would make an overarching "circum-Pacific" paradigm meaningful;[19] nor does it feature the deep integration of the Mediterranean world, nor, indeed, the density of long-established communications between the port cities and emporia of the Indian Ocean zone.[20] Rob Wilson and Arif Dirlik acknowledge the definitional problems posed by the Pacific region's "deterritorializing power of oceanic vastness" whose "circumference is everywhere and center nowhere."[21] As large as both the Atlantic and Indian Oceans together and larger than all of the planet's landmasses combined, the Pacific confronts us with a scale "of a different order than that of any other global division,"[22] whereby conventional notions of regional coherence begin to splinter. The sheer immensity and heterogeneity of the area, its discursive and spatial uncontainability, and the multitude of competing, overlapping, and contradictory classifications means that this fecund space of crossings forever threatens to spill into other domains, thwarting objective delineation. Dirlik rightly discerns that "the Pacific is as much a realm of fragmentation as of unity, which therefore deprives any effort to describe it with the narrative unity that might lend a guise of comprehensiveness to an otherwise diffuse subject."[23] Inevitably, we must wrestle with the fact that common chorographic descriptions—"Pacific Ocean," "Pacific Basin," "Pacific Islands," "Pacific Rim," "South Pacific," "Asia Pacific," or "Oceania"—are not stable geographical realities but imposed ideational constructs that operate as "part of the very struggle over the Pacific they seek to describe."[24]

Part of what stymies efforts to imagine the Pacific as a coherent ecumene is the apparent dichotomy between the islands that populate the vast ocean and the continental peripheries of Australia, Asia, and the Americas. The archipelagoes constitute the Pacific's unique geography as the planet's truly oceanic environment, yet the vast area of sea relative to land has long generated assumptions about its ostensible emptiness. R. Gerard Ward summarizes this top-down viewpoint:

> From the communications satellite in geostationary orbit over the Equator at 149°W, almost the whole visible surface of the globe is water. Apart from eastern Australia, New Zealand, Central America and a strip of the USA, the Pacific Ocean fills the hemisphere. From Los Angeles to Sydney is 12 000 kilometres; from Tokyo to Valparaiso 17 000. There are scattered islands, mostly in the south-west quadrant, but their total [land] area is tiny. The impression is of an earth empty of land and people.[25]

As Hawaiian scholar Amy Kuʻuleialoha Stillman has observed, these extremes of immensity and smallness in the Pacific resist scaled mapping altogether: "The islands in the ocean are so miniscule that the dots representing most are already greater in scale than the actual landmasses."[26] From the moment that Iberian explorer Ferdinand de Magellan completed European knowledge of the globe's circumference and inaugurated "the Pacific" as a named feature with his lonely and violent transit from Cape Horn to Guam in 1520–21 — sighting only one coral atoll along the way[27] — the Eurocentric concept of the Pacific Ocean as a deserted expanse to traverse was consecrated, and the ocean has been strategically "emptied" for various political, economic, and military purposes ever since.[28]

Known by its Indigenous peoples by many names, the Pacific Ocean is a rich matrix of social habitation. Some of these names are expansive and encompass an oceanic imaginary that stretches far beyond one's respective islands, such as the New Zealand Māori appellations *Te Moananui-a-Kiwa* (the great ocean of Kiwa, the ancestral navigator) and the domain of Tangaroa (the sea deity); or for ʻŌiwi Hawaiʻi (Native Hawaiians), *kai Pōpolohua mea a Kāne* (the purplish-blue, reddish-brown sea of Kāne [principal deity]), or *Moanaākea* (the broad, wide, full, large ocean).[29] At the same time, as Māori scholar Alice Te Punga Somerville reminds us, there are "as many oceans as there are languages here,"[30] indicating over twelve hundred overlapping oceans in simultaneous occupation.[31] The twenty-five thousand islands ranging across twenty-six countries and territories represent some of the world's most intense linguistic and cultural diversity, as well as a dizzying patchwork of economic and political statuses.[32] The geospatial reach of the zone encompassed since the nineteenth century by Polynesia, Melanesia, and Micronesia[33] — extending over one-quarter of the earth's surface from Hawai'i to Aotearoa New Zealand, Palau to Rapa Nui (Easter Island)—would, if transposed onto northern coordinates, traverse an area stretching from London to Johannesburg, Boston to Beijing. Martin W. Lewis notes, however, that in other oceanic intercultures such as the Mediterranean and Atlantic worlds,[34] islands are crucial, even emblematic elements of the larger system, and thus there is little disjunction between studies of the ocean and the rim. In the Pacific, conversely, "The disconnection between the Oceanic island realm . . . and the perimeter is profound" to the extent that "the oceanic archipelagoes and the rimlands of the Pacific Ocean often seem to form separate regional worlds."[35] While, as I shall show, this division derives from a repertoire of inherited disciplinary assumptions that legitimate certain topics and geographies while subjugating others, it is nevertheless the case that this prevailing view pervades approaches to the study of the Pacific; hence, discussions tend to focus on islands or continents but rarely both.

This contemporary view can be attributed in no small measure to World War II–era and Cold War–era regional thinking that has persisted or reemerged in new formulas long after the putative breakdown of those structures. The modern idea of the "South Pacific" was a European artifact, a postwar project motivated by Cold War concerns that attempted to draw regional boundaries to protect the interests of dominant colonial powers in the islands. Invested as a formal region at the South Seas Conference in Canberra, Australia, in 1947, the "South Pacific" experiment aimed to create a regional identity among the emergent Indigenous elite in territories stretching from Dutch New Guinea (the Papua region of Indonesia) to Tahiti. In 1951, the parameters were redrawn to include the Micronesian islands north of the equator, although the name remained the same until eventually becoming the "Pacific Islands" region.[36] According to Greg Fry, whereas these origins of postcolonial regional identity might be understood to have sown the seeds of Indigenous self-determination and presaged the era of decolonization that began in the 1960s, the scheme can also be read as a gambit to use regional trusteeship to maintain empire in the face of anticolonial impulses among the postwar international community,[37] and to prohibit possible links to "Asiatic Communism"[38] by keeping native leaders focused toward a Western political and social style.[39] This Euro-American domination has had a lasting impact on Pacific Islanders' perceptions of Asia and Asians, delimiting Pacific peoples' opportunities, in African American and i-Kiribati scholar Teresia Teaiwa's words, to "make their own independent assessments of the Asian presence in their region."[40] Furthermore, the tension between ideas of self-determination and control has continued to underlie attitudes toward Pacific Islands regionalism, especially in relation to the southern hemispheric neocolonial powers of Australia and New Zealand, which emerged with independent leadership aspirations in this period[41] and which remain dominant today.

As Teaiwa's comment suggests, attempts to regionalize the Pacific on Western terms submerge the long history of East Asian, Southeast Asian, and South Asian migration and settlement in Oceania, which in several places is more prevalent than the European presence. Asia's influence in the Pacific has been on the rise since the 1970s, a period of Asian economic expansion and confidence that coincided with the decolonizing of many South Pacific nations. Asian countries (especially China, Taiwan, and Japan) have used an outflow of investment in Pacific countries as a way of gaining access to commodities such as minerals, fishing rights, and other natural resources, while for many independent island states, Asian investors represent an alternative to traditional—and more demanding— Western aid partners.[42] Consequently, these demographic, political, and financial entanglements might be understood, from one perspective, to break down island-rimland dichotomies.

Yet, from another point of view, the burgeoning capitalist rise of Asian economies and the development of the Asia-Pacific ideal of financial co-prosperity between neighboring rim nations has in fact further entrenched the cartographic division between "basin" and "rim." This scheme, driven by the United States' commercial ambitions, largely depends on collapsing the ocean into *aqua nullius*—compressing, ignoring, or exploiting it in thrall to integrated economic continental powerhouses with an attendant focus on macro-level relations that evacuate attention to local specificities. Liz DeLoughrey explains that this strategy, an extension of US frontier expansionism, was abetted by US naval militarization during and after World War II. In the wake of America's territorial acquisition of the Micronesian islands from Japan, the National Research Council's Pacific Science Board partitioned its islands into isolates, eliding the complexities of regional exchange to overlay a US network of military bases and administrative controls and to facilitate an aggressive nuclear weapons testing program.[43]

Initially, the "Pacific Rim" idea of the late twentieth century was predicated on the post–Cold War decentering of Euro-American dominance in the region, following the emergence of Japan, and later Taiwan, Singapore, and South Korea as global powers, along with the collapse of the Soviet Union between 1989 and 1991, which unhinged the bipolar superpower grid that had justified the US military presence in the region.[44] Triumphant about these new challenges to US economic and political power, cultural critics of the mid-1990s could look back on former US president Ronald Reagan's 1984 prophecy that "the Pacific is where the future of the world lies"[45] and write optimistically that its teleological assumptions of Euro-American progress, global hegemony, and capitalist integration were "breaking down from multiple directions."[46] Notably, however, the era's prognostications of a more multilateral "Pacific Century" were stridently rearticulated in the 2010s as "America's Pacific Century," following then US secretary of state Hillary Clinton's 2011 *Foreign Policy* article.[47] Translated into official policy by the Obama administration in 2012, Clinton's essay identified the crux of the United States' diplomatic efforts in the turn to the Asia-Pacific, expanding and overtaking from the web of transatlantic institutions and relationships that had characterized America's post–World War II commitments. Responding to the perceived threat to American influence posed by newly ascendant Pacific nations like China, Clinton recast the United States once again as "a Pacific power,"[48] whose future over the next ten to sixty years would be "intimately intertwined"[49] with the region and would encourage regional consistency with American interests and values.[50] Clinton's neo–Cold War Pacific overtures located America's manifest destiny in harnessing the free flow of trade with a growing and dynamic Asia, subtended by a reinforced military infrastructure demanding increased US operational access across the region.[51]

These midcentury paradigms also continue to influence the way we render these geographical areas comprehensible as disciplinary objects of study, with direct relevance to theater and performance studies. It is widely known that the world regional framework that formed the basis of postwar "area studies" employed in American government departments and universities stems from the United States' entry into World War II and the work of the Ethnogeographic Board, an intellectual mobilization geared toward foreign landscapes that could be studied for their strategic purpose and value.[52] Yet, surprisingly, as Martin W. Lewis and Kären Wigen point out, "despite the prominence of Oceania in the global conceptualization of the old Ethnogeographic Board" and indeed, the vast upsurge of scientific interest in and research on the Pacific Islands during the Cold War decades, once the area studies complex was institutionalized in the American academy under the aegis of the federal government and the Social Science Research Council in the 1950s, "The islands of the Pacific did not appear on the map of area studies at all."[53] Even after the much-touted contemporary "crisis" in area studies due to global modernities, increased transnational and migration flows, new geopolitical formations, and Indigenous culturalisms that destabilize the epistemic foundations of US globalization,[54] this world regional grid—comprising North America, Russia and Eastern Europe, East Asia, Southeast Asia, South Asia, the Middle East, Western Europe, Africa, and Latin America—continues to hold considerable sway in the academy and has acquired a life of its own far beyond American institutions.[55]

There are, in fact, various Pacific (Island/er) studies discourses that have developed since World War II and that have produced important and groundbreaking work, but as Teaiwa avers, such scholarship remains "small-fry" in the global scheme of area studies and interdisciplinary projects,[56] and is conceived of and practiced rather loosely, with no disciplinary or methodological consistency.[57] For its part, Chamorro scholar Keith Camacho observes, the tendency for Pacific Islands studies to focus almost exclusively on peoples and islands *in* the Pacific is one reason why it has failed to materialize in the continental United States.[58] Similarly, the propensity for Indigenous decolonization movements in the American Pacific to portray the challenge of US imperial and military formations as "solely island-centric, but not as relational or transnational in scope, has thus resulted in a literature that avows U.S. empire in the Pacific only to disavow it on the continent,"[59] exacerbating the lack of Pacific Islands research, resources, and narratives of sovereignty in the US academy already produced by strategic erasure and national amnesia.

These inherited models have had a profound influence on the way that theater and performance studies conceptualize global performance. Whereas scholars in various academic fields (including our own) have invoked island spaces in order to trouble and intervene in existing area studies, in our discipline this move has yet to gain traction in regard to the Pacific beyond the insights of individual authors. Likewise, the very welcome transnational turn in theatre and performance scholarship has not yet translated into a revision of scholarly practices as far as Oceania is concerned. Although the Pacific has certainly been imagined in different ways, it is one of my contentions that a primary reason why international scholars in our field typically *don't* think about the island Pacific as a space of knowledge or academic inquiry—why material from the region is so frequently excluded from curricula and textbooks, why we so rarely hear from Pacific scholars at our conferences, and why the few published studies of its performance are so often seen as stand-alone contributions is not because of lack of output, lack of quality or analytical richness, or even—in this age of digital streaming, social media, and online purchasing—lack of documentary access, but because of this flaw of taxonomic logic that places Oceania "off the map" and beyond intellectual and pedagogical regimes of intelligibility. This lacuna, moreover, is not ideologically neutral but has demonstrable bases in (predominantly) US strategic military and economic interests that profit from an "empty" Pacific. Even though my project does not seek to reify a Pacific area studies paradigm but rather to complicate one, it is hard to challenge a scheme when it is not visible in the first place. It is not difficult to see this world regional structure replicated in major reference books such as Oscar G. Brockett and Franklin J. Hildy's *History of the Theatre*, popularly tagged "the 'bible' of theatre history,"[60] in which the absent Pacific Islands are relegated to apocryphal status; similar priorities are interwoven into less conventional but equally authoritative publications like Bruce McConachie et al.'s *Theatre Histories*, and at other times authors get around the problem of global coverage by subsuming Oceania into Asian performance.[61] This problem also holds true for performance studies; despite the broad geographical horizon that characterized its approach from the beginning (and that positively invigorated theater studies),[62] recurrent debates about performance studies' internationalization and related anxieties over its hegemonic reach have largely sidestepped consideration of this regional framework and its implications for knowledge production.

So axiomatic is this model that it even recurs in studies that deliberately set out to reconfigure the geographical foundations of Eurocentric assumptions about world performance. In his 2011 *Theatre Survey* article, "Conceptualizing Space: The Geographic Dimension of World Theatre," Steve Tillis laments the tired reliance on the continent and the nation as basic units for theatrical analysis.[63] Arguing for more sophisticated geographic concepts adequate for interpreting the density and variety of theatrical traditions in different parts of the world, Tillis proposes a series of "theatrically organized world regions"[64] that would open up possibilities for overwriting prevailing geopolitical and colonial boundaries to highlight mobile artistic and cultural relationships that are latticed, multisited, and multidirectional. Tillis's categories and his single map of "contemporary world theatre regions" has been praised (and the map reproduced) as one of theater studies' foremost critical responses to its conventional, Western-influenced use of mapping.[65] It is striking, therefore, how dependent he remains on the cartography of Cold War area studies. Tillis's map has obvious similarities with Lewis and Wigen's earlier "heuristic world regionalization scheme," which likewise attempts to refine the geographic determinism of world regions with a more processual and relational conceptual approach. Even so, the authors admit that "in its contours, this map does not differ dramatically from the standard depiction of world regions already employed in geography and other disciplines; with a few important quali- fications, we endorse the global architecture that has emerged within the North American academic world."[66] Thus, whatever else one might make of Tillis's scheme vis-à-vis other parts of the globe, of relevance here is how these prior templates prevent him from apprehending the Pacific Ocean world as a performative space.

Despite Tillis's appeal to scholars to examine water-based connections as an alternative to the land-based bias in many theatrical studies,[67] the Pacific is here treated as a convenient vacancy. In fact, it is almost impossi- ble to visualize the area because the map repeats and reinforces Eurocentric cartography by bisecting the Pacific Ocean so that it forms a marginal frame for a centralized Europe and its surrounding continents, becoming so huge it disappears (when I show people this map, they tend to feel sorry for Greenland). New Zealand is annexed to Australia due to its "neo-European" features, but this partial view does not suggest how Indigenous Māori the- ater might have greater historical, formal, and collaborative commonalities with theater and performance in other parts of Polynesia (not shown here) than with Australian Aboriginal performance forms, nor does it register the city of Auckland as one of the world's foremost Pasifika theater centers. "Melanesia" appears as a bounded entity, but its wider cultural and theat- rical links to other parts of the Pacific, to Australian South Sea Islander com- munities, to Torres Strait Islanders, or to Fiji as a vital regional nexus are unclear. How might one account for Hawai'i, which is not marked (not even, if problematically, as part of North America), yet is a potent and mul- tivalent node for localized Asian, Pacific, and neo-European cultural pro- duction? How does one map Samoan theater, which is one of the most prominent components of Pasifika performance, and yet is produced mostly in off-island locales? These challenges are not designed to nitpick at this one scholar's model, but to draw attention to an omission that is typical of the field more broadly. Indeed, it is *precisely because* this oversight occurs within a thoughtful, revisionist study dedicated to displacing a Eurocentric purview that its redress seems particularly urgent to me.

REORIENTATIONS: OR, LOOKING OUT THIS WAY

By way of a reorientation, I'd like to turn to a different cartographic perfor- mance, one that sought to instantiate an articulated transpacific imaginary on the cusp of World War II, and that foregrounds the role of Latin Ameri-

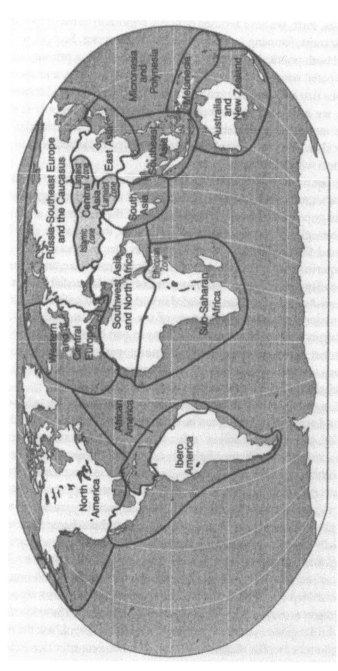

Map 1. "A heuristic world regionalization scheme." In contrast to earlier world regions schemes, the map acknowledges the presence of the Pacific, but its orientation obscures an integrated view of the Pacific world. Note the inclusion of "Melanesia," but also the lumping together of "Micronesia" and "Polynesia" off to the right (with Polynesia placed inaccurately). From Martin W. Lewis and Kären Wigen, *The Myth of Continents: A Critique of Metageography* (Berkeley: University of California Press, 1997), 187. Reproduced with permission of the University of California Press.

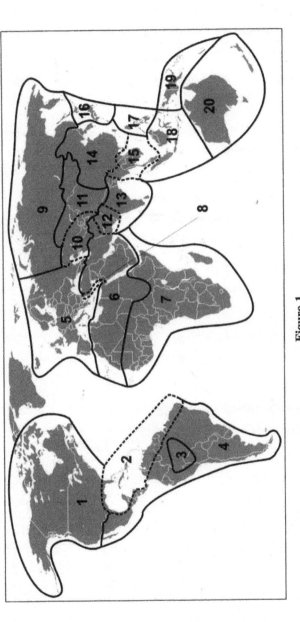

Figure 1.

Contemporary world theatre regions. Boundaries between the regions of world theatre are shown as solid lines. Where regions are contiguous, the boundaries should understood as *border zones* where the influences of the adjoining regions can be found. *Border regions* are demarcated by dashed lines. My suggestions for the regions and border regions of contemporary world theatre are as follows: (1) North American Region (neo-Europe); (2) African–American Border Region; (3) Ibero-American Region (neo-Europe); (4) Indigenous Ibero-American Region; (5) European Region; (6) Southwest Asian–North African Region; (7) Sub-Saharan African Region; (8) Eastern Mediterranean Border Zone; (9) Northeast Russian Region (neo-Europe); (10) Euro–Central Asian Border Zone; (11) Central Asian Region; (12) North Indian Border Region; (13) South Asian Region; (14) East Asian Region; (15) Continental Southeast Asian Border Region; (16) Japanese Region; (17) Philippine Region; (18) Insular Southeast Asian Region; (19) Melanesian Region; (20) Oceanian (Australia–New Zealand) Region (neo-Europe).

Map 2. Steve Tillis, map of "Contemporary world theatre regions." Figure 1 in his article "Conceptualizing Space: The Geographic Dimension of World Theatre," *Theatre Survey* 52, no. 2 (November 2011): 310. Reproduced courtesy of Cambridge University Press.

can artists and intellectuals in conceptualizing an interconnected Pacific world in the context of expanding US interests. In 1938, as Adolf Hitler was ramping up the German offensive in Europe with the annexation of Austria and the planned invasion of Czechoslovakia's Sudetenland, members of the Department of Geography at the University of California, Berkeley, were creating one of the world's first maps to represent the Pacific Ocean and Islands in the center with Asia, Southeast Asia, Australia, and North and South America along the left and right sides.[68] These charts, using the van der Grinten projection (which reduces the distortions of the Mercator projection to show land areas more in proportion), were a revised version of the inaugural map of "The Pacific Region," drawn using Goode's homolosine equal-area projection and introduced in 1927 by the Institute of Pacific Relations (IPR). The IPR, an organization founded in Honolulu in 1925 to study issues endemic to the cultures of the Pacific world (and which would strongly influence the development of Asian and Pacific academic studies),[69] came into being, as Etsuko Taketani explains, as part of a drive to internationalize the Pacific in service of a hemispheric regional order initiated and led by the United States.[70] This vision "gave rise to a nascent Pacific-centered perspective on the world, transforming the region from the periphery of Europe to a central stage in international politics,"[71] a spatial reordering of the world that the map symbolized.

The Berkeley geographers' maps formed the templates for the *Pageant of the Pacific*, six large-scale, densely illustrated mural maps (nine by thirteen feet and fifteen by twenty-four feet) created by Mexican cartoonist, theater and dance director, set designer, and anthropologist Miguel Covarrubias (1904–1957). The maps depicted, respectively, the native peoples, flora and fauna, art forms, economy, dwellings, and means of transportation of this newly visualized Pacific area for the Golden Gate International Exposition (GGIE) in 1939–40. Held on Treasure Island, a four-hundred-acre artificial islet constructed on the shoals of Yerba Buena Island in San Francisco Bay, the GGIE epitomized California's predilection to look west rather than back to the East Coast and Europe, and sought to "make San Francisco the hub of what civic leaders imagined as an emerging Pacific civilization that would supplant the Atlantic world."[72] In contrast to the New York World's Fair of 1939–40 with its future orientation toward a "World of Tomorrow," the GGIE's theme of "Pacific Unity" expressed a geospatial imagination that fashioned an alternative, idealized unfolding world of interconnected trade, peace, and harmonious cultural rapprochements across the broad domain of the ocean; a necessary antidote, organizers declared, "since the

Old World has embarked into savage, suicidal wars that will leave it maimed, if not destroyed, to convalesce for many years to come."[73]

There is no doubt that this broad vision of the GGIE encompassed an imperialist agenda—in train in US policy since the nineteenth century and prefiguring the Pacific Century—that promoted the dominance and superiority of an American presence in an integrated economic region. The exposition's guidebooks[74] and official public spaces made clear, in Andrew Shanken's words, "just how much the Pacific, understood as a region, was a European invention tied to the heroic colonial project of civilizing, if not possessing, the Other,"[75] relying on cultural stereotypes and expressions of racial miscegenation that cohered in Ralph Stackpole's eighty-foot statue of Pacifica, "goddess of the Pacific Ocean," in which Otherness melted into a single, ethnically indistinct, presiding monument that both appropriated and erased indigeneity in the name of progress and profit. But just as world's fairs have long functioned as enmeshed sites of contradictory and intersecting perspectives and projects, Covarrubias's performative artistic vision of the Pacific operated in tension with the GGIE's commercial ideology. The mural maps were displayed inside Pacific House, a zone of intercultural interaction in the GGIE's Pacific Area, which was overseen by and advanced the mission of the IPR. It was constructed on an atoll in the center of the "Lagoon of Nations," a miniature representation of the Pacific Ocean where the exposition's seventeen million visitors could spatialize the region kinesthetically by walking between the pavilions of Pacific nations and territories arranged around its shore. Although Covarrubias's visualizations helped manifest the notion of the Pacific area as a comprehensible and thus controllable chorographic unity, the other arguments contained in the illustrated subject matter, design aesthetic, and metaphors of his maps enlisted audiences in alternative co-participatory acts of world-making.

Covarrubias and his assistant Antonio M. Ruíz infused the *Pageant of the Pacific* with a specifically Latin American intercultural aesthetic that merged European caricature and Indigenous Mesoamerican visual culture, especially Mixtec ideographic painting.[76] Across the six murals, the 1,001 figures inducted viewers into a vibrant, prismatic world of connectivity, bringing diverse sites, temporalities, goods and technologies, practices, and populations into dynamic and critical relationship, and creating active links between islands and continents. The Pacific Islands are presented as an integral and fecund space of plentitude bridging the region, pulsing with motion and reciprocity as well as contradiction and change: an iridescent palette wrought with humor and pain. Central to Covarrubias's worldview is his privileging of the local and the Indigenous and their place within larger schemes. Commodities that conscript Pacific economies into world markets and galvanize large-scale diasporic flows are pictured alongside goods essential in the maintenance of local kinship and social exchanges; elsewhere, the visual scheme accords a container ship equal value with a water buffalo, and a breadfruit with an oil rig. At times, the maps' visual arcs are celebratory, tracking the transmission of vigorous art and performance traditions; at others, the pageant's theatricality is tragic, registering detrimental historical processes of foreign colonialism on native bodies and environments. Although informed by (now obsolete) anthropological theories of his time, and necessarily reliant upon the metonymic and emblematic, Covarrubias's imaging of the prewar Pacific world abjures the homogenizing currents of capital and encourages spectators to trace transformative interactions between different communities, visualizing islands as dynamic, fluid systems embracing multiple cultural affinities: implicated in broader forces while owning distinct knowledges and genealogies.

The networks that entwine across the *Pageant*'s six maps are suggestive of a concept of the Pacific embraced more recently by scholars and that is congruent with the approach taken in this book. In his magisterial study *Pacific Worlds: A History of Seas, Peoples, and Cultures*, which traces the interconnectedness of Asian, Oceanian, European, and American peoples, Matt K. Matsuda makes the case for the existence of many Pacific worlds rather than a single one. While I maintain that there is heuristic value in reading an ocean *as* an ocean—as a historical force and entity that mobilizes peoples' collective efforts and that can be studied as such—I agree with Matsuda that this is "not the same as locating the Pacific Ocean and then identifying the lands, littorals, and islands within its embrace. For Pacific worlds are not synonymous with one declared and defined 'Pacific,' but with multiple seas, cultures, and peoples, and especially the overlapping transits between them."[77] Matsuda proposes that instead of beginning with Magellan's sixteenth-century vision of "the Pacific" as an immense space of endless water to cross, we conceive of the area as a "historical assemblage of smaller elements,"[78] of interlocking navigations, migrations, settlements, and cultural interchanges that comprise a plurality of locally connected histories.[79] Although the Pacific can be conceptualized and analyzed in terms of the activities of global transnationalism, this alternate perspective privileges particularities, focusing on a multiplicity of translocal sites and communities: "specific linked places where direct engagements took place and were tied to histories dependent on the ocean,"[80] and containing stories that only take on their full meanings when connected to other stories and places.

Let me index some of the dynamics of a series of translocal communities that feature centrally in what follows by looking more closely at Covarrubias's map depicting "Native Means of Transportation in the Pacific Area." Although not the most fulsomely illustrated and often the least considered of the six murals, it is the most symbolically resonant for my purposes. In homage to the Pacific area as home to "the greatest navigators of all,"[81] the central section of the map animates the cerulean spread of the ocean with an array of piloted Indigenous voyaging craft, from coastal canoes to long-distance double-hulled and outrigger vessels. Following their sweep from insular Asia across the oceanic archipelagoes to the coastlines of the Americas, the viewer is encouraged to draw visual comparisons between these shared yet distinctive vehicles. As complex syntheses of religion, art, science, and technological transfer among different island societies, such vessels were responsible for the human colonization of the Pacific Islands, pursuing itineraries of expansion, settlement, and new cultural iterations that express a fundamental characteristic of life across much of the Pacific; namely, the dialectic between dwelling and traveling, indigeneity and diaspora, roots in land and routes across the sea.[82] Placing the ancient and modern in coeval time-space, the canoes are juxtaposed with the larger vignette of an airplane taking off from San Francisco; as the prospectus describes it, "The greatest contribution to transportation of our time, the giant China Clipper[83] stands as a climax and a symbol of the aims of the Pacific Area—bringing Asia to America and America to Asia in just five days."[84]

On the one hand, this imagery might threaten to collapse the ocean into the ultimate flyover zone of utopian Asia-Pacific co-prosperity, seeding the GGIE's capitalist ambitions in a paean to American triumphalism and aeronautic prowess that lauds the Clipper as "native" invention and export. However, Covarrubias's transtemporal figurations push back against teleological supersession, compressing simultaneity into his 2D planar arrangement. The vessels actively occupy the ocean, encircling and embedding the airplane; likewise, their performative feats of noninstrument navigation pose a challenge to the dominance of the compass rose positioned in the southeast quadrant of the sea. Rather than entrench a dichotomy between an evolving world of Western modernity and a romantic memory of legendary voyaging from the distant past (as Indigenous Pacific seafaring was largely viewed in 1939), Covarrubias remits a genealogy of an Indigenous cosmopolitanism that remains remarkably salient. In this regard, it is fruit-

Figure 1. Miguel Covarrubias, "Native Means of Transportation in the Pacific Area." Plate VI, *Pageant of the Pacific*, for the Golden Gate International Exposition, 1939–40. Lithograph by H. S. Crocker Company and Schwabacher-Frey Company. San Francisco: Pacific House (SF Bay Exposition Company), 1940. Image reproduced courtesy of Maria Elena Rico Covarrubias and David Rumsey Map Collection, David Rumsey Map Center, Stanford Libraries. https://purl.stanford.edu/xh131zd2127.

ful to consider the proleptic possibilities of cartography; that is, how the performative, world-making capacities of maps operate via the imagined futures that inhere in them, alluding (intentionally or otherwise) to an alternative world "that will exist once the possibilities entailed in the map are performed."[85] In my present-day encounter with the archival lithograph, I am struck by how—to me—the map expresses a vision for a contemporary Pacific world that registers the tensions and relationships between the unfolding performances of transnational capitalism and Indigenous revitalization.

More than fifty years after Covarrubias's *Pageant*, another Indigenous artist and scholar from the Pacific world, the Tongan visionary Epeli Hau'ofa, would famously characterize the Oceanic region as a "sea of islands."[86] Shifting the emphasis from land to the vast relational medium of the ocean, Hau'ofa eschews the connotations of tiny, powerless, remote surfaces contained in the notion of "islands in a far sea" and instead champions a "holistic perspective in which things are seen in the totality of their relationships."[87] This grassroots regional imaginary is based in the self-directed, vernacular activities of Pacific Islanders in an expansive and expanding world replete with the mixing and moving of peoples and cultures. It refutes both the Asia-Pacific conglomerate and the neocolonial framework of South Pacific regionalism, and offers a powerful challenge to the macro-level discourses of politicians, bureaucrats, and officials with their derogatory fiscal and developmental concerns. Drawing dual inspiration from the pelagic voyages of the past and the diasporic trajectories of the present, Hau'ofa, like Covarrubias, presents an empowering, transhistorical vision of Islander world-making involving dynamic exchange and the establishment of wider zones of community and belonging. It is a vision of solidarity that works for the advancement of Islanders' collective interests while still championing "our diversity" as "necessary for the struggle against the homogenizing forces of the global juggernaut."[88]

Covarrubias's own vision would be shattered by the Japanese bombing of Pu'uloa (Pearl Harbor) in 1941, which dragged the United States into World War II; instead of becoming the envisaged municipal airport, Treasure Island was repurposed as a naval station to help manage the flows of men and munitions as the Pacific area was remapped as a theater of conflict. Yet in ways that Covarrubias could likely not have anticipated, his map art in the twenty-first century gestures to aspects of a newly interconnected Pacific world where postcolonial Indigenous voyaging craft once more ply courses toward sovereignty across the region and around the globe, and where airborne Islanders plot the itineraries of an expanded

Oceania in complex interaction with different societies and locales. With its complicated co-imbrication of economic and cultural flows, and its representation of local Indigenous movements alongside global economic shifts, Covarrubias's image is richly suggestive of the multiple mobilities and reconfigurations, as well as the inevitable discontinuities and contradictions, of the Pacific, whose performatic expressions form the basis of this book.

ISLANDS AND CONTINENTS: OCEANIA ON THE MOVE

If the Pacific Ocean world is best understood in terms of the crosscurrents of its human activities, then what critical paradigms might help us to talk about them? What are their possibilities and limitations? What models and discourses might be productive for theater and performance studies to engage more expansively, and how, in turn, might the tools of performance analysis invigorate those conversations? What new paradigms are needed?

Scholars have been grappling with these issues since the field of Asia/Pacific cultural studies started to gain traction in the 1990s. Coeval with the wider cultural studies turn as well as challenges to discrete area studies modeling in favor of more malleable views of culture and identity,[89] this new critical orientation contested the compartmentalization of Asia, the Pacific Islands, and the Americas into divergent entities. In their germinal 1995 edited volume, *Asia/Pacific as Space of Cultural Production*, Rob Wilson and Arif Dirlik argued that the preoccupation with the integrated economies of regional powerhouses means that the "so-called Pacific Basin countries contained in the region are habitually excluded from mapping and contesting these megatrend visions of 'economic cooperation' and 'cultural exchange' that bear down upon their heteroglossic well-being and threaten their local survival as distinct cultures and alternative histories."[90] Looking to the promise of cultural production to illuminate more fluid and multiple maps and networks of migration and transcultural innovation that might operate beyond or counter to the circulations of hegemonic power and the paradigms presented by market planners and military strategists,[91] Wilson and Dirlik raised the question of how scholars could acknowledge "the cultural micropolitics of the region as a source of dynamic opposition and local difference worthy of international recognition."[92] *Asia/Pacific as Space of Cultural Production* is notable for its inclusion of Pacific Islander perspectives—including Hau'ofa's essay—alongside poetry, essays, and activist texts from Asia, Australia, and

America in a "new regional conceptualization."[93] The potential of this approach, however, has not been fully realized during the subsequent generation, with studies still tending to coalesce around island interests or rimland interests, despite the development of new theoretical approaches that promise more integrated possibilities.

One such paradigm is the emerging academic field of "transpacific studies,"[94] which has garnered increasing currency since the mid-2000s as an arena for innovative scholarship. In its dominant conceptualization as an interdisciplinary "space of interaction"[95] that represents an outgrowth of Southeast Asian studies, Asian studies, and American studies, and draws from diaspora, transnational, and cosmopolitan discourses, the transpacific "both extends and exceeds the earlier categories of 'Asia Pacific' and 'Pacific Rim.'"[96] Moving beyond these more singular designations, a transpacific analytic has the potential to chart with more nuance "the ways that different Asian, Pacific Island, and American cultures and communities mutually shape one another as they circulate throughout the region."[97] This "cross-hemispheric turn"[98] has been stimulated by the recent shift in the world's strategic and economic epicenter from the North Atlantic to the western Pacific, whereby the transpacific is now vying with the transatlantic in contemporary discourses of globalization.[99] For scholars of the 1990s, Japan's burgeoning economy galvanized critical engagement with the region (growing up in New Zealand during this period, I clocked up eight years of Japanese language study—some of it mandatory—at school and university). In the 2010s, the United States' preoccupation with China's rise and the attendant Obama-era "pivot to Asia"[100] has sharpened the necessity for critical methodologies that can historicize and interrogate the United States' militarized presence in Asia and the Pacific Islands, particularly the structuring legacies of World War II and Cold War geopolitics and knowledge that undergird the Cold War sensibilities reemergent at this contemporary juncture.[101]

For my purposes, the promise of transpacific studies as an evolving intellectual and political project lies in its multilateral and multisited research approach, which incorporates voices and perspectives from different locations, histories, and epistemologies. In addition to its perceptual shift from anchored spaces to the movements of peoples, materials, and ideas, transpacific studies focuses on the broader infrastructures and circumstances that produce or constrain local movements, contacts, and exchanges, and attunes us to the core tensions between mobility and fixity.[102] It is also valuable for its attention to histories and flows across the Pacific that support minoritarian connections, encouraging us to examine how the poor, oppressed and disempowered, dispersed across different populations and locales, can enact their own resistance and agency against the hegemonic globalizing forces shaping the contours of the region.[103] Beyond its resignification of movements and interfaces across the Pacific area, what lends a critical transpacific studies its heft as a distinctly emergent epistemology is its ability to "clarify the specific geohistoric conditions under which that space has been constituted as an object of knowledge and nonknowledge," which involves scrutiny of the "Pacific turn" itself "and considers the interventions and contestations it may reveal or conceal."[104]

That said, there are limits to the transpacific imaginary as it is currently taking shape, especially in US academic discourse. In much of the work in the field published since the mid-2010s, the fixation on the Asia-America dyad remains dominant, with affiliatory webs spanning the ocean rather than engaging with its contents, reifying ongoing positions of primacy and subordination. Echoing Wilson and Dirlik, transpacific commentators have readily acknowledged the problematic absence of Pacific Islander interventions, indicating the forms of knowledge production that are obscured by what Lisa Yoneyama calls the "epistemic violence of crossing over" contained in the prefix *trans*.[105] Yoneyama emphasizes the need to rechart transpacific studies' inherited "cartographic legacies of militarized global capitalism and its political rationality that have long vacated the people and histories of the Pacific Islands,"[106] thereby erasing the long-term engagements and exchanges by which native Pacific Islanders have sought to unravel colonial, neocolonial, and neoliberal practices.[107] Likewise, foundational volumes in the field have called to place transpacific studies within a wider array of Indigenous practices and knowledge systems and to incorporate oceanic thinking.[108] Tina Chen's overview of the field identifies indigeneity as a key "turn" in transpacific scholarship,[109] although this discourse is still fairly nascent and is an area in which this book seeks crucially to intervene.

An important example of this new research, and one that resonates strongly with my own approach in *Moving Islands*, is literary scholar Erin Suzuki's monograph *Ocean Passages: Navigating Pacific Islander and Asian American Literatures* (2021). Drawing inspiration from Hau'ofa, Suzuki reads across the fields of transpacific Asian American and Indigenous Pacific studies "to trace out a literary theory of transpacific entanglement that places the deconstructive critiques foregrounded in Asian Americanist texts with the intellectual, social, and aesthetic frameworks based on perspective and relationality that have been addressed in literary and scholarly works by Indigenous scholars and artists."[110] By examining how Asian

American and Pacific Islander subjectivities have been constructed along-side and against each other across a shared ocean, Suzuki seeks to decolo-nize transpacific paradigms by centering the Pacific and by illuminating fresh understandings of networks, alliances, and formations.

In a related vein, Yuan Shu, Otto Heim, and Kendall Johnson's 2019 edited volume *Oceanic Archives, Indigenous Epistemologies, and Transpacific American Studies* brings scholars in Oceanic studies into conversation with scholars in transnational American studies to introduce a "transpacific American studies" as a new critical paradigm.[111] Methodologically, its wel-come attention to island spaces and Indigenous/non-Western perspectives within the American Pacific chimes with the recent "archipelagic turn" in American studies, with its decontinentalizing swerve toward theorizing the Americas in terms of their constitution by and accountability to an assemblage of interconnected islands, shorelines, continents, and oceans.[112] Timely and necessary as these interventions are, however, they tend to favor translocalities bound by a common cause of resistance to US expan-sionism or otherwise entangled with American cultural priorities and con-cerns. My project calls for a wider transpacific imaginary. I am fully in tune with Suzuki's observation that "there is not just one transpacific, but mul-tiple transpacifics that conflict, intersect, and overlap."[113] To this end, despite the signal importance of scrutinizing America's imperial and mili-tary legacies and its overseas ventures in the newly enunciated Pacific Century—which this book does—these are not the only questions and sen-sibilities that can be illuminated through a transpacific lens.

One tactic that *Moving Islands* pursues is to detach the United States as a cardinal point for transpacific cartographies, in order both to place the United States within more heterogeneous matrices and to trace entirely dif-ferent networks across vast tracts of the Pacific. Paul Giles is absolutely right to push back against uniform figurations of US hegemony in the region, arguing that "it is much too one-dimensional, in every sense of that word, to suggest that such imperializing narratives have only ever extended westward from California."[114] In addition to views of the region that extend from Asia, as Giles makes clear, "The transpacific circuit has always been made up of imperial crosscurrents as well as aquatic flows and island domains, with these imperial pressures flowing back across the Pacific, from Britain's settlement of Australia and New Zealand and from Germa-ny's involvement in New Guinea and Samoa."[115] To these I would add the francophone Pacific, a rich and politically exigent arena of cultural and artistic output that remains woefully sidelined by anglophone production stimulated by British colonialism and American militarization.

Useful models of this sort have been proposed by European and Antipodean scholars. In *Transpacific Americas: Encounters and Engagements between the Americas and the South Pacific*, German anthropologists Eveline Dürr and Philipp Schorch treat the Americas as a transhemispheric space, tracing multiple connections stretching from Canada to Chile that excavate less visible southern linkages with the Pacific Islands and with networks of Indigenous actors.[116] Likewise, in *Coast to Coast: Case Histories of Modern Pacific Crossings*, Australian cultural historians Prue Ahrens and Chris Dixon identify transpacific interactions connecting North America, Pacific Island peoples, and the settler societies of Australia and New Zealand.[117] These vital southern ties focus attention on the networks sustained outside the American Pacific by Australia and New Zealand as major Pacific Islander diasporic nodes and neocolonial presences, and opens space for a deeper interrogation of their leadership roles and their changing identities in the Pacific. This is especially the case for Australia as the predominant southern power, whose own constructions of the Asia-Pacific region tend to privilege its relationships with neighboring Asian nations, excluding the Pacific Islands.[118] These selective affiliations might be understood to have their history, as Fry has observed, in Australia's attempts to realize its own form of manifest destiny by appointing itself as the natural leader of the postcolonial South Pacific. Couched in a rhetoric of benevolent concern, Australian bureaucratic discourses on the Pacific Islands frequently trade in subordinating depictions that justify Australia's continued hegemony, characterizing the region as inferior, vulnerable, and economically nonviable, in contrast to an internationally successful and adaptive Australia: "failing to become part of the Pacific century," "falling off the map," and "the hole in the Asia-Pacific doughnut."[119] As Hau'ofa has argued passionately, these belittling portrayals have weighty implications for policy outcomes as well as for the self-image of Pacific peoples, calling crucial attention to how Pacific Islanders might frame more equitable and agential conceptions of their pasts and futures.[120]

This book is profoundly in sympathy with these expanded and reorganized approaches, yet presses further with its performance-centered engagement with Pacific Islander interventions within, across, and beyond the Pacific Ocean domain. This focus also enables me to draw upon the body of dedicated anthropological work on Islander movements, migrations, and multiple place-making modalities that remains largely in parallel rather than in dialogue with these other conversations.[121] Importantly, however, such extensions and redefinitions of transpacific theory demand thoughtful negotiation and a careful awareness of the distinct disciplinary formations, epistemologies, and regional imaginaries that risk being inundated by a transpacific surge. Concerns of this kind have been strongest in US contexts, where Pacific studies frequently finds relevance by being articulated with Asian and Asian American studies,[122] and where Pacific Islanders are typically grouped into the panethnic category of "Asian Pacific Islander (American)." Indigenous scholars such as Teresia Teaiwa, Vicente M. Diaz, Amy K. Stillman, and J. Kēhaulani Kauanui have made ongoing calls to keep Pacific Islands studies protected from disciplinary elision, arguing that uncritical associations "will always raise the specter of unequal power relations,"[123] imperiling long-term, conscious efforts "to demarcate Pacific Islanders and Islands from the generic and totalizing 'Asia-Pacific' category."[124] At stake in these debates is not just a concern about demographic invisibility but also about epistemology: the different knowledges, histories, identities, and struggles that are denied when terms are used "irresponsibly and interchangeably."[125] These scholars have advocated for studies of encounters, interactions, and links between various peoples of the Pacific world in ways that emphasize comparison rather than conflation, and productive engagement rather than inclusion.[126] While this is a methodology that a critical transpacific analytic may be able to accommodate, it is imperative that any paradigm be attentive to differentiated histories, cultural localities, interpretive frameworks, and terms of engagement.

Such an approach also needs to recognize other Indigenous paradigms for understanding relational mobilities in the region. The arguments mounted by the aforementioned scholars were also motivated by the development of a Native Pacific cultural studies (in contradistinction to an Asian Pacific cultural studies) that likewise took root in the 1990s and flourished in the twenty-first century. Conceived initially by Diaz and Kauanui, the discourse triangulates native, Pacific, and cultural studies with their "kindred but distinct lines of critical questioning."[127] A Native Pacific cultural studies explores "notions of Pacific indigeneity as they circulate through geographical, cultural, political, and historical forms of people(s), things, knowledge, power—between islands and continents,"[128] and has generated a great deal of important work that examines the roots and routes of Islander identities and practices. This critical move was part of a wider effort to decolonize the interdisciplinary field of Pacific studies, decoupling it from its associations with supporting research on the Euro-American discovery and conquest of the region, which figured the Pacific as a tabula rasa for imperial and colonial concerns and for unequal encounters through the dominance of Western philosophies and pedagogical traditions.[129] Emerging alongside the "new Oceania" or "new Pacific" of postcolonial independence movements, native struggles for self-determination, and mass diasporic flows generated by the impact of postwar global economic shifts on small island states,[130] these calls advocated for a change in Pacific studies' emphasis from island-centered to Islander-centered paradigms. Accordingly, scholars aimed to trouble the Pacific as a Western concept, to emphasize Indigenous orderings, and to pursue research outcomes attentive to the needs of Pacific communities.[131]

All of this brings us back around to Hau'ofa and his "sea of islands" thesis, because I want to touch briefly on how his empowering vision of archipelagic solidarity, reciprocity, and interdependence rests on a preference for the term "Oceania" over "the Pacific Islands." For Hau'ofa, the former denotes a world of people connected to each other and sharing a common oceanic heritage, while the latter reinforces the official world of states and nationalities.[132] Hau'ofa's utopian intervention emerges—and operates in tension with—a complicated and fractured world frequently characterized by narrow national self-interest, ethnic schisms, and the failed autonomy of the postindependence era. It represents a counterdiscursive resignification of d'Urville's Océanie and its derivation from Enlightenment-era formulations of geography that fostered imperial knowledge and formed the basis for official policy and economic discourses, rebranding it from an Islander-centered perspective deriving from ancient formulations of Indigenous relationality.[133] As such, it advances the relational turn in island studies that views "island spaces as mutually constituted, co-constructed and inter-related,"[134] involving "networks, assemblages, filaments, connective tissue, mobilities and multiplicities."[135] Hau'ofa invokes Oceania, as Chris Ballard puts it, "in its topological rather than topographic sense";[136] that is, "as a space that remains preserved under continuous (re) formations: Being bended and stretched but not torn apart, remaining connected within shifting boundaries."[137] Hau'ofa's "expanded Oceania"[138] measures its circulations and resources by the places where mobile Islanders are located, creatively imagining a moving ocean world "connected to Asia, to the Americas,"[139] and which "certainly encompasses the great cities of Australia, New Zealand, the United States, and Canada."[140] In this respect, as Suzuki also suggests, Hau'ofa's Oceania can be understood as a structure and concept that can be productively articulated with a transpacific one, supporting enquiries committed to remapping the Pacific as a less Eurocentric and homogenous space and a more labile, complex arrangement of translocal assemblages; and as an arena for analyzing the wider discourses of the Pacific Century as well as more particular questions and contestations over Pacific place-making and identities.[141]

The range of contexts and conversations that I have outlined above, moving toward a potentially expanded and adapted notion of the transpacific, represents a rich arena of debate and enquiry that theater and performance studies scholars have yet to engage in a substantial or sustained way. Similarly, scholars of the Pacific have rarely availed themselves of the objects and frameworks of our field. There are certainly researchers in theater/performance and cognate disciplines (anthropology, art history, ethnomusicology) working on Pacific drama, dance, and various other performance traditions, and their work is cited throughout this book. Yet, to date, much of this work tends to focus on single sites and suffers from a paucity of full-length published studies, especially of contemporary performance.[142] Disciplinary paradigms in Pacific studies have often prevented scholars from committing to theorizing performance, even as they acknowledge its omnipresence in Pacific worlds. Pacific studies' primary grounding in the social, political, and natural sciences has tended to preclude performance qua performance as a subject of critical inquiry. Instead, performance has been enlisted as a metaphor for understanding ethnohistorical encounters and processes;[143] or the performance event is captured in an ethnographic account as a means of illuminating other social practices and structures. Even the flourishing discourse of Pacific literary studies, which has provided me with several inspiring models of scholarship, runs largely in parallel rather than in conversation with discussions of performance; when they occur, readings of performance works are usually literary and textual, with little attention to questions of audience, embodiment, staging, or production context that animate theater and performance studies.

This situation needs to change, because the analytic tools and perspectives of theater and performance studies are admirably equipped to interpret how the intercultural interactions and their attendant social processes described above are worked out in everyday life and in aesthetic contexts. Performance studies thus has a significant conceptual contribution to make to Oceanian scholarship by showing, for instance, how theoretical abstractions and macrostructural forces can be grounded in performance's sociomaterialities, and by offering new methods for examining how the intricacies of race and culture are expressed corporeally. Further, Pacific scholars may benefit from our field's capacity to track the mobilization and reworking of artistic forms across different sites and spaces, and to anatomize intricate power dynamics among performers, audiences, collaborators, institutions, and other stakeholders. We might then, as this book intends, better understand how performance functions as a means by which Pacific peoples navigate the vagaries of the globalizing Pacific Century in ways that emphasize creative agency and innovative alternatives to the evolving status quo.

To this end, I position my analyses within the "new intercultural turn" in theater and performance studies that has emerged since the late 2000s and early 2010s. The "intercultural" has always been a critical keyword entwined with the development of performance studies as an interdiscipline, primarily through its grounding in Richard Schechner's and Victor Turner's cross-cultural, ethnographically based performative theories and experiments in the 1970s and 1980s.[144] Interculturalism has also been one of the field's most contested terms, not least because of its problematic associations with auteurs of the Euro-American avant-garde who strove to revitalize their moribund theatrical aesthetics by appropriating non-Western performance forms and traditions. In the 1980s, this manifested in what Daphne Lei calls "hegemonic intercultural theatre" (HIT), "a specific artistic genre and state of mind that combines First World capital and brainpower with Third World raw material and labor, and Western classical texts with Eastern performance."[145] The legacy of HIT and its discontents has been comprehensively rehearsed in a number of recent publications,[146] so it will suffice to say that HIT's cultural politics came under necessary postcolonial fire in the 1990s, and that at the turn of the twenty-first century a new wave of critical scholarship, calling for more politically astute, culturally inflected, and equitable praxes and interpretive approaches, motivated the "new interculturalism" of the succeeding decade.[147]

"New interculturalism" in performance responds to the perceived urgency of intercultural engagement in the contemporary moment, when the diversifying of cities and nations, the increase in global human traffic, and the acceleration of neoliberal capitalism have engendered both new forms of interculturalism and a sharpened need for critical reexaminations of the ways that cultural exchange is performed.[148] The new intercultural turn is resolutely distinguished from HIT by its ethical, political, and methodological invigoration from a confluence of discourses; among them, new developments in performance studies, critical multiculturalism, critical race theory and whiteness studies, new cosmopolitanism, diaspora and migration studies, and postcolonial and (trans-)Indigenous studies.[149] It has also benefited from the assemblage thinking and actor-network theory that have energized relational methodologies in several branches of the social sciences and humanities. From these discursive intersections emerge tools for the analysis of what Ric Knowles calls an "intercultural performance-from-below"[150] that is rhizomatic, multimodal, and nonhierarchical, operating as "one of many nodes in a relational network."[151] It eschews assumptions of monocultural audiences and the binaries of East-West and source-target models of analysis, and instead "involves collaborations and solidarities across real and respected material differences within local, urban, national, and global performance ecologies."[152] Thinking beyond the semiotic-representational encounter between two or more (discrete) performance forms, this revamped discourse privileges the human relations that performances negotiate, characterize, and instantiate, reading performances as "politicised sites for the constitution of new, hybrid, and diasporic identities in space":[153] crucibles within which new subjectivities and social orderings can be forged.

The utility of the new interculturalism for my project includes the productive emphasis on collaborative models of exchange and dialogue that are inaugurated and propelled by local, vernacular, minority, and subaltern voices and viewpoints. In its embrace of interconnections across relational and multisited nodes, this framework has great potential to map new performance geographies that unseat the more intractable legacies of area studies. Also valuable is the new interculturalism's attention to how performance serves as a vehicle for analyzing the negotiations of multiple identity positions and cultural genealogies as they are expressed corporeally, and how performance can reveal culture's inherent hybridity.[154] Additionally, I find useful the concerted emphasis on performative becoming; that is, the inherently processual nature of intercultural relations that, as opposed to one-off aesthetic experiments, have a transformational role in the creation of cultural values and individual and community identities. In so doing, the perspectives of new interculturalism help us to recognize the often-fraught complexities of these spaces of interaction; for example, how (neo/post)colonialism, imperialism, racism, and other power dynamics produce and influence these relationships across different polities and production contexts.

At the same time, we need other models of interculturalism to understand contemporary performance from the Pacific world. We need means of talking in sophisticated ways about the performative conditions that arise from the Pacific's unique circumstances: the varied means by which small, vastly dispersed island communities spread across and beyond an oceanic domain use performance to create and maintain coalitions across great distances, heterogeneous societies, and uneven circumstances to critique broader forces affecting the region and to advocate for change. This approach also requires attention to disruptions, disjunctions, and immobilities. These topics demand more robust frameworks for looking at related performances in multiple sites, and for analyzing how multiple and multisited identifications are worked out, along with their implications for broader social transformations. They require that we pay attention to genealogical ties across the Pacific and, especially, the signal intersection of indigeneity and diaspora, which are imbricated for many Pacific Islanders yet are treated as separate categories in many accounts of intercultural performance. We must, in addition, draw upon theories from the Pacific rather than relying upon the presumed universality of terms and concepts derived from the Western academy. How can we, as Erika Fischer-Lichte asks, break open the homogenizing of discourse and diversify international performance theory by "interweaving discursive cultures,"[155] allowing the Pacific / Oceania to stand as a source of theoretical innovation rather than merely as a point of application? Such questions point to how thinking from the Pacific might productively enhance intercultural theater and performance studies.

It should be clear at this point that I see significant overlaps between the evolving discourses of transpacific studies and studies of interculturalism in performance, in terms of both their analytical promise and their critical gaps. Consequently, I want to mediate between these broad paradigms while insisting on their continued revision, because no single extant framework adequately addresses the range and priorities of the performances examined in this volume. In the spirit of Kauanui's call for productive engagement rather than blanket inclusion, I'd like to mobilize an alternative concept and model derived from a Pacific artistic context that brings these regional and performance discourses into more meaningful conversation, and that I outline in the following section.

TRANSPASIFIKA: PERFORMANCE IN A PACIFIC CENTURY

I explore the potential of transpasifika as an optic and reading strategy that conceives of the contemporary Pacific world relationally, that privileges Islander-centered perspectives, and that offers a way to talk about the performative interculturalisms that arise from that nexus. The term is not presented as a catchall for Pacific performance or a programmatic rebranding but as one of "several alternative transpacifics"[156] that enables more nuanced ways of approaching certain kinds of cultural production from Hau'ofa's expanded Oceania. This work embeds movement in its content, form, production, and circulation; centers the concerns, perspectives, knowledge structures, and aesthetics of Pacific Islanders; and is often produced in interaction with collaborators, participants, and audiences from outside of the Pacific region. Transpasifika also avoids the exclusionary and colonialist imputations that remain embedded in terms like "transpacific" and "intercultural." My uptake of the term is inspired by the artist profile in the spring 2010 issue of the Pacific Island studies flagship journal, *The Contemporary Pacific*, featuring Norfolk Islander artist Sue Pearson. "Sue uses trans-Pasifika symbols and motifs to illuminate the cultural connections that exist between Norfolk Islanders, Tahitians, Pitcairn Islanders, and other peoples in the wider Pacific—connections that have for many years been overshadowed by the Island's political links with Australia."[157] This précis of Pearson's work is promising in its emphasis on the strategic deployment of patterns and images shared by many Pacific Islander (Pasifika) communities across the area to express and reinforce a networked identity that operates as creative resistance to Norfolk's containment within the neocolonial ambit of its mainland neighbor.

Yet the example of Norfolk Island identity itself, I suggest, opens transpasifika to wider possibilities. Although the evolving story of Norfolk Island is—again—only one of manifold narratives and overlapping circuits coursing through the Pacific, it is richly indicative of the layered complexities generated by the processual entanglements of cultures-in-relation. The Norfolk population stems from the vivid events of the 1789 *Bounty* mutiny against Captain William Bligh (a topic much beloved by Hollywood filmmakers); specifically, the British sailor mutineers and Tahitian women who fled to remote and unpopulated Pitcairn Island and over several generations created a closely interrelated community of plural European and Polynesian heritages. To accommodate the growing population, in 1856 the British government granted the people leave to relocate to the more spacious Norfolk Island in the Tasman Sea (previously uninhabited except for abandoned British convict settlements), which most elected to do. Over time, these fused trajectories have led to new expressions of indigeneity (formally declared in 1994) based on certain Islanders' assertions that they are the first whole, intergenerational population to settle Norfolk; they maintain a surviving and evolving culture developed on Pitcairn by their ancestors; and they speak their own language.[158] Such claims are in part motivated by an equivalent logic to genealogical settlement in other parts of the Pacific; namely, like early Polynesian settlers on their *vaka* (voyaging canoes) they sailed to an island and over time became a new and separate people:[159] they arrived there *and* they have always been there.

These claims have been rejected by the Australian government, which initially annexed Norfolk as an external territory in 1913 in an expression of Australia's new national identity and self-assumed leadership role in the southwestern Pacific. It doubled down in 2015 by revoking the island's legislative autonomy, leading to Norfolk Islanders' pro-independence appeals to the British Parliament and the United Nations, citing civil and political rights breaches and their oppression by a larger settler society.[160] These unfolding positions point to the interleaving and (re)formulation of Indigenous, diasporic, settler, and colonial influences and identities. Artistic work that maps ancestral genealogies reaching from Norfolk to Pitcairn to Tahiti not only asserts Pasifika ties that simultaneously cut across and mesh with Australian, British, and French jurisdictions, but also highlights the complex relationships between groundedness and movement, hybridity and autochthony, regionalism and nationalism, and the strategic investment in wider webs of belonging and the urgency of local, specific claims to place. Tracing such transpacific and global telemetries indexes the intricate dynamics of cultural production that an intercultural paradigm must be able to address.

Transpasifika's relexicalizing is attentive to the disciplinary and cartographic legacies of erasure that "transpacific" contains, shifting focus from "the epistemic violence of crossing over" the Pacific to highlight Pasifika, the peoples of the Pacific Islands.[161] It is thus less a spatial designation (traversing an area) than a relational one (a way of talking expansively about a series of relationships among the peoples and cultures of the Pacific world). "Transpasifika" is a term that embeds multiple interculturalisms. "Pasifika" ("Pasefika" in Samoan) can denote the ocean, but it is more commonly a term designating Pacific Islands peoples in general, while eluding the (derogatory) aggregate of the generic "Pacific Islander" category. In certain sites such as Australia and New Zealand it also describes resident diasporic Pacific Islander populations arising from the mass mobilizations of the postwar Pacific.[162] "Pasifika" is therefore a collective, relational term, specifying no single culture or essential trait but indicating communities linked through common ancestries or experiences (sometimes amicably, sometimes in deep conflict), and involving multiple habitations, transits, identifications, and modes of place-making. As an indigenized term but not an Indigenous one (unlike, for example, the Māori *tino rangatiratanga*, which steadfastly refuses direct translation),[163] "Pasifika" references and critiques a hybrid history: it both refers to and resists Magellan's *Mar Pacifico*, acknowledging the legacy of European knowledge and power in constituting the region while insisting on an Indigenous substructure and reemergence, and avowing the agency of Pacific/Oceanian peoples to define space, place, and identity in the present.

This move from Pacific as empty space to Pasifika as multiplicity of translocal communities has implications for the work that the prefix *trans* might do. To begin with, it divests *trans* of its dominant meaning of "crossing over" or "on the other side of," and suggests a more productive addressing of diverse and complex identities via a culturally and theoretically richer and less determinedly geopolitical mode of *reading across*. In this regard, it resonates with Chickasaw literary scholar Chadwick Allen's deployment of the prefix in his concept of trans-Indigenous,[164] where *trans* "may be able to bear the complex, contingent asymmetry and the potential risks of unequal encounters borne by the preposition *across*. It may be able to indicate the specific agency and situated momentum carried by the preposition *through*. It may be able to harbor the potential of *change* as both transitive and intransitive verb, and as both noun and adjective."[165] Accordingly, "transpasifika" foregrounds the notion of moving purposefully through, across, and among communities and individuals, placing carefully contextualized and praxis-oriented analyses of specific concerns and traditions within larger frames and different kinds of conversations. It points to the generative possibilities of transformation from one state to another, highlighting the processual potential of social becoming. It furthermore signals the possibilities of larger coalitions (as does Pearson) in its sense of uniting; and—significantly—the prefix *trans* in its sense of surpassing or transcending invites consideration of the collaborations, connections, and itineraries that expand the Pacific world, linking communities and projects to peoples, places, and fields of enquiry *beyond* the geographical Pacific to embrace a more global intercultural reach. This last approach corresponds to a mode of the trans-Indigenous that, Allen writes, "operates across and through texts produced not only by Indigenous, but also non-Indigenous writers, artists, and intellectuals."[166] It "centers on Indigenous texts and contexts, but positioned among a range of 'other' voices, perspectives, and interpretative frames. This understanding of the trans-Indigenous continues to indicate an Indigenous itinerary, . . . one that is multiply aligned and multiply relational, never sited in isolation."[167]

In its focus on performance, transpasifika accords with theatre scholar Rossella Ferrari's argument that the semantics of *trans* "do not simply denote transfers across the geopolitical borders of nation-states but also conjure a host of phenomenological, ontological, and metaphysical borderlands which are traversed, transgressed, and transcended by multiple kinds of trans-actors."[168] Further, in stressing the agentive capacity of *trans*—not solely as a prefix but also as an action—Ferrari's work evokes performance scholar Amelia Jones's meditations on how the relational connotations of *trans* are "intimately linked to the claims for performativity and performance" and nuance our "understanding of how performance *works*"[169] by attuning us to how performative behaviors and practices come to mean across time and space, human and non-human, bodies and performers, and across various identifications and linguistic modes.

As a mobile spatial imaginary and an archipelagic approach to performance analysis, transpasifika provides a capacious yet targeted lens for illuminating the diverse artistic expressions of a globalizing Pacific on the move. In reading performance across varied polities and circumstances, it answers Diaz's call for "a framework that can flex nationally, internationally, transnationally, sub-nationally, supra-nationally, and even extra- and post-nationally, and in such a way as to accommodate the many 'nations' involved."[170] This framework allows me to trace the malleable contours of Pacific Islander migrations, venturing beyond regional boundaries to consider how performance facilitates cultural maintenance and change in situations of global dispersal, as well as mapping possible performance constituencies that do not conform to established areal designations. It also keeps in mind the various ways in which non-Pacific participants enter the picture, and that, due to cultural and migratory flows, colonial dispossession, and the designs of empire, one's closest affinities might not in fact be with other Pacific Islanders: as Kauanui observes within the American Pacific, "Samoans (at least on the West Coast), for example, might find much more in common with African Americans, Hawaiians with American Indians, and Chamorros with Chicanos."[171] Significantly, a transpasifika perspective also pursues a critical cosmopolitics by remaining attentive to social, political, environmental, and human differences in the Pacific region that remind us how frequently "'oceans disconnect' even more than they 'connect.'"[172] These various considerations are drawn together through a focus on how transpasifika performance projects reflect and effect the "sea changes" of this vast region under the evolving pressures of the (American) Pacific Century. This focus guides my examination of works that reclaim and refill an "empty" ocean through acts of Indigenous voyaging; take action against climate-induced sea-level rise in a region bracketed by the US and China, the planet's two largest greenhouse gas emitters; effect cultural maintenance and transition in island populations widely separated by the impetus of the late capitalist economy; and navigate new pathways in the wake of widespread urbanization, militarization, and nuclear testing.

CONSTELLATED READINGS

Like the Pacific Ocean itself, the content of this book encompasses both breadth and depth, moving across wide geographical and cultural terrain but with specific attention to the minutiae of performances staged mainly between 2000 and 2020 as I have experienced them as a reader, spectator, activator, and invited participant and documenter. As a non-Indigenous scholar from Oceania, I am very aware of how my research in and on Oceania is more often than not an intercultural process, a negotiation of different positions that must acknowledge my own biases and blind spots. Consequently, where possible, I maintain my practice in this book of engaging creative artists as expert interlocutors through *talanoa* (conversation, exchange of ideas).[173] In this regard, I also develop a dialogic relationship between Pacific and non-Pacific theories as complementary traditions. Although the book's body chapters stand on their own, different artists and themes overlap and flow through them. In my arrangement of the case studies, I pursue a method of "constelled reading"; in other words, I juxtapose texts from different genres and sites, bringing them into formation to reveal new patterns and assemblages that divulge what might not be evident otherwise.

Pragmatically, this approach responds to Teresia Teaiwa's call for a Pacific studies methodology that "reflect[s] a commitment to making comparisons across the region,"[174] that goes beyond a single nation or ethnicity, and that strikes a balance between attentiveness to local intellectual genealogies and a continuing engagement with traditions and trends in the broader humanities and social sciences.[175] Drawing various sites and struggles into larger frames lends relational relevance to otherwise neglected materials and locations—a necessary strategy given the situation outlined in this chapter. John Carlos Rowe states his point from an Americanist perspective, but it applies more widely: "When considered merely as discrete entities, small, underpopulated islands like the Marshall Islands hardly deserve our attention in the already crowded liberal arts curriculum. But when understood as crucial parts in the larger movement of the United States across the Pacific . . . , these neglected areas gain significance not only in the study of U.S. imperialism but also in terms of their own struggles for cultural identity and geopolitical sovereignty."[176]

Metaphorically, in creating these various mappings across the chapters, I take guidance from the *etak* model with its dynamic triangulation of oceans, stars, and islands. As explained above, in the context of this book, *etak* offers a productive trope for Pasifika artists' creative agency in navigating vicissitudes of production and reception as well as the wider upheavals of the Pacific Century. The concept also serves as a scholarly method of moving through/by the performances discussed herein. Following a lead in Pacific thought, we could conceive of this book itself as a voyaging canoe, a repository and vehicle containing a diverse cargo of contributions and ideas, which are variously picked up and dropped off, enriching the canoe as it journeys through each chapter. Consequently, the design of this book comprises a series of voyages undertaken across the geographic, topological, and discursive expanse of the Pacific, guided in each instance by a series of case studies that help me plot the journey, and leading to different destinations that culminate in new understandings of our contemporary moment. Hawaiian scholar Renee Pualani Louis reminds us how genres of performance cartography like Pacific navigation shift the notion of cartography from a "science of representation" to a "science of practices"[177] and, accordingly, from a representational/ontological understanding of maps (what things are) to a processual/ontogenetic one (how things become).[178] In developing a contemporary body of knowledge around *ka ho'okele* (Hawaiian navigation), master navigator Nainoa Thompson devised a series of "star lines," patterns that connect several stars in the celestial sphere to assist oceanic wayfinding, with the navigator using the stars as directional clues as they rise and set.[179] These star lines have different configurations and purposes from Western constellations; rather than static astral pictures, these are dynamic patterns that unfold performatively and in process as the wayfinder connects different points in motion, traveling point by point toward a destination. As such, they offer an instructive, potent symbol for how I link up the various guiding case studies as I unfold the argument in my own performative movement through each chapter toward new outcomes.

In doing so, however, I am conscious of settler Canadian academic Pauline Wakeham's judicious advice to interrogate the forms of critical agency that are exercised when non-Indigenous scholars juxtapose Indigenous texts. To guard against "cultural appropriation or tokenistic cultural tourism,"[180] she argues, we need methods that "prevent different texts and contexts from being 'plac[ed] together' in ways that are determined arbitrarily by the critic."[181] Wakeham recommends that scholars build, as I attempt to do throughout, the ground from principles drawn from the texts themselves, "carefully considering the intricate ways in which texts themselves speak—as well as the contexts out of which these textual commentaries emerge and the layered ways they may generate meanings in relation to multiple readerships."[182]

My hope in what follows is that readers will be able to navigate their own passages throughout the book from their situated perspectives, rather than feeling like passengers on a turbulent journey. To assist with this experience, I describe the arc of the book's journeys, setting sail with a focus on the canoe itself. Chapter 2, "Pelagic Performances: Pacific Voyagers on the Sea and Stage," examines how contemporary Pacific Islanders have resisted strategic characterizations of the Pacific as a nonsignifying expanse or as a partitioned series of territories and nation-states by drawing on the long history of seaborne exploration and landfall by which the ocean world was initially populated. I map varied geographic and performance cartographies in Oceania by scanning the interface between two recent regional cultural revival efforts: the renaissance of Indigenous seafaring vessels and navigational technologies, and the development of local forms of modern artistic performance. The resurgence of *vaka moana* (oceangoing canoes)—Oceania's signal cultural artifact—has nurtured national pride and regional affiliations across the Pacific, and the performing arts have contributed to that discourse by transmitting, challenging, and imaginatively elaborating information and attitudes and by actively staging intercultural encounters. The chapter considers multiple ways in which the *vaka* encourages transpasifika connections, charting a range of voyaging projects, dances, plays, and performance art pieces that highlight various translocal assemblages within this critical regional structure. Starting with the reassertion of ethnic ties across an extensive Polynesian "nation," I look at how oceanic relationships are performed between Aotearoa New Zealand and its South Pacific neighbors, and between Hawai'i and Tahiti. I then turn to translocal circuits between Australia and western Melanesia, and then to multisited connections forged throughout central Oceania that revivify Fiji as a vital nexus of exchange. Finally, I examine a series of works by Asian, Pacific, and American artists that track imbrications and tensions between Micronesian and Polynesian voyaging from East Asia to California, drawing attention to complex Islander identities and interactions within the long reach of the American Pacific.

These case studies illustrate how artists and activists have embarked on real and imagined voyages to pursue questions of identity, autonomy, attachment, and agency in the Pacific Century. I show how theatricalized versions of Pacific voyaging can offer insights into tensions between models of regional identity and local sovereignty, especially when voyaging tropes are deployed to emphasize genealogical connections that work against national schisms caused by military coups, ethnic oppression, or imperial domination. I also explore how the works navigate relationships between precolonial interisland mobility and modern migrancy, and treat representations of gender in voyaging scenarios. The case studies, moreover, drive forward discussions in theater and performance studies about historical reenactment and the dynamics of site-specificity in intercultural performance. By charting exchanges and alliances along with exclusions and disjunctions, this discussion acknowledges Oceania as a complex, heterogeneous, and volatile region, inviting consideration of how transpasifika methodologies work across various forms of power and authority, and encouraging a more nuanced appreciation of how identities are negotiated in Oceanian performance.

Chapter 3, "(Dis)appearing Islands: Climate Change and the Future Geographies of Oceanian Performance," shifts the sense of "moving islands" by asking what happens when, in an era of "carbon colonialism," the ocean ceases to be an empowering highway and instead becomes an existential threat. Since the millennium, the Pacific Islands region has assumed an urgent significance in debates about anthropogenic climate change as rising oceans and associated impacts pose an increasing danger to the lifeways and sovereignty of low-lying island states. Here, I examine how artists, activists, and performers have become part of a broader cohort of traveling Pacific citizens engaged in a range of climate-change negotiations in international contexts, and how they have deployed various aesthetic strategies to draw specific attention to the crisis and to leverage international partnerships in responding to it. Refuting characterizations of climate-exposed communities as helpless victims or as climate heroes in a relationship of dependency on the developed world, the performances tread a strategic path between vulnerability and agency. Drawing upon performance's ideational capacity to instantiate imagined movements and future scenarios, these works create proleptic embodiments, images, and environments that engage foreign publics materially and virtually.

My case studies include activist projects by the Pacific Climate Warriors, a grassroots coalition from fifteen Pacific Island nations, with a particular focus on their Mat Weaving Project (2015). This pilgrimage to the Vatican and the gift of a fine mat to Pope Francis draws upon a complex heritage of ceremonial gift exchange in the Pacific, whose reciprocal obligations stretch into the past and reach into the future, symbolically enlisting the Catholic Church in the fight against climate change. I then consider very different deployments of Oceanian theatrical aesthetics in stage presentations that place Pacific performers within divergent climate-change narratives and outcomes: the Fiji-based Oceania Centre's European tour of their musical spectacle, *Moana Rua: The Rising of the Sea* (2015) on the festival circuit and to the European Parliament; and New Zealand / Samoan MAU dance company's *Birds with Skymirrors* (2010–14). My final two examples, which analyze the Tuvalu and Kiribati Pavilions at the Venice Biennale, differ in that Pacific Islander performers are not physically present in the mise-en-scène; instead, the onus is on the visitor to activate the work. In the i-Kiribati-Slovenian coproduction *Sinking Islands, Unsinkable Art* (2017), participants face off against a digital avatar of a traditional i-Kiribati warrior in a battle over climate change; and in *Crossing the Tide* (2015), a collaboration between Taiwanese artist Vincent J. F. Huang, the Tuvaluan government, and New York's Guggenheim Museum, visitors traverse a flooded pavilion that encourages a global environmental consciousness linking the Adriatic and the Pacific. By rehearsing different possibilities for global futures, these works link Oceania with the wider world in their form, content, collaboration, and circulation. These international networks complicate restrictive and stereotypical depictions of "disappearing" island communities and offer alternative prospects for natural and cultural sustainability based in Oceanian traditions and worldviews, while providing insights into new mobilities of contemporary transpasifika performance.

The journey undertaken in chapter 4, "Performing Transnational Samoa: Remittance, Resistance, Community," involves a detailed view of how transpasifika dynamics operate through performance by charting theatrical relationships between multiply situated nodes of the Samoan diaspora, one of Oceania's most demographically visible and artistically prolific populations. My key critical concept here is "cultural remittances," which, as distinct from financial remittances, refers to the ideas, behaviors, narratives, values, and social capital that are relayed back and forth between home communities and diasporic locales, and that function as local-level forms of cultural diffusion in contrast to the macro-level dissemination of global culture. I adapt this sociological concept to create a framework that better accommodates and illuminates the operations of theater and performance practice and that attends more closely to the decentered and multipolar character of Pacific migration, which frequently activates intradiasporic and indirect transnational transactions that function beyond the homeland/hostland dyad. My purpose is to analyze how theater stimulates cultural exchange across vast and variegated geographic and social terrain, and how it enables diasporic community building.

Although this critical framework can be applied to various diasporic communities from Oceania and elsewhere, my discussion centers on Samoa, an island group partitioned into an independent nation ([Western] Samoa) and a United States territory (American Samoa). Both Samoan populations are characterized by a high degree of out-migration and by artistic production that takes place predominantly in off-island contexts. Enriching the notion of cultural remittances by linking it to the Samoan concept of *vā*, the relational space between people, places, and things, I read a constellation of performance pieces produced by different Samoan artists based in major diasporic nodes across the Pacific. These are Tusiata Avia's *Wild Dogs under My Skirt* (New Zealand, 2007/2019), Polytoxic ensemble's *Teuila Postcards* (Australia, 2006–9), Michel Tuffery's *Siamani Samoa* (*German Sāmoa*, 2015), Dan Taulapapa McMullin's *Pink Heaven* (United States, 2000), and Victoria Nalani Kneubuhl's *The Holiday of Rain* (Hawai'i, 2011). I examine how their cultural remittances—sometimes affirmative, sometimes subversive—operate to sustain relations between dispersed communities while at the same time contributing to new, transnational permutations of Samoan culture.

The rapid changes to Pacific Island cultures caused by mass migration to urban centers after World War II also form the backdrop for chapter 5, "Destination Urbanesia: Cityscapes, Militarization, and Islander Identities," which takes up "Urbanesia" as a spatial configuration, creative arena, and mode of lived experience. Coined by New Zealand–based Cook Islands / Samoan performance artist Courtney Sina Meredith, the term "Urbanesia" describes the new physical mappings and social formations that emerge from the energetic, polyglot Pasifika cultures of contemporary metropolises, where island and city are brought into profound collision and act as the crucible of fresh global identities. As an elastic cartography that takes the modern city as its common ground, Urbanesia emphasizes Pasifika identities shaped by expansive, mobile cultural fields and offers a counter to the artificially imposed and colonially restrictive geocultural categories of Polynesia, Melanesia, and Micronesia. Urbanesian cultural production can, I argue, also be fruitfully extended to examine how Pacific artists frame broader coalitions with different communities across global, urban spaces to interrogate histories of mobility, colonialism, and violence.

I begin by looking at how young, urban-raised Pacific artists such as Meredith, Mīria George, and John Vea explore evolving forms of urban selfhood, treating aspiration and affiliation but also alienation and disidentification. The chapter's linchpin is a study of three filmic artworks by Fijian New Zealand artist Luke Willis Thompson, presented as a single exhibition: *How Long?* (2018), *Cemetery of Uniforms and Liveries* (2016), and *autoportrait* (2017). Suturing the cities of Suva, London, and St. Paul, these pieces link discourses of militarization in the Pacific and the militaristic structures of urban police brutality, registering performances of violence on Black bodies across Pacific Island (Fijian), Black British, and African American contexts, and yoking emergent discourses on the Black Pacific with the globalizing movement of Black Lives Matter. This focus on militarization draws crucial attention to how certain spaces within the Pacific have become urbanized through military infrastructures. The final section of the chapter explores this process through the legacy of "nuclear performativity" in the Pacific, focusing on the play *Les Champignons de Paris* (Tahiti, 2017) by Emilie Génaédig and La Compagnie du Caméléon, which moves between metropolitan France, North Africa, and French Polynesia to critique the urban logics and detrimental impacts of France's thirty-year bomb-testing program.

Taken together, these itineraries through Pacific worlds disclose important insights into the urgent aesthetic forms and social functions of contemporary Pacific cultural production, and advance our comprehension of the globally embedded nature of this diverse and mobile region. I want to be clear that the emphasis on creative agency, while a deliberate and constant bearing of this study, does not default naively to an assumption of political efficacy. Not all creative acts—perhaps not many—result in a subversion or even a recalibration of the formidable forces faced by Pacific peoples in the twenty-first century. Nevertheless, these works *are* generative and transformative in their foregrounding of alternative worldviews, their creation of new collaborations and communities, and their modeling of different modes of thinking and doing. When brought together, they provide compelling evidence of creative activity that can shift the way theater and performance scholars apprehend the Pacific, and that holds the potential to reposition our discipline's mappings and its theories and methods at large. Dissolving the pervasive boundaries between islands, seas, and continents, a transpasifika performance studies offers new frameworks for reading the Pacific Ocean domain while expanding and enriching our understanding of the scope, concerns, and strategies of world performance.

TWO

Pelagic Performances:
Pacific Voyagers on the Sea and Stage

BEGINNINGS, ENDINGS, BEGINNINGS

In 1929, while conducting research on the island of Rakahanga in the northern Cook Islands, the prominent Māori ethnologist Te Rangihiroa (Peter
Buck) attended the performance of a *nuku* (historical pageant), which
depicted the origin and settlement of the atoll.[1] The afternoon performance
took place on the main village street representing the South Pacific Ocean,
with the audience lining both sides of the thoroughfare and guests of honor
seated on the veranda of the chief's house. Costumed actors reenacted the
deeds of the historical ancestors through verbal recitation and pantomimic
actions, accompanied by a sung chorus and an orchestra of wooden gongs
and goatskin drums. The four-act nuku opened with the Rarotongan ancestor Huku the Discoverer on a deep-sea fishing expedition, sighting the
nascent atoll in the form of a coral upgrowth beneath the water and then
returning to his home island (represented by a dilapidated house at one
end of the street). The second act embarked from another house representing the sacred homeland of Hawaiki,[2] portraying two voyages by the demi-
god Māui-muri (a local version of the pan-Polynesian trickster figure and
culture hero, Māui) as he schemed with the old woman at the bottom of the
sea, Hina-i-te-papa, to bait the coral upgrowth and fish up the island.[3] The
nuku then dramatized Huku's voyage back to the risen atoll to drive off
Māui-muri, followed by a third voyage to supply the new island with coconut plants. Finally, the nuku depicted Huku's fourth voyage to expel his
interloping compatriot Wheatu (in a clowning role), who had been carving
a canoe channel through the reef: in the myth, this expulsion enabled
Huku's own family to begin the human colonization of Rakahanga; in the
play, Huku also returned to Rarotonga.

The drama of *Huku the Discoverer* was one of several Cook Islands nuku
that Te Rangihiroa witnessed in the late 1920s during his field research for
Hawai'i's Bishop Museum, and that he identified as an Indigenous form

traditionally enacted throughout the Cook Islands, the Society Islands, and the Tuamotu Archipelago.[4] Many of these historical enactments featured ancestral sea journeys of migration and settlement, adventure, and familial obligation; as Te Rangihiroa remarked at the time, "Such dramatic representations help to preserve the history of the past, and, being uninfluenced by European stage managers, they interpret the true spirit that moved the old-time voyagers to dare and succeed."[5] *Huku the Discoverer* is noteworthy, however, because of the interleaving of human history and mythology in the origin narrative, the repeated feats of voyaging and navigation undertaken by the human characters between Rarotonga and Rakahanga (a distance of almost eight hundred miles of open ocean each way),[6] and—especially—the particular approach to representing the voyaging canoes in the mise-en-scène. Te Rangihiroa explains that Huku's canoe

> was formed of a 6-foot length of coconut leaf split down the midrib and plaited in the same manner as two roof sheets. With the midrib strips uppermost to form the canoe gunwales, a sheet was placed on either side of Huku's waist and tied in front and back so that the ends projected fore and aft to represent the bow and stern of his canoe. To prevent the canoe from slipping down, a loop of bast tied to the gunwales before and behind was passed over one shoulder. . . . Huku's mud-painted legs projected down through the bottom of the canoe and supplied the real motor power as he wielded a canoe paddle to propel his canoe toward the middle of the stage.[7]

Similar canoes were worn by the other principal actors, including an extra-large one to accommodate Māui-muri and his two older brothers together.

Aside from the practical value of the *vaka moana* worn as a costume, which enabled the performers to enact physical confrontations with gales, troughs, and seething waves, as well as to produce various humorous effects as they made the twenty-yard "ocean" passages to and from the tiring-houses to the main playing area, the vaka as embodied extension holds additional symbolic connotations. In this tribute to the village's originary forebear, the symbiotic enmeshment of human body and canoe evokes the vaka as a genealogical vehicle, a synthesis of material, cultural, and somatic history that binds the bodies of those in the present to those of their seafaring ancestors. Far more than a mere "object" or "prop," the canoe here indexes the "symmetry and continuity between object and human worlds" so crucial to Oceanic life, acknowledging the vaka as a vital co-performer that acts with a will and a destiny on the sea as well as the stage.[8] Corporeal performance activates and reinforces these historical and ongoing relation-ships, creating an epistemological and ontological continuity that sustained the local community as it navigated a rapidly changing Pacific.

Indeed, by the time this nuku was presented, various internal factors combined with the colonial parceling of territories in the Pacific and wide-spread foreign intervention into social and cultural life meant that in most areas of Oceania purposeful, long-distance sailing and navigation in Indig-enous vessels existed only in performative representation—in dramatic enactments, legends, dances, and other ritual protocols—rather than as lived practice. As Te Rangihiroa's own process of collecting and recording for the Bishop Museum attests, these fading traditions were increasingly considered subjects for salvage ethnography. A grainy field photograph exists of the performance and reveals the village's colonial setting, a model "of orderly arrangement and cleanliness" under New Zealand's govern-mental administration on behalf of Britain.[9]

The audience, sporting starched shirts and sundresses, cloche hats and panamas, is arranged demurely in front of the whitewashed facade of the church.[10] Against this backdrop, the nuku performs its own version of Indigenous colonization, positing the Islanders as agents of discovery and settlement. By portraying an origin narrative that begins with acts of migra-tion, the performance speaks to a characteristic feature of Pacific Islander identity that demonstrates dynamism between emplacement and mobility, local affiliations and networked sites, and grounded genealogies and mul-tiple landfalls. This dialectical relationship between sea and land is per-formed spatially by overlaying the village's cartography with that of the Pacific Ocean; the main street highlights the ocean as a highway rather than a barrier or hindering vacancy. As this thoroughfare is walked/sailed by people/demigods/canoes—many times, in different directions—the nuku's action repudiates the colonial notion of the bounded Islander and weaves the people of Rakahanga into a mobile system that includes Rarotonga, expands across Oceania, and spans human and divine realms.

Te Rangihiroa's interest in this performance is not surprising in light of his own work as an Indigenous ethnologist. His pioneering contributions to scholars' and general readers' appreciation of Polynesian cultures in the first half of the twentieth century can be understood as a performative proj-ect that was as personal as it was intellectual. His voyages and interactions as a Māori researcher were premised on a recognition and reinforcement of familial ties. While this emphasis, as well as the academic culture of the period in which he wrote, problematically inflected his theories of Polyne-sian migratory origins with areal and racial biases (themes that I shall take

Figure 2. Huku, dressed in a "canoe" costume made from plaited coconut leaves, sights the coral upgrowth of Rakahanga in the nuku performance *Huku the Discoverer*, Cook Islands, 1929. In Te Rangihiroa / Peter Buck, *Ethnology of Manihiki and Rakahanga* (Honolulu: Bishop Museum, 1932). Photograph by Te Rangihiroa, reproduced courtesy of Bishop Museum Archives, www. bishopmuseum.org

up variously throughout this chapter),[11] his work is notable for seeking to instill pride in a shared heritage—especially the accomplishments of deliberate voyaging—across a subregion whose people had been divided and disenfranchised by colonial intercession. In the epilogue to his 1938 popular ethnography *Vikings of the Sunrise*, Te Rangihiroa's elegiac acknowledgment of the departed world of precolonial Polynesia is tempered by a provocation to his readers:

> The old world created by our Polynesian ancestors has passed away, and a new world is in the process of being fashioned. The stone temples have been destroyed and the temple drums and shell trumpets have long been silent. Tane, Tu, Rongo, Tangaroa and the other members of the divine family of the Sky-father and the Earth-mother have left us. The great voyaging canoes have crumbled to dust and the sea captains and the expert craftsmen have passed away to the Spirit-land. The regalia and symbols of spiritual and temporal power have been scattered among the museums of other peoples. The glory of the Stone Age has departed out of Polynesia. . . . The old net is full

of holes, its meshes have rotted, and it has been laid aside. WHAT NEW NET GOES AFISHING?[12]

By citing the proverb of the net—often employed in Māori self-determination contexts—Te Rangihiroa lays a challenge for coming generations: how might the strategic recuperation of ancestral knowledge chart a course out of a milieu of loss and dispersal, stimulating future forms of social and cultural agency? A generation afterward, palpable responses would start to emerge from decolonizing efforts across Oceania more broadly, as Indigenous mobilizing in politics, science, cultural affairs, and the arts began to reshape the physical and social contours of the region, among them a revival of Indigenous shipbuilding and navigational skills. This renaissance, its confluence with the performing arts, and their regional and global dynamics in the twenty-first century are the subject of what follows in this chapter.

VOYAGES OF REDISCOVERY: CONTEMPORARY INDIGENOUS SEAFARING AND CONNECTING ACROSS OCEAN SPACES

As Paul D'Arcy affirms, "Oceania was, and still is, one of the few places on earth where the sea figures so prominently in human activities and thoughts."[13] Containing over 80 percent of the world's islands in a body of water greater than all the land in the world and that could easily accommodate all the world's remaining oceans, the vast area of sea relative to land has given rise to cultures inflected intimately by these geographical dimensions.[14] The settlement of the region, particularly of "Remote Oceania,"[15] represented the last original human migration and the first to require technology to accomplish it, in the form of oceangoing vessels capable of traveling great distances across open water and guided by sophisticated navigation systems based on acute observation of natural phenomena.[16] Over time, due to numerous internal and external factors, many communities throughout Oceania experienced an atrophying of long-distance voyaging ability and an increased focus on land-based identities and concerns. Yet localized interisland sea travel, international voyages on foreign vessels,[17] and a sustained and intricate involvement with the ocean as medium, resource, and genealogical reservoir have continued to characterize island societies. This point is important to acknowledge: Richard Feinberg observes that while "most writing on Pacific seafaring and navigation has focused on the spectacular exploits of those peoples who have managed to retain a large proportion of the old technology and skills," one must not lose sight of the fact that "few Pacific Islanders today make lengthy canoe voyages."[18] Far more common are quotidian acts of maritime engagement (for food, transportation, trade, leisure, and art), which nevertheless speak to the deep significance of the sea for Oceanian communities, including those "islanders who have abandoned—or who never had—great voyaging traditions."[19]

It is in the period since the 1970s—a fecund phase of revival and revision in many aesthetic, social, and political domains throughout Oceania—that a scholarly, practical, and artistic awakening of Indigenous voyaging has taken place. David Lewis's monograph *We, The Navigators* (1972) was one of the first texts to draw upon ethnographic research and empirical experimentation to make the case for the existence—in pre-European times and more sparsely in the present[20]—of "highly organized systems of complex navigational lore"[21] that suggested far more extensive acts of purposive voyaging, greater possibilities of interisland population mobility along ocean highways, and stronger relationships between Oceanian peoples and the aquatic world than had been granted by European commentators.[22] A key development was the founding of the Polynesian Voyaging Society (PVS) in 1973 and its construction of the *Hōkūle'a*, a Hawaiian *wa'a kaulua* (double-hulled canoe) based on historical designs, which made a groundbreaking twenty-five-hundred-mile voyage to Tahiti in 1976, guided by Satawalese[23] navigator Pius (Mau) Piailug. Since then, the region has witnessed a renaissance of Indigenous shipbuilding and navigational culture, including the establishment of voyaging societies in numerous Pacific sites; oceangoing vessels making various transpacific journeys; and the enmeshment of voyaging technologies and symbolism with a raft of cultural revival efforts and forms of production, which Paul Sharrad has coined a "pelagic post-colonialism."[24] These grassroots activities have even captured the attention of the Walt Disney Corporation, which fashioned its latest "Princess" as a plucky Polynesian girl voyager in the blockbuster movie *Moana* (2016).[25]

Broadly speaking, postcolonial voyaging exemplifies Epeli Hau'ofa's figuration of Oceania as a "sea of islands" that enables Islander activities to be understood relationally and as contributing to a regional community of potentially global proportions.[26] Yet the construction, launching, and sailing of *vaka moana* comprise a complex array of performances that speak to deep, and sometimes not easily reconciled, investments in and questions of Oceanic being and belonging. Whereas the mix of traditional and modern building materials and design concepts has led some critics to dismiss the revival's "authenticity" and its utility for understanding past practices, Ben

Finney argues that this attitude "miss[es] the main point of what is now primarily a social movement."[27] Rather (as with modern theatrical performance), the phenomenon is better understood as part of a long continuum of Pacific peoples' adaptation and creation of new cultural forms from blended influences, of "drawing selectively from their past, bringing forward ancient elements—be they in voyaging, dance, art, epistemology and above all their native languages—for contemporary social, cultural and political purposes."[28] This approach resonates with Hawaiian scholar Stephanie Nohelani Teves's eloquent argument that "the power of Indigenous performativity is its ability to create, modify, alter, and revive practices or to make completely new ones out of a reverence for your culture while also critiquing the need to perform a pure indigeneity."[29] As performative historical reenactments that seek both to materialize and to imagine beyond a remembered past in order to invest in new coalitions and collaborative projects, vaka and their voyages signify origin and destiny, ancestral and contemporary continuity, local sovereignty and political struggle. Moreover, as Renee Pualani Louis explains, "The canoe is considered a living being with purpose, responsibility, and intelligence and with whom the navigator and crew form a lifelong and timeless bond, as each cares for the safety of the other."[30] Rejecting notions of the Pacific region as *aqua nullius*, a strategic zone of foreign militarization, or a space of transit swamped by the Asia-Pacific conglomerate, the social and physical movements of vaka generate potent genealogical and geographic networks that can remap (neo)colonial cartographies and offer powerful expressions of solidarity, teamwork, and environmental responsibility.[31]

The vaka's historical and ongoing emphasis on suturing transpasifika ties across Oceania shifts the frame away from the colonizer/colonized, settler/indigene, and Western/non-Western binaries of traditional postcolonial inquiry. As maritime historians Peter Nuttall, Paul D'Arcy, and Colin Philp contend, to focus on Oceania's precolonial-era vessels (and their latter-day manifestations) "mov[es] the predominant lens beyond the obsession with European priorities and European interactions with Pacific Islanders"[32] and recenters Indigenous accounts of "mobile interaction between fluid social and political groups forever mediated by their relationship to the sea."[33] This approach finds affinities with Chadwick Allen's move away from conventional comparative analysis and the Eurocentric "obsessions of orthodox studies of literatures"[34] to a "trans-Indigenous" model that aims to "invite specific studies into different kinds of conversations, and to acknowledge the mobility and multiple interactions of Indigenous peoples, cultures, histories, and texts."[35] Such multiperspectival analyses demonstrate the persistence and resurgence of Indigenous cultures and reach across tribal and national boundaries to advance an intellectual and artistic sovereignty potentially global in scope.[36]

Scholars in various disciplines have taken a multisited approach to mapping acts of Pacific voyaging and their expressions in other media, including Paul D'Arcy in environmental history, Vicente M. Diaz in Native Pacific cultural studies, and Paul Sharrad, Elizabeth DeLoughrey, and Michelle Keown in literary studies, and I am indebted to the insights of these colleagues in the pages that follow. Yet there is more to be said, and differently, about how the performing arts elaborate information and attitudes about voyaging past and present, and how they intersect with the performative claims of voyaging missions. The collaborative, embodied, and theatrical aspects of Oceanic cultural production shed new light on what is at stake in these endeavors. In this chapter, I constellate several case studies from sites throughout Oceania that exhibit different forms of Pacific Islander collaboration and regional relationships to voyaging histories. Bringing together expeditions by reconstructed vessels, plays and stage spectacles, dance works, and performative art installations, I explore how artists and activists have embarked on real and imagined journeys to pursue urgent and often contentious questions of identity, autonomy, attachment, and agency in the Pacific.

The combined case studies sketch a regional topography of Oceania that both acknowledges and complicates the imposed geocultural subcategories of Polynesia, Melanesia, and Micronesia.[37] Looking first at the reassertion of ethnic ties across an extensive Polynesian "nation," I begin with two works, the photographic installation *The Raft of the Tagata Pasifika* (2014–16) and the dance piece *Vaka* (2012), which perform back against colonial histories that disavowed the abilities of Indigenous navigators, especially their claims to the deliberate settlement of Aotearoa New Zealand, positioned distantly at the southernmost point of Polynesia. Drawing subversively on castaway and shipwreck imagery from nineteenth-century art, both works invoke histories of Indigenous colonization that unsettle New Zealand's European settler-colonial dominance by emphasizing genealogical networks that link Māori to other island groups such as Samoa and the Cook Islands, while tracking New Zealand's shifting identity as a Polynesian society, a British colony, and (back to) a Pacific nation. The next pairing of case studies continues the focus on how native sovereignties have been produced and advanced through transoceanic affiliations. I read reciprocal performances between Hawaiian and Tahitian communities that emerged from the Hawai'i to Tahiti leg of the Polynesian Voyaging Society's Mālama Honua Worldwide Voyage (2014) and the *heiva* spectacle *Te Feti'a 'Avei'a/L'étoile guide* (2014) performed by Tahitian dance group O Tahiti E, which depicted a migratory voyage to Hawai'i. My analysis examines how the multiple intersections of sailing, cultural performance, and theatrical performance support local coalitions while building mutual relationships that cut across US and French colonial jurisdictions to strengthen ties between "Polynesian cousins."

Subsequently, the discussion moves beyond the familial structures of Polynesian membership to consider how, and to what ends, communities in other parts of Oceania (especially Melanesia) have engaged voyaging histories. This section includes the reminder, as in Crossroad Arts' community theater piece *No Two Stones* (Australia, 2006), that some Pacific Islanders bear histories of coerced sea passages, not just voluntary ones. Principally, I take up vexed questions of participation and representation in my reading of the Oceania Centre's music-dance-dramas *Vaka: The Birth of a Seer* and *Drua: The Wave of Fire* (Fiji, 2012), which theatricalize the regional cooperation among Fiji, Samoa, Tonga, and Kiribati that enabled the development of the Fijian *drua* vessel in the late eighteenth century. The projects foreground historical and artistic federations that offer alternatives to Polynesia as a privileged regional topography, and that work implicitly to transcend the exclusionary Indigenous nationalism and regional schisms engendered by Fiji's military coups.

The connections between precolonial interisland mobility and modern migrancy form a through line for several works in the latter part of the chapter. This final series of texts interweaves gender and geography, pointing to the possibilities and occlusions of both emphases within the context of the American Pacific. These works also bring together Indigenous and non-Indigenous perspectives and participants through transpasifika collaborations with Asian and American playwrights and theater companies. Honolulu Theatre for Youth's *Navigator* (Hawai'i, 2010) eschews the predominantly masculine bias of the voyaging discourse by featuring dual female protagonists who limn a powerful line of women seafarers and navigators. Yet when *Navigator* is read alongside two other HTY-sponsored works, *Song for the Navigator* (1986) and TeAda Productions' *Masters of the Currents* (2017), which attend to the salient but underacknowledged role of Micronesian navigational traditions in the recent resurgence of Indigenous voyaging in Oceania, we see how the play's attempts to write an Americanized Hawai'i back into Polynesia threaten to evacuate Micronesian voices and contributions. Theater is thus indicative of the competing tensions brought about by the ongoing states and relations of subjugation for Pacific Islanders under the United States' imperial and militarized purview.

Reading across and through various complementary works "close together placed"[38] enables a determined focus on specific cultures and traditions while highlighting correlated bodies of social and artistic practice across a broad and diverse region. The approach avoids, on the one hand, the myopic scholarly tendency to study individual island communities in relative isolation,[39] and on the other, homogenizing views of Oceania that arise not only from foreign clichés, but also from the unifying rhetoric of affirmative regionalist paradigms. The case studies in this chapter offer ways to think about how the often contested and contradictory discourses of regional identification in Oceania have been engaged through nautical and theatrical linkages. By charting exchanges and alliances along with exclusions and disjunctions, this discussion situates Oceania as a complex and volatile region that has been characterized as much by discrete national and political formations, colonial circumscriptions, military uprisings, and other social and ethnic fissures as by cognatic, bureaucratic, and artistic fraternities, and that is constituted by widely differing Indigenous demographics, social circumstances, and forms of authority. Accordingly, the following discussions shed fresh light on the political and social role of Pacific Islands performance, its interculturalisms, and the important contribution of artistic and cultural production to our understanding of the contemporary Pacific.

LEGACIES OF LANDFALL:
VISIONS OF ARRIVAL AND SURVIVAL IN AOTEAROA

The discourse of partition and belittlement to which Hau'ofa's "sea of islands" vision responds, especially the colonial tendency to view the ocean as an expanse to be traversed, a resource to be exploited, or a space to be contained and surveilled, has been remarkably pervasive and persistent. Until the mid-twentieth century, in the absence of empirical evidence to prove or disprove deliberate Indigenous voyaging and noninstrument navigational ability, European responses tended to fall into two camps: an acknowledgment often tied to naively romantic ideas of a noble (now vanished) past, which in some situations involved the manipulation of oral traditions to produce particular theories of migration and settlement; or outright rejection, writing off exploratory landfall as the serendipitous result of storms or accidental drift.[40] This was particularly the case in Aotearoa New Zealand, where critical debate about Māori origins dominated scholarly and public discourse at the turn of the twentieth century as New Zealand was cementing its identity as a settler-colonial nation. Both historical positions are taken up critically from Pacific perspectives in two contemporary works by New Zealand–born Samoan artists, which cite these European attitudes to Indigenous voyaging histories and art's role in reinforcing them: Greg Semu's performative photo installation *The Raft of the Tagata Pasifika (People of the Pacific)* (2014–16); and the dance work *Vaka* (2012), choreographed by Neil Ieremia and performed by his company Black Grace. These two independent projects are linked by their reworking of dominant images from two iconic history paintings that bookended the nineteenth century: Louis J. Steele and Charles F. Goldie's *The Arrival of the Maoris in New Zealand* (1898), which took its primary inspiration from French romantic painter Théodore Géricault's *Le radeau de la Méduse (The Raft of the Medusa*, 1818–19).

Both paintings reimagine voyages of colonization: Géricault's work depicts the shipwrecked passengers of a French naval frigate en route to Senegal in 1816 to reestablish French governance of the African territory after British cession; Steele and Goldie's shows the ancestors of the Māori making their initial landfall in Aotearoa (in their schema, somewhere in the fourteenth century). The artworks share major similarities in form and composition (British immigrant Steele and New Zealand–born Goldie made studies of *Medusa* when they visited France), including European conventions for representing struggle and miraculous survival at sea. Both emphasize the physical suffering of the seafarers, the extremity of dead and dying figures, the ghoulish insinuation of cannibalism, the crumbling vessels, the tenebrous sky and tortured ocean, and the appalling despair of the ailing survivors punctuated by a flash of hope: the rescue ship in *Medusa* and the tip of coastline in *Arrival*. But whereas Géricault was responding to a contemporary, politically charged event in post-Napoleonic French society, even if he abstracted his specific subject to address the more universal theme of monumental and symbolic struggle,[41] Steele and Goldie were participating in a different project of appropriating Indigenous history to validate an emerging European New Zealand (Pākehā) national consciousness. As Leonard Bell explains, *Arrival* played into the era's rhetoric of liberal nationalism, whereby Māori were figured as a "dying race" while aestheticized Māori subjects, history, and culture were absorbed into Pākehā identity as a key way to distinguish Anglo-Saxon colonists from their European forebears.[42] The dramatic spectacle of *Arrival*, with its ethnographic errors, anachronisms, and cultural faux pas, aimed less for historical fidelity than an expression of European feelings and attitudes about

Figure 3. Louis John Steele and Charles F. Goldie, *The Arrival of the Maoris in New Zealand* (1898). Oil on canvas. Auckland Art Gallery Toi o Tāmaki, gift of the late George and Helen Boyd, 1899.

seaborne struggle and endurance that resonated with a nineteenth-century pioneer mentality. With its biblical references to salvation and the Promised Land, *Arrival* situated New Zealand as a new secular paradise, co-opting Māori landfall to prefigure white migration from Britain.[43] The skeletal figures in a state of near death aboard the ripped and broken *waka* posit the Māori arrival as tenuous rather than triumphant; in effect, Goldie and Steele suggest, it almost didn't happen, thus lending legitimacy to the subsequent wave of European settlement.

Interdisciplinary artist Greg Semu is known for a corpus of large-scale staged photographic work in which he collaborates with Indigenous or ethnic minority groups to produce meticulously detailed, provocative tableaux. Semu's images explore experiences of colonization in order to interrogate demoralizing and displacing portrayals of Indigenous peoples, drawing subversively on the classical tradition of history painting in "political acts of re-appropriation."[44] In his response to *Arrival* (and, by extension, *Medusa*), Semu worked with twenty-two local artists and performers during a four-week residency in Rarotonga, Cook Islands, to create dramatically intense compositions captured in digital C-type photographs, which were edited and produced as large-format light-box installations for a dark exhibition space.[45]

Semu explains that he wanted the gallery presentation to evoke a ship-

Figure 4. Greg Semu, "The Arrival Full Cast Hero," from *Raft of the Tagata Pasifika* (*People of the Pacific*), 2016. Rarotonga, Cook Islands. Type C transparency on transparent synthetic polymer resin. Reproduced courtesy of the artist.

wreck experience, with the different light boxes arranged on various internal walls to give an impression of objects and groups of people breaking up into multiple parts in the dark. At the same time, for Semu, each light box represented the idea of an island scattered in the ocean; thus, as the visitor traverses the dark space between each piece, they also reenact the idea of migratory connection. True to its oceanic theme, therefore, the installation is conceived of an experience that is at once fragmented and cohering.[46]

Experiencing *The Raft of the Tagata Pasifika* at the National Gallery of Victoria in Melbourne, Australia,[47] I was captivated by how the illuminated boxes emerge from their shadowy backdrop like lit scenes in a black-box theater; the chiaroscuro of the backlit images casts into sharp relief the subjects' musculature, eyes, and facial expressions, seizing the human drama of the voyage. The painstakingly reconstructed *waka taua* for the *Arrival*-based studio scenes (later stripped back to a raft for the *Medusa*-inspired compositions) is backed by dark blue plastic sheeting to simulate the seamless merging of sky and sea, and the crackling and surging of thundercloud and ocean. Significantly, Semu does not present us with a romantic legend of effortless passage, but pays respect to the difficulty of the endeavor: I witnessed a palpable struggle and hardship in the wracked, prone, and praying bodies pressed into proximity and pushed to their physical limits. The tableaux contain scenes of death, yes, but also scenes of childbirth: these are not tragic figures stained with the emaciated pathos of the *Arrival* painting, but inhabit a spare and vigorous physicality—a prepared and purposeful group of skilled navigators and seafarers. The powerful pose of the man who sights land with confident delight epitomizes this visual reworking, which presses against Pākehā mythmaking while literally fleshing out the lacunae of Indigenous oral traditions.

These reenactments of past events and (re)playing of/with precedent artworks, which weave back and forth between text and embodiment, recall Rebecca Schneider's observation that reenactors not only restage the past to get it right as it *was* "but to get it right as it *will be* in the future of the archive to which they see themselves as contributing."[48] Semu's work does not only look backward but also laterally and forward, responding to the Victorian-era art historical reenactment through recourse to the validating discoveries of the contemporary voyaging revival, whose recent experiments have proven the claims of deliberate South Pacific migration to New Zealand. Importantly, however, present-day voyaging praxis also partakes of reenactment, but the kind of historical work and imagination it entails offers something more or other than the way that reenactment has been theorized in theater and performance studies as "an intense, embodied inquiry into temporal repetition, temporal recurrence."[49] Instead, its performative inquiry centers on scientific and sociocultural hypotheses about submerged or lost practices and technologies—gesturing to manifold "events" unfolding over centuries and millennia in the peopling of the Pacific—and involves systematic efforts to test and reconstitute them in the present in order to advance Indigenous sovereignty. This wider historical frame and purpose appears in Semu's reworking: instead of a "re-do" of a purportedly precise (and contingent) event—"*the* arrival of the Maoris [*sic*]"—his "*raft* of the people of the Pacific" broadens to conceptualize multiple waves of migration, recuperating "raft" from its connotations of a flimsy, makeshift, emergency vehicle to privilege its sense of "a lot or a large amount of something," corroborating the fullness, multiplicity, and longevity of Pacific migration.

Central to Semu's revisionist imagery is a compelling expression of collaboration, community, and collective will, borne out in the intergenerational dynamics of the tableaux and in the genealogical lineaments of *tatau* (tattoo), which write place, history, and identity potently on to skin, in contrast to the generic, etiolated bodies imagined by Goldie and Steele. These affiliations across space and time are essential to Semu's relational images, which construct a critical dialogue not only with New Zealand's colonial past but also with its multicultural present. Specifically, Semu's restaging reinscribes the history of Pacific Islanders in Aotearoa by connecting precolonial and contemporary diasporas. This move is itself an offshoot of the discourse of contemporary seafaring, which has encouraged modern Pacific diasporas to be theorized as extensions of volitional voyaging. *The Raft of the Tagata Pasifika* highlights the significance of Rarotonga as what Pacific artist Michel Tuffery has called a "BP station,"[50] a recognized fueling stop and historical embarkation point for migratory voyages to Aotearoa, thus positing Cook Islanders as ancestors of the Māori people. Yet the tableaux also acknowledge other intercultural interactions that included different passengers on these southward journeys, such as Samoans. Semu's self-portrait, which depicts him supine, center, in one of the *Medusa*-inspired scenes with his *pe'a* (Samoan male tattoo) on full display from navel to knees, is what the artist terms a "political statement" and a "date stamp"[51] that attests to an earlier history of Samoan settlement in Aotearoa. This testament is particularly pertinent given the overwhelming association of Pacific migrants with accelerated regional mobility following World War II, and their challenges in navigating a sense of belonging within New Zealand's avowed bicultural Māori/ Pākehā social structure. As a New Zealand–born Samoan, Semu places himself within a different genealogy: instead of being "fresh off the boat," as the epithet goes, Semu's body of evidence cites ancestral connections to Indigenous New Zealanders, contributing to the future archive of New Zealand's evolution as a Pacific nation.

Notably, such a claim does not renounce the status of Māori as the Indigenous people of Aotearoa with specific relationships to history, land, and place. This is significant because, as Alice Te Punga Somerville has argued in a major work on the topic, politicized enunciations of New Zealand as a "nation of immigrants" all coming from elsewhere can be detrimental for Māori self-determination.[52] Observing that Hau'ofa's "insistently regional focus allows little room to problematize the relationships between Indigenous and immigrant Pacific peoples in particular spaces,"[53] Te Punga Somerville points out that in contemporary Aotearoa New Zealand Māori and Pasifika peoples connect differently at the level of region and nation. Whereas Māori are genealogically and geographically part of the wider (Indigenous) Pacific, *within* the nation, Māori and Pasifika communities fall into an Indigenous/immigrant dichotomy that blurs the complexities of their past and present connections.[54] Viewing this dichotomy as facilitated by the prejudicial logic of the settler-colonial nation-state, Te

Punga Somerville sees productive potential in Māori articulations with the Pacific in which the nation-state is relegated to only one strand in a matrix of relationships in which Māori operate.[55] Accordingly, Semu's tableaux usefully push back against dominant Pākehā national imaginaries past and present to weave alternative affiliations that encourage Māori connections with Oceania, both rooted and routed. This approach suggests how Pacific contexts can teach us something about intercultural performance, especially when Semu's restaging of this phenomenon is less about actors taking roles and more about a genealogical continuity (more than a temporal repetition or recurrence per se) in which performers may legitimately appear as manifestations of ancestral forebears. In this light, Semu's deployment of *tatau* (tattoo) gains further import. It is noteworthy that the *pe'a* itself contains the figure of a va'a/vaka inscribed across the lower back, a symbol of the *'āiga* (extended family), which the wearer of the *tatau* must protect.[56] The *mise en abyme* of the community within the vaka within the body within the vaka within Semu's image speaks once again to the sophisticated performative enmeshment of bodies, vehicles, and genealogies on the move. These dynamics highlight multiple ways in which indigeneity and diaspora/migration become coconstituted in historical and contemporary situations, simultaneously layered in the subject's identity, but also subject to complex negotiation.

If Semu's tableaux push back against a social and aesthetic history of dismissing Polynesian expeditionary achievements by focusing on corporeal specificity and (re)documenting the apodictic body of the voyager and the visceral solidarity of the voyaging community, then Black Grace's *Vaka* takes up this task by exploring the more expansive connotations of the *vaka moana*. One of New Zealand's leading contemporary dance companies, Black Grace was established in 1995 by artistic director Neil Ieremia, also of Samoan descent, and originally comprised an ensemble of Māori and Pacific men. The company now incorporates a greater diversity of genders and ethnicities that represent a broader cross-section of New Zealand and the Pacific. Black Grace tours widely internationally, deploying a choreographic vocabulary that blends customary Māori and Pacific dance forms with contemporary dance registers. As well as responding to the racist politics of *Arrival of the Maoris*, the one-hour dance performance also draws inspiration from another artwork influenced by Géricault's *Medusa*: US video artist Bill Viola's *The Raft* (2004).[57] In this video installation, a collection of strangers from various backgrounds accumulates in a space. Suddenly, they are cannoned by a massive onslaught of water; some are bowled over, while others try to fight against the violent deluge. Then, almost as suddenly, the water stops, leaving breathless, pummeled, soaking, bewildered bodies. Slowly, they start to connect, to reach out, to help each other up, and to embrace. As a piece about people's collective experience of wars and natural disasters, *The Raft* emphasizes our ability to find communion in the wake of trauma, to survive, and to persevere.

Vaka (originally titled *Waka*, the Māori term) figures the canoe as a metaphorical vehicle for survival and a potent symbol for hope. The driving questions of the work are what constitutes a "vaka" in contemporary society, how we conceive of and protect the contents of our vaka, and why and with whom we might share those contents.[58] These prompts emphasize the social dimensions of voyaging, centering humans themselves as vaka (vessels of history, culture, and identity), and charting a journey of the social life of Aotearoa and of humanity in general. The dancers express this notion of support, this vital link between the individual and the collective, in an opening sequence by stepping slowly and smoothly across the dimly lit stage to plangent guitar chords, each one carrying a fellow company member on their back. Subsequent group compositions that showcase Black Grace's characteristic athletic style feature the group coming together to form complex tableaux and to execute finely coordinated running maneuvers and sustained lifts, exhibiting a meticulous precision and synchrony that conveys a powerful assertion of group fusion and teamwork. The narrative segues into a depiction of sea journeys to Aotearoa, as the company unfurls a vast blue cloth to represent the ocean's labile integument, shaping it into a variety of tensile and enveloping configurations. They pass over a stage floor embossed with outlines of frigate birds (a boon to ancient navigators for their ability to make landfall in a vast ocean) and diagrams of *etak* triangulation—directly referencing the Micronesian technique of navigational reckoning whereby the voyager inhabits a "stationary" canoe while the islands and cosmos "move" toward and around them, and which serves as a powerful metaphor for the traveling subject who monitors and maintains control of their position in a constantly changing relation to a dynamic world. The ensemble performs an honest relationship to the ocean that is at once personal and perilous; while the dancers' perseverance and solidarity refute the assumptions of *Arrival*, as with Semu's work, not everyone survives: a recumbent female dancer positioned at the edge of a triangle of projected light revealing the coast of Aotearoa gestures poignantly to those who did not complete the journey.

Successive sequences represent the history of settlement and European colonization of Aotearoa New Zealand with its legacy of westernization and urbanization. More literal group choreographic images of the rugby scrum, the macho drinking culture, the specter of Christianity, and city skyscrapers course fluidly through the middle section of *Vaka*, with the ensemble dressed in Western-style costumes. These social changes are accompanied by a shift in the tone of the piece: an urgent, electronic beat undergirds more frenetic, violent movements as the dancers shove and fight one other, beating down their competition and kicking away the vanquished as they stumble and stomp, zombie-like. This apocalyptic crescendo culminates in a darkened stage: out of the gloom, we hear news broadcasts of modern natural and manufactured disasters, including the New York 9/11 terrorist attack, the Tokyo subway sarin incident, nuclear bombing in the Pacific, and international wars, selected to highlight New Zealand's place in a conflicted global milieu. The aural snippets are accompanied by related projected images that glide over the backs of three female performers, along with text that articulates unfinished statements of identity: "I am / I am from / I am a carrier / I am a vessel / I am a vaka / I believe in / I am . . ." This moment of global reckoning, in which the promise of the vaka as a cultural container grapples with the existential crises of the present, gives way to a final sequence that cycles back to the costumes and choreography of the precolonial Pacific world: Pacific drumbeats and gentle guitar strains cue lithe group phrases that return us to the more harmonious social integration of the early stages of the show, with the ensemble once again transporting each other and traveling together.[59]

Vaka's message of survival and hope thus also serves as an allegory for Indigenous cultural revival and resilience, reinforced in the very form and being of the work. The dance phrases that bracket *Vaka*, however, are not identical, suggesting that for Pasifika peoples, cultural voyaging into a fraught and uncertain future might be sustained and enriched by a carrying of tradition, but always in strategic and complicated negotiation between past and present, local and global. Notably, the company's publicity photograph for the production also restages Géricault's *Medusa* scene, drawing upon the allegorical potential that the painting so rapidly accrued.

While the model is obvious, the differences are striking: in contrast to the confusion and lack of common purpose expressed by Géricault's *naufragés*, the tableau contains clever compositional syntheses to turn Géricault's scenes of anomie into comforting acts, discernible in the gracefully arranged outstretched arms, tender glances, and embraces of the muscular crew. Most strikingly, the scene is posed not against an oceanscape but against the concrete detritus of a former Auckland factory.[60] Rather than

Figure 5. Jean-Louis Théodore Géricault, *Le radeau de La Méduse* (*The Raft of the Medusa*), 1818–19. Oil on Canvas. Collection of the Musée du Louvre, Paris.

across the water, then, Ieremia's work indicates that the paths navigated by contemporary Pacific Islanders in New Zealand and the world are as likely to be charted along urban streets and in its industries. Significantly, there is no equivalent to Géricault's far-off *Argus* in this image: who or what is the man at the head of the raft hailing? If the scene isn't fixed on a salve, then perhaps this isn't a scene of rescue (or abandonment) at all. From this perspective, it is less an image of the end of the world, of world destruction, as art critic Michael Fried has famously argued of Géricault's romanticism,[61] and instead suggests one of persistence and promise; even if these "floating islanders," as Makerita Urale has termed them, are at times unmoored and adrift, then they also inhabit a liminality between different social groups and practices that energizes cultural production.[62] Black Grace's image accentuates the vessel itself, in distinction to the critical preoccupation with the people on the *Medusa* raft or the painting's relationship to the beholder. Separating the raft from its watery immersion at once heightens the raft's metaphorical capacity (it can serve no literal purpose here) and draws specific attention to its role as a character, extending the inter(in)animation of canoe and voyager[63] to suggest its potential as a cultural and spiritual sup-

Figure 6. Black Grace, *Vaka* (2012). Artistic direction by Neil Ieremia, photograph by Duncan Cole. Image courtesy of Black Grace.

port and a fellow sojourner in an ongoing journey weighted with aspiration and ambivalence.

Taken together, *The Raft of the Tagata Pasifika* and *Vaka* demonstrate how current genres of corporeal performance can explore and express the somatic and symbolic resonances of vessels and voyaging. Both works retrace the contours of New Zealand's national history and its links to the South Pacific and the wider world, while pointing to the range of ways that voyaging legacies and metaphors have been deployed by Pacific artists, from the minute to the macrostructural, the historical to the contemporary, and the literal to the figurative. These transpasifika collaborations that connect, in Semu's case, Aotearoa, Samoa, and the Cook Islands; and, for Black Grace, the diverse peoples who congregate in the world's largest Polynesian city, foreground the performances as sites of mobility that reflect and reinforce Oceania's complex reticulations.

The most evident challenge to the colonial dismissal of voyaging ventures has been in the widespread resurgence of Indigenous shipbuilding, sailing, and navigation itself. In some cases, these pioneering vessels have played an artistic role in theatrical performance projects, whose spectacular pedagogies underscore historical and contemporary connections between island communities. A case in point is *Kupe*, presented as part of *A Waka Odyssey* for the opening of the 2018 New Zealand Festival, which retold the story of the Pacific explorer Kupe and his originary arrival in Aotearoa. In this large-scale "theatrical pōwhiri" (welcome), Te Whanganui-a-Tara / Wellington Harbor by New Zealand's capital city served as the watery stage for the choreographed movements of a fleet of actual voyaging canoes from Aotearoa, Samoa, and the Cook Islands, while actors, a mass choir, and a thousand-strong haka group welcomed them to land. By honoring Kupe's legacy and celebrating Aotearoa's shared voyaging history, the event combined and showcased nautical and theatrical performances to present a momentous, affirmative public statement about New Zealand's place in the Pacific.[64] The following section investigates aspects of this international and interdisciplinary potential in other parts of Polynesia by juxtaposing complementary performances by and between Hawaiian and Tahitian communities that took place in 2014: the first leg of the Polynesian Voyaging Society's Mālama Honua Worldwide Voyage, and the ensemble spectacle *Te Feti'a 'Avei'a* by O Tahiti E at the Heiva i Tahiti. In pursuing a reading that crosses locations, languages, and genres I examine how voyaging and its ancillary performances spur transpasifika reciprocities that simultaneously advance local sovereignty initiatives and regional alliances.

KE ALA I KAHIKI: NURTURING HAWAI'I-TAHITI RELATIONS VIA THE MĀLAMA HONUA WORLDWIDE VOYAGE AND THE HEIVA I TAHITI

The Mālama Honua Worldwide Voyage might be understood as the culmination of the voyaging revival to date and the beginning of a new phase of global engagement. Following a statewide Hawaiian tour in 2013, *Hōkūle'a* and her sister vessel *Hikianalia* embarked on a three-year, sixty-thousand-nautical-mile journey to 150 ports in twenty-three countries between May 2014 and June 2017. In addition to promoting Hawaiian values and perpetuating traditional navigation skills, Mālama Honua ("to care for the earth and its people") was charged with an ecological imperative to nurture sustainable environmental practices drawn from Indigenous principles, as well as a social mission to cultivate enduring, strategic alliances with Indigenous peoples throughout Oceania and around the globe.[65] As an icon of the contemporary voyaging revival and the attendant Hawaiian cultural renaissance, *Hōkūle'a* is a storied receptacle of ancient memory and postcolonial history, freighted with the triumphs, tragedies, and tensions of forging a viable voyaging praxis and propagating its international legacy. *Hikianalia*, built in Aotearoa in 2012 especially for the voyage, served as a platform for scientific experimentation and for documenting the project,[66] dispatching live tracking information and uploading photographs, videos, and online stories via a host of internet and social-media outlets that constituted the voyage's "third canoe"[67] and swelled the number of participants in the Mālama Honua experience to incorporate a potential audience of millions of virtual voyagers.

At the heart of this project is an ongoing reassertion of a coalitional Polynesian identity and what we might call in this context a Polynesian-centered globalism. In an overview video about the voyage on the PVS website, we are told that "in a generation, *Hōkūle'a* has sailed over 140,000 nautical miles to reunite the world's largest oceanic nation." Polynesia is defined here as an "oceanic country bounded by Hawai'i in the north and New Zealand in the southwest and Rapa Nui in the east. Ten million square miles—bigger than Russia."[68] In line with Hau'ofa, ocean (aquatory) rather than land (territory) becomes the measure for determining national expanse and resources, and for advancing a decolonial cartography that bypasses latter-day borders to privilege Indigenous ethnic, linguistic, and social similarities; moreover, it provides an empowering recuperation of d'Urville's nineteenth-century geocultural categorization. In this respect, the PVS harkens back to—and provides an answer for—British explorer Captain James Cook's marveling statement in February 1778 after encountering Hawai'i:

"How shall we account for this nation's having spread itself, in so many detached islands, so widely disjoined from each other, in every quarter of the Pacific Ocean! . . . How much further, in either direction, its colonies reach, is not known; but what we know already, in consequence of this and our former voyage, warrants our pronouncing it to be, though perhaps not the most numerous, certainly, by far, the most extensive nation upon earth."[69] At stake, then, is a strategic remapping of Pacific space that repositions Hawai'i—an appropriated Pacific polity on the margins of the United States—as a fulcrum and agent of an Indigenous nation that is "bigger than Russia": an imagined community, the correlation implies, that is a force to be reckoned with.

Writing in the close historical wake of the Mālama Honua, it is difficult to predict what lasting impact might be made by a Polynesian global circumnavigation: how captains of vaka might confront the captains of industry, or how "island wisdom" might subvert the obduracy of capitalist ambition. Nevertheless, the most insightful and meaningful aspects of the voyage, I suggest, lay in the micro-level, intimate, reciprocal social acts that characterized and cumulatively comprised the overall endeavor. Whether working with local communities on environmental restoration projects, undertaking educational outreach with neighborhood schools, conducting mutual science experiments, making visits to sites of cultural significance, participating in exchanges of dance, oratory, song, and ceremonial ritual, or inspiring the creation of related artworks, the vessels and their crews were engaged in intricate processes of remembering, reinforcing, and redefining Indigenous-Indigenous relationships that enriched the potential for future forms of action.

The worldwide voyage expanded the reach of Pacific voyaging through the networks forged with Indigenous communities in Australia, Indonesia, South Africa, Brazil, the Caribbean, the United States, Canada, and Panama.[70] Given Hōkūle'a's basis in suturing a Polynesian ecumene, however, certain relationships were of special importance. The trans-Indigenous dynamics of the voyage can be cast into specific relief by examining the vessels' visit to Tahiti, which marked the end of the first international section of Mālama Honua in June–July 2014. While representing the first step on a new mission, the passage also marked a series of homecomings, honoring both the relationship with Tahiti that began with Hōkūle'a's arrival in Pape'ete Harbor on her maiden voyage in June 1976, and a much deeper historical relationship that began with the settlement of Hawai'i by Tahitian voyagers. As Pwo navigator[71] and voyage leader Nainoa Thompson explained, "Hawai'i to Tahiti, to me, is one of the two most important voyages of the Worldwide Voyage because it's ancestral, it's family, you're going back to the homeland."[72] Post-1970s reinscriptions of the ancestral sea-path *ke ala i Kahiki* (the path/way to Tahiti) have lent new semantic accretions to the ancient migratory route. The 1976 passage became significant not only as the journey that lent credence to ancient legends and genealogies, but also as the course by which the troubled disjunction between *Hōkūle'a* as a scientific research experiment in navigation and as a vehicle for Indigenous sovereignty was encountered and eventually worked through to stimulate a Hawaiian, and subsequently a broader Polynesian cultural resurgence.[73] Over the past forty-five years Tahiti and neighboring islands have been frequent ports of call for voyages that cut across imposed jurisdictional boundaries and constructions of nationalism to assert autochthonous kinship networks; they have also operated as a training ground for latter-day navigators, as well as marshaling points for a variety of collaborative voyaging projects that have honed the critical, symbolic, and agential purchase of fleets of reconstructed vessels.[74]

It is necessary to point out that these "water-ties"[75] have sought to bind sites that, politically and demographically, are highly distinct from one another. Hawai'i, an archipelago united as an independent kingdom in the late eighteenth century, suffered the overthrow of its Indigenous monarchy in 1893 by a group of American businessmen assisted by the US military, followed by annexation as a US territory in 1898 and statehood in 1959. Within both the state of Hawai'i and the ambit of the US settler-colonial nation, Kanaka Maoli (Native Hawaiians) constitute an Indigenous minority (21 percent in-state, less than 0.1 percent nationally), and sovereignty representatives have been active in coming together with other self-identified Indigenous peoples as part of a globalizing Indigenous rights movement since the 1960s. In French Polynesia, however, as Natacha Gagné reports, the situation is "configured in an extremely different fashion than in the anglophone Pacific."[76] French Polynesia (encompassing several island groups of which Tahiti, in the Society Islands, is the capital seat) was united as a French protectorate in 1889 and currently comprises an overseas collectivity of the French Republic with administrative autonomy. French Polynesia retains an 80 percent Indigenous majority, and the local population remains split between a desire for more autonomy and for direct administration by metropolitan France. French Polynesian representatives have come late and irregularly to international meetings on Indigenous issues, and the 2007 United Nations Declaration on the Rights of Indigenous Peoples passed almost unnoticed there.[77]

Gagné attributes these stances to pejorative associations with the word

"Indigenous" (*indigène*) and a reticence about identifying with what are perceived to be marginalized and disenfranchised communities elsewhere. She likewise notes the general ambiguity and vagueness of the term for Mā'ohi people;[78] as well as the French conception of citizenship founded on "right of birthplace" (*jus soli*) that entails "being a member of a political community, which has no ethnic foundation and has nothing to do with ancestry and a 'blood right' (*jus sanguinis*)," but rather "involves a sense of being *autochtone* to France."[79] Beyond conventional political parties and channels, however, a number of grassroots and volunteer associations have been at the forefront of advocacy for Indigenous identity and rights in French Polynesia, motivated primarily by cultural production (literature and the arts) and the preservation of cultural heritage, and have worked to establish cultural networks with people throughout the Pacific region.[80] The examples discussed below are located in these cultural and artistic arenas, and thus they highlight the productive possibilities for Indigenous mobilizing in this area of Oceania. At the same time, the local administrative context affects the expressive strategies that are deemed to be appropriate, raising the question of how the vaka might act as a strategic device for navigating these political passages.

The two weeks that the Hawaiian crews spent on Tahiti and nearby islands in 2014 were marked by numerous fungible performances that offer insights into the correlation between bridging cultures and advancing local self-determination, and the role of a constituted multitemporal past in creating renewed space for future action. In addition to the chants, dances, and songs that greeted *Hōkūle'a* and *Hikianalia* on their arrival in Pape'ete, the section of Pā'ōfai Beach where *Hōkūle'a* had first made land in 1976 was remade as a mnemonic site dedicated to the vessel and the social links and meanings that she had inspired. Renamed Plage Hōkūle'a, the site featured a *va'a* (canoe) landing, a marae,[81] a monument to the vessel with a plaque, and an *'unu* (totem)[82] and served as the venue for the main ceremonial events of the welcome. Beside the monument, Hawaiian representatives left a gift of *vai* (water) and a *pōhaku* (stone) from *Hōkūle'a*'s birthplace in Hakipu'u on O'ahu. More intangible, affective exchanges took place in the oratories. The contemporary Hawaiian sailors, several of whom were children of the 1976 crew members, received the same speech delivered to members of *Hōkūle'a*'s original cohort, inducting the young voyagers into this history and inviting them to be part of (re)making it. Thompson made a specific gift of acknowledgment in his address to the crowd on the beach, speaking to the very strong reciprocal bond that had been reestablished between the two communities over the past generation and paying tribute to Tahiti's role in the Hawaiian renaissance: "I was here in 1976. The people of Tahiti gave us great gifts. And they told us to be proud of who we are as Pacific people, be proud of our culture, and hang on to who we are. Tahiti changed Hawai'i for the better, forever."[83]

The celebrations also recalled the important role that *Hōkūle'a* had played in Tahiti's own sovereignty efforts. Finney notes that in 1976 the Tahitians were locked in a bitter struggle with the retrograde French administration over the granting of internal autonomy to French Polynesia. The arrival of *Hōkūle'a* gave people courage, asserted their pride as Polynesians, and inspired a mass demonstration in Pape'ete that led to a change in governmental structure, which became a contributing factor in subsequent social changes.[84] In 2014 this mutual indebtedness was further acknowledged when French Polynesia's president at the time, Gaston Flosse, made Thompson a Commander of the Order of Tahiti Nui (the highest award given for outstanding merit in service of French Polynesia), which Thompson accepted on behalf of the teachers and navigators involved in the previous four decades of voyaging and took as recognition that *Hōkūle'a* was a canoe that also belonged to the Tahitians. Elsewhere on Tahiti and the adjacent islands where the vessels called, Hawaiian visitors and Mā'ohi hosts engaged in similar interactions to promote the Mālama Honua effort and invest in lasting relationships. These activities also involved attending the annual *heiva* (a sporting, cultural, and performing arts competition and exhibition) and making pilgrimages to significant cultural sites. Such sites included Taputapuātea Marae on Ra'iātea, an island traditionally identified as Havai'i (Hawaiki), the cradle of the eastern Polynesian migrations; Fare Hape in Papeno'o on Tahiti, the birthplace of the canoe *Fa'afaite* (which accompanied *Hōkūle'a* and *Hikianalia* around the archipelago) and mythic abode of the fire deity Pere (Pele) before her migration to Hawai'i; and the village of Tautira, *Hōkūle'a*'s adopted home in Tahiti, historical canoe-building center, and a model of sustainable living.[85]

Together, these performances attempted to bring into being a new community, in important respects based on a historical past both actual and engineered, while representing pioneering expressions of solidarity and agency that inhered in lateral networks rather than in an overt critique of hierarchical governmental structures. The Mālama Honua events exemplify how the ongoing efforts of present-day Pacific voyagers to refashion the break with the past as a recognition of continuity and to reestablish embodied knowledge as social practice are not merely citational, but also generative. Yet, in line with Nicholas Thomas's avowal that "exchange is always, in the first instance, a political process, one in which wider relationships are expressed and negotiated in a personal encounter,"[86] the strategic entanglement of objects, affects, and gestures through this series of votive, site-specific acts also indicates how the recuperation and construction of community is mediated by, and positioned relative to, contemporary political agendas. It is noteworthy, for instance, that in these scenes of renewed encounter and active historicization, it was not the endurance of Micronesian navigation that was acknowledged as having reversed Hawai'i's cultural fortunes, but *Hōkūle'a*'s destination point, Tahiti; thus, the specifics of history slipped into service of a different schema whereby genealogy was of prime importance in brokering trans-Indigenous ties.

The dynamics of these direct and indirect exchanges can be examined in greater depth by considering one performative enactment designed as a homage to *Hōkūle'a*'s return visit: *Te Feti'a 'Avei'a* / *L'étoile guide* (Guiding Star), a song, dance, and visual spectacle that tells the story of a *va'a* and its crew setting out from Tahiti on a migratory journey to Hawai'i.[87] Jean-Claude Teri'iero'oterai, a Mā'ohi cultural revitalization advocate, wrote the scenario for the performance. A member of the Pacific Voyagers project,[88] Teri'iero'oterai helped organize the Pape'ete and Tautira receptions for the Mālama Honua Worldwide Voyage, served as a cultural ambassador during the visit, and sailed on the second leg of the voyage from Tahiti to Samoa on *Hōkūle'a*. *Te Feti'a 'Avei'a* was coproduced by the Mā'ohi dance group O Tahiti E under the direction of Marguerite Lai, along with the Conservatoire artistique de la Polynésie française (Te Fare Upa Rau), a school of traditional plastic and dramatic arts headed by Fabien Mara Dinard, and featured sets and props by students from the Centre des Métiers d'Art for the annual Heiva i Tahiti in July 2014.

The Heiva i Tahiti opens space for a more specific analysis of the confluence of Indigenous revival efforts in the performing arts and the voyaging discussed so far, especially within French Polynesia's unique context. Although the *heiva* existed as a program of entertainments during the precontact era, the modern version (first called "La Fête Nationale" or "La Bastille") dates from the late nineteenth century, and its initial function was to celebrate French independence.[89] Karen Stevenson explains that the modern *heiva* emerged from, and has continued to be characterized by, a delicate balance between French and Tahitians, with the festival managing a working relationship that allows for the perpetuation of two disparate cultural traditions and the satisfaction of apparently contradictory agendas.[90] Renamed the Heiva i Tahiti in 1986, the festival has become an important factor in developing a distinct, modern-day Mā'ohi identity; it is a symbol of sovereignty, but acknowledged as a "new cultural tradition" that recognizes contemporary Tahitian identity as a creation and that is "meaningful in terms of both the traditional past and the reinterpreted culture of the present."[91]

The genre of Te Feti'a 'Avei'a is indicative of this interplay between past and present influences, agendas, and ideals. As a marae reenactment, it is not a category that has direct historical antecedents in Tahitian culture, but is one of several events introduced during the 1950s and "rooted more firmly in current political and economic manipulations."[92] Unlike historical marae ritual, which was sacred and restricted to a few special participants, modern heiva reenactments are commercial entertainments regarded as theatrical pieces and typically staged at Marae 'Ārahurahu, which was reconstructed for educational and tourist purposes by the Société des Océaniennes in 1954.[93] The primary role of these presentations is to "instruct the contemporary community about traditional Tahitian society" by offering "manifestations of a traditional heritage transformed into currently meaningful interpretations."[94] Bruno Saura describes how the past few decades have witnessed evolutions in the style and composition of these spectacles; this trend is especially visible in the work of O Tahiti E (founded in 1986), which, since the 1990s, has pushed formal boundaries with its innovations in the balance of dancers and choir, as well as in the introduction of new dance steps.[95]

Te Feti'a 'Avei'a is a useful demonstration of how the artistic deployment of the vaka trope and voyaging histories might negotiate this delicate balance of disparate cultural traditions and agendas in Tahiti. Seated on rows of plastic chairs at the base of the lushly forested valley at Marae 'Ārahurahu, audiences looked out over the playing area, which integrated the rectangular, volcanic stone terraces of the marae as well as the flat, grassed area in front of it. The show enlisted the efforts of over two hundred actors, singers, dancers, musicians, and designers. In addition to the lavishly costumed principal actors, who mainly portrayed members of the royal court, a complement of sixty male and female dancers depicted the preparation for the voyage and the voyage itself. A choir of a hundred singers and chanters, adorned with flowered headpieces and greenery, was seated along the marae edge of the playing area and accompanied the action with a variety of himene;[96] near them, a group of musicians maintained percussive rhythms throughout. The major feature of the mise-en-scène was a forty-foot, double-hulled voyaging canoe constructed of wood and painted plywood that had a raised platform for actors to appear on, as well as hoistable sails based on Society Island models, and that was positioned on the grass adjacent to the marae structure and upstage of the dancers.

Figure 7. After surviving a tropical tempest and the doldrums, the voyagers are delighted to catch a first glimpse of their destination, in *Te Feti'a 'Avei'a* (2014), performed by O Tahiti E and directed by Marguerite Lai. Marae 'Ārahurahu, Tahiti. Photograph by, and courtesy of, Hélène Barnaud.

The ninety-minute performance unfolded in three parts: "Te fanora'a" (departure), "Te 'avei'a" (heading for a new land), and "Te taura'a o te va'a" (arrival of the canoe). It told the story of Pa'ao, the younger son of the *ari'i nui* (paramount chief) Tutera'i of Vavau. After his older brother assumes power, Pa'ao is forced to leave the island with his retinue, including his wife Tehani and the priest Tepori, to found a new society on a suspected though yet undiscovered island. Once built and provisioned, the *va'a* departs; after some peaceful sailing for several days following Tahiti's zenith star Ta'ura-fau-papa (Sirius, Alpha Canis Major), for which the canoe is named, they encounter a tempest: the vessel is blown about and drifts, food rots, and the voyagers are hungry and frightened and pray for deliverance. Eventually, thanks to Tepori's invocations, the storm clears, the guiding star reappears, and the people notice birds, clouds, and marine debris that indicate the presence of land. With great joy, they spot a mountainous island, which Pa'ao calls Hava'i after his grandfather's land.[97] The settlers disembark and begin to build a new marae and enrich the land with plants, animals, and people. Pa'ao and Tehani become the new ruling family.

The form and content of *Te Feti'a 'Avei'a* exemplify the dynamic between expanding social matrices and sustaining local identity. On one level, the show presents a general parable about how communal balance is maintained by the younger generation's extension into new territory once the existing island reaches capacity, a story applicable to the past settlement programs of many Pacific societies and that emphasizes a perpetual history of familial reproduction and societal replication in the peopling of Polynesia.[98] The narrative, however, might also be interpreted as evoking the historical figure of Pa'ao, a Tahitian high priest and *ari'i* who journeyed from Ra'iātea to Hawai'i in the twelfth century and introduced a number of significant religious and cultural changes to Hawaiian society based on Tahitian paradigms. Pa'ao founded a priestly lineage and constructed several *heiau* (marae), including Mo'okini at Kohala on Hawai'i's Big Island; he also traveled back and forth between Hawai'i and Tahiti to broker alliances between the two island groups, importing a Tahitian high chief, Pili, who became an ancestor of the Hawaiian royal family.[99] Through recourse to this historical narrative (adapted in the performance to emphasize the voyaging experience and situate Pa'ao's journey as a discovery expedition), *Hōkūle'a*'s pioneering voyages from Hawai'i are reinforced as returns and reciprocated symbolically through a dramatic representation that (re)imagines a Hawai'i-bound voyage that embeds familial links between the two archipelagoes.

Genealogy is highlighted strongly in the performance: when Pa'ao farewells his family, his father gives him a knotted genealogical cord that connects him to his ancestors and that he will pass on to his children. The bond between the voyagers and the home community is also sustained through the ritual of *'aha moa* (sleeping sennit). In this tradition, a priest would place a piece of sennit that had been passed beneath the hull of the canoe under a sacred slab of the marae; when the estimated time of the voyage had elapsed, the priest would examine the cord, and its condition (straight, crooked, or twisted over) indicated the condition of the vessel and crew (straight: all is well; crooked: having met with contrary winds though still safe; twisted over: capsized and lost).[100] When the Tahitian priest finds the sennit lying straight at the end of the performance, it confirms Pa'ao's successful arrival and binds the two locations together via the ritual and the stage. Additionally, since Pa'ao has been charged to build his new society on the model of the old one, he transports a foundation stone (*'ōfai faoa*) from his home marae and places it on Hawaiian ground to establish his new marae/*heiau*, foregrounding a patrilineal logic whereby Hawai'i is reiterated as the "child" of Tahiti. This action simultaneously recalls the past and the present-day return journey of the stone from *Hōkūle'a*'s birthplace to the new Tahitian marae at Plage Hōkūle'a, drawing the traffic in symbolic objects into a figurative rapprochement.

Te Feti'a 'Avei'a also draws pedagogical attention to aspects of Tahitian social history, and by extension Hawaiian history, through its concentration on canoe construction and launching rituals—an emphasis typical of Polynesian voyaging sagas whereby information about the fitting out of the vessels usually takes precedence over details of sailing and navigation.[101] After representing the ritual of the carpenters asking permission from the forest to sacrifice a tree for the *va'a*, the performance depicts the ceremony of *ha'amoe ra'a to'i* ("putting the hatchet to sleep") in which the craftsman would place his adze in a recess of the marae overnight and invoke the presiding gods to consecrate it.[102] Thirty male dancers represent the carpenters, each wielding an adze of local stone and guava wood made by students from the Centre des Métiers d'Art. Subsequently, once the vessel is provisioned and ready for launching, a complementary group of female dancers holds aloft large rectangles of patterned cloth that suggest strips of *'aute* (paper mulberry), which were customarily cast over the waves as the canoe set sail to encourage clear skies and favorable winds.[103] In a self-reflexive move that acknowledged the central cultural role of shipwrights in ancient Tahiti, director Marguerite Lai incorporated a number of the center's students who constructed the *va'a* centerpiece into the show to play canoe-builders and help hoist the sails and work the rigging of the vessel, thus drawing conscious links between form and function in the performance.[104]

Indeed, the recuperation, reframing, and relaying of past practices through new aesthetic frameworks have valuable repercussions for the contemporary expression of Indigenous arts, especially in extensive spectacle entertainments like *Te Feti'a 'Avei'a* that serve as major community events and bring together artisans from different disciplines to advance local arts efforts. Working on *Te Feti'a 'Avei'a* spurred new initiatives for students at the Centre des Métiers d'Art, one of several Mā'ohi cultural institutions established during the period 1967–80 and dedicated to the preservation and continuity of Polynesian and Oceanic visual and plastic arts.[105] In a media interview, Viri Taimana, the center's director, explained that his students were encouraged to become involved with large-scale projects in which they could showcase their skills and products meaningfully. Pieces like *Te Feti'a 'Avei'a*, which call for modern incarnations of customary objects and of substantial set pieces (especially the *va'a*), open up new pathways for employment within the event industry, and offer new genres and contexts for the expression of Mā'ohi identity through artistic production.[106]

As with the voyages of *Hōkūle'a*, *Te Feti'a 'Avei'a* offers an instructive illustration of how indigeneity can be, as James Clifford puts it, "both rooted in and routed through particular places,"[107] deriving sovereignty from pathfinding, journeying, movement, and exchange. As a collaborative Indigenous project that recalls the history of the great Polynesian migrations, the piece, like the returning Hawaiians, reasserts Tahiti and the Society group as the cradle of Polynesia, sourcing and supporting a network of ancestral and genealogical links throughout eastern Oceania that constitute the identity of the local. Just as *Hōkūle'a* and her descendants help chart new horizons for Hawaiian identities beyond the restrictive rubric of the US nation-state, *Te Feti'a 'Avei'a*'s social-expansion narrative emphasizes Indigenous kinship affiliations that present a powerful alternative to the colonial dyad and countervail the geographical structures and ideological imperatives of French imperialism. The voyaging theme, moreover, can be seen to play a strategic role in managing French Polynesia's specific political dynamics within the context of the *heiva*. The show's generalizable narrative, its inclusive pedagogical slant, and its focus on the intrepid deeds of the distant past are designed to appeal to Mā'ohi and non-Mā'ohi alike, with advertising material situating festival audiences equally as "amoureux de culture polynésienne et des sagas heroïques" (lovers of Polynesian culture and heroic sagas), and inviting them to enter "un univers épique et époustouflant!" (an epic and breathtaking universe).[108] In this manner, *Te Feti'a 'Avei'a* sells an empowering Polynesian regionalism as sanctioned cultural appreciation and evades the authoritarian pushback that has beleaguered some other Indigenous dramatists whose work has pursued a direct critique of French administrative frameworks.[109] Reading the performance with and through the Mālama Honua Worldwide Voyage traverses languages, genres, polities, and thousands of miles to illuminate not only ethnic articulations, but also interdisciplinary articulations, highlighting synergies among various Indigenous revitalization efforts in navigation, linguistics, the visual arts, social customs, religion, politics, and the performing arts. While the modern histories of Hawai'i and Tahiti have produced them as very different sites, the artistic and practical reconstruction of voyaging legacies strengthens their multiple connections across a diverse sea of islands.

TEMPESTUOUS HISTORIES: NAVIGATING NATIONAL AND REGIONAL IMAGINARIES BEYOND THE POLYNESIAN TRIANGLE

Heroic seafaring histories are seductive. In November 2006, Australian community theater company Crossroad Arts created *No Two Stones*,[110] a dance, music, and installation performance devised collaboratively by Aboriginal, Torres Strait Islander, and Australian South Sea Islander participants in the local Mackay, Queensland, area. Aboriginal peoples have an indigenous relationship with continental Australia that reaches back tens of thousands of years, and Torres Strait Islanders are Melanesian peoples from the waterway separating northern Australia and Papua New Guinea whose islands were annexed by Queensland in 1879. Australian South Sea Islanders are descendants of people from numerous islands in the western Pacific (mainly the Solomon Islands and Vanuatu) who were recruited, often forcibly, as plantation laborers for Queensland's sugar industry during the nineteenth century, when US Civil War upheavals collapsed North American cotton and sugar production and led to the rise of Queensland as a "second Louisiana."[111] Although the Australian government deported many of these laborers with the advent of its White Australia Policy in the early twentieth century, the descendants of those who remained are part of the Pacific Island diasporic community in Australia and now form the basis of Australia's largest non-Indigenous Black ethnic group. The troubled histories of the Melanesian "labor trade" serve as a trenchant reminder that in the Pacific, too, the sea has been a space of subjection. Designed as a means of alleviating social tensions between the three groups and asserting and maintaining cultural mores through new artistic intersections, *No Two Stones* located identity purposefully on the seashore through the large woven shells, fish, and nets used as props and set pieces, and through its physical location on Lambert's Beach. The littoral setting suggested flux, movement, and interrelation, as well as the possibility of a hopeful passage to new understandings and conditions,[112] but it also set the stage for a more direct evocation of voyaging histories through a major installation of a hundred miniature outrigger canoes fashioned from bamboo and cloth, which were brought to the shore and placed on the waves to come in with the tide.

According to the director Steve Mayer-Miller, for Australian South Sea Islanders especially, this segment "involved a process of imagining 'What if?' What if, instead of coming as kidnapped victims in the holds of ships, they came voluntarily in outriggers? Like the Māori to Aotearoa."[113] This engineered version of triumphant encounter, which positioned the Australian South Sea Islanders and Torres Strait Islanders as travelers with the Aboriginal cohort on the beach welcoming them, presented a co-opted alternative to the performers' distinct, yet shared legacies of forced migration, cruelty, and dispossession in ways that were affirmative though ambivalent. The moment sat somewhere between an avowal of the groups' water ties—of maritime customs embodied and practiced in Vanuatu, Solomon Islands, and the islands of the Torres Strait, as well as the vital "sea Dreaming" of coastal Aboriginal peoples[114]—and a wishful desire to be part of the reification of a romantic history of volitional migration and long-distance landfall associated with Micronesian and Polynesian voyagers. Voyaging's mobile matrix supplied a useful metaphor for connecting place with place and culture with culture to serve a collaboration that helped bypass the physical boundaries, discursive fixtures, and divisive policies of the Australian nation-state. At the same time, however, the imagining of a different history through performance's ideational structures raises the questions of how other notions of agency-in-mobility might be acknowledged beyond the framework of epic voyaging, as well as the extent to which holistic regional claims arising from voyaging discourses are borne out in practice. I mention this example as a preamble to this chapter's next case study because it prompts consideration of how voyaging might be marshaled less as a celebration than a critical conceit, and sharpens our awareness of the possibilities of the theatrical medium in addressing the paradoxes of real and imagined voyaging across the vexed postcolonial terrain of the Pacific.

As Margaret Jolly asks of Hau'ofa's sea-of-islands thesis, "I wonder how far this is a compelling vision for *all* Islanders"[115]—noting in particular concerns about "an undue emphasis on the ocean and navigation" expressed by members of Pacific communities who have "no sense of ancestral connections to the ocean, [and] no knowledge of how to make canoes."[116] Jolly's observations once again draw important attention to Islanders' differentiated situations relative to the geopolitics of state forms, demographics, and migration patterns. While she is cautious not to translate Clifford's dialectic between roots and routes into an essentializing dichotomy that separates Pacific Islanders, Jolly argues that "*where* they live, the specific places of their being, also matters" because divergent colonial histories and Indigenous configurations of interest "mold how roots and routes are 'articulated.'"[117]

These concerns are also relevant for those communities with seafaring histories that have not been enveloped within the genealogical mantle of Polynesian voyaging. In this regard Elizabeth DeLoughrey wonders whether such familial discourses might invoke originary models of ethnic identity that contribute to contemporary discrimination.[118] Despite the fact that voyaging histories might seem to emphasize connections among "Moana [ocean] cultures" over nationalist affirmation, she avers that a utopian emphasis on Indigenous vehicles of sovereignty "does not necessarily lead to a unifying model for regional identity. In fact, the concept of the region, even when stitched together by the transpacific vaka, cannot provide a panacea for the ethnic and gender hierarchies that flow over from colonial and national frameworks."[119] DeLoughrey attends to the distinction between the shared history of a relatively unified Polynesia versus an ethnically diverse Melanesia, and the legacy of colonial prejudice that figured Melanesians as culturally and physically inferior to Polynesians. In particular, she refers to colonial inscriptions that positioned Fiji outside the Polynesian triangle, separated from its neighbors despite its historical and tectonic linkages.[120] As she remarks, "Fiji, with its long history of trade and exchange, has always challenged these ethnic maps of the Pacific, a position that became more salient after its series of racialized coups" starting in the 1980s.[121]

These histories have had implications for Fiji's voyaging visibility: Nuttall and colleagues affirm that "neither Fiji's *drua* [canoe] culture nor the related culture in central Oceania has been the subject of the intensive research of Eastern Polynesia."[122] They call for the production of "a Fiji-centered history based on Fijian priorities as a seafaring people," which "requires a more generous assessment of Fijian voyaging ability and history than currently exists."[123] So far these assessments have focused on the memory of the *waqa drua*, a Fijian double-hulled voyaging craft posited as "the largest and finest sea-going vessel ever designed and built by natives of Oceania before contact with Europeans."[124] Since the *drua* could be constructed only by chiefs who could commission the services of highly trained, hereditary canoe-builders (called *Mataisau*), it was considered a *waqa tabu* (sacred ship), the province of the aristocracy.[125] Capable of carrying up to two hundred armed warriors or fifty tons of cargo, the one-hundred-foot-plus vessel enabled significant voyaging for war, trade, and political expansion during the late 1700s and early 1800s, but was eclipsed by colonial vessels and circumscribed by administrative boundaries during the nineteenth century.[126]

These topics are brought to the fore in two collaborative performances undertaken by the Oceania Centre for Arts, Culture and Pacific Studies at the University of the South Pacific (USP) in Fiji: *Vaka: The Birth of a Seer* (2012) and *Drua: The Wave of Fire* (2012), both of which treat the construction, navigation, and interisland journeys of the *waqa drua*. Produced especially to demonstrate how knowledge of Indigenous technologies can enhance Oceanian cultures, and relatedly how the performing arts can function as a vital conduit for communicating cultural and historical information, the "music-dance-dramas"[127] were informed by academic investigations undertaken by USP's research cluster on Pacific cultures and societies and a center-sponsored documentary and ethnographic study of *drua* history and culture conducted by the Fiji Islands Voyaging Society in 2011. These interrelated projects were underpinned by a shared belief that "revitalisation of drua-related culture would be an immensely empowering and desirable objective, both for Fiji and the wider related Pacific community."[128]

In this respect, however, *Vaka* and *Drua* also emerge as revelatory texts for examining enduring frictions between regionalism and nationalism in the contemporary Pacific. The shows highlight how Fiji as a nation is trying to negotiate the disjunction between its role as a regional arts hub and a long-established site for pioneering Oceanian cultural production, and its troubled reputation as an exemplar for regional disunity due to its coup-ridden recent history and traumatic legacy of Indigenous-led racism. I suggest that the performances' focus on a linked Oceania premised on transoceanic voyaging, and their reinforcement of Fiji as a crucial crossroads and custodian in the region, might be read implicitly as a dramatic strategy that seeks to suture a fragmented nation with a tenuous hold on democracy, to recuperate Fijian indigeneity in positive and empowering ways, and to foreground Fiji as an integral and integrated component of the South Pacific community.

Epeli Hau'ofa founded the Oceania Centre in 1997 as a material and artistic extension of his vision for a connected, expanded, and invigorated Oceania. It is located on the university's main campus in Suva, Fiji's capital, the headquarters of USP's pan-regional network of satellite campuses and centers,[129] and is host of the UNESCO Pacific Heritage Hub. From the outset Hau'ofa conceived of the center as an institutional space devoted to the imagination and a pocket of resistance against the university's predilection for vocational training and activities tailored to meet the demands of the global economy. His aims were for the center to nurture art forms that are "unmistakably ours" as a route to cultural autonomy,[130] and to reinstall USP as a vehicle for a critical localism, as it had been during the 1970s, rather than an instrument for a globalizing hegemony. The center pursues visual and performing arts practices inspired by various Pacific forms, but that adapt and respond to the changing international environment; and that are based in Oceanian ideals of reciprocity, cooperation, and the embodied transmission of knowledge and skills. Importantly, such practices are invested with a profoundly regional purview that draws on the ocean as a unifying thematic and ideological concept and as a rationale for the dissemination of the center's work. As Hau'ofa explains: "Taking a cue from the ocean's ever-flowing and encircling nature, we will travel far and wide to connect with oceanic and maritime peoples elsewhere, and swap stories of voyages we have taken and those yet to be embarked upon."[131]

Vaka and *Drua* are evidence of a coming to fruition of the Oceania Centre's aesthetic, political, and institutional aims since Hau'ofa's passing in 2009. Vilsoni Hereniko, a Rotuman scholar, playwright, and filmmaker,[132] recalls that he felt compelled to travel from Hawai'i to Fiji to take management of the center in 2010 after Hau'ofa's spirit appeared to him in the form of an owl.[133] The performances were conceived by Hereniko in collaboration with Hawaiian choreographer Peter Rockford Espiritu and Samoan composer Igelese Ete, whose own choreographed choral work based on voyaging histories, *Malaga: The Journey* (1998–), has been produced widely across the Pacific, changing each time to fit the stories of each place and to include the work of local composers.[134] The big-budget, large-ensemble productions represent a rich corpus, but for the purposes of this discussion I shall concentrate primarily on the second episode, *Drua: The Wave of Fire*, which depicts the *drua*'s voyages, intercultural design, and social ties. In this segment a group of young Fijian men set out on the *drua* to search for new lands. They are shipwrecked in Kiribati, where a Fijian navigator, Uli, falls in love with the local chief's daughter, Nei Te. Nei Te teaches Uli about the superior designs of Micronesian outriggers, and she and the Fijian crew set sail for Fiji. The *drua* encounters a storm and is blown off course, landing in Samoa. There, the voyagers connect with a Tongan chief and a Samoan *Lemaki* (canoe-builder), who are impressed with the *drua* and, along with the bird-woman Gogosina, accompany Uli and his cohort back to Fiji's Lau archipelago (the historical center of shipbuilding in Fiji). Everyone returns to the descendant of the *vesi loa* (*Intsia bijuga*) tree from which the original *drua* was fashioned. The tree urges them to respect the sacrifice made by her forebear by sharing their combined knowledge to improve the design of the *waqa drua*, and the whole community builds the new model together. Gogosina prophesies the coming of a "wave of fire," revealed as the colonial influx of missionaries, diseases, and foreign vessels that put *drua* culture into a slumber. The finale celebrates the revival of *drua* culture with a contemporary song in English that emphasizes that "we are one" and "together we're stronger," with "the ocean our avenue" as we sail throughout the "beautiful sea of islands."

One of the performance's key functions is to communicate how the *drua* drew on and in turn advanced shipbuilding technologies from many different Pacific societies. Nuttall and colleagues admit that "just how the innovations of several cultures were amalgamated into an ultimate drua design remains a matter of debate," as does the extent of the *drua*'s operation and influence, but it is understood that the "drua catchment" incorporated a large part of central Oceania.[135] Through the odyssey of Uli, Nei Te, and their companions, the performance dramatizes the particularly fecund technology transfer among Fiji, Kiribati, Tonga, and Samoa, including the Fijians' historical adaptation of i-Kiribati and Carolinian canoe designs; the subsequent influence of the superior hybrid craft on Tongan and Samoan seafarers, who by the late eighteenth century had begun to discard their own double-hulled vessels for Fijian prototypes; and how the shipbuilding industry stimulated the movement of Tongan and Samoan craftsmen to the Lau archipelago, where they settled and intermarried with local Fijians.[136] The characters thus serve as metonymic signifiers who enact a microcosmic history of the transpasifika traffic of materials, peoples, and ideas across an area that, significantly, traverses the artificially imposed subregions of Melanesia, Micronesia, and Polynesia, rescripting cartographies and reinforcing alliances that are both pre- and postcolonial.

The communal construction of the revamped *drua*, as in *Te Feti'a 'Avei'a*, conveys epistemologies and ritual protocols related to canoe manufacture, but in a more specifically politicized way that foregrounds social cohesion. The scene depicts the large cast seated in various groups on the stage; they pass around lengths of sennit, leaves, and bark to weave into sails and cordage while projections upstage show canoe diagrams, clips of craftspeople constructing traditional canoes, and a *drua* fully laden with passengers. The motif of strength-in-unity resurfaces in a song in which the performers draw correlations between the canoe and the populace, singing of how the sennit cords that bind the *drua* together are like the bloodlines that bind the people. Nuttall and colleagues explain how the *drua* as a symbol of pride and solidarity is embedded historically and etymologically. The term *drua* comes from an amalgamation of the Fijian words *dua* (one) and *rua* (two), therefore meaning "two but one," with two "different" hulls coming together as one vessel.[137] By extension, given that building a *drua* was a long-term undertaking that involved the entire village (including foreign carpenters, who had become an intimate part of the polity), "the building of a *Drua* had a uniting (*Duavata*) effect and brought the village together with one goal to finish the canoe and bring pride to the community." Indeed, "A smart chief would order the building of a *Drua* when he sensed disunity amongst his people [because] at times when a community was divided (*Rua*), the building of a *Drua* would bring everyone together as one."[138]

The regional collaboration among the authors of the *Vaka/Drua* projects; their extensive multicultural casts and crews drawn from artists, students,

Figure 8. The ensemble honors the Fijian *waqa drua* (voyaging canoe) in the Oceania Centre's *Vaka: The Birth of a Seer* (2012), devised by Vilsoni Hereniko, Peter Espiritu, and Igelese Ete. Japan-Pacific ICT Theatre, University of the South Pacific, Suva. Photograph by, and courtesy of, Naoki Takyo.

and unemployed youth in the community; their creative development according to Oceanian principles of reciprocity; and their interweaving of various Pacific performance cultures via the focus on cooperative precolonial voyaging practices are all designed as a powerful assertion of historical fraternity, contemporary regional unity, and future collective action. Given how the particularities of place bleed into the performance event, however, I probe further into what it might mean to stage this narrative in and through Fiji. Given the *vaka*'s association with Indigenous sovereignty as much as regional connectivity and the fact that the *drua* is one of the most commonly recognized symbols of Fiji, how does the performance negotiate national identity apropos these intercultural ties? What is at stake in new forms of regional performance that emanate from Fiji? In a history of voyaging that centralizes Fiji as a vital nexus? An acknowledgment of Fiji's turbulent contemporary history highlights the fissures between the hierarchies of the nation-state and regional imaginaries and sharpens our understanding of the sorts of intercultural interventions the performances attempt.

In the contemporary Pacific Fiji has a split reputation, which derives from its role as a significant regional catalyst for postcolonial artistic activ-

ity since the 1970s, and, conversely, its image as an index of ethnic divisive-
ness and regional fragmentation since the 1980s. In May 1987 Fiji's demo-
cratically elected government was ousted in a military coup, whose leaders
abrogated the 1970 constitution that had been in place since the country's
independence from Britain and instituted Fiji as a republic in October of
that year. Carried out under the rhetoric of Indigenous nationalism, the
coup (as well as subsequent coups in 2000 and 2006) ruptured Fiji's profile
as a model multicultural nation and represented a key sociopolitical schism
that eroded the idealist regionalism of the Pacific Way.[139] A key target of the
Fijian nationalists was the Fiji Indian community, descendants of Indian
plantation laborers brought to the islands by the British colonial administration between 1879 and 1916, redoubling Fiji Indians' own fraught memories of crossing *kala pani* (the dark waters) and the ordeal of indenture.
These conditions have also had a significant impact on cultural and artistic
expression. Hau'ofa recalls that at USP the postcoup environment threatened the very establishment of the Oceania Centre, as certain groups within
the university felt its proposed emphasis on Pacific cultures to be at odds
with liberal democracy and human rights, smacking of the Indigenous racism associated with the coups.[140]

Indeed, recuperative theories and practices of regionalism, emanating
from USP, have been important in responding to the divisive legacies of
Fiji's coup-cycle phenomenon. If, as certain scholars have, one takes
Hau'ofa's famous "sea of islands" essay and his attendant critical oeuvre
as an attempted antidote to a contemporary history of ethnic bias and
social splintering,[141] we might also read the work of the Oceania Centre
and the *Vaka/Drua* performances in particular as intervening in a national
imaginary as much as a regional one. This agenda has not been a visible
aspect of the performances' public objectives, with the producers prefer-
ring to focus on, as DeLoughrey has put it in another context, "water ties"
rather than "blood vessels."[142] The fluid metaphors of Oceanic relations
seek to absorb and dissolve legacies of division, yet the avowed narrative
is that of foreign colonialism and globalization (the "wave of fire")—an
external adversary against whom Pacific Islanders can band together strategically. The other, coup narrative, which speaks of internal discrimination, nativist xenophobia, and the renewed exile of an immigrant population whose own historical mobility was framed by the architecture of
British capitalist enterprise, is not openly declared, but it arguably subtends and informs these productions.

From this perspective, there is crucial social and symbolic purchase in
locating national history in the voyaging canoe rather than the soil, and in

emphasizing the persistent dialectic between roots and routes encapsulated in the history and destiny of the *vesi loa* tree. The *drua*—an icon of Fijian nationalism and chiefly authority—is shown strategically to have its basis in intercultural exchange, rendering it a multistate phenomenon and foregrounding the ocean as a shared and cooperative space that downplays the land and its particularized contestations. Similarly, ancient models of chiefly leadership that support community collaboration offer a historical alternative to postcolonial corruption. The performances, then, which relay and enhance *drua*-related knowledge for public audiences, operate as means to restore national pride while decoupling Fijian indigeneity from its negative associations with ethnic exclusionism, and they deploy the arts as a counter to a repressive governmental regime.[143] Ultimately, the recuperation of national history through a determinedly regional lens attempts to resecure Fiji's place within an Oceanic imaginary, reinforcing the country as an active and pioneering participant in, and location of, various cultural revival efforts in Oceania.

It is revealing, from this point of view, to place *Vaka* and *Drua* more squarely within a modern Fiji theatrical tradition, especially Fiji's self-representation on the regional stage. We can compare the center's works, for instance, with *The Visitors* by Fijian dramatist Larry Thomas, which was staged at the Festival of Pacific Arts in American Samoa in 2008. The festival, inaugurated in Fiji in 1972, was conceived initially as an intra-Pacific cultural showcase to foster a regional sensibility in resistance to homogenizing global cultural forces and is held every four years in a different Pacific location. Thomas's plays since the 1987 coup have maintained predominantly realist techniques to enact incisive social criticism regarding Fiji's climate of fear, division, and intolerance.[144] *The Visitors* used the device of the home invasion to comment on the country's ethnic tensions, and as the director, Ian Gaskell, recalls, it exemplified how political theater from Fiji has posed problems for the constructed sense of regional identity conveyed through events like the festival, challenging its ideological underpinning whereby "Indigenous identity and solidarity are central to promoting a sense of 'Pacificness.'"[145] There was strong resistance from the Fiji Arts Council to taking *The Visitors* to American Samoa, with fears it would reflect badly on Fiji, and indeed it reminded audiences of the social problems in many Pacific nations that undermine the image of regional bonhomie. As Gaskell says, "Just as the play depicts a marginalised section of the Fiji population—the 'visitors' of the title—and interrogates their sense of belonging, when it came to the Festival the production itself did not belong.

It was an unwelcome visitor spoiling the party; its sense of 'Pacificness' ran counter to the accepted version."[146]

The difference between *The Visitors* and USP's presentation of *Vaka* and *Drua* at the subsequent Festival of Pacific Arts in the Solomon Islands in 2012 was conspicuous.[147] Ethnic conflict, contemporary social critique, and gritty realist mimesis in *The Visitors* were replaced by the mytho-historical past, the scheme of the romantic quest, experimental creative genres, and affiliatory paradigms that, on the face of it, eschewed adversarial postcolonial politics in favor of a reification of community. The final song from the *Vaka* episode (as with *Drua*) accentuated approved concepts of "Pacificness" through its emphasis on the suturing potential of interisland voyaging and of lyrics that upheld the ideal of unity-in-diversity with "Our eyes that see as one, / One people we are strong, / One cause, one family, / United together, / Together forever as one."[148] To read the *Vaka* epics as expressing a postcoup poetics is to anchor the work of the Oceania Centre within a complex field of historical and sociopolitical relations that cast into relief the multivalent stakes and strategies of regional identification in the Pacific. Through its collaborative and interdisciplinary engagement with *drua* voyaging, especially the specific alignment of Fiji with countries like Samoa, Tonga, and Kiribati (all independent Pacific nations whose Indigenous struggles lie primarily in their status as Small-Island Developing States within a broader global context), *Vaka* and *Drua* nurture tangible connections that endeavor to break down the boundaries of colonial prejudice and autochthonous political partisanship, and to reposition Fiji within coalitional configurations that can act purposefully on the world stage.

DIASPORIC DIRECTIONS, CONTESTED STATES: PACIFIC VOYAGERS IN THE CONTEMPORARY WORLD

Hau'ofa's optimistic vision for Oceania is also motivated by "the contemporary process of what may be called world enlargement that is carried on by tens of thousands of ordinary Pacific Islanders right across the ocean."[149] Linking the exploratory migrations of the past to the mobilities occasioned by the expansion of the global economy in the second half of the twentieth century, Hau'ofa argues that postwar conditions have "made nonsense of artificial boundaries, enabling the people to shake off their confinement. They have moved . . . [,] doing what their ancestors did in earlier times" by "establishing new resource bases and expanded networks for circulation."[150]

Accordingly, I turn now to a tranche of plays that diverge from historical seafaring pedagogies to explore Oceanian identities on the move in the modern world. Hau'ofa's (strategically) utopian generalizations notwithstanding, the works that follow, which concern the United States' connections to the "American Pacific," remind us of the fact that Pacific diasporic trajectories are frequently mediated by (quasi-)colonial administrative, commercial, religious, and military pathways that influence where and how Pacific Islanders journey and migrate.[151]

In shifting the focus from social collectivities to the experiences of individual protagonists, the plays demonstrate a corresponding shift from an emphasis on shipbuilding and the communal act of voyaging to the specific figure of the navigator, drawing on the vessel as a metaphor for the vagaries of the life course as its pilot pursues a direction toward personal and cultural actualization. Written and performed in a context where the greatest concentrations of Pacific Islanders are now located in large, industrialized cities of the Pacific periphery rather than in the island Pacific, these works are preoccupied with the tensions between roots and routes in the "expanded world" of Oceania,[152] and tender more ambivalent characterizations of flux and fluidity. So far, I have traced regional interculturalisms in performance by considering transpasifika ties sutured through the widespread chronotope of the vaka, focusing on relations among and across different Pasifika communities that emphasize Indigenous collaborations and the centering of an indigenized Pacific Ocean. These next three works position transpasifika dynamics somewhat differently by prioritizing Pasifika experiences and viewpoints in intercultural projects that include non-Indigenous participants from beyond the Islands, engaging Asian and continental US theater-makers and companies to forge links stretching across the Pacific from Micronesia to California.

In this section, I also want to address more directly the gendered dynamics of voyaging, which flow over into theatrical and artistic portrayals. Despite the popularity of Disney's Moana character, a dominant trend in Pacific seafaring discourse is its emphasis on male protagonists, expeditionary achievements, and (self-)discoveries. Notwithstanding the robust presence of female voyaging figures in Oceanian mythology, and records of female navigators in places like Kiribati and the Marshall Islands, navigation across Oceania is traditionally figured as a primarily masculine occupation.[153] Richard Feinberg likewise points to the widespread gendered division of sociospatial symbolism in the Pacific that associates men with sailing and women with the land.[154] In her novel L'épave (The Wreck, 2005), Kanak (New Caledonian) writer Déwé Görödé uses the recurring and shifting image of the wrecked ancestral canoe as a metaphor to critique a male-dominated custom that carries an age-old oppression of women.[155] However, symbolic frameworks of vessel production and voyaging have also been important for conceptualizing more positive feminine identities and Indigenous women's writing and art-making in Oceania. In the introduction to their special journal issue of *Pacific Studies*, "Women Writing Oceania: Weaving the Sails of Vaka," Samoan scholar Caroline Sinavaiana and Hawaiian scholar J. Kēhaulani Kauanui explain that "while traditional voyaging is often presumed to be a male domain in many parts of the Pacific, we here invoke a female lineage of sailors exemplified by Pele, Nafanua, and Ne'i ni Manoa, for example, as voyagers in command of their own vessels."[156] Moreover, women make further contributions to genealogies of mobility in their special role in constructing the vessel: "As the weavers of sails, that is wind-powered 'engines,' women's social power is materially associated with the actual generation of mobility itself. The divine associations are there as well, as women can be understood to partner with the heavens in the negotiation of kinetic power through various types of winds."[157] Consequently, the vaka as a metaphor for ongoing literal and figurative journeys is linked just as much to "a historical continuum of women's cultural labor, both intrinsic and emergent, across vast reaches of space and time."[158]

Accordingly, it is useful to consider *Navigator* (2010), scripted by Susan Soon He Stanton, a Hawai'i-born playwright of Korean descent, in consultation with Hawai'i's Polynesian Voyaging Society and with Hawaiian theater director Harry Wong for Honolulu Theatre for Youth (HTY). Since its establishment in 1955, HTY has been one of the United States' foremost centers for professional theater and drama education programs aimed at young audiences, and since the 1980s has taken an increasingly proactive role in developing youth theater throughout Oceania in keeping with its stated identity during that decade as "a theatre leader for America's Pacific Islands and the related island nations."[159] Theater for youth is a significant contributor to theatrical production in contemporary Oceania and offers a view of social and artistic influences and interactions that might not be evident in a study confined to performance targeted primarily at adults. Consequently, an examination of how the voyaging discourse is framed artistically for young audiences[160] yields additional insights into the intersections between these revival movements and the larger social currents that they traverse.

HTY's *Navigator* features two female protagonists and triangulates Kahiki, Hawai'i, and the mainland United States. The drama follows two twelve-year-old girls: Moana, from an island in Kahiki (possibly Tahiti) in circa 1000 CE, and her descendant Moana (who goes by Annie) from present-day Sausalito, California. Featuring simultaneous action and fluid temporality, scenes from the ancient and modern worlds are consistently interleaved within a playing space configured as a double-hulled canoe, whereby different spatiotemporal enactments on either hull are unified through the vessel's composite structure. The girls' stories, therefore, become one story via their interwoven sea journeys that fix Hawai'i as a geographical and personal destination. Moana, who—despite gender prohibitions—aspires to become a *ho'okele* (navigator) like her father, stows away on a voyaging canoe and gets to prove herself when she takes over from her injured father to guide the *va'a* to Hawai'i. Annie, an off-island Hawaiian, is displaced from her Indigenous heritage, but when her parents' marital troubles see her flown out to stay with her grandfather in Puna on Hawai'i's Big Island, she experiences a cultural reconciliation that includes an initiation into traditional sailing.

Despite their similarities, the two girls intervene in the historically masculine world of navigation in differing ways: Moana is immersed in her cultural milieu but must negotiate restrictive gender norms, whereas Annie does not face gender discrimination but must come to terms with her cultural inheritance, part of which involves her recognition of her place in a lineage of *wahine maoli* (Native Hawaiian women) on the move. In Kahiki of a thousand years ago, Moana stands out: rather than learning to pound *kapa* (barkcloth) with the village women, she yearns "to travel to the unknown!" (2).[161] Moana begs her father to teach her wayfinding; despite his insistence that "the art of navigation must be passed from father to son," he has a dream in which a young woman (whom he thinks is Moana) sails "a canoe to islands beneath a bright star" (2) and so he agrees to give her secret tuition. When a great expeditionary voyage is planned, Moana is forbidden to go; viewing the new vessel, she realizes that her navigation lessons have removed her from regular women's labor and thus a contribution to building the canoe: "She is the only girl in the village who did not help weave the massive sails" (10). Hiding herself on the *va'a*, Moana is discovered on the open ocean and is outcast for having disrupted the careful balance of the canoe and its allocation of resources. After her father is struck by the ship's *paepae* (boom) during a storm, however, she uses her knowledge to assert herself as a traveling subject and to "bring the island to the canoe" (42), marking her passage to Hawai'i and into legend.

Annie's story is more complex because of the cultural alienation that she faces. As a part-Hawaiian born and raised in the California Bay Area, she declares, "I don't look Hawaiian, I don't feel Hawaiian" and disavows her "super embarrassing name," Moanalipolipoakaho'okele (5). Thoroughly estranged from her grandfather's traditional Hawaiian lifestyle, Annie's sea change occurs when she seeks to escape by taking his canoe and plotting a course back to the US mainland, but loses her GPS and must survive by setting a home course for Hawai'i. As Annie strives to find her way back, she hears the voice of her ancestor Moana guiding her to land, and it is revealed that Annie is in fact the subject of the prophetic vision experienced in Kahiki centuries before. In addition to beginning Hawaiian navigation lessons with her grandfather, Annie's new journey toward her Kanaka Maoli identity is marked by inheriting a shell lei that symbolizes the forebears named in her family's genealogical chant, including Moana. It is at this moment that Annie also learns the meaning of her full name: "The deep, mysterious ocean travelled by the navigator" (44). Although Annie's older cousin Koa voices the common assumption, "I thought dere weren't any wahine navigators" (47), the play's ending validates women's historical routes and links them to women of the contemporary Pacific diaspora: in the final scene, Moana ties the shell lei together and places it around Annie's neck, ritually confirming Annie's position in a genealogy of female voyagers that brings past and present full circle.

It is notable that (as in Disney's *Moana*) the most determined theatrical portrayals of female navigators occur in youth genres, and indeed, the young protagonists—adolescent girls rather than mature women—perhaps offer greater possibilities for pushing against customary boundaries and venturing beyond ascribed adult social roles (besides avoiding obvious issues that arise from the mixture of sexual desire and shipboard propinquity). The trope of the new generation also holds symbolic relevance for a regional voyaging revival that is still young and realizing its potential, and which has brought social changes to traditional practices: not a replica of the past but a strategic reconstruction that synthesizes ancient and modern elements, contemporary Indigenous voyaging has also made room for greater women's participation. *Navigator* thus pays homage to a wave of real-world female navigators who have emerged across Oceania in the past few decades.

As the very (complicated) concept of a "cultural renaissance" indicates, however, it is vital to remember that twenty-first-century Hawai'i is hardly a virgin land but a contested, politicized space intersected by Indigenous, diasporic, and settler-colonial claims; and that Native Hawaiian sovereignty has been characterized by a history of erasure and by struggles for hard-won access to place-based resources and rights. Consequently, it is not only Annie but her grandfather, too, who has experienced estrangement from Indigenous culture under US imperialism. Grandfather's mission to live his life "connected to da old way" (16) has been a conscious process of relearning and a quest for belonging that precedes and parallels, rather than counterposes, Annie's. In figuring Hawai'i as Annie's origin and destiny, *Navigator* revises not only the gendered discourse of navigation but also the image of Hawai'i itself. This latter goal signals a turn that I want to make to explore the regional cultural work that Stanton's play undertakes, especially in the context of HTY's goal over the past generation of writing and performing Hawai'i back into the Pacific. Alongside *Navigator*, I examine how other intercultural theater projects sponsored by HTY reveal tensions between the perimeters of the US nation-state and concepts of Oceanic regionalism that emphasize the evolving self-determination of Indigenous communities within America's imperial purview. These tensions are thorny and are shot through with multiple, competing trajectories, affiliations, and identifications, particularly across the imbricated geocultural domains of the United States, Polynesia, and Micronesia. Theatrical depictions of voyaging, I argue, effectively expose the promise and the ambivalence of these relationships.

To better understand how representations of traditional seafaring reflect changing notions of Indigenous sovereignty brought about by that very renaissance, it is revealing to read *Navigator* next to the earlier HTY play that inspired it. *Song for the Navigator: A Story of Micronesia* (1986) follows the journey of sixteen-year-old Gabby, a young man from Saipan in the Northern Mariana Islands, who attends a private boarding school on O'ahu, Hawai'i. Arriving home for vacation, he learns that his parents have separated and that he is being sent to live for the summer with his mother's family on isolated Satawal atoll in the central Caroline Islands (now part of Yap State in the Federated States of Micronesia). Scenes detail Gabby's culture shock as an Americanized Pacific Islander thrust into a traditional Micronesian society, and his growing bond with his grandfather Samal, a blind navigator (*palu*). Samal's lessons in navigation enable Gabby to save his own life on the ocean and that of his cousin Tilifag, and result in Gabby's enriched sense of culture, family, and self.

Featuring local Hawaiian and Micronesian actors, *Song for the Navigator* was the first US play to tour the Micronesian islands. The NEA-funded project was designed initially as a celebration of Micronesia at a historic moment when the Mariana, Caroline, and Marshall Islands were leaving the United Nations Trust Territory of the Pacific Islands (administered by the United States from 1947 to 1986) and becoming independent nations.[162]

HTY focused on voyaging and navigation because it was such a prominent feature of societies across Micronesia but also because it was the cultural influence that had profoundly impacted Hawai'i's own resurgence of Indigenous identity through Hōkūle'a's role in reconnecting communities throughout Oceania. The theme developed during several prolonged conversations between American playwright Michael Cowell and the famed Satawalese navigator Mau Piailug (crucial to Hōkūle'a's successful 1976 voyage), who inspired the character of Samal.[163] Piailug's cousin Lino Olopai from Saipan—also a celestial navigator—served as Micronesian cultural consultant and aided the extensive fieldwork undertaken by the HTY team in preparation for the production.[164]

Song sought to spark a desire among non-Micronesians to learn more about the languages and lifeways of the more than two thousand islands in the northwestern Pacific spread over an ocean area the size of the contiguous United States.[165] Reciprocally, HTY wanted to present theater as a gift for a region without a modern theatrical tradition in the hope that Micronesian audiences would "discover theatre as a vital, dynamic means of exploring their own history, legends, and contemporary lives."[166] In pursuing these aims, the project can be read as an act of decolonial remapping: while the tour traced and traded on US imperial routes, it also cut across those lines, gesturing to the potential dismantling of prohibitive areal designations promised by the loosening of US trusteeship and Hōkūle'a's voyages, while offering a new art form that could be adapted by different communities to enhance local pride, knowledge, and skills. In this way, Song can be situated as part of HTY's plan to weave Hawai'i back into Oceania artistically and politically, overhauling Hawai'i's postwar reputation as an Americanized site with a distal relationship to the sea of islands. A generation later, Navigator continued this work by positioning Hawai'i in dynamic relation to both Polynesia and the continental United States.

Whereas Song sought to advance Hawai'i's reputation as a Pacific-centered theater node, the play still figures 1980s Hawai'i as a resolutely American space, synonymous with the commercial world of "tall buildings, and cars, and McDonald's" (37).[167] After three years at high school in Honolulu, Gabby is au fait with the world of body surfing, video games, and popular dance moves—accoutrements of Hawai'i's modern American lifestyle. Yet he is also defined by his difference as an "other" Pacific Islander and a citizen of a "'Third World' America":[168] as Gabby's roommate Guts declares, "Wow, so you're finally going home to that island you're from in Microknees; Saimin or something . . . What do you folks do down in Micronesia, anyway? Make microwave ovens, or what?" (13).

Guts's puerile jibes at the top of the play set the scene for *Song*'s underlying commentary on how colonial girdles that bind states and territories can craft modes of belonging in Oceania that are more disparate than holistic. Indeed, as we shall see, this situation continues to be particularly charged for immigrants from Micronesian sites, who are moving to Hawai'i in increasing numbers for work, education, and healthcare, and who frequently experience racism and discrimination.[169] On Satawal, the play's action turns on Gabby's reeducation as the "son from America" (23) and his process of acculturation to Satawalese customs and social life. At the end of the play, when Gabby prepares to return to Hawai'i to complete his Western schooling, he does so with knowledge of, and pride in, his Micronesian heritage, holding out the promise that he might resist US assimilation and navigate a clearer course within the matrix of the American Pacific.

Produced twenty-five years later, *Navigator* depicts off-island Hawaiians returning to their Native Hawaiian roots. In this adaptation, Hawai'i is presented as an assuredly Polynesian space that can salve the cultural effacements of the "real" America. When paralleled with the historical narrative of settlement from Kahiki, the play legitimates Polynesian precursors rather than the United States as the origin and defining feature of Hawai'i. However, whereas *Song*'s portrayal of Satawal is of a cohesive and continuing atoll culture that has maintained its history and traditions, remotely insulated from the impact of US trusteeship, Stanton's play shows Native Hawaiian culture in a process of recovery and rediscovery. The characters openly acknowledge the ruptures caused by US annexation, territorialization, and statehood, with their detrimental social and linguistic eradications. In *Song*, Gabby offhandedly describes Hawai'i as anglophone:

SAMAL: Don't speak Hawaiian?
GABBY: Nah, Hawaii's part of America, they just speak English. (23)

In *Navigator*, this topic opens to a far more heartfelt confession from Annie's grandfather: "During small kid time, I was taught for be ashamed for be Hawaiian. My sistahs and I not allow for speak Hawaiian in school. Like you, we wen by our haole[170] names" (21). Thus, "I lost my way. Den I met a group of people who was learning how for bring da art of Hawaiian navigation back to life without one compass or maps. I wanted to learn how for speak wit my ancestas" (29).[171]

Connecting with the ancestors, in person and in spirit, is an integral component of Annie's journey, in which grounded routes and ocean routes are conjoined through the metaphor of the kalo (taro), a vital part of the agricultural and cultural traditions of the Hawaiian people. Kalo connotes life, growth, and community, and binds together concepts of past heritage and future development. In a sequence that interpolates scenes from the ancient and modern worlds, Annie and Koa plant taro in Grandfather's garden, while on the *va'a*, the boy Kalina (who looks after plants and animals on the voyage) teaches Moana about it. The embedding of roots in the soil, juxtaposed with the passage of the taro seedling across the sea, reinforce Koa's and Kalina's interlocking explanations that "no matter how many shoots come off the 'oha / They are all part of the same plant. / The members of the 'ohana, / No matter how distant, / All come from the same source" (25). As Filipino-Pohnpeian scholar Vicente M. Diaz and J. Kēhaulani Kauanui further note, the taro plant as a symbol for the kinship ties between people and land can be extended to encompass a contemporary Hawaiian diasporic subjectivity. They explain that the Hawaiian word for family, *'ohana*, derives from *'oha*, the taro corm or generative offshoot grown from older roots or the stalk of the plant, and is a term also used to describe "off-islanders": "As Hawaiians living outside Hawai'i are often referred to as 'transplants,' one might argue that this label assumes the familial and genealogical connection between those living on and off the islands."[172] This metaphor is evoked primarily in relation to the maintenance of a transnational network of support for Hawaiian sovereignty struggles, "mark[ing] the possibilities in taking root and growing in a different soil while continuing to maintain an originary location and emphasizing indigeneity as a central form of identification."[173] The fracturing of the conjugal family structure symbolized by the separation of Annie's parents here opens to the possibility of extended kin relationships, centered in Hawai'i, that bolster Annie's Kanaka Maoli and Pacific Islander identities.

Song gestures to the gathering momentum of Hawai'i's own Indigenous cultural renaissance a decade after *Hōkūle'a*'s maiden voyage, but places the credit squarely in the realm of Micronesian knowledge and technology, particularly Mau Piailug's expertise. In *Song*'s final sequence, Samal paddles his canoe out to sea and disappears. As Gabby's aunt Ilaemal reassures him, "Samal no die on land, he too proud; Samal stay paddling that canoe right now, forever" (53). During Gabby's voyage back to Saipan on the field boat, Samal's voice manifests over the radio waves and he becomes an omniscient presence. Gabby's conclusion, "I don't know where he is exactly. He's probably somewhere over the ocean, or maybe all around us" (56), functions as an apt analogy for the role of Satawalese seafaring skills in galvanizing Hawaiian voyaging, as well as the greater dispersion, proliferation, and adaptation of this knowledge across Oceania. The overlapping dramatizations of Moana's ancient landfall and Annie's contemporary homecoming serve a rather different purpose. Although *Navigator* presents a productive repositioning of island-mainland hierarchies to place a reindigenized Hawai'i at the artistic and cultural nerve center of the Pacific, the debt to trans-Indigenous knowledge transfer between Micronesian and Polynesian communities is strangely absent from this updated narrative. Indeed, *Navigator's* additional historical thread (which has no counterpart in *Song*) reiterates the privileged Hawai'i-Kahiki relationship, bypassing obligation to Micronesian methods of navigation for Hawai'i's cultural resurgence and instead reaching back to a naturalized, familial genealogy that is handed down rather than laterally reacquired. While the play accurately affirms a continuum of Hawaiian epistemology that is crucial to acknowledge, turning a story of Micronesia into a story of Polynesia nevertheless threatens to relegate Micronesia to a space of alterity once again—an approach that is troubling in the context of contemporary migration from the Micronesian islands to Hawai'i, which is exacerbated by the inequalities of US imperialism.[174]

These issues are taken up in *Masters of the Currents* (2017), a devised, ensemble community theater work that explores the contemporary vicissitudes of the Micronesian community in Hawai'i. Developed in collaboration with performers from the Micronesian islands, the piece focuses on the experiences of people from nations bound by the Compact of Free Association (COFA) with the United States—the Federated States of Micronesia (FSM), the Republic of the Marshall Islands (RMI), and Palau—examining how the compact determines the circumstances under which these populations move and their challenges and opportunities in the United States as nonimmigrants (neither migrants nor citizens/nationals).[175] The persistent and pervasive impact of American infiltration into Micronesian cultures is expressed by the character of Tamana, an elder from Chuuk (a state of the FSM), who laments, "We were once masters of the currents, now we are slaves to the US dollar."[176] The decline from currents to currency registers the shocks of US neoliberalism and militarism: from canned fish to cement to the excoriating fallout from the sixty-seven nuclear bomb tests conducted in the Marshall Islands between 1946 and 1958, Tamana calls out the damage to lifeways, health, land, and resources that have pressed Islanders to leave their homes. Lambasting the COFA commitment to assist local communities with rebuilding, education, and medical services as "broken promises!" he pinpoints the United States' complicity in a rising tide of immigrants who are subject to stereotyping and discrimination in the host country but who cannot return to certain islands because of climate-change effects and radioactive contamination.

Masters of the Currents was created by Leilani Chan and Ova Saopeng, theater-makers of Chinese-Malay and Laotian heritage, respectively, who are the artistic directors of the Los Angeles–based TeAda Productions. It was coproduced with Kalihi's T-Shirt Theatre, Pacific Voices Oceania, the Micronesian Health Advisory Coalition, and Honolulu Theatre for Youth, with key creative directorship from Chuukese community leader and cultural navigator Innocenta Sound-Kikku. The workshop-devised play premiered at HTY's Tenney Theatre before embarking on a neighbor island and US mainland tour, where it opened in San Francisco as part of Brava Theater's Asian Pacific Islander Performance Series. In an interesting circuitry, whereas *Song* was described as the first US play to tour Micronesia, *Masters* was billed as "the first nationally touring play about Micronesians in the U.S."[177] In line with TeAda's profile as "a nomadic theater of color rooted in the stories of immigrants and refugees, committed to healing and honoring the lives of the displaced, exploited and overlooked,"[178] *Masters* sought to educate audiences about the vast linguistic, cultural, and sociopolitical diversity contained within the huge and arbitrary category of Micronesia (as we are reminded: "There's nothing micro about Micronesia") and to encourage a productive interrogation of neocolonial partitions and prejudices to (re)establish vital connections between Micronesian islanders and Hawai'i's Indigenous and other ethnic groups, and especially between Micronesians themselves.

Performed in English and Chuukese, the various community stories gathered during the production process are distilled into vignettes and channeled through five characters: the Chuukese elders Tamana and Tinana, and three teenagers: Alanso from the Marshall Islands, who came to Hawai'i as a young boy; Eva, born in Hawai'i to a family from Kosrae and Pohnpei (states of the FSM); and Soso, a girl newly arrived from Chuuk. Their experiences demonstrate, like *Song* a generation earlier, that despite the renaissance of native Hawaiian language and culture that *Navigator* celebrates, for many other Pacific Islanders Hawai'i remains as American as ever. In a common narrative of diasporic adjustment, Soso's new friends delight her with tales of twenty-four-hour malls, strong Wi-Fi, indoor toilets, public transport, and on-demand access to food, clothing, and medicine. But there is the inevitable trade-off: since Soso is "in America now," she must "only speak English, not your native language" and wear Western attire, not "that shower curtain" (a pejorative term for the *urohs*, or Micronesian embroidered skirt that records the histories of the wearer and her family). Projected images behind the actors depict Honolulu's urban geography of skyscrapers and bustling traffic, dressing O'ahu in the replicable garb of downtown America. Even those characters raised in Hawai'i suffer derogation when they are discovered to be "Micro": Eva's academic accomplishments are questioned ("She's Micro *and* she's smart . . . like Microsoft!"), and Alanso is physically assaulted by his former friends. If the promise that *Song* celebrated after the dissolution of US trusteeship in the 1980s is revealed here to be a set of broken promises, then little has changed in thirty years. The work of *Masters*, then, is to model possibilities for the young people to structure connections between island communities and across generations to develop pride in their heritage as Micronesians. At an extended family gathering to decide whether an elder's body should be buried in Hawai'i or repatriated, Alanso, Soso, and Eva discover that—Marshallese, Chuukese, Kosraean, or Pohnpeian—they are all related to one another, sparking interest in their shared homelands and traditions. The play's central message that "the ocean is our highway, it connects us, it does not divide us" forms the basis for a network that lends internal solidarity to, and charts new paths for, a fractured community in the diaspora.

The metaphor of the voyaging canoe is key to this scenario. Although the young characters do not learn canoe navigation in the play, the identity of Micronesian islanders as ocean custodians, sailors, and navigators is vitally reinforced, with the performance paying homage to the legacy of "Papa Mau" (Piailug) and foregrounding various associations between voyaging histories and contemporary cultural navigation in the diaspora through the canoe that comprises the central feature of the set. Positioned on a stage floor painted to resemble the ocean, the large-scale model is built in the style of a Chuukese fishing vessel, reoriented and adapted for stage business. The characteristic triangular sail, found in many sites throughout Micronesia, indexes shared yet distinct traditions and lends visual support to the play's leitmotif that although the travelers are from different lands, they are "all in the same boat." Its most striking feature is the sail employed as a canvas for projected images and film footage, which illustrates the characters' experiences, memories, and aspirations, as well as the heavier cultural and emotional freight with which their journeys are weighted. As characters share stories of their homelands, the sail's images shift between Honolulu's gray-skied cityscape and the landscapes and villages of the islands; the canoe thus allows the characters to "travel" back and forth in a space of memory and imagination, and in some cases, to inhabit what has been rendered uninhabitable.

Figure 9. From left: Jayceleen Ifenuk (Soso), Ova Saopeng (Tamana), Emeraldrose Hadik (Eva), Innocenta Sound-Kikku (Tinana), and Mikendon "Mike" Raed (Alanso) in the world premiere performance of *Masters of the Currents* by TeAda Productions in association with Honolulu Theatre for Youth, Kalihi's T-Shirt Theatre, Pacific Voices Oceania, and the Micronesian Health Advisory Coalition. Tenney Theatre, Honolulu, 2017. Photograph by, and courtesy of, Brad Goda.

This device enables some arresting juxtapositions. During the sequence when Alanso is being attacked by his schoolmates, he enacts the choreography of the fight in a series of stylized solo dance moves while the canoe sail behind him depicts images of smoldering embers and a traditional stick dance. The other cast members stand silhouetted upstage against a red backdrop, beating long staffs on the floor in ironic time to the stick dance and rhythmically chanting the insult "Cockroach, cockroach." As the assault reaches its apex, we are confronted—suddenly and disturbingly— with historical footage of an American atomic bomb vaporizing a Marshallese atoll. The detonation obliterates the dance scene and registers the devastating rupture of custom; the canoe becomes a site of, and witness to, the deep trauma of the nuclear diaspora in the Pacific, carrying the histories of destruction, deracination, and contamination occasioned by US militarization, and demonstrating how the injuries of exile are redoubled in this Marshallese boy's violent rejection in Hawai'i. As the cultural work of *Masters* suggests, however, the canoe is a capacious and generous vessel that is also an engine for healing, holding the possibility for new subjectivities, kinship ties, and pathways to tradition. As the characters journey toward new coalitions, home spaces, and solidarity networks, the play extends the promise for Hawai'i to be a node in that network: a productive transposition that not only dismantles the divisive logic of the US border but also bridges the contentious separation of "Polynesia" and "Micronesia" to emphasize commonalities among Pacific Islanders across the region.

Read together, *Song for the Navigator, Navigator,* and *Masters of the Currents* display HTY's investment in theatrical interrogations of the American Pacific over the past generation, from the ostensible end of US trusteeship in northwestern Oceania to new anxieties about borders and immigration occasioned by the Trump administration. The voyaging canoe and the navigator in modern diasporic contexts serve as hopeful symbols for cultural cohesion and social purpose, yet their deployment also draws trenchant attention to overlapping and competing narratives, and varying autochthonous claims and opportunities, which highlight, once again, how the sea of islands is marked by fractious, traumatic, and divergent histories, as well as affirming and multiplex connections. These "close together placed" readings of what the vaka reveals and what it effaces testify to the heterogeneous nature of identification, contemporary reality, and Indigenous sovereignty in Hawai'i and in the wider subregions of Oceania under the aegis of American power.

●　●　●

Waka carry stories, art, science, knowledge, whakapapa and performance.
　—Māori master navigator Hoturoa Barclay-Kerr[179]

The entwined journeys of *vaka moana* on the sea and the stage provide a productive framework for exploring some particular ways in which communities connect socially and artistically across Oceania's vast and heterogeneous terrain. Examining the interface between the voyaging renaissance and modern genres of Indigenous theatrical expression reveals important insights about the social role of Indigenous cultural expression in reasserting Oceania as an interconnected and mobile space. These overlapping translocal circuits refute dominant ideas of an "empty" ocean and highlight what Damon Salesa calls a "Brown Pacific" produced from Islander movements, transits, and interactions.[180] By focusing on the *mode* of travel—

the oceangoing canoe as a central instrument of oceanic life—I have charted a regional topography of Oceania that acknowledges the presence and tenacity of colonial domains, partitions, and pathways, yet reveals alternative ways of tracing Islander roots and routes that point to the decolonizing potential of the canoe as model and metaphor, and to the promise of Hau'ofa's complicated sea of islands.

The transpasifika perspectives employed here rework the dominant cartographic priorities of transpacific studies to privilege the concerns and contributions of Island societies; they also nuance discussions of interculturalism in performance by drawing attention to Oceania's unique archipelagic geographies and genealogical structures. The choice and arrangement of the works discussed in this chapter draw attention to how transpasifika exchanges are negotiated across very different matrices of power and political determination. They highlight tensions between structures of regional identity and local sovereignty, navigate relationships between precolonial interisland mobility and modern migrancy, and scrutinize representations of gender in voyaging scenarios. Accordingly, the case studies illustrate how performance's mechanisms move in, through, and beyond voyaging to address pressing issues of belonging, affiliation, and agency in the Pacific—several of which will be taken up in more detail in subsequent chapters. Ultimately, the destination point of this journey brings us to a clearer appreciation of Oceania's irreducible complexity, with the vaka perhaps less symbolic of Oceania's holism and more revealing of the intricate and differentiated ways in which Pacific communities negotiate their relations with respect to a host of historic and contemporary conditions. As John Carlos Rowe urges, "Imperialism, indigeneity, and migration or diaspora must all be read together in their layered simultaneity; they are the currents of the transpacific region."[181] Analyzing these micro-level acts of connection and exchange against the generalities of macro-level flows foregrounds how performance can frame a response to the forces shaping the globalizing Pacific Century.

CODA: PHANTOM VESSELS, VIABLE FUTURES

You hear them before you don't see them. The first impression of George Nuku's *Bottled Ocean 2116* at the Pātaka gallery in Porirua, Aotearoa, is aural: the rhythmic chant of a man's solo voice in *te reo* Māori, the slosh and splash of paddles scything seawater, and the slow beat of a deep drum. Entering the shadowy exhibition room, shot through with pinpoints of azure, green, and purple light to evoke the shifting hues of the ocean depths, we encounter a double-hulled *Wakapounamu* levitating eerily in the gloom, its milky translucence ghostlike, as though imbued with its own luminosity. Walking around the waka, which is suspended at hip height, I study the intricate construction of this vessel devoid of crew as I listen to the repeated echo of their being. Each hull is buoyed by an elegant line of water-cooler containers adorned with transparent plastic top-strakes, and intricately incised acrylic canoe sternposts soar above my head. Atop the decorated crossbeams sits a glowing *wharenui* (meeting house), a highly symbolic structure that, like the canoe, is suffused with history, body, and community and serves as the rooted counterpart to the canoe's routedness, topped with a *tekoteko* (carved human figure) that takes the place of the waka's figurehead. This uncanny vessel, with its haunting beauty and strange sterility, is not alone. It is flanked and guarded by mutated sea creatures fashioned from soda and water bottles: schools of small fish with colored plastic tails and fins, four hammerhead sharks with elongated tails and jagged jaws, and three sentinel jellyfish, their globular tentacles catching the light luxuriantly, cascading like sub-aqua chandeliers. These voyaging companions converge on the waka's guiding stars, the constellation of the Southern Cross, represented by four acrylic cubes. A looping digital projection on the back wall of the installation features a carved visage that slips in and out of watery focus, a portal to the underwater realm of the ocean divinity Tangaroa, who watches over the canoe on its ethereal journey.[182]

This bottled waka, as it voyages through our sea of plastic, inhabits a Māori temporality that brings past, present, and future into a coeval relationship. Both portent and evidence, the waka cites the tradition of sighting phantom vessels as omens of catastrophe—most prominently, the apparition of the Māori canoe on Lake Tarawera in 1886, just prior to the devastating eruption of the adjacent volcano—predicting the disaster of environmental degradation. Yet the waka also looks back from this impending position as it travels across a polluted ocean a century in the future, searching for the last human community in a world covered by water.[183] But Nuku, a New Zealand Māori artist currently based in Paris, encourages a more active response to the installation beyond seeing it only as a warning or a jeremiad. Curator Reuben Friend observes that by engaging ritually with plastic in the same way as with traditional materials such as wood or jade, "Nuku encourages an indigenous methodology that considers our genealogical connection to the natural environment,"[184] informed by a *whakapapa* (layering of ancestry) that treats environmental resources as living entities and breaks down oppositions between "natural" and "manu-

Figure 10. George Nuku, *Bottled Ocean 2116*. Installation at Pātaka Art + Museum, Porirua, for the 2016 New Zealand Festival of the Arts. Photograph by, and courtesy of, Mark Tantrum.

factured" materials. Nuku's strategic recycling and aestheticizing of plastic supports sustainable resource management while offering a vision of possibility and beauty rather than ignorance and fear.[185] *Bottled Ocean 2116* ultimately draws on the waka motif as a hopeful symbol. This is reinforced in the *whakairo* (carved patterns) inscribed on the vessel: spiral, ziggurat, and chevron designs that denote evolution, continuity, unity, tenacity, and vigor; in the caretakership of Tangaroa; and in the disembodied voices that pulsate through the spirit of the *Wakapounamu* as it pushes onward toward its destination. It is also present in the performative interactions that have informed the installation as it has voyaged to France, Aotearoa, New Caledonia, Australia, and Taiwan, where Nuku has worked closely with communities to make the exhibit unique to each site by sourcing and repurposing local materials. The next chapter of this book likewise voyages beyond a regional framework to explore the international collaborative efforts of Oceanian artists and activists to address the planetary crisis of environmental abuse. I constellate projects that tackle the peril of climate change and rising sea levels by emphasizing Indigenous philosophies and cultural perseverance while deploying varied performance vocabularies that engage and enlist foreign audiences and stakeholders.

THREE

(Dis)appearing Islands:
Climate Change and the
Future Geographies of
Oceanian Performance

On 17 October 2014, climate-change activists from twelve Pacific nations brought a flotilla of hand-carved canoes to the world's largest coal port in Newcastle, Australia. After performing ceremonial observances, dances, and songs to launch the vessels, and flanked by hundreds of local and international supporters in kayaks, the protesters paddled their small craft out into the channel, where they engaged in a peaceful direct action to prevent massive coal ships from entering and leaving the port. The blockade, organized by the Pacific Climate Warriors, a subset of the environmental activism network 350 Pacific,[1] was a response to more than twenty years of Pacific Islanders' unsuccessful pleading and negotiation with neighboring countries like Australia to curb fossil fuel production and emissions that have devastating impacts on Pacific Island ecologies, particularly sea levels. The action communicated the strong message that Pacific Islanders are not passive victims of First World consumption choices but are proactive and strategic advocates for the future survival of their homelands and cultures. Despite being dwarfed by the gigantic ships they faced down and purposely intimidated by the Australian police force (who endangered paddlers and kayakers with their jet-ski wake and repeatedly rammed the ni-Vanuatu canoe until its outrigger broke off), the Climate Warriors maintained a calm and dignified demeanor that enabled the action to remain nonviolent, later retiring to the beach to pray for the police.[2]

The Newcastle coal blockade demonstrates how, beyond long-distance voyaging, Indigenous Pacific canoes may be marshaled for other political purposes. In this case, the construction of the smaller traditional vessels, which occupied several months' work in participating communities, represented an important cultural revival project while serving as a strident articulation of resistance to the prevailing mechanisms of global warming.[3]

More generally, however, the Pacific Climate Warriors' activities highlight several important aspects of Pacific Islander mobilizing and mobility in relation to climate change, which I explore through a variety of case studies and performative genres in this chapter. I am interested in how, in addressing one of the most pressing issues facing the Pacific region and the global community, island microstates are working together and with international publics to gain traction on climate-change awareness. I examine how cultural and artistic production is bound intimately with these endeavors, often forming a crucial component of their rationale and expression, and frequently recalibrating and recontextualizing Indigenous cultural repertoires in ways that expand the forms and functions of contemporary Pacific performance. Likewise, just as the work of the Pacific Climate Warriors has taken them from Istanbul to Australia, and across Oceania and North America to Paris and the Vatican, these expanded aesthetic frameworks operate in concert with enlarged geographic itineraries, providing new contexts for the strategic construction of Pacific perspectives, identities, and modes of conduct on the world stage.

Since the millennium, the Pacific Islands region has assumed an urgent significance in debates about anthropogenic climate change as rising oceans and associated impacts pose an increasing threat to the lifeways and sovereignty of low-lying island states. Wolfgang Kempf and Elfriede Hermann suggest that the existential challenges posed by these conditions are a primary gauge for the extent to which Oceania is integrated into global flows.[4] As the previous chapter made clear, mobility and connectivity have long been important for understanding the dynamics of Pacific Islander ways of life, but the changing circumstances prompted by global warming — particularly the impending threat of displacement due to sea-level rise — force reassessments of processes and practices of movement, place-making, and forms of belonging.[5] Since the full physical impacts of climate change remain uncertain, consigned to varying scientific predictions in more or less distant futures, climate-change effects in the present have a strong discursive dimension. It has been widely acknowledged that although certain regional communities are already experiencing climate-related environmental degradation, with implications for island morphology, natural resources, livelihoods and infrastructures, predominantly it is *narratives* of climate change to which Pacific citizens are subject and to which they respond, and it is within this context that I position my discussion of artistic performance.

Throughout this chapter, I examine how imagined *future* movements propel performers' *current* movements: their international collaborations, journeys, and representations. These are usually in the form of artistic appeals to the world community to prevent enforced relocation through the reduction of harmful emissions—appeals that frequently include rehearsals of those speculative future displacements and mobilities. These movements are themselves regulated by and/or intervene in the structures and agendas of political congresses, the theater industry, the international art market, and various sponsors, while referencing existing, historical, and anticipated patterns of Oceanic movement and interrelation. The intercultural case studies discussed here illuminate a transpasifika framework in the sense of collaborations between different Pacific Islander communities, offering a performance-centered elaboration of Peter Rudiak-Gould and Tony Crook's observation that "climate change has had an important regionalising effect across the Pacific, providing a new basis for emphasising common cause across a range of scales."[6] The examples also take up transpasifika collaborations between Pacific and non-Pacific partners, extending beyond the region to curate a new, global reach and visible presence. My concern, then, is less with ecocriticism per se than with the dynamic relationships that Oceanian artists, activists, and governments leverage with each other and with counterparts in Asia, Australia, Europe, and the Americas to encourage action on global warming, and what these efforts help us to understand about the aesthetic strategies, cooperative energies, and circulatory capacities of contemporary Pacific performance.

RISING OCEANS, RISING ARTISTS

In the twenty-first century, cultural, activist, and artistic performance has been assembled variously across Oceania's broad and diverse domain to address a multitude of environmental issues from Indigenous land and resource rights, deforestation, urbanization, coral reefs, and protection of endangered species, to drought, water pollution and waste, as well as the devastating effects of nuclearization. But the topic that has garnered the most artistic attention, especially in international arenas, is climate-induced sea-level rise. Because of their geophysical characteristics and demographic patterns, the Pacific Islands are particularly vulnerable to the effects of global warming, especially the rising ocean. Although there is a great deal of regional and local variability in terms of island geography and environmental impact, low-lying atoll countries such as Kiribati, Tuvalu, Tokelau, and the Marshall Islands are considered to be "existentially threatened,"[7] already facing inundation in the case of a major storm or tsunami, and subject to gradual immersion that will see the islands become uninhabitable within the next fifty years.[8] The 2014 assessment report of the Intergovernmental Panel on Climate Change observes that "to date there is no unequivocal evidence that reveals migration from islands is being driven by anthropogenic climate change";[9] however, projections that by the year 2050 between 665,000 and 1.7 million Pacific Islanders (of an estimated total of 18 million) will have migrated or been forcibly displaced due to climate-change effects[10] foreground questions about the legitimacy of "non-territorial state entities" and "portable sovereignty," as well as calls to officially recognize displaced people on the grounds of climate-change status.[11]

There are, therefore, clear reasons why this particular issue has been spotlighted. Primarily, sea-level rise has crucial implications for Islander identities constructed though an intimate, genealogical connection to the ocean, posing the question of what it might mean when that ocean as heritage, resource, and connective tissue is reframed as an existential threat. At the same time, it highlights the jeopardized land, whetting the discourse of home, belonging, and ancestral relation to place. These urgent questions of Pacific futures centralize a contrast between, on the one hand, affirmative models of migrancy inspired by oceanic metaphors of fluid identities and networked relations across sea-paths, and, on the other, more troubled notions of dislocation brought about by the impending threat of lost land and culture—a dialectic between routes and roots that is not always easily reconciled in theory or in practice. In the context of the global art and performance market, moreover, sea-level rise has proven a more bankable topic than, for instance, performances about acidification and coral bleaching or the salinization of freshwater reserves, even though in some places these are actually more immediate and relevant concerns than sinking beneath the waves. It is a subject that dramatizes well, translating its exigency and extremity effectively to the material stage and soliciting affect; it engages big metaphors, allegories, and stories (the deluge, the apocalypse) that cross epistemic frameworks (Western science, Christian eschatology, and Indigenous cosmology). The topic provides an effective platform for activism and embodied resistance, and also serves as a vehicle for Pacific citizens to advocate for related issues to do with human and more-than-human rights.

Moreover—and most significantly—sea-level rise has most frequently been the focal point around which climate-change narratives from afar are constructed; namely, disappearing islands and Islanders. As environmental anthropologist Carol Farbotko asks: what are the politics and ethics of international attention to atoll communities that have been largely absent from Eurocentric cultural and touristic imaginings of the Pacific and that "have become meaningful spaces in cosmopolitan discourses only as they disappear?"[12] In the global media conversation on Pacific climate-change impacts, metaphors abound. Imperiled island communities "assigned the role of confronting on a small scale what the whole world will soon be confronting"[13] are described variously as being on the "front lines" of climate change:[14] a "canary in the coalmine,"[15] a "barometer,"[16] a "laboratory and litmus test,"[17] a "microcosm,"[18] a "synecdoche: a representation of all threatened islands and greenhouse disasters,"[19] and drowning climate refugees facing the imminent "end of the Pacific."[20] In their figuring of the Indigenous island subject as an endangered species, these attitudes constitute what Liz DeLoughrey calls a "salvage environmentalism,"[21] whereby white Westerners mourn a paradise lost of their own making.[22] As Farbotko and Heather Lazrus contend, when "a climate-exposed population is being problematically positioned to speak for an entire planet under threat,"[23] it can be leveraged into ventriloquizing a Western "crisis of nature" that speaks on behalf of other, foreign interests, and that displaces the emphasis from Islanders' specific concerns to highlight their service to a larger (global) purpose as proof of the climate crisis.[24] In addition to trading on a broader discursive history of conflating the interests of "nature" with the Indigenous or rural poor,[25] such constructions recapitulate reductive island mythologies that present the island as an ideal test site — isolated, hermetic, simplified, and expendable; or that tie the island to a place-based essentialism whereby loss of physical territory is equated with loss of sovereignty and culture. Framed by this "eco-colonial gaze,"[26] Pacific citizens risk circumscription within a narrow range of subject positions — climate hero or helpless victim — in a dependent relation with powerful groups in the "developed" world.[27]

How, then, can Pacific Islander perspectives be taken more squarely into account to provide more inclusive, equitable, and agential articulations of climate change and population mobility issues?[28] For Pacific citizens evince a diversity of interpretations and appropriations of climate-change discourse. The "spectral" character of climate change, as Crook and Rudiak-Gould put it, describing "both a present reality and an imagined future that is still in the process of materializing," means that "Islanders are responding to the idea as much as the thing, the future as much as the past or present,"[29] and reveals climate discourse — even more than its physical manifestations — as a force that has real effects, does concrete work, and inspires significant action. Even if the various channels of communication about climate change tend to relay similar messages to Islanders (an impending calamity with a catastrophic end-point), there are many ways in which these messages are received and recalibrated.[30] Moving beyond the polarities of acceptance or refutation, responses range from tactical adoptions of vulnerability that harness dominant messages and available roles as opportunities, to a sharpening of the discourse of home and heritage that amplifies Indigenous conceptualizations of an "integral connection between place, person, culture and way of life,"[31] to differently empowering identifications that emphasize resilience, networks, and adaptive strategies. In communicating these reframings back to Western and scientific audiences, Pacific peoples hold the potential to subvert dominant technocratic characterizations of climate change, as well as complicating more radical anthropological narratives of global warming, giving voice to both counternarratives and counter-counternarratives.[32]

Curiously, DeLoughrey asserts that "climate change is not the major subject of Pacific Island literary, cultural, and visual production. When it is addressed it is largely through the initiative of development and arts grants that originate from the larger carbon emitters, like the United States and Australia."[33] While that may be the case in other genres,[34] I argue that the picture changes considerably when we take seriously *performance* as a mode of Pasifika cultural production. Indeed, in Oceania, performance has emerged as a potent—perhaps exemplary—form of Islander-driven action inspired by the discursive effects of climate change. This regional performance output includes a variety of solo and ensemble works produced in local contexts. Just a sampling reveals New Zealand–based Tongan performance artist Kalisolaite 'Uhila's *Ongo mei Moana* (2015), performed at Wellington's Oriental Bay, in which the artist danced with and conducted the sea from low to high tide, following its rhythm for a week, to express an affective, genealogical connection with the ocean and to comment on climate-induced sea-level rise. Red Leap Theatre's *Sea* (Aotearoa, 2014), uses devised physical theater and sumptuous puppetry to tell the story of a community cast adrift after their Pacific island is inundated by an ecological disaster, presenting a poignant plea about the plight of the ocean. A similar logic underpins Tuvalu/Samoan dramatist Tavita Nielsen-Mamea's *Au Ko Tuvalu* (2019), which portrays a family's heart-wrenching decision to leave Tuvalu in the face of rising seas, and their concerns about relocating to New Zealand. Māori playwright Aroha White's dystopian "cli-fi" play *2080* (2015) speculates on a future in which 1.5 million Pacific Islanders have been relocated to New Zealand due to sea-level rise, forming a backdrop for fraught interactions between Māori and Samoan characters in a partitioned, surveillance state that gives a nod to George Orwell's nightmarish "Oceania."[35] Māori / Cook Islander Mīria George's performance installation *Fire in the Water, Fire in the Sky* (2017) treats the complicity of colonization and climate change across the Pacific; and Australian-born Tongan *punake* (body-centered performance artist) Latai Taumoepeau has developed a series of pieces that explore the impact of climate change on Pacific communities, such as *i-Land X-isle* (2011), *Repatriate I and II* (2015), *Stitching (up) the Sea* (2015), and *Disaffected* (2016), frequently placing her performing body under duress to allegorize the threat of global warming to land and culture.[36]

These are powerful and provocative works and have much to disclose in their own right, but my primary focus in this chapter is somewhat different. Rather than attempt a comprehensive survey of this burgeoning corpus, I consider how performance operates as a means of articulating and disseminating competing climate narratives in international contexts of climate-change appeal. In this regard, I take up what Kempf and Hermann identify as "a promising area of study, [and] one that has received little attention to date": an emerging "terrain of movement formed by travelling Pacific Islanders who are propelled by the discourse of global warming."[37] These comprise the growing number of Pacific government and church representatives, NGO members, technical experts, activists, and artists, who "give their own accounts of the special vulnerabilities and existential perils facing islands and island states in the wake of global climate change"[38] in various international forums and contact zones. Engaged in complex processes of representation and negotiation in these contexts, "with a view to securing the attention, empathy and support of the international community,"[39] these performative appeals introduce new vectors for Islander mobility and visibility, and add to the existing ways in which climate-change knowledge is circulated within transnational networks.

So far, that largely social scientific conversation has paid scant attention to how Pacific citizens use artistic performance or create aesthetic experiences to inform, challenge, and complicate conceptualizations of the climate crisis in their interface with international publics. Nor has this field of analysis really considered venues beyond conventional political negotiation contexts. Consequently, I want to expand the discussion by exploring a range of internationally situated cultural and artistic performance projects that have taken place at charged sites of religious observance, at arts festivals, and in galleries and theaters. I begin with the Pacific Climate Warriors' Mat Weaving Project (2015), which entwines cultural and performance activism. The Warriors' pilgrimage to the Vatican and their gift of a fine mat to Pope Francis draws upon a complex heritage of ceremonial gift exchange in the Pacific, whose reciprocal obligations stretch into the past and reach into the future, symbolically enlisting the Catholic Church in the fight against climate change. I then examine two very different deployments of Oceanian theatrical aesthetics in stage presentations that place Pacific performers within divergent climate-change narratives and outcomes. The Fiji-based Oceania Centre's European tour of their musical spectacle *Moana Rua: The Rising of the Sea* (2015) on the festival circuit and to the European Parliament charts the passage between vulnerability and agency, calling for mitigation while rewriting the possibility of forced migration as a self-directed expansion of Oceania. New Zealand / Samoan Lemi Ponifasio and MAU dance company's avant-garde presentation *Birds with Skymirrors* (2010–14), on the other hand, invites us into a ritual experience where we become aware of the apocalypse as already upon us, and as an inevitable phase in the cyclical making and remaking of the world. My final two examples, which analyze the Kiribati and Tuvalu Pavilions at the Venice Biennale, differ in that Pacific Islander performers are not physically present in the mise-en-scène; instead, the onus is on the visitor to activate the work. In the i-Kiribati–Slovenian coproduction *Sinking Islands, Unsinkable Art* (2017), participants face off against a digital avatar of a traditional i-Kiribati warrior in a battle over climate change; and in *Crossing the Tide* (2015), a collaboration between Taiwanese artist Vincent J. F. Huang, the Tuvaluan government, and New York's Guggenheim Museum, visitors traverse a flooded pavilion that encourages a global environmental consciousness linking the Adriatic and the Pacific.

This constellation of case studies contributes productively to evolving dialogues in theater and performance studies about what theater and performance can be and do in a climate-changed present and future, especially those conversations that seek to amplify Indigenous practices and perspectives.[40] For example, the discussions throughout this chapter show how Oceanian viewpoints can help illuminate and nuance the important questions posed by Lisa Woynarski et al. in their "Dossier: Climate Change and the Decolonized Future of Theatre" in the July 2020 issue of *Theatre Research International*. The authors ask—as I do here—how theater and performance can reckon with the uneven violence of climate-change impacts, take a more critical stance on what kinds of futures are imagined, draw on Indigenous ways of thinking to intervene in notions of futurity, and decolonize narratives of extinction.[41]

More specifically, the case studies demonstrate how performance can help address the question of what happens when populations conventionally viewed as "marginal" in global terms are positioned at the humanitarian, political, and aesthetic vanguard of international debates, especially the implications for the ways that islands and Islanders appear and disappear within that representational economy. The performative projects discussed here resist the plotlines of climate determinism and the concomitant disappearance of Islander subjects cast as remote, pastoral, precapitalist, and prelapsarian peoples who function as harbingers but with limited capacity to respond to the modernity of global warming. Instead, these artists explore performance as a situation in which people can appear and be recognized as political subjects; likewise, they complicate the reductive rendering of Pacific actors and activists as embodied evidence by experimenting with the strategic value of appearance and disappearance in the *form* of the performances, including spirituality, virtuality, absence, and the disruption of conventional viewer-performer relationships. Taken together, these projects encourage a range of encounters and conversations that engage human, nonhuman, more-than-human, and posthuman elements of the Anthropocene. By rehearsing different possibilities for global futures, these works link Oceania with the wider world in their composition, content, collaboration, and circulation. These international networks further defy restrictive and stereotypical depictions of isolated and vanishing island communities and offer alternative prospects for natural and cultural sustainability based in Oceanian traditions and worldviews, while providing insights into new mobilities of contemporary transpasifika performance.

"WE ARE NOT DROWNING, WE ARE FIGHTING": THE PACIFIC CLIMATE WARRIORS AND CLIMATE-CHANGE RESILIENCE

> Our message to the world is that we are more than just broken-down seawalls, dead breadfruit trees, and fewer fish. We are also resilience, sheer courage, and shared hope in the face of climate change!
> —Fenton Lutunatabua, Pacific managing director, PCW[42]

The Pacific Climate Warriors are a youth-led, grassroots coalition that spans fifteen Pacific nations.[43] The organization was conceived at the "Global Powershift" conference in Turkey in 2013 when 350.org representatives from around the world gathered in Istanbul. Aaron Packard and Koreti Tiumalu, who had been working to build a Pacific climate movement from New Zealand, sought the opportunity to expand the network to encompass a regional framework.[44] As is predominantly the case with regional initiatives in Oceania, the Pacific Climate Warriors are defined by diversity, encompassing multiple languages and cultures, and so their rationale and activities attend both to local specificities and to broader commonalities. Regional coordinators work with representatives in each country, who are closely connected with local community organizations and committed to following customary protocols. In complement, the Warriors' activities also have a transpasifika element, in Pearson's sense of practices and images that connect people across the Pacific, such as canoe culture, mat making, and warrior traditions, which encourage coherence and solidarity.[45] This pairing of on-the-ground community organizing and international mobilizing facilitated by digital interconnectivity has contributed to the resurgence of what Jason Titifanue et al. term a "bottom-up regionalism" that fuels climate-change advocacy among ordinary people, not just among state representatives, and that transcends ethnic and political borders to promote a unified Pacific identity.[46] The Warriors' undertakings, which involve workshops, performative protests, story-sharing, and other expressive genres such as sailing, weaving, dance, spoken-word poetry, and photographic tableaux, introduce new vectors for the transmission of Indigenous views of global warming while performing dynamic, interconnected regional identities that refute belittling and isolating characterizations of climate-exposed communities. By creating new cultural productions that circulate internationally on land, sea, and in cyberspace, the Pacific Climate Warriors contribute to our understanding of contemporary forms and mobilities of Oceanian performance.

The notion of "resilience" as a human response to the challenges posed by global warming has become an increasingly prominent topic in scholarly and policy discussions, signaling a more affirmative turn away from the focus on risk and vulnerability. Kirsten Harstrup observes that despite the lack of consensus on definitions of resilience, the term "conventionally points to the amount of perturbation a particular society or community can absorb and still be recognizable, also to itself."[47] The problem with this approach, she argues, is that it requires a bounded social or ecological system in order to make sense. Human social communities, however, are not closed systems but are perforated, permanently in flux, and open to impulses from elsewhere.[48] Harstrup suggests that rather than inhering in a well-defined system, resilience resides in human action and agency. In the context of climate change, this approach calls for a renewed understanding of "social resilience" that links global processes and local perceptions, and that attends to people's practical and conceptual flexibility, especially their capacity to "change practices without jeopardizing their sense

Figure 11. A promotional image created by the Pacific Climate Warriors and 350.org Pacific as part of a 2015 campaign to encourage people to #StandUp-ForThePacific against climate change. Featuring Lagakali Tavaiqia, contemporary *masi* outfit designed by Epeli Tuibeqa. Photograph by, and courtesy of, Navneet Narayan.

of belonging and knowing,"[49] and to "create and combine knowledge in new and creative ways to best prepare themselves for the future."[50]

I would take Harstrup's useful intervention further to consider, as Jane Bennett does, how "agentic capacity is now seen as differentially distributed across a wider range of ontological types."[51] Rather than insist on the primacy of the human, this observation highlights how techniques and strategies of social resilience involve human action in relation to the material agency or effectivity of nonhuman things; as Bennett notes, "The locus of agency is always a human-nonhuman working group."[52] This approach is sympathetic to understandings of resilience in Indigenous environmental studies, which emphasize "moral relationships of responsibility, spirituality, and justice"[53] that connect humans to animals, plants, and habitats, and that function as "complex systems working to promote adaptive capacity,"[54] drawing upon long-standing practices and philosophies to generate wisdom to sustain future generations. In assessing the Climate Warriors' projects, I am attentive to this interplay, examining how new iterations of customary practices and new assemblages of knowledge actively entwine human agency and material agency, as well as, significantly, the motive forces of immateriality.

The Pacific Climate Warriors' activities provide a productive example of a multiply enmeshed concept of resilience across a globally entangled Oceania. The Warriors' campaign emphasizes *mitigation* of climate-change impacts rather than accepting inevitable population displacement.[55] Their guiding principle is that Pacific Islanders are not victims doomed to disappear but warriors defending their homelands, an attitude encapsulated in their slogan, "We are not drowning, we are fighting." This resistance to prevailing narratives is based on particular modes of conduct attached to a revamped idea(l) of the warrior. As the organization's online profile describes it:

> A warrior is resilient. A warrior is not aggressive or violent, but is assertive. A warrior serves to protect their community, culture, land and ocean. A warrior is always learning. A warrior responds to the needs of those around them and of the greater good. A warrior nonviolently stands their ground against an adversary, against injustice and against oppression. A warrior respectfully embodies their local culture and traditions. A warrior is accountable for their actions and words. A warrior serves those who cannot fight for themselves—future generations, animals and plants, environments.[56]

This conception of the strong, yet peaceful, warrior-activist (which includes female warriors) refutes pejorative depictions of "savage" islanders as well as contemporary images of the hyper-combative soldier from the militarized Pacific. This rebranding, which undoes patriarchal masculinity by way of "traditional feminine characteristics of nurturing and collaborating" to promote "more peaceful pathways to change,"[57] is central to what former regional coordinator Koreti Tiumalu termed a "Pacific style of activism," which emphasizes dignity, integrity, and upholding Pacific beliefs and traditions and making them relevant for today.[58] It is also an attitude strongly informed by Christian principles, which, since the nineteenth century, have become important aspects of many Pacific cultures.

This posture also constitutes a public identity that can be distinguished from other versions of the Pacific warrior-activist that circulate in counterdiscourses on climate change, such as in *The Turquoise Elephant* (2016) by postcolonial Australian dramatist Stephen Carleton. Carleton's award-winning play is especially relevant here because it resists both the clichés of classic colonialism and the narratives of carbon colonialism projected on to Pacific Islanders, and is addressed to the same Australian big business and frustrating political denialism that motivated the Warriors' blockade of Newcastle Harbor. Owing a debt more to Ionesco than UNESCO, *The Turquoise Elephant* diverges from the earnest tone of most climate wake-up calls to use black humor as an ideological weapon. Its near-future scenario features the Pacific Islander characters of Visi and Vika, identical twin sisters who came to Australia as environmental refugees when their island drowned. Members of the militant Cultural Front for Environmental Preservation, they force social change by employing terrorist tactics: both sisters become suicide bombers whose sacrificial detonations cripple leading political figures and destroy Sydney's core infrastructure.[59] Whereas Carleton's absurdist farce offers a searing indictment of current mendacity and inaction from the theatrical stage, the Pacific Climate Warriors' alternative counternarrative does a different sort of cultural work that is keenly attentive to the upshot of their public actions for external perceptions of Pacific Islanders, especially those living abroad.[60] The Warriors' approach also exhibits an alternate female influence that, Karen McNamara and Carol Farbotko argue, "demonstrate[s] the importance of prayer, kinship and connections to ancestors as tools in climate change activism."[61] I find useful Hawaiian scholar Noelani Goodyear-Ka'ōpua's identification of such activists as "*protectors, not protestors*"[62] who transform settler-colonial relations with the environment and enact an "Indigenous futurity."[63] By renewing intergenerational pathways that link ancestors with descendants, these actions resist "the future" as Western telos and protect the possibilities of multiple futures.[64]

I explore what this "Pacific style of activism" might add to our understanding of the scope and strategies of performative climate-change resilience, especially tactical linkages among Islanders and non-Islander allies, and among the human, the material, and the immaterial, by examining the Warriors' subsequent regional action after Newcastle: the Mat Weaving Project. For this initiative, which took place in October 2015, the Warriors partnered with the most climate-affected communities in each of the organization's fifteen nations, inviting the women to weave a mat that incorporated that community's particular story of climate change. These mats were taken to Europe to connect with thousands of people mobilizing ahead of the UN COP 21 Climate Summit in Paris in December 2015. Ultimately, the Warriors took the mats to Vatican City for a three-day vigil involving storytelling and prayer. Dressed in black mourning garb, the group fasted and prayed for their islands and their leaders convening at the Paris Climate

Figure 12. The Pacific Climate Warriors prepare to present a fine Tongan mat to Pope Francis during their pilgrimage to the Vatican in October 2015. Photograph by, and courtesy of, George Nacewa.

Summit, for fossil fuel executives, and for Pope Francis's proactive stance on climate change. The mats themselves, and the stories they contained, were central to the proceedings. Spreading out the bright mats on the gray, cobbled paving of St. Peter's Square under the colonnades, the group sat on or around each mat and acknowledged where it came from. Representatives from each community related the narrative of climate impact worked into the mat, followed each time by a period of dedicated prayer for that place. During their vigil, the group attracted attention from, and welcomed, passersby and journalists, as well as several Pacific priests, some of whom arranged for the Warriors to attend the papal audience. The Warriors took this opportunity to give a particularly fine Tongan mat to the pope, presented by Silivesiteli Loloa, the grandson of the weaver.[65]

This contemplative event represents an action distinct from the canoe blockade, with its more obvious deployment of the warrior ethos in the drama of its David-and-Goliath standoff. But as Tiumalu explained to me, if the canoes project was about the "bigger picture," that is, the organization's public profile and enlistment strategy, then the mats project was more introspectively focused on the people themselves, and that both approaches are essential.[66] At first glance, this overture to the pope might seem odd, given the Catholic Church's historical reputation as a bastion of conservatism and colonialism. I posit, however, that to fall back on colonial binaries and a dyadic opposition between "foreign" and "Indigenous" risks a reductive apprehension of the highly syncretic, nativized, and polydox character of Pacific Christianities, their widespread and significant place in Pacific communities, and by extension, the role of such beliefs in a dynamic understanding of "local, heterogeneous responses to climate change, involving . . . various religious traditions, oral history, myth, and secular ways of knowing."[67] I am also in accord with Cecilie Rubow's argument that resilience literature needs to pay greater attention to religious and ethical aspects of communities' comprehension of climate change,[68] beyond doomsday scenarios that forecast an eschatological future, perceptions of natural disasters as divine interventions of a punishing God, or "denial" scenarios that cleave to faith in the rainbow as a symbol of God's promise never to send another universal flood.[69]

The Mat Weaving Project can be understood as a reciprocal action, a reply to Pope Francis' encyclical letter *Laudato Si': On Care for Our Common Home*, published in June 2015. A papal encyclical, a circular letter designed to be spread throughout a community, is one of the most authoritative statements that the pope can issue on his own, and *Laudato Si'* ("Praise Be to You," from St. Francis of Assisi's thirteenth-century "Canticle of the Sun") is the first papal encyclical devoted to the environment.[70] Pope Francis's substantial critique of environmental exploitation and the technocratic regimes, throwaway culture, and profit-driven anthropocentrism that fuel it is couched in a concept of "integral ecology," which emphasizes the mutually interdependent nature of all things. From the perspective of integral ecology, social and environmental crises are not separate, but represent "one complex crisis,"[71] hence the pope's particular focus on social justice and environmental responsibility to the poor and marginalized, and his call for special dialogue with Indigenous peoples on the sustainability of natural and cultural resources.[72] A major statement and performative act, *Laudato Si'*, "now added to the body of the Church's social teaching,"[73] positioned the Catholic Church as a leading moral voice and institution in holistic debates about global warming, and the Vatican as a site for climate-related action.[74] In this regard, Pope Francis reveals himself as an exponent of "green theology," a field constructed as a rejoinder to critiques of Christianity's collusion with humans' dominion over and exploitation of nature. This eco-theological stance identifies the earth and sea as gifts from God to be cared for in perpetuity, emphasizing human embeddedness in nature and the value of nonhuman entities in the cosmos.[75] Consequently, green theology suggests how Christianities might offer sustainable ways to cope with climate change.[76]

I want to analyze the Warriors' performative, reciprocal action in terms of the operations of their mats as interpretive texts and as items of gift exchange. This requires some preliminary information about the meanings and roles of mats in Oceania. As diverse as they are ubiquitous, woven objects—mainly of coconut, pandanus, or hibiscus fibers—are central aspects of material and social life across the Pacific. Woven mats (technically, they are plaited) are one of Oceania's most significant cultural products, serving a wide range of functions from the quotidian and the commercial to the ceremonial. Whereas, except for the woven sails, canoe construction is largely a male province, mat weaving in Oceania is almost exclusively women's work. Some mats serve as everyday household items, but others are intricately worked pieces that are not used like regular mats and may represent a society's most treasured cultural artifacts. They may become paramount heirlooms bestowed with names and invested with ritual importance, ancestral genealogies, and even sacred powers. In certain areas of Oceania, especially Samoa and Tonga, such "fine mats" constitute items of gift exchange in major life event and dedication ceremonies, connoting prestige, respect, gratitude, recognition, and obligation, while dramatizing social and cosmological relationships.[77]

In view of the agency and animacy ascribed to certain material things in many Pacific societies, the (fine) mat's evocative power is sharpened by the notion that it has a "soul," which—like the canoe—enriches its status as an "effective object";[78] that is, it *performs*. Customarily, the process of weaving was frequently understood to invest the mat with the essence of the weaver(s); in some sites, such as Vanuatu, the nature of the weave imbued the mat with special potency,[79] and in other situations, as formerly in Rotuma, the act of mat weaving symbolically constrained and ameliorated potentially malevolent spiritual forces, bringing them into the moral order and domesticating them.[80] In areas of the contemporary Pacific where woven mats almost died out due to the importation of foreign cloth, the revival of traditional weaving constitutes an important act of cultural resilience. In the case of the Marshall Islands, the weaving circle has reemerged as a crucial venue for the intergenerational exchange of knowledge and cultural values within a matrilineal society; the performance of weaving celebrates women's unique creative abilities, while the mats' designs encode stories of identity and heritage, linking personal endeavor and the unbroken bond with community and ancestors.[81]

The mats that traveled to the Vatican fell, generally speaking, into the "fine mat" category. The symbolic associations and performative potential of mats help us to think about what understandings of social resilience might be performed through the notion of the mat as emissary, and through narrating climate change within and alongside the form of a mat. Because customs and beliefs vary throughout Oceania and have changed over time, and since so many mats were brought to the Vatican from so many places, the possibilities for meaning-making were manifold and culturally situated, but one can venture some ideas. As materializations of landscape, place made into thing, the mats have reflexive relationships to the woven stories of climate change that contribute to their unique aesthetic form. This encourages consideration of the ways that constructing a story in and through a mat—pairing the ordering and selecting operations of narrative organization with the repeated act of physical entwinement—might, if not symbolically constraining or ameliorating the effects of climate change, at least materialize its abstractions and capture and communicate experiences, worldviews, fears, and hopes in potent ways. As texture, textile, and text, the mats' stories were activated by the oral storytelling that accompanied their display. These actions demonstrate cultural resilience through the complementary use of two heritage art forms to express the urgency of a changing present, interweaving local wisdom and global issues, and giving voice to communities frequently marginalized from international debates on climate change.[82]

Formally, the plaited mat is an apt object to represent the philosophy of a holistically interdependent world. As Heather E. Young Leslie puts it: "Like a mat which is strong because individual elements are combined and intertwined into a single unit, society is strongest when persons' actions and destinies are entwined and overlaid upon others', making families, community, potentially all humanity, from the disparate wefts of individual lives, time after time."[83] Indeed, the concept of a "woven world"[84] encompasses not only the nurturing of social relations but also environmental and spiritual ones; in this way, the Warriors' mats find an affinity with, and serve as a material analogy for, Pope Francis's notion of an integral ecology in *Laudato Si'*. The mats' construction thus symbolizes resistance to the polarizing and distancing view of Pacific Islanders in certain climate discourses, and advocates for mutual involvement and responsibility in planetary concerns. This reciprocal drive inheres not only in the form of the mat but also in its function as a circulating prestation. The act of gifting converts the mat's symbolic meanings into action—Bruno Latour would call the mat an actant[85]—emphasizing its capacity to make something happen, to bring something about. The gifted mat has a central role in establishing strategic, ongoing, and mutually binding relationships in both local and international settings. There is a long history of fine mat exchanges linking different Pacific communities, sometimes extending inter-archipelagically to strengthen ties across what are now national boundaries.[86] Today, mats also play a crucial role in maintaining diasporic relations, participating in an international ceremonial economy in which "vast numbers of fine mats circle the globe in aircraft linking island and overseas communities."[87]

These contexts feed into how we might interpret the Warriors' gift of a Tongan mat to Pope Francis. The weekly papal or general audience, which takes place outdoors in St. Peter's Square, typically attracts ten to fifteen thousand visitors and pilgrims. The pope processes in his popemobile, delivers a homily and prayers, and blesses Bibles and rosaries. The gift of the mat under these circumstances is significant not only because of the substantial throng that witnessed it, but also because of the pope's conscious, public desire to accept the unusual offering. Loloa made his way through the crowd with his grandmother's mat and was thrice rejected by Vatican security. On Loloa's fourth attempt, the pope noticed him, motioned for him to come forward, and accepted the mat.[88] According to Young Leslie, Tongans expect, generally, to give to higher-ranked individuals and to receive from lower: they provide respect and in turn receive beneficence.[89] On one level, this differential reciprocity is played out whereby the Warriors provide respect and gratitude for the pope's encyclical and leadership on climate change, which is returned with the apostolic blessing during the papal audience. But this relationship goes further: the gift of the mat also secures, with the pope's acceptance of it, an obligation to follow through on his encyclical with a further gesture of support. Since this exchange is part of weaving the social fabric, with the givers entwined with the gift, one can view it as a performative act that interweaves not just the two microstates of Tonga and Vatican City but also the broad, overlapping networks of Oceania and the Holy See into a mutual association based on a common commitment to combat global warming. As God's earthly representative, the pope is a vehicle of divine agency. As a representative of the Pacific Climate Warriors, Loloa comes not as a victim but as an ambassador bearing a hallmark of identity and heritage, continuity and presence from a female elder, with the performative power to secure strategic alliances through an intermingling of people, souls, and things. Just as Pope Francis argues for the need to "grasp the variety of things in their multiple relationships,"[90] Tcherkézoff similarly affirms that "this is what the 'Pacific Way' is about: by constantly giving one certainly does accumulate; it is not objects that are accumulated however, but relationships."[91]

We can say more about what is enacted here by attending to the layering of epistemologies that characterize both mat and encounter. Given the mat's simultaneous uses as (at least) Christian prayer mat, product of Indigenous feminine labor, and hybrid text, we could think about it not simply as a woven object but also as an *entangled* one. I refer here to Nicholas Thomas's use of the term, in which he goes beyond "Maussian stereotypes of the gift economy"[92] to analyze the more intricate and imbricated ways that objects "become" what they are through the cross-cultural systems and interactions engendered by colonialism in Oceania.[93] As both a Christian symbol and an Indigenous one, the gifted mat leverages Christian faith as a strategic mode of solidarity and resilience. At the same time, it gestures to the complementarities between paradigms of green theology and certain Indigenous Pacific cosmologies with their mutual investment in holistic ecologies and environmental stewardship. Although, to be sure, the receipt of the mat may amount to little more than a passing acknowledgment on the pope's part, it is the symbolic resonance of the act that is of primary significance for this more intimate action, and points to the need to appreciate notions of efficacy from Pasifika perspectives. The energy of the action flows back to the Pacific along with the other mats that return to their home communities, enriched by their cumulative itineraries and charged by the blessings, shared stories, and encounters that aid resilience by binding climate-exposed communities into larger networks of support.

The Mat Weaving Project is meaningful because it reveals the value of more subtle notions of Pacific activism based in dignified conduct, prayer, ancestral connections, and respectful customary protocols, and suggests alternative ways in which transpasifika cultural production can demonstrate resistance and resilience while maintaining unity in diversity. The Warriors' action at the Vatican revised the canonical sites, spaces, and structures of climate stories, shifting the emphasis from conventional political forums, media platforms, and research arenas. It also offered new insights into the use of Christian rhetoric and practice in climate negotiations. Moreover, the action foregrounded models of connection and interrelation that functioned both to internally consolidate and strengthen the diverse regional organization, as well as to encourage external symbolic and material relationships between island communities and world leaders, while modeling forms of social resilience that situate human agency within the more-than-human realm. Not drowning but fighting, the Warriors' activist and cultural performances draw from the past and reach into the future, binding the traditional and the contemporary, the social, aesthetic, and metaphysical, and the Indigenous and the foreign in ways that embed deeply held ways of knowing and belonging within broader matrices, and that create affiliative structures to reveal Pacific communities not as closed systems but as multiply interpenetrated. This stance resonates with Epeli Hau'ofa's configuration of Oceania as an expanding sea of islands whose potential is understood according to the totality of its relationships. As Heather Lazrus remarks, "In the context of climate change, [Hau'ofa's] thesis is about the resilience and adaptive capacities of island communities that leverage global networks in the face of local environmental devastation,"[94] pointing, as the Pacific Climate Warriors do, to the creative initiative of Pacific peoples in plotting precarious futures.

MAKING WAVES ON THE INTERNATIONAL STAGE: THE OCEANIA CENTRE'S *MOANA: THE RISING OF THE SEA*

Moana: The Rising of the Sea, devised by the Oceania Centre for Arts, Culture and Pacific Studies at the University of the South Pacific (USP) in Fiji, was the third major collaborative project in a series of new works in 2012–13 designed to showcase the Centre's revamped leadership and artistic expertise. As such, *Moana* forms a complement to the music-dance-dramas *Vaka: The Birth of a Seer* (2012) and *Drua: The Wave of Fire* (2012), treated in the previous chapter, but *Moana*'s distinctive subject matter, cooperative development, and production trajectory mean that it is best discussed as a separate project. Created by Rotuman playwright Vilsoni Hereniko, Hawaiian choreographer Peter Rockford Espiritu, Samoan composer Igelese Ete, Samoan lyricist and cultural consultant Allan Alo, and Norwegian anthropologist Edvard Hviding, *Moana* premiered in December 2013 to open a conference at USP titled "Restoring the Human to Climate Change in Oceania," organized by the European Consortium for Pacific Studies, an EU-funded international climate-change project bringing together research and higher education institutions in Europe and Oceania. The thirty-five-minute film made from the performance was screened and discussed in numerous regional and international venues, as well as being streamed online.[95] Motivated by the conviction that, in Hviding's words, "it is in the performing arts that we meet with the most immediate, most powerful expressions of how Pacific ways of life are threatened by the effects of climate change," and that performance presents the most potent way for "creating understanding at the crossroads between the local and the global,"[96] the creative team substantially revised the piece into a full-length live performance for a European tour, which I joined as an invited interlocutor and documenter. In May–June 2015, thirty-two Pasifika performers (some of whom were also Pacific Climate Warriors) traveled from Fiji to present the show in Norway, Scotland, Denmark, and Belgium, including a performance at the European Parliament in Brussels. A live recording of the production, entitled *Moana Rua* (that is, *Moana No. 2*), was screened at COP 21 in Paris in December 2015. Although both live shows had the same title, I shall use *Moana Rua* to differentiate the extended and developed European version—my primary focus—from the original 2013 *Moana*.[97]

Moana Rua deploys its embodied and affective mechanisms to make relevant and proximate the crisis of global warming and to facilitate an urgent, communal conversation with European patrons. In this respect, *Moana Rua* is similar to previous productions in international arenas that leverage the emotional impact of corporeal performance to alert First World audiences to the exigencies of a climate-exposed Pacific. The "heartbreaking presentation"[98] that comprised the Kiribati delegation's side event at COP 15 in Copenhagen in 2009, for instance, combined climate science with poignant personal addresses, film footage from Kiribati, songs, and traditional dance;[99] while the US tour of *Water Is Rising: Music and Dance amid Climate Change* (2011) featured thirty-six performers from Tokelau, Kiribati, and Tuvalu, who presented a program of customary songs and dances accompanied by projected documentary images to showcase the cultures threatened by sea-level rise.[100] *Moana Rua*, however, places its appeal within a more cohesive dramatic and narrative structure. Whereas the 2013 version was targeted mainly at Pacific audiences, the 2015 revision was designed for reception largely within European festival contexts, a visible site of cosmopolitan traffic that tends to attract affluent and seasoned theatergoers. It was a spectacular, technically sophisticated production that both demanded the full apparatus of a state-of-the-art performance space and assumed an audience with little or no prior knowledge of Oceania.

As such, *Moana Rua* is a useful starting point for thinking through some of the dynamics of using forms of theatrical presentation for international climate-change appeal. The festival context, conventionally associated with corporate sponsorship and commercial consumerism, raises the perennial questions of the kind of performance involved in seeing a show like this, and of whether the audience's affective response comes to stand in, for some, for truly ethical spectatorship and action beyond the theater. However, as Keren Zaiontz has argued, we should not underestimate the capacity for festivals to serve as "spaces of pressing social and political debate," nor "how cultural performances of resistance that have their basis in festivals can migrate to other contexts."[101] If festivals often cultivate what Andy

Bennett and Ian Woodward call a "cosmoscape," a spatialized and social-ized zone "for representing, encountering, incorporating and understand-ing aspects of cultural community and cultural difference" alongside the local and rooted,[102] then it is illuminating to investigate how *Moana Rua* manages its medium and message accordingly.

The plot concerns a regionally diverse group of Islanders, including a pregnant woman, Mele, and her family, led by a *fa'aluma* (shape-shifter, trickster) figure called Chief Telematua. The people are frightened by the rising sea (represented on stage by a voluminous blue cloth activated by five performers) and fearful for their future. A series of vignettes presents songs and dances from the Solomon Islands, Samoa, Kiribati, and Fiji,[103] while the ocean's violence and violation increases. Despite the Chief's advocacy on behalf of the Pacific community, including an address to the United Nations, the situation becomes so perilous that the people turn to the old ways, building a vaka (voyaging canoe) to journey from their islands in search of new options. A devastating hurricane and storm flood strike, killing all but a few survivors; exhausted, Mele dies in childbirth, but her child lives. In their new location, the Chief and the people vow to fight for the child's future and for that of Pacific Islanders and the world.

Notably, although the preservation of island environments and cultures lies at the heart of *Moana Rua*'s appeal, the piece rehearses rather than rejects the possibility of displacement and relocation. Indeed, the show's emotional crux turns on the dilemma of how to frame an ongoing relation-ship with one's ancestral place once that place becomes uninhabitable. This crucial commitment to home is expressed at the beginning of the perfor-mance in the lines that Chief Telematua speaks from Kathy Jetñil-Kijiner's poem, "Tell Them": "we don't want to leave / we've never wanted to leave" and "we / are nothing without our islands" (ll. 95–98).[104] While accentuat-ing the irretrievable losses of climate-induced relocation, however, the poem suggests something more. Like the basket of Marshallese goods that Jetñil-Kijiner sends to her friends in the United States to spark conversation about the islands among broader publics, the poem—and the performance itself—are emissaries that travel out from the Pacific to touch a wider world, situating local lifeways within a more elastic and expansive cultural plexus woven from migration and other social alliances, and pointing to a greater potential for cultural resilience that might be enacted across a larger, off-island domain. In contrast to those appeals that focus solely on mitigation strategies, *Moana Rua* negotiates a different tension between asserting vulnerability and proposing Pacific-centered responses that fore-ground Indigenous agency. By eliciting pathos yet consistently refusing a position of victimhood, explicitly placing island communities within larger networks, and activating those networks in a self-directed response to the crisis, the production refutes derogatory stereotypes of threatened Pacific Islands and invites European audiences to take a more reciprocal stance on addressing climate concerns.

Designed for a large-scale proscenium stage, *Moana Rua* combines acting, live and recorded music, poetry, song, and dance, as well as multimedia projections and aerial performance into a spectacular pedagogy that crystallizes diffuse arguments and multiple perspectives on climate change. The performance's generalizable parable, whereby the multiscalar effects of global warming are narrativized through anthropomorphic actants, archetypal characters, and symbolic actions, is influenced by Pacific oral tradition and mythology, which enables a rendering of the epochal and cosmological without relinquishing attention to the Indigenous local as articulated through the specific choreographies, vestments, and languages of the bodies on display. But what interests me here is the way that—in my interpretation—the show cultivates an empathic connection with European theater audiences by trading on the affective techniques of European melodrama, which are wedded to its Oceanian form. By this I don't simply mean that the show includes melodramatic elements, which it does in abundance, from the embattled but worthy protagonists, the sacrificial mother, the tormenting villain of First World industrial modernity, and the expulsion from the home space of pastoral innocence, to the sensational depiction of natural disasters, the emotive musical cueing, and even the benevolent comic role in the *fa'aluma*.

Rather, what I find more compelling is how the performance co-opts the theatrical vocabularies of *melodrama as a genre* to reframe environmental narratives that routinely utilize the *melodramatic as a mode*. This mode takes effect not only in popular journalism that employs the concept vaguely and indiscriminately to lend a hysterical edge to prognostications of impending disaster, but also in consciousness-raising campaigns by certain climate-change activists.[105] In the latter case, Shannon Davies Mancus observes how melodrama has been deployed "as a *performative framework* for a certain kind of environmental citizenship" that solicits appropriate affective and embodied responses to moral prompts.[106] Here the climate situation is figured through the triad of a virtuous, suffering victim of persecution (who can also be a hero if their suffering confers sufficient moral authority), a persecuting villain, and an imminent tragedy that can only be averted by intervention from the viewer-hero who is called upon to take action.[107] Narratives of this sort (of which Al Gore's 2006 film, *An Inconvenient Truth*, is exemplary) disrupt melodrama's familiar arc by curtailing the final act, turning responsibility for the resolution—frequently in the form of a "nick-of-time" rescue—over to the audience.[108] The problem with this framing, Mancus argues, is that it sets up the interpolated audience to fail (the hero can never finish the story), and it displaces social problems that require sustained collective action on to the individual. It also tends to reify the colonialist and gendered assumptions in both in the melodrama genre and climate-change discourse through its privileging of the white (male) hero in contrast to the diminished agency of the racialized, feminized, and infan-tilized others experiencing the most immediate effects of climate change.[109] *Moana Rua* works within and reworks these conventions and their atten-dant expectations, taking advantage of melodrama's rhetorical structures and the sensate immediacy of its stage techniques, but infusing them with Oceanian worldviews in ways that pursue a more sophisticated dialectic of vulnerability and agency, and that avoid the polarized and limited posi-tions of emblematic climate hero or helpless victim.

Moana Rua heightens its emotional impact through the melodramatic technique of having the spectators live the crisis more than once, repeat-edly. Carolyn Williams identifies "melodrama's rhythmic patterning of affective response,"[110] especially its temporality defined by periods of absorption "pierced by suddenly intensified moments of shock, terror, or sentiment."[111] This dynamic is epitomized in the agon between the people and the sea, the structuring logic of the performance by which the escalat-ing impacts of sea-level rise can be dramatized in human-scale terms while centering Pacific epistemologies. In keeping with a holistic cosmology, the ocean is a constant presence in *Moana Rua* (recall that *moana* means "ocean" in several Pacific languages) and is depicted as a character with its own moods and motivations; throughout, the sea spirits' intricate choreogra-phies imbue the vast azure fabric with the ocean's manifold tempers, from benevolent undulation to roiling catastrophe. The sea itself, while an aggressor, is also shown to be a victim of environmental abuse, trauma-tized and made monstrous by its own pushing to extremes. In this case, ecological science and Oceanian paradigms press into alignment with melodramatic stagecraft, which is adept at portraying the affective state of ostensibly mute entities; "the environment as mise-en-scène absorbs the psychic energy of the earth and allows it to 'speak,'" making legible its inef-fable distress.[112]

The melodramatic development of the performance is organized according to the Islanders' increasingly embattled displays of cultural buoyancy versus the sea's destructive incursions. The show presents captivating cultural exhibitions from various Pacific nations in colorful and brightly lit scenes, with vibrant costumes, energetic songs and dances, addictive beats, and large-scale projected images of local life. It's a shock each time the sea rises suddenly as a menacing antagonist, breaking the grace and camaraderie of the Samoan women's *siva*, leaping malevolently between the dancers in the Kiribati vignette and swallowing up two of the performers to terrified screams, and overwhelming the virility of the Fijian men's *meke* in a groping, clasping cascade that drowns all of the dancers. Alarming chords reverberate sonorously through the electronic soundscape, and the engaging views on the backdrop morph into a morass of black, swirling floodwaters, inundated villages, ruined homes, eroded beaches, and the crying faces of the dispossessed crowded in temporary shelters. It is noteworthy that the performance undercuts the audience's desire to applaud the cultural presentations by deliberately refusing time for a conventional response between the dancing and tidal surges.[113] Exemplifying melodrama's serial aesthetic that oscillates between affective sensation and spectacular shock,[114] *Moana Rua*'s rising action offers a particularly apt illustration of Juliet John's observation that "the emotional economy of melodrama is best figured as a series of waves."[115]

In a context of climate-change appeal and negotiation, this strategy has the dual benefit of patterning and intensifying affect, enhancing empathy for the Islanders caught in an adversarial and tragic scenario, but it also provides multiple opportunities for those characters to demonstrate resilience and cultural plentitude. In this way, the production manipulates the conventions of melodrama to actively resist the victimhood that such dramaturgical and narrative frameworks often ascribe. After each attack from the sea, the dancers return time and again with a new presentation, a new community formation, another attempt at a solution. Consequently, *Moana Rua* conveys the message that through the pain there is strength, survival, and adaptation; even if the Islanders are fighting a losing battle, it is a fight nonetheless, and one in which contemporary Pacific performance itself plays a part in refusing a fixed role of dependency.

Perhaps the most striking engagement with melodrama comes in the show's own final act (revamped substantially from the 2013 version for the European tour), which breaks from these generic conventions in a move that is all the more effective for having established those prior expectations. The concluding arc of *Moana Rua* neither offers audiences the happy ending of community resolution (nor calamity), but nor does it capitulate to the incomplete ending whereby European audiences might be called upon to absolve themselves by turning hero. Instead, the performance scripts a more complicated, ambivalent outcome in the people's eventual decision to leave their decimated islands and relocate globally in the vaka. This approach, I argue, encourages audiences to take more equitable and mutual roles as advocates and partners in supporting Pacific-centered solutions to the climate crisis. At first glance, the choice to depict migration as an adaptive strategy might appear surprising—even controversial—in light of the predominant attitude expressed by ambassadors for Pacific nations that "focussing on migration instead of mitigation [is] not only defeatist but a globally irresponsible vision for the future"[116] because it risks circumventing international and local efforts to reduce future global climate-change impacts. The Pacific Warriors campaign adopted "sailing not sinking" along with "not drowning, but fighting" as a critical disposition, but primarily as a strategy for staying put. The concern that a preoccupation with discourses of displacement might thwart both international and local efforts to prevent forced migration has led to Pacific citizens' increasing emphasis on protecting their sovereign identity and ensuring their continued community sustainability and survival. As we have seen, these representatives call for a reduction of future global climate-change impacts, stressing "the integrity, uniqueness, and indispensability of place, identity and nation, which must at all costs be preserved from destruction and loss."[117]

Certainly, *Moana Rua* does not disavow the necessity of continued combat against global warming. The show's closing lines reinforce this position in Chief Telematua's performance of Jetñil-Kijiner's poem "Dear Matafele Peinam," first delivered by Jetñil-Kijiner at the UN Summit on Climate Change in New York City in 2014. Here, the language turns to global activism: "there are those / who see us // hands reaching out / fists raising up / banners unfurling / megaphones booming" (ll. 60–65), who "are spreading the word" (l. 78). Jetñil-Kijiner's promise to her infant daughter that "we will all fight" (l. 46) so that no-one else will lose their homeland and "wander rootless / with only a passport to call home" (ll. 18–19)[118] becomes, in this scene, the Chief's promise to Mele's mother[land]less baby, spurring a collective call to action. Nonetheless, *Moana Rua*'s future vision of forced relocation is important for understanding how that ethical call is framed and understood; likewise, the vaka becomes important for navigating the contours and priorities of that potential movement and, concomitantly, the performer-audience relationship.

In chapter 2, I discussed at length the vaka as a powerful symbol of purposeful mobility and exploratory agency in Oceania, and as a primary vehicle for community identity, collaborative synergy, and global connec-

Figure 13. Surrounded by sea where there once was land, Pacific Island-
ers consider their future options after a devastating storm flood. From the
Oceania Centre's *Moana: The Rising of the Sea* (European tour, 2015), created by
Vilsoni Hereniko, Edvard Hviding, Peter Rockford Espiritu, Igelese Ete, and
Allan Alo. Photograph by, and courtesy of, Edvard Hviding.

tivity. It is valuable, however, to return briefly to this trope for a different
perspective and to clarify *Moana Rua*'s intervention. After a shattering hurricane has killed many members of the regional community and inundated
the islands, the small group of survivors gathers on stage, led by Chief
Telematua. Singing an uplifting anthem to the vaka, they process slowly
around the bare stage as full-scale projections upstage show a double-
hulled vaka sailing alone over a broad oceanic expanse; subsequent images
depict more and more vaka sailing, charting courses together. The vaka,
then, becomes instrumental in offering up a discourse of migration that is
empowering and positions Pacific travelers as self-determined navigators
with something to contribute to the world.[119] This climate-change counternarrative is especially pertinent in the context of global media and policy
scenarios in which the category of the fleeing "climate refugee" is increasingly applied "in a naturalised, unproblematised way to entire nationalities of people in the Pacific region."[120] Couched in a discourse of trauma
and dependence, the climate refugee reifies perceived relationships of
inequality with the "developed world" and emphasizes passivity and

weakness, positing Pacific citizens as "helpless victims of a provoked and inhospitable future."[121] *Moana Rua* renounces this reductive identification; as Chief Telematua says in his speech to the United Nations that forms the show's structural fulcrum: "Should we be forced to relocate, our desire is to be able to leave with our DIGNITY intact. / Do not call us climate change refugees. We do not deserve that label. Instead, call us migrants to a new land, where we will rebuild our lives, piece by piece, slowly, but surely."[122]

This antipathy is neither surprising nor unique; as Michael Balfour makes clear, "No one chooses to be a refugee, and certainly it is a tag that new settlers seek to transcend as swiftly as possible."[123] Although *Moana Rua* has strategies in common with other theater works that perform state-lessness in Europe,[124] the speculative, future-oriented performance of what we might call a "proleptic statelessness" has a different valence, disrupting the paternalistic characterization of the Global North as savior to the southern migrant and asking less for protection than for partnership. The production situates itself carefully in relation to current discourses in Europe on migration, refugeeism, and asylum seeking. This includes an awareness of how environmental migrants have been framed as threats to national security,[125] but attends especially to the heightened public visibility of drowned Mediterranean refugees, mainly from North Africa. According to Steve Wilmer, from 2014 to 2016, more than three thousand people died each year by drowning in the Mediterranean trying to reach Europe.[126] The performers thus identify themselves not as people making desperate forays on makeshift rafts but as journeying in ways that engage the full capacity of the vaka as model and metaphor.

In this regard, the production prompts consideration of how Hau'ofa's concept of an enlarged, globally connected Oceania might fare in light of the new challenges posed by climate change. While acknowledging that Hau'ofa's affirmative model of oceanic relationality is complicated by new realities of the ocean as a threatening and dislocating medium, *Moana Rua* also proposes that these understandings need not necessarily be oppositional. Wolfgang Kempf suggests that Hau'ofa's emphasis on practices of entwinement and enlargement—worked out in *Moana Rua* through the symbolism of the vakas' combined journeys—might function as ways to combat projections of belittlement and smallness that circulate in climate-change rhetoric.[127] As Kempf argues, "If Pacific Islanders were, in future, to become more strongly affected by the inroads of climate change and if displacement, forced migration and/or mass evacuation were to become realities, there is no reason why this should not also be seen as an enlargement of Oceania."[128] This approach maintains the positives in Hau'ofa's thesis as a specific form of empowerment in the face of depictions of inferiority and hopelessness without losing sight of the many hardships and losses that relocation would entail. From this perspective, *Moana*'s symbolic enlistment of the vaka as a metaphor for self-determination within a context of loss, death, and trepidation presents a counternarrative that navigates a course between plight and potential, vulnerability and agency, which can be understood as central to the production's attempt to partner strategically with European audiences to advance Pacific-centered solutions to the climate crisis.

The concept of the vaka as a vehicle of salvation also references the biblical story of the Noachian flood; namely, Noah's preparation for surviving the deluge by building the ark. This narrative has gained considerable traction in the heavily Christian Pacific in relation to local responses to the conjoined issues of climate change, sea-level rise, and migration; and has—as Kempf shows—been subject to a range of interpretations for political, religious, and scientific purposes. In one iteration, scientific projections of climate impacts are invoked to encourage local populations to prepare for change: "If, in the Biblical narrative, the rainbow stood for salvation, so now science is constituted as playing the same role, pointing the way to salvation of a different kind."[129] I suggest that the deployment of the vaka/ ark in *Moana Rua* represents a further reinterpretation of how different epistemologies might be brought into mutual correlation—one that is specific to the design of the double-hulled canoe. As I have explained, the vaka's two hulls, worked into a single vessel, have long signified the coming together of two different constituents or perspectives into one paradigm. In this case, salvation hinges on a possible combination of Western science and Indigenous knowledge to chart a course out of the climate crisis, reinforcing the pitch for the multilateral, Pacific-centered collaboration that motivates the performance project.

Moana Rua usefully elucidates one way in which theater from Oceania has been used as an experiment in climate-change negotiation and advocacy in international arenas, particularly within contexts of theater festival production and reception. The piece is valuable for its blending of theory and practice, its interdisciplinary collaboration between scholars and practitioners in the sciences and humanities, and its mapping of new Oceanic performance cartographies that activate social and institutional connections. As a vaka that crosses oceans to bring the voices of the Pacific to the centers of power and global consumption, the show's theatrical evocation of a Pacific world, its imaginative enactment of alternative future scenarios, and its experimental blending of heritage arts, contemporary fusion aesthetics, and Western genres make it an illuminating case study for examining ways in which climate-change counternarratives may be expressed through form as well as content, and highlights the role of transpasifika performance in actively creating new discourses about climate-change impacts in Oceania.

CEREMONIES FOR THE END OF THE WORLD:
LEMI PONIFASIO AND MAU, *BIRDS WITH SKYMIRRORS*

A very different climate-change counternarrative, aesthetic, and governing philosophy occurs in *Birds with Skymirrors* by New Zealand–based Samoan multidisciplinary artist and choreographer Lemi Ponifasio and his company, MAU.[130] An international coproduction between theaters and festivals in France, Germany, Belgium, the Netherlands, Spain, and New Zealand, the piece premiered at the Theater der Welt 2010 RUHR festival in Berlin, and toured widely throughout Europe, North and South America, and the Asia-Pacific region until 2014. Established in 1995, MAU (named after the Samoan independence movement founded in 1908 and meaning "a declaration to the truth of a matter" or "revolution") is New Zealand's most prolific and internationally recognized dance and theater company, featuring regularly at major venues around the globe. A renowned auteur and celebrity in the dance world, Ponifasio has prompted comparisons with Pina Bausch and Robert Wilson, and in 2016 he was chosen by UNESCO to author the International Dance Day message.[131] The fact that MAU is better known and acclaimed overseas than in New Zealand and the South Pacific[132] is a deliberate strategy; as Ponifasio explains: "I found that it is more powerful to go and dance in the powerful places where the powerful people are, who are making powerful decisions about us. They will sit for 90 minutes and watch and listen—so for me it is much more effective than to dance under the tree, in the garage or on the beach."[133]

After a decade performing as a solo dance artist in Japan, Europe, and the Pacific, Ponifasio returned to Auckland, New Zealand, to work in a community context, founding an ensemble of artists of various South Pacific heritages with the intention to present stories, myths, and legends from the region.[134] Most MAU performers possess no Western dance or theater training and reflect Ponifasio's inclination toward "troublemakers and outsiders,"[135] including school dropouts, juvenile offenders, political provocateurs, and recent immigrants. Ponifasio's radical oeuvre has sometimes been described as a version of theater, dance-theater, or contemporary dance, yet his performance interventions resist ready identification with any of these discrete genres. Ponifasio has tended to prefer the term "avant-garde" over the narrower category of "Pacific dance" as a more flexible descriptor for his work, which is marked by its experimental interculturalism, formal hybridity, and divergence from extant choreographic forms.[136] Ponifasio's aim to bring audiences to new states of awareness is central to his idea of the artist not as a passive observer but as "a player in the society, a leader, and catalyst for change,"[137] and is a manifestation of his own responsibilities as a Samoan high chief. In discussions about his work, Ponifasio has repeatedly de-emphasized his performances as "entertainment," accentuating instead their poetic, philosophical, cosmological, and metamorphic capacities,[138] and his view of the theater as "a sacred space, a gathering point for the ceremonies that will bind us together in a community of understanding and purpose."[139]

Birds with Skymirrors was inspired by Ponifasio's visit to the island of Tarawa in the central Pacific nation of Kiribati in 2009, where he was profoundly affected by the peril of the low-lying atoll community and by the sight of a flock of frigate birds with strands of videotape in their beaks garnered from beach litter, which glinted in the sun (the "skymirrors" of the title). For Ponifasio, this was an apocalyptic vision and prompted him to create an artistic response to the crisis. Featuring performers of New Zealand Māori, Samoan, and i-Kiribati descent, *Skymirrors* offers a multimodal form that features mixed soundscapes, chant, poetry, Pacific ritualistic and performance traditions, and contemporary dance practices, tied together in taut formality and focused intensity at the level of mise-en-scène and bodily discipline. Oblique human/more-than-human hybrid figurings appear instead of actual characters. Ponifasio favors a monochromatic visual scheme in a layered play of darkness and light imbued with abstract symbolism, and images and ceremonies that are startling, mesmerizing, and vatic. The result is a Pacific aesthetic of spare beauty and haunting austerity, which, bereft of chronological narrative or strict spatiotemporal boundaries, creates a prolonged, meditative space of reflection.[140]

Skymirrors differs from *Moana Rua*'s grounding in anthropological debates and its rehearsal of a near-future scenario of agency-under-duress that folds back into the present to remit affirmative iterations of "Pacificness" to encourage more equitable negotiations toward local solutions to a global crisis. It presents no pedagogy and places no call for active advocacy, no depiction of or appeal for mitigation strategies or alternative adaptation scenarios. Instead, it invites its audiences to enter into an uncompromising encounter with an ecological tragedy that, in Ponifasio's words, "is not an apocalypse about to happen. It is already here."[141] Ponifasio's statement taps into a strain of Indigenous thought that understands the Anthropocene not as a hitherto unanticipated occurrence but, for Indigenous peoples, as an extension of a violent and unresolved historical past. As Potawatomi scholar and activist Kyle Powys Whyte phrases it, the ecological crisis is "an intensified repetition of anthropogenic environmental change inflicted on Indigenous peoples via colonial practices that facilitated capitalist industrial expansion."[142] Due to the catastrophic processes of empire, "Indigenous imaginations of our futures in relation to climate change . . . begin already with our living today in a post-apocalyptic situation."[143] From this position, Whyte suggests, one can productively "challenge linear narratives of dreadful futures of climate destabilization"[144] by drawing on insights and perspectives offered by temporal structures central to various Native epistemologies (including the Pacific) in which pasts, presents, and futures flow together.[145] Ponifasio's work spirals out beyond the future anterior tense of much climate-change prognostication (that which will have been), to embrace a holistic temporal structure that enfolds creation, descent into destruction, and rebirth into a coeval Pacific timespace (tā/vā). Ponifasio takes seriously the notion of eschatology, doomsday, or apocalypse, which is often understood in media discourse according to a predominantly linear, Christian schema leading to a tumultuous end-point, and repositions it from a cyclical, Polynesian viewpoint. What we might be brought to awareness of, then, is the current degradation and crisis as a continuation of dispossession and disaster caused by empire[146] and, viewed from the perspective of the work's blended and dilated temporality, the need for complete renewal as part of a more expansive process of making, unmaking, and remaking the world.

The specific philosophical regime that I argue informs Skymirrors is articulated more explicitly in Ponifasio's later work, Lagi Moana, for the 2015 Venice Biennale Arte. Although the project was not fully realized due to lack of funding, the ceremonial rites had been performed and the foundations for the installation were publicly visible when I visited, as were the detailed exhibition notes, which shed useful light on the Skymirrors performance in terms of its Indigenous response to climate change's complicity with capitalism and imperialism. Here Ponifasio's approach might be understood as a counter-counternarrative in its dual refusal of dominant climate-change accounts as well as more radical anthropological views of global warming. Taking as its starting point "the inevitable collapse of human life under global warming" and a "re-ordering of the world power systems as we know them,"[147]

Lagi Moana proposes that the rising ocean is not a curse to humanity but is an opportunity to welcome our ancestor Moana to take back what is itself. Within these times of crises when there is an atmosphere of being trapped by natural and man-made disasters, rising inequality and rampant consumerism, *Lagi Moana* proposes to think unthinkable ideas and propose the rising sea level as the freeing and cleansing agent of change. Under its influence, empires acquire new status in which they will not be just in ruins but are dissolved and become watery.[148]

This deluge narrative resonates with the Noachian one to the extent that the sea's rise does not represent the ultimate end of the world, but an evolution beyond the Anthropocene epoch, a resetting for a new and better era in which "the cosmos might be reformed," we are returned to "genearcheological matter," and in which death is part of a cycle. Significantly, the artistic works themselves become ceremonies to prepare for change and, in fact, to help bring it about, constituting "a song that is sung at the end of the world, a call which brings about a new beginning."[149]

In a similar vein, *Skymirrors* is underpinned by ten poetic texts from historical and contemporary Pacific archives. These words are not spoken in performance but inform the work's eddying cyclical structure from creation to degradation, the descent into death, and a message of peace from the ancestors that urges a gathering together and a renewal. The curtain recedes to reveal a darkened stage; in the shadows we can make out a large central obelisk that rises through the space on a slight right diagonal, tapering toward the top. Slowly, a shaft of white light begins to illuminate the obelisk, bringing light into the space. Ponifasio identifies this sequence as a representation of the Māori creation genealogy that begins with Te Pō (the unknown darkness of creation), followed by Te Kore (the primal source, potential) and Te Ao (the light). It culminates in the separation of the sky (Ranginui) and the earth (Papatūānuku) by their children, principally Tāne, god of forests and ancestor of human beings and birds (represented here by the central post), who broke his parents' embrace and pushed them apart, thus bringing light and space into the world.[150] Creation lineages form the basis for all other Māori *whakapapa*, a genealogical framework that links people to all other living things, as well as elemental and spiritual phenomena, and traces the universe back to its origins.[151] The emergence of life out of the darkness is a common motif in many creation stories throughout and beyond the Pacific, including in Kiribati (*te bo*) and in Samoa, where the void is seen as the source and potential of *vā* (the relational space between loci, people, and entities). Accordingly, the mise-en-scène serves to high-light the central elemental concepts of the production, encouraging audiences to understand themselves as part of a relational space and an interconnected universe, with obligatory relationships to each other, to the earth and sea below, the trees, the sky above, and the past, present, and future.

This shift from darkness to light is an uneasy transition, however, imbued with an eschatological sensibility that simultaneously foreshadows the end of the world. The abrasive, immersive rumbling of the soundtrack, like a jet engine or industrial machinery, and which becomes cacophonic later in the show, registers the sinister, pervasive hum of modernity and establishes the sense of an environment stretched to breaking point. The feeling of being welcomed into a world that is under intense, apocalyptic stress is reinforced by a Māori woman who emerges from the darkness into the downspot, naked except for a pair of black briefs and high heels, her hair in a topknot, her lips painted red. She glares at us brashly, eyes wide. She flexes her shoulders, rolling them back to ripple her upper body, but there is nothing sensual or languid about her tautly suppressed energy. All of a sudden, she belts out a *karanga*:[152] the yell is aggressive, challenging, protocol strained to its tensive limits by some oppressive pressure; it alerts us, unsettles us—she finishes with a brief scream. Her eyes are dilated in a *pūkana*[153] as she leans back from the waist, hands fluttering in a *wiri* that evokes a persistent yet faltering animacy.[154] Here, Māori ceremonial and *kapa haka*[155] performance is syncretized into a disturbing contemporary ritual that structures an encounter of deep unease, and indexes the history and culture of a Pacific world that is about to implode.

This *karanga* embeds a tone of urgency and peril that pervades the performance in various ways. A dominant motif is the association of the human performers with birds, especially the frigate bird, which has symbolic significance throughout the Pacific and is a national icon for Kiribati, appearing on its flag. Dressed in black costumes reminiscent of Chinese kung fu uniforms and with shaven heads, the six i-Kiribati dancers weave in and out of the performance in a version of i-Kiribati traditional dances that imitate the walking and flying movements of the frigate bird (*te eitei*), with rapid, shuffling feet, arms spread, crisp circular gestures, and fingers flickering in martial synchronization. Once again, these cultural traditions are forged into new expressive forms under Ponifasio's aegis; as MAU performer Teataki Temango, an i-Kiribati dancer and former member of a dance group in Tarawa noted, "It's not the kind of dance we know, it's a combination of different artistic work,"[156] yet the birdlike rhythms and symbolic resonances of the dances are palpable. In Kiribati, the frigate bird functions as a navigational guide, a harbinger of weather changes, and a sign of peace and harmony, but it cannot swim or rest in the ocean. At the UN Climate Change Conference in Mexico in 2010, the Kiribati delegation presented a poignant song about a frigate bird that flies the ocean to find food for her chicks but returns to find its island lost beneath the waves,[157] and this prophetic text reverberates implicitly here. In an early sequence, bird cries join the rumbling soundtrack along with the sound of running water, and a solo male Samoan performer occupies the downspot, arms outstretched. His dance is slow and undulating, with his sinuous upper-body movements sharpened periodically by a quick movement, a slap to the chest or a clap. His arms suggest a bird's wings stuck in something, trying to fight something, falling down, drowning, while he employs the Japanese *butō* technique of his eyes rolled back in his head to express a state of extreme suffering. His mesmerizing performance is full of restrained power but also pain, a feeling of victimization made visceral. Watching, I am also reminded of the devastating tsunami that struck Samoa in 2009 and those that have since struck Oceania with increasing frequency, an association that lifts Kiribati's concerns to a wider regional level.

The connections between a regional and a global crisis are most evident in the projected image that flashes up periodically on a large screen upstage, showing a brief loop of CBS footage from the 2010 British Petroleum oil spill in the Gulf of Mexico.[158] A distressed pelican rises up out of the water, its wings glugged with oil. It splashes frantically, helplessly, head and massive beak contorted and flailing as it tries to take flight but cannot, pulled back into the sea by the oil's miry viscosity. Within the production's temporal abeyance, the long-dead bird rises again and again in its desperate effort, its agony prolonged and elaborated in this giant representation. Inevitably it will succumb to its oily prison, weaken and die, but the struggle is repeated here, tragic yet persistent. The mapping of pelican and frigate bird creates a semiotic layering whereby the embodied performers and the multimedia, the Pacific and the non-Pacific, and ancient myth and petrocapitalist realpolitik are brought into philosophical counterpoint, encouraging audiences to recognize and take responsibility for a mutual, holistic, and violated environment. Although this is an ethical exhortation that extends to and incorporates us all, the struggle of the pelican against its overwhelming odds prompts continual recollection of the human subjects who stand to lose the most from global practices. The correlation between bird and human casualties is reinforced in a sequence where the solo Samoan performer appears in a static pose, arms outstretched, naked except for his *pe'a*[159] and a green, stylized bird mask reminiscent of the elongated avian/anthropomorphic forms of New Zealand painter Bill Hammond, whose work frequently references vulnerable environments under threat and the complex relationships between Māori, Pākehā, and nature. Against this backdrop, the six i-Kiribati dancers silently emerge from the wings, perform their specific dance, and then sit in a single row downstage facing the audience: torsos bare, exposed, dominating the space. Their expressions are neutral but their stares are not unconfrontational: these men from Tarawa whose very existence is threatened—perhaps irreversibly—by the ongoing actions of wealthy Westerners challenge us by their presence, their performance, their standoff.

The final vignette of *Skymirrors* suggests the ending of the current world and an ancestral regathering for a new beginning. A single male performer walks into the space, holding a white *poi*.[160] Deliberately and methodically, he begins to shake out white dust from the poi onto the stage floor. Some of the dust rises, smoke-like, into the gloom of the auditorium, but most coheres like a light snow on the ground. Very slowly, more people with similar poi join the man on stage and proceed to cover the entire stage floor with white dust. This prolonged and meditative sequence, largely silent apart from the occasional notes of a *kōauau* (bone flute), sets the audience in a trancelike state (broken only by the pelican, which rises again on the screen). The stark white against the blackness is focusing, clarifying, and confronting if we take the time to reflect on possible meanings: the fallout from nuclear weapons testing in Kiribati and elsewhere in the Pacific; phosphate hollowed out from Banaba—the dust of the ancestors—scattering the farms of Australia, New Zealand, and Great Britain; or a rising Pacific covering all to "take us back to the matter that makes up our ancient genetic origins."[161] A more soaring soundtrack with a rumbling undercurrent introduces the black-clad i-Kiribati dancers for their final dance; as birds flying over the Pacific Ocean, what do they see? What routes do they traverse? Where will they land? What kinds of imprints might i-Kiribati make in foreign soil (their soil)? Is this a new start? When they have finished, the braided lines of their shuffling footprints, lingering in the dust, produce aesthetic pleasure but also a deep sense of ambivalence.

Birds with Skymirrors is a haunting jeremiad, a stark warning, an oneiric vision, and a sacral meditation developed through focused precision and expanded temporality, which attempts to bring the audience to a new state of consciousness regarding their networks of coexistence within a more-than-human world that includes their inexorable place within a cyclical cosmogenic scheme. In probing the intricacies of this internationally

Figure 14. From left, Ria Te Uira Paki, Kasina Campbell, and Rosie TeRau-awhea Belvie perform in the US premiere of *Birds with Skymirrors* by Lemi Ponifasio and MAU. Howard Gilman Opera House, Brooklyn Academy of Music, New York, 2014. Photograph by Andrea Mohin / *The New York Times* / Redux.

acclaimed work, I want to attend to some of its ambiguities and contradictions, especially between what is explicitly presented and implicitly performed, and thus to pose more pressing questions about the critical corollary of the performers' self-representations. Ponifasio has repeatedly cautioned that the production should not be read as "an environmental lecture"[162] but as a piece about the i-Kiribati people he works with, several of whom have appeared in previous MAU performances since 2003. Given Kiribati's status as a metaphor for global warming, as well as a major voice in international climate-change activism, there are intriguing disjunctions between the corporeal realities of the bodies in front of us and their insistence upon survival—their petition to appear as political subjects—and the more abstract frame of deep time within which they threaten to disappear. This effect is a by-product of reading the work as it is sited within different frameworks of climate-change discourse and counterdiscourse, and highlights how the competing narratives at play on and beyond the stage world exhibit a core tension between a crisis with a *human solution* and a crisis with a *cosmic solution*.

What one reviewer described as the work's "contemplation on the certain, unrelenting movement towards death"[163] threatens to play into other extant climate narratives by casting the i-Kiribati performers in the image of doomed Pacific Islanders from disappearing islands. This finds grounding in Ponifasio's motivating question, "What would it be like when the islands are gone? What would be the last dance, the last song of these people?"[164] along with his suggestion that if global warming continues on its current course and "these guys disappear in 50 years," then *Birds with Skymirrors* may well represent the last dances of this kind.[165] Consequently, there is little overt acknowledgment in the performance or its framing conversations of the contexts in which i-Kiribati (or other Pacific Islanders) might resist disaster, adopt more empowering forms of mobility, or maintain agential connections beyond grounded contact with the (home)land, although these possibilities continually irrupt within the work. Tellingly, another reviewer interpreted the performance's central obelisk not as a tree trunk in situ but as "the mast of a traditional vessel travelling through the Pacific cosmos,"[166] foregrounding the relationship between a rooted indigeneity and a routed mobility and prompting us to consider, in ways that the performance as a whole perhaps does not, how deterritorialized cultures might be practiced, maintained, and modified in various ways and places. The aforementioned song of the frigate bird, "Koburake" ("Rise Up"), notably, was originally composed not as a lament on climate loss, but in advance of Kiribati's independence from the United Kingdom in 1979, indicating how the new atoll state should rise up to the level of other countries and secure the help it needs from the outside world in order to be viable in the international arena.[167] This sentiment flows over into climate solidarity, conveying not just pity but unfolding agency in its encouragement to "rise up" above climate change through strategic connections.[168]

Traditional dance is of key importance to i-Kiribati history, culture, and identity. A popular understanding is that "we are known as I-Kiribati from the way we dance,"[169] and this is also how MAU's contemporary performers see themselves in diasporic enclaves and within global artistic circuits. As one performer averred, "Wherever we go, we carry the name of Kiribati with us."[170] Indeed, it is through these particular dances in *Birds with Skymirrors* that we witness the intriguing friction between the work's doomsday scenario and the performance of a contemporized form of i-Kiribati dance—enabled by the transnational collaboration with Ponifasio—that enfolds customary vocabularies while connecting to other cultural repertoires. There is a doubleness in the performance that occurs at the moment of articulation: as the dancers perform their ostensible "last dance," they disavow this finality with a sequence of net-worked gestures that choreograph a cosmopolitan i-Kiribati culture through their internationally moving bodies. It is in these moments that we see the negotiation between an investment in a grounded homeland and national sovereignty, and a distributed, transterritorial movement that is also an inherent part of i-Kiribati identity.

In contexts of climate-change exigency, *Skymirrors* demonstrates per-formance's potential beyond conveying "a message," and reveals how performance—especially through the richness and contradictions of embodiment—can trace the ebb and flow of multiple narratives that con-verge and collide. There is a persistent tension in *Birds with Skymirrors* between a holistic sensibility and the particularity of its performers; the aspiration toward the transcendent and noumenal and the gravitation toward its human stories; its chthonic drive and the performers' defiant presence; the extradiegetic circumstances of the show's circulating bodies and the projected circumstances of those portrayed; and the radical cho-reographies that debunk South Pacific clichés while reinforcing some pre-vailing viewpoints. The ambivalences that permeate *Birds with Skymirrors* open up the piece to wider conversations that not only examine creative responses to current climate-change debates but also move toward more sophisticated discussions of Pacific performance praxis, including a sub-tler investigation of how Indigenous self-representation is negotiated in Pasifika performing arts intended for international consumption, and the politics of intercultural collaborations between Pacific Islanders that go beyond a view of such partnerships as "antidotes" to Western intercul-tural exploits. I pivot now to the final two case studies in this chapter, which focus on the Venice Biennale as an emerging venue for interna-tional climate-change performance from Oceania. They extend these questions of representation and negotiation by turning to more open-ended engagements with audience-participants that demand their haptic interaction and that require them to become active collaborators in com-pleting the work.

VIRTUAL BODIES AND CLIMATE CHA(LLE)NGE: KIRIBATI IN VENICE

The Venice Biennale was inaugurated in 1895 as part of a plan to revive the city economically and culturally after its rapid nineteenth-century decline following its conquest by Napoleon in 1797. For a thousand years prior, the sovereign state and maritime republic had been one of the preeminent thalassocracies of the Mediterranean world, dominating commercial and cultural traffic between Europe, North Africa, and Asia. Civic leaders sought to restore Venice's fortunes by establishing a permanent international venue for art, which has since become the oldest and most prestigious artistic institution in the world.[171] The Venice Biennale is distinguished and enabled by its national pavilion structure, whereby participating countries bear the cost of building and setting up their exhibitions, thus contributing financially to the event. This has resulted, increasingly from the mid-twentieth century and especially since the 1990s, in the effective participation of a large number of foreign countries, making the Biennale truly global and cementing its role in establishing the state of contemporary art.[172] The twenty-first century has witnessed the formal participation of the Pacific Islands; in addition to solo artists like Ponifasio, national representation began with New Zealand in 2001, followed by Tuvalu in 2013 and Kiribati in 2017. In recent years, the Biennale has become a venue and platform for Pacific-led projects on climate issues, with artists often using performance or performative interactions to engage their international audiences. Although the Biennale has been subject to criticism that its structure reifies the forms and hierarchies of the nation-state,[173] the collaborations discussed in the final sections of this chapter transcend national borders, brokering transpasifika partnerships that enable the representation of populations and local perspectives normally excluded from the elite art market.

The Republic of Kiribati comprises thirty-three atolls and coral islands straddling all four hemispheres for over thirty-one hundred miles across the western Pacific Ocean. Home to 110,000 people, the Micronesian nation has emerged as a vocal advocate for climate-change mitigation at a range of international summits and conventions. It has, in addition, made some of the most active strides toward implementing adaptive strategies in the face of impending loss of territory, including training its citizens to be skilled migrants, petitioning Australia and New Zealand to accept its people as permanent refugees, and purchasing offshore land in Fiji.[174] Kiribati's first two outings at the Biennale in 2017 and 2019 were partnerships between the Kiribati Ministry of Internal Affairs, which commissioned the projects, and Slovenian multidisciplinary artist Daniela Danica Tepes, and were presented at the European Cultural Center in the sixteenth-century Palazzo Mora in Venice's Cannaregio district.[175] Tepes is known for a body of activist art-making that addresses crimes against humanity and the environment, and that typically layers video, photography, interactive animation, performance, readymade, and installation.[176] This approach characterized the two pavilions, which shared a similar aesthetic, logic, and content: both combined Tepes's work and the joint efforts of multiple Kiribati artists from different generations and branches of art; and, principally, both used interactive installations that merged the material and virtual, augmenting a theatrical mise-en-scène with video-game technology. This participatory component reveals a different dimension of how international audiences become engaged in Pacific climate concerns, especially Biennale visitors, who are typically affluent, cosmopolitan, and well-educated tourists, more than half of whom are under the age of twenty-six.[177]

As Katja Kwastek notes, interactive media art places the action of the recipient at the center of its aesthetics, and this activity is also the primary source of their aesthetic experience; the recipient responds actively to an interaction proposition and becomes a performer.[178] In the case of the 2019 pavilion, *Pacific Time—Time Flies*, commissioned by the Ministry of Internal Affairs' senior cultural officer Pelea Tuhumu and curated by Kautu Tabaka and Nina Tepes, visitors were prompted to reflect on Kiribati's endangered existence through their spatial presence within an immersive environment layered with cross-referential elements. Kiribati photographer Kaeka Michael Betero's arresting documentary images of crumbling seawalls, partially submerged roads, and buildings eroded by an encroaching ocean found congruence in Daniela Tepes's physical construction of a disintegrating, low block wall that bisected the small exhibition room, and in the casement windows affixed to the left-hand and right-hand walls, which depicted our precarious inundation through the digital waters that lapped high against the panes. We were called into action when we stepped into the sensor area behind the block wall and a Kinect camera captured our motion, rendering it as a mirror figure of a male i-Kiribati dancer (two participants could activate two of them, side by side) who hovered high above an aerial view of Tarawa atoll projected opposite us. There was a visual echo between the avatarial figure(s) and the video-recording on a monitor directly below of the Kairaken Betio (Youth of Betio) Performance Group, which maintains local song, dance, and performance traditions connected to modern performance approaches. In this circumstance, visitors assumed an active and self-reflexive relationship to performance; we were not merely witnesses to a separate cultural presentation but were required to perform ourselves, to choreograph a relationship to the virtual figures (digital and filmed) and their dance repertoire. While, perhaps, urging a conscious meditation on artistic performance itself as a medium for advocacy and cultural resistance in climate justice contexts, the interactive encounter embedded us in a curious play of solidarity and alterity, translating the local into new forms of somatic experience, interpretation, and expression.

This physical and digital interplay of self and other, sameness and difference, is complex, and I want to delve into it in more detail through a close reading of the debut 2017 pavilion, which employed comparable strategies but elicited a differently complicated performance from visitors through the mimetic figure of the warrior. *Sinking Islands, Unsinkable Art*, curated by Pelea Tehumu and Nina Tepes, featured an immersive audiovisual environment created by Daniela Tepes with digital projections on three walls and the floor. To the left and right, occupying the entire walls, are video-recorded, life-size dancers from Kairaken Betio in customary dress, performing song and dance on Tarawa's Red Beach. They surround us, fading in and out in a slow filmic dissolve against the ocean backdrop so that they seem to appear from and disappear into the sea. Projections on the floor present the illusion that we are standing in a shallow, pellucid lagoon: turquoise waters wash our feet while vibrant yellow and orange fish meander and dart around them. Around the edges of the space, fine sand punctuated with shells and starfish marks the edge of the reef. Along two of the walls, there are sandbags piled to prevent flooding; on them are arranged black-and-white photographs of Kiribati individuals and families, marking a personal connection to place. On the third wall, facing us directly as we enter the room, the Kinect motion capture technology activates an image (again, up to two) of an armed i-Kiribati warrior in traditional garb—a version of a Pacific climate warrior—floating above the stacked sandbags and against the aerial atoll backdrop. A placard by the screen invites us to participate: "A seawall made of sandbags protects the Republic of Kiribati from the rising Pacific Ocean. How long will it last? Can Kiribati warriors protect the seawall? Yes, they can! What the mankind [sic] is going to do, the Kiribati warriors will do it too." In this interface, called "Kiribati Warriors," what is afforded by the dynamics of human and virtual bodies in relation? How might we read this dialectic of combat and cooperation? What might it mean to turn the urgent concerns of climate change and its representation into a game?

The virtual body reorients the theme of appearance and disappearance running through the case studies in this chapter. To a large extent, it is simply logistical to have performers virtually present rather than living in Venice for the six-month run of the Biennale, but from the outset I want to trouble any notion that a virtual body interacting with a live visitor somehow involves a less robust, real, or effective intervention. I side with new-media dramaturgs like Peter Eckersall, Helena Grehan, and Ed Scheer, for whom "the body/technology nexus in performance functions to amplify rather than negate bodily and affective experience," and who argue that

Figure 15. Visitors interact with digital avatars in the Kiribati Pavilion at the Venice Biennale, a partnership between the Kiribati Ministry of Internal Affairs and Daniela Danica Tepes. Above: a warrior avatar features in the 2017 installation *Sinking Islands, Unsinkable Art*. Below: dancer avatars appear in the 2019 installation *Pacific Time — Time Flies*. Photographs by Diana Looser, with permission of Andrei and Samuel Baltakmens.

such interactions can indeed intensify both media and performance.[179] When the only live component in the installation is the spectator (activator, visitor, viewer, recipient, user, player), then it can result in a subtler repositioning of bodily presence, and may productively dislocate familiar roles assigned to viewers and performers.[180] The possibility of dislocation and repositioning is especially pertinent to the interactive situation being staged and unfolded in "Kiribati Warriors," with its entwined focus on climate-change appeal, indigeneity, and unequal relationships of power and consumption between different communities. How might interactive art's capacity for an aesthetic experience that, in Kwastek's words, "manifests itself in a process of oscillation between flow and reflection, between absorption in the interaction and distanced (self-)perception,"[181] as well as its potential for "provoking disruptions that include conscious reflection on the process of interaction itself,"[182] provide productive engagement but also friction or dissonance that might unsettle the recipient's own cultural, socioeconomic, and ethical position, and encourage them to view the situation afresh?[183]

Players who accept the interaction proposition of "Kiribati Warriors" face off against the Warrior avatar that is dressed in historical martial attire of brown body armor fashioned from tightly woven coconut fiber, with a helmet from the dried skin of a puffer fish, and armed with a three-pronged wooden sword lined with shark's teeth. Untethered enigmatically in the sky, is it a figure from the past carrying tradition into the present, evoking the power of the spirits of the ancestral warriors, or a more ominous vision from the future (the afterlife), ancestor spirits witnessing the future history of climate change? Locked in our literal and metaphorical combat over the iconic seawall, we are "watched" by other visitors as well as the filmed dancers who become spectators as well as objects of our scrutiny, another of many ways in which the pavilion manipulates the traditional gaze of viewer to performer. Microsoft's Kinect for Xbox is a motion-sensing camera peripheral whereby players can experience digital gameplay without prosthetics or handheld controllers. It provides a sense of enhanced and unmediated player agency and engagement, encapsulated in Kinect's advertising slogan: "You are the controller." Of a genre Jesper Juul calls "mimetic interface games,"[184] Kinect encourages full-body action, as nothing happens on screen (except for an unresponsive avatar) unless the player participates physically, animating avatars by moving their bodies in a mirroring relation in what feels like real time. By privileging proxemic movement and embodied performance, Kinect's bridging of virtual and visceral experience shifts attention from ambient space more to player space.[185]

How might "playing with oneself" lead to awareness of the other? The relationship between player and avatar trades on the contradictions and unstable categories of identity, presence, and subjectivity opened up by gameplay. Bob Rehak observes that the video-game avatar, as the human player's double, "merges spectatorship and participation in ways that transform both activities."[186] The encounter of difference and potential alliance through the not-quite-other, not-quite-self exemplifies how players "exist with their avatars in an unstable dialectic" that oscillates toward and away from the other as part of the formation of subjectivity: the avatar is both self and other, symbol and index.[187] The Warrior highlights this ambivalence: neither an obvious extension of the player (that is, an intermediary helping to navigate the virtual world as in many video games), nor a model for mimetic behavior like many music or sports games for Kinect, it meets the player head-on, forcing an encounter or confrontation that involves decision making. In many ways, the Warrior insists more on alterity than identity through the agon of the gamespace, amplified by the fact that both player and avatar are assigned differential roles: the Warrior with his own history, identity, and agential task, and the player as "mankind" (a designation that might prompt reflection on their place within that category).

Of course, there are dozens of ways in which this interaction could backfire, from patronizing overidentification, stereotypical objectification, and racial ventriloquism, to outright antagonism. In his review essay of the same title, Paul Manning poses the central question: "Can the avatar speak?" Although cited in a different context, this cue from Gayatri Spivak's famous essay appears particularly pertinent in a situation where the avatar might be understood to index or assume subaltern status.[188] There is always the danger that the visitor's absorbing, even profound, experience might, like the Western academics and postcolonial scholars Spivak critiques, reinscribe and reinforce imperatives of imperial dominance, standing in and speaking for the Other in a solipsistic manipulation that delimits dialogue. But rather than shut down lines of inquiry prematurely, I remain open to ways in which the avatar might "speak" through modes of critical self-consciousness potentially afforded by the interface, and through an interrogation of the technology that subtends and enables the encounter.

When the very gestures that bring the Warrior into being seem to make the avatar work against the player, it might force a more self-conscious relationship than one where the self flows seamlessly into an imagined other. With no scoring mechanism, the fighting is potentially endless, which might reflect the indeterminacy or intractability of present climate-change efforts, yet might equally testify to efforts to stave off a negative outcome, thus orienting players to the larger stakes of the game. I think there is the possibility, as Kiri Miller argues, for a distributed subjectivity through bodily engagement with immersive technology that bridges space and time and creates connections "between dispersed and diverse individual human experiences."[189] Drawing from phenomenology and psychology, Jennifer Parker-Starbuck likewise sees potential for a subject freed from the notion of the classical humanist unitary subject, an embodied "becoming-subject that might better represent processes of mutation, migration, and transformation,"[190] and that understands its race, class, ability, and sexuality as strands that interconnect with other humans and nonhumans.[191] This tilts toward a more ethical goal of "bodies embodied and aware of the transformations around them," aptly, "to remind us of the presence of 'real life' bodies that threaten to 'be disappeared.'"[192] On the one hand, the installation sets up a combative interaction where the Warrior/avatar matches whatever "mankind" throws at them, giving as good as it gets. But it also goes the other way: the interaction could be read as cooperation or commitment—in order to defend our nation, whatever you do to help, whatever you put in, those of us in Kiribati will likewise contribute our efforts. Thus, in effect, we are *fighting together*. The player is transformed into a (climate) warrior, too: meeting the challenge, playing with, not against, and in the spirit of gaming, overcoming obstacles.

But I would like to push further to think specifically about the ideology of the interface, and how a consideration of the technology itself can furnish deeper insights about the dynamics and politics of this type of engagement. Following scholars who have asked how interactive media art might function as an analytical, critical, or deconstructive model of activity by drawing attention to media-based interaction systems that characterize modern society,[193] I explore how the interactive installation might respond critically to the Kinect apparatus, especially the narratives about indigeneity, imperialism, islands, and technology that were part of Kinect's marketing story from the outset and that continue to shape and sustain the product's logic and target audiences. This began with Kinect's launch in June 2010 with a giant immersive theatrical spectacle, a collaboration between Microsoft and the Canadian entertainment behemoth Cirque du Soleil, at the Galen Center in Los Angeles for the Electronic Entertainment Expo (E3).[194] Gina Bloom is right to view the show as trading on the imaginative topos of the island—ubiquitous in the scientific imagination—as a discrete, performative space of fantasy, experimentation, and discovery, of worldmaking and mastery of nature, presided over by the scientist-technologist as a Prospero-like figure.[195] This disposition, it must be said, has had disastrous ramifications for certain Pacific Island ecologies and communities. Whereas this mythos has been well scrutinized by critics of technoculture,[196] just as the (post)colonial politics of Shakespeare's *Tempest* have been tirelessly rehearsed on pages, stages, and in classrooms for at least the last generation, the story that Microsoft and Cirque du Soleil tell about Kinect is striking for its unabashed embrace of these conjoined narratives. In the epilogue to her monograph *Gaming the Stage*, "Participatory Spectators and the Theatricality of Kinect," Bloom describes this performance in detail, yet her account is curiously devoid of any analysis of the imperialist intercultural problematics of the E3 production. But these are worth excavating, because I posit that any fuller discussion of the theatrical affordances of Kinect—especially in regard to "Kiribati Warriors"—cannot be divorced from the hierarchies of race and power so blatant in the launch performance and in the Western technocracy it represents.

Upon entering the Galen arena, the three thousand audience members become a uniform entity by donning identical white ponchos over their clothes. En masse, they invade the space already occupied by the native inhabitants (played by the Cirque du Soleil performers), which comprises a material and virtual mise-en-scène of lush jungle, rocks, pools, and tropical flora. Lorded over by an orchestrating Prospero character and his Ariel sidekick, the "islanders"—sporting ornate headdresses, garlands, and brown unitards—beat drums, dance, and otherwise cavort for audiences in the digitally enhanced water in rituals of encounter. The show expresses an evolutionary narrative of gaming controllers and, by extension, the telos of Western modernity. A sonorous male voice-over declares that "with each leap forward for civilization, more people are left behind." It becomes increasingly clear that those left behind are the Indigenous inhabitants, as a parade of dancing natives selects a Caucasian boy and a young Caucasian woman to represent the past and future of Kinect gaming demographics. This allochronicity is translated into the spatial hierarchies of the set and reinforced as another young white boy ascends a series of large boulders through space and time, trying out various controllers in the progression of gaming until he stands—sans controller—in front of the colossal Kinect screen, to meet yet another Caucasian nuclear family inside the screen, whose son will assume a role in the show's finale as a next-generation Prospero. The islanders, significantly, do not ascend to this level or manipulate the technology, remaining on the lower boulders and watching in wonder at the demos taking place above. While they engage in vicarious spectatorial play, their movements are often less controlled, and they frequently seem bewildered and overwhelmed by this locally sited resource whose potential the foreigners have unlocked. In regard to the human body as controller, the voice-over's final question, "Is it possible that the future of humanity is humanity itself?" leaves us with our own uncomfortable question of who might count as fully human within this scheme.

That is hardly a subtle analysis, but it doesn't have to be, because the show offers such a spectacular ratification of Western technology's privileging of the white, male, middle-class, conventionally able-bodied, and heteronormative subject, as well as an explicit positioning of technology's "others": who acts and who is acted upon. This reading has clear implications for the way we think about Kinect as a theatrical technology in the Kiribati Pavilion encounter and its climate-change context. I don't suggest that addressing this specific legacy was necessarily the creative team's intention when designing the pavilion, but it is worth reflecting on how the interactive artwork's very theatricality might encourage a reflexive take on technology and its discontents. In the ludic interaction between the player and avatar, what capacity might "Kiribati Warriors" have to decolonize Kinect? The installation, I argue, doesn't *reverse* these colonial dynamics, but it does play with them and complicate them in intriguing ways. The remediation of the game into the performative installation has potential to break down the binaries reinforced by imperialist narratives of technoculture. If Kinect is an instrument of the white Prospero figure, what might it do to see oneself differently through one's engagement with the Indigenous Warrior? It is conceivable for the player to develop a self-consciousness about their role in an unequal relationship through the encounter (especially in a situation in which one is "acting upon" a figure rendered as "not fully human") and to think critically about the veracity and responsibilities of one's putative role as a "controller." For instance, the experience might prompt reflection on the fact that the player, as a wealthy westerner, is *making* the Warrior fight to defend the seawall—a symbolic representation of how they are in some way responsible for the Warrior's plight, creating the conditions whereby the Warrior has to act. In this way, the player becomes aware of the nature of interaction itself, and their own behavior becomes the object of analysis. The nature of the action, moreover, in which the avatar just keeps fighting, might also attune us to critical issues of labor and race so often excluded from technological discourse.

Primarily, however, the loaded issue of "control" is worked out through the materiality of the technology. Just as "Kiribati Warriors" is not inviting the player to inhabit the Warrior's identity so much as to engage with it, manipulation of the interface is not always met with the avatar's obedient response. Although Kinect promises the sensation of spontaneity and unmediated access, Kinect generates much weaker data than more elaborate and costly motion capture systems; the image generated is rather crude, and, most significantly, the avatars don't precisely mirror their players.[197] My experience of observing players with the Warrior and of engaging it myself is that it failed to keep up with rapid gestures: it could do something unexpected (something I didn't do), disturbingly freeze or flicker as if having a seizure, or disappear altogether if one moved out of range of the sensor; additionally, if another, inadvertent, "player" moved into the sensor space, they caused the second avatar to materialize, interrupting the flow. When avatars do things their players don't anticipate, it underscores the extent to which avatars, although largely controlled by players, are separate entities, enhancing our existing tendency to attribute to the avatar different dispositions and desires, and characteristics of an acting subject. Furthermore, the avatar might be understood to have its own scriptive agency. Alison Gazzard argues that beyond player-led exploration, mimetic interface games like Kinect can also retrain our real-world actions.[198] By rewarding and provoking particular gestures and behaviors, the Warrior conditions the player's kinesics: the user is extended in the artwork, which in turn changes the user.[199] In the interplay as it unfolds, there are thus situations in which the player might assume a responsive, even mimetic relation to the avatar. Parker-Starbuck urges us to be "wary of a seamlessness that too easily elides gender, sexuality, race, class, ability, and the qualities of humanness that immersion within technology often misses."[200] For her, the *relinquishing* of control—which these glitches, scriptings, and feedback loops might constitute—helps develop this more flexible subjectivity, so troubling the assumption that "you are the controller" might find one differently immersed.

The play of self and other that merges and emerges in "Kiribati Warriors" captures the vulnerability/agency dynamic discussed throughout this chapter, but this time transposes it to the player instead to embody both complicity and cooperation. It is here that a self-awareness might hold decolonizing potential, which, ideally, might translate to proactive commitment beyond the gaming situation. The orientation of the 2017 Kiribati Pavilion resists the persistent "desire for an ahistorical, escapist gamespace,"[201] subverting video games as "paradigmatic media of Empire," and harnessing their potential as sites of creative practice, cultural critique, and political action.[202] Arguably, this kind of open-ended, inconclusive engagement with virtual bodies (while involving more potential risk and misunderstanding) might urge greater critical self-reflection on climate justice issues than live theatrical performances that are more didactic and rehearse specific outcomes, signaling the importance of this emerging genre for Pacific performance repertoires.

TOTAL IMMERSION? *CROSSING THE TIDE* IN THE TUVALU PAVILION

My final case study offers a further way of thinking about how small island communities mobilize international linkages to encourage action on climate change by analyzing the dynamics of *Crossing the Tide*, an interactive art installation that comprised the Tuvalu Pavilion at the 2015 Venice Biennale. The project was an alliance between Tuvalu's foreign affairs and environment minister Taukelina Finikaso, who commissioned the piece, curator Thomas Berghuis from New York's Guggenheim Museum, and Taiwanese eco-artist Vincent J. F. Huang. The installation, touted as the first flooded pavilion in the history of the Biennale, represented a negotiation between the Pacific, Asia, the United States, and Europe at the collaborative level and in the form and content of the work; specifically, it emphasized the environmental and discursive interrelationships between Tuvalu and Venice as "sinking islands" in ways that aimed purposefully, in Finikaso's words, to "magnify the national pavilion into a global pavilion."[203] In a step beyond the Kiribati Pavilion's virtual presencing, *Crossing the Tide* featured no human performers save for the activating visitor, pushing us to consider how Pasifika mobility and advocacy can function through staging acts of disappearance.

Situated midway between Hawai'i and Australia, the Polynesian country of Tuvalu encompasses nine islands and coral atolls covering sixteen square miles of land spread across 350 miles of ocean. Just four hundred yards across at its widest point, its highest vantage is fifteen feet above sea level, with the majority of land resting at less than ten feet. The world's fourth smallest nation, Tuvalu gained independence from Britain in 1978. Almost half of the national population of approximately ten thousand people lives on the island of Funafuti, the capital and only urban center. Tuvalu has been declared by the IPCC to be among the most vulnerable to climate-induced sea-level rise, and joined the United Nations in 2000 primarily to spotlight the issue and to call for a curtailing of emissions to protect the country's unique culture, history, and lifeways. The form of these appeals has extended into art and performance, with an increasing emphasis on brokering international transactions that place Tuvalu's concerns at the center of a mondial matrix. *Crossing the Tide* was Tuvalu's second outing at Venice and is one of a series of installations and performances that Vincent

Huang has developed since 2010 that reflect on the effects of global warming on the South Pacific nation in a transnational context. Much of this work has been undertaken in Tuvalu itself, where Huang has established close links with the government; he has served as an official delegate for Tuvalu at UN climate-change conferences around the world since 2012, and in 2019 he was formally appointed Tuvalu's ambassador for climate emergency.[204]

Huang's presence at these conferences was a doubly significant move, both for Taiwan's enlistment of support for its international representation, and for Taiwan as a regional island nation struggling for diplomatic recognition. Taiwan has Austronesian links to certain Indigenous Pacific Island communities and has formally attended the flagship Festival of Pacific Arts since 2008. But the People's Republic of China (PRC) also claims sovereignty over Taiwan (Republic of China, ROC), which it views as a breakaway province that will eventually be united within "one China," although many Taiwanese want an independent nation. In 1971, the United Nations recognized the PRC over the ROC, leading Taiwan to attempt to offset the diplomatic victory and retain an international voice by securing relations with developing counties, especially in the South Pacific. Tuvalu is one of four Pacific Islands Forum members that currently recognizes Taiwan over China. This ongoing Beijing-Taipei rivalry in the region, sustained through various forms of diplomacy, especially financial aid, has had substantial implications for Pacific Island economies and political stability.[205] A transpasifika viewpoint that breaks down island-rimland binaries, especially one that attends to Asian-Pacific crossings that highlight artistic collaborations instead of policy tensions, can elucidate crosscurrents often overlooked in other regional and disciplinary frameworks. In addition to this specific engagement, as with the Kiribati exhibitions, Iping Liang notes that Huang is one of a number of noncitizen artists in national pavilions at Biennales who have addressed recognizably global issues,[206] indicative of his self-identification as a "global environmental citizen."[207]

Crossing the Tide, which appeared as part of the Biennale theme "All the World's Futures," was visited by over one million people during its installment from May to November 2015.[208] The installation's design represented a shift from the satiric stance in Huang's former work toward a more conceptual, relational approach. It was one of several national pavilions located in the Artigliere at the Arsenale, which has been one site for Biennale exhibits since 1980. Presently used as a naval base, the Arsenale is a complex of former shipyards and armories that, from the thirteenth century until Napoleon's takeover, pioneered mass production methods to produce the bulk of Venice's naval and merchant vessels that generated most of Venice's military and economic wealth and power. The sixteenth-century Artigliere comprises a long, single-story brick building with a trussed roof consisting of several large rooms (former workshops) connected by internal doorways. *Crossing the Tide* took up one of these rooms. A shallow pool of clear water, lined with turquoise vinyl to simulate a limpid tropical lagoon, covered the floor. It was traversed by two Venetian footbridges—the kind used during the city's *acqua alta,* or high tide, when the city floods—that were level with the surface of the water. A main thoroughfare bisected the space, and a secondary footbridge created a T-intersection with the first. Both bridges consisted of two panels placed immediately side by side but not fixed in the middle, so that when they depressed under the weight of people's footsteps, water was forced up, flooding the footbridge and flowing back under. Every few minutes a smoke machine sent up a geyser of mist, which replenished as soon as the former jet had diffused; through this, a data projector at floor level cast up an aurora pattern with shifting shapes of colored light. These manufactured lights merged with the natural, reflected light from the pools that occurred when sunlight filtered in through the building's large windows.[209]

Described in this way, *Crossing the Tide* sounds (deceptively) simple. And to some degree its apparent minimalism was designed to offer up, at first encounter, an integrated vision: a stark, elemental space that reduced the world to—or produced the world as—water, sky, and cloud. Unlike many of the other pavilions that I visited, there was minimal text to read beyond the framing explanation at the main entranceway that cued us to the installation's rationale; there were no films, photographs, or displays of artifacts: here, Huang conjured in microcosm a total national vision of a vanished future that spilled over into a future global vision, prompting us to render the implications of unchecked climate change. But this response was precipitated by, and generated, further complexities that split this ostensibly singular vision, refracting and synthesizing multiple sites and spaces. The key way in which the installation encouraged a more global apprehension of climate change was through its specific connections between Tuvalu and Venice as lagoon archipelagoes destined to "go under" this century, producing an aesthetic experience that brought "here" and "there," *acqua alta* and king tide, Europe and Oceania, and the Adriatic and the Pacific into mutual engagement. It sutured the sinking nation and the sinking city in ways that spoke to a transhemispheric environmentalism that transcended the distancing and objectification of threatened Pacific Island communities to help make the crisis relevant and present for visitors.

Figure 16. Vincent J. F. Huang. *Crossing the Tide*, 2015. Water, fog, Venetian footbridges, projectors, aurora video. 600 × 1,700 × 1,600 cm. In the Artigliere at the Fifty-Sixth Venice Biennale Arte, "All the World's Futures," Venice, Italy. Photograph by, and courtesy of, Vincent Huang.

I will concentrate on the performative operations of the installation itself to consider *how*, precisely, we might come to a comprehension of the co-imbrication of Tuvalu and Venice in service of a global environmental imaginary, and *how* we become inspired to reflect (and possibly act) on the sustainability of modern civilization as a result of it. Aside from the installation literally "crossing the tide" via its transnational production, how does it and do we cross the tide in other ways? These questions, which foreground the installation's phenomenological and experiential qualities, focus on the role of the visitor/immersant whose experience within the space constitutes the performance. Central to this analysis is a serious consideration of the work's site-specificity, which involves reading the Artigliere as a crucial feature of the work's mise-en-scène and semantics. Venetian materiality and history are woven intimately into the piece through Huang's decision not to cover the walls of the Artigliere to create a hermetic, transporting totality. Instead, the large windows are unadorned and admit fulsome natural light; an open doorway to the thoroughfare outside invites traffic and the ebb and flow of the immediate environment; and the crumbling interior of the structure—with its statigraphy of whitewash, plaster, bricks, and mortar, its patches of vegetation, and its trusses, pipes, and metal rungs—is embraced as a core component of the immersive experience, reflected in the ocean pool and, through the ongoing disintegration of the 450-year-old wall during the months of the Biennale, gradually dispersing into it. (Perhaps this becomes an inadvertent commentary on the detritus of European industry in Pacific waters?)

To investigate the relationships between the built structure and the artistic project it houses, I find it useful to take up Joanne Tompkins' scholarship on heterotopia, a concept that has undergone considerable retheorizing since Foucault proposed it in the 1960s. In Tompkins's formulation, heterotopias are "alternative spaces that are *distinguished from* the actual world, but that *resonate with* it."[210] Heterotopias can be actual or imagined spaces; they can appear in multiple forms and/or may be fleeting, transitory, or ephemeral, or they may not be able to be mapped in any conventional or cartographic way (they may be psychic or conceptual), but they are encountered in "performance" space.[211] While heterotopias don't intervene directly in the actual world, they offer models for (re)fashioning the present and the future, and might affect audiences by demonstrating how change for the social good might take place.[212] Heterotopias are therefore hopeful: they encourage audiences to ask "What if?"[213] and refuse to foreclose the future as a teleological inevitability.[214]

Site-specific performance is especially conducive to heterotopic analysis, Tompkins argues, because the performance/installation is more directly entwined with its social context.[215] "Heterotopic space" is located within a tripartite structure, emerging from, or discerned between or in relation to what she calls a performance's "constructed space" (the "extra-theatrical" spatial environment or location that frames the production) and its "abstracted space" (the contrasting spatial environment, which operates more metaphorically, and typically constitutes the production's diegetic world). It is through the delineation of different types of spaces, concrete and metaphoric, that heterotopia may become apparent. In the case of *Crossing the Tide*, then, the heterotopia would potentially become perceptible in the interface between the constructed space of the Artigliere with all its historical, capitalist, and maritime resonances and the abstracted space of an imagined, future, oceanic world that both is and is not Tuvalu, and that explodes the spatial constraints of the Artigliere and its trans-Mediterranean purview to encompass a global milieu. It would emerge from the manifold durational rhythms of the piece: the crumbling Arsenale marking the time of human civilization (especially the cultural and political vicissitudes embedded in Venice's fortunes) compared with the much longer geological span of existence represented by the aurora and the preceding and succeeding ocean. And it would emerge through the tension between the assumed centrality of Venice/Europe, with its weight of imperial power, wealth, and "world heritage," and the assumed remoteness of Tuvalu / the Pacific, extending, blending, and complicating this dichotomy by bringing the putatively incongruous locations into one space. The act of traversing the footbridges (whose sodden surfaces index—with precarious immediacy—the cumulative impress of anthropogenic climate impacts) evokes simultaneously the experience of walking Venice's flooded streets and piazzas, of wading across a submerged atoll, and of inhabiting a space between and beyond that charts broader transoceanic trajectories.

And what might we come to understand as a result? Arguably, there is potential—although not every visitor will experience this, and not necessarily in the same way—for the activating immersant to apprehend an alternate ordering of spatial practices, which dissolves the Eurocentric compartmentalizing of the globe and makes one aware of one's situation within a more interconnected, holistic scheme. This posture is sympathetic to Ursula Heise's notion of an "eco-cosmopolitanism," which concerns itself with how "local cultural and ecological systems are imbricated in global ones,"[216] and constitutes "an attempt to envision individuals and groups as part of planetary 'imagined communities' of both human and nonhuman kinds."[217] This awareness—aligned with the logic of climate change as a planetary concern—stimulates a conceptual crossing of the tide, and, in that moment of crossing, that appreciation of mutual relation and relevance, perhaps a new or renewed inspiration to respond more actively to climate-change impacts. The heterotopia, perceived in the space between and beyond Venice lagoon and Funafuti lagoon, is thus a more personal map, the space of the individual to intervene and react to the events around them in ways that raise the possibility of a different version of global futurity. As the title of the installation suggests, in crossing the tide (spanning watery realms), we may, eventually, *cross*—stem, stymie, defy—the rising tide. Thus, while appearing to present an absolute vision at first glance, *Crossing the Tide* is not apocalyptic: it is not a cry for help from victims in a remote wilderness, nor is it an act of climate heroics; rather, it is an invitation to enter into a relationship founded on a recognition of a common urgency. It does not promote a homogenizing sameness but a complementarity that presents an alternative to geopolitical binaries that entrench notions of inequality and alterity, and that posit the Global

North as a moral and juridical arbiter and as a custodian for a chaotic and needy Global South.

• • •

Global media and policy discourses on anthropogenic climate change have tended to depict members of "sinking" or "disappearing" island communities in limiting ways: as early warning systems for industrialized nations and as victims sentenced to a future of displacement and dependency. The case studies profiled in this chapter demonstrate how Pacific citizens have staged numerous performative interventions in international forums that resist foreign attempts to define future outcomes for Islanders and that replenish agency to local actors. Although some of these examples have taken place in conventional climate-change negotiation settings, I have mainly explored the work that they undertake in cultural and artistic contexts (religious rituals, theaters, galleries, and arts festivals) so as to allow for a deeper and more subtle analysis of their performance praxes and strategies of engagement with those publics. Moving from cultural performance activism to anthropologically based performance, to avant-garde ceremony and experiments with abstraction and absence, my voyage through these sites of performance highlights their different philosophical foundations and contributions, while tracing strategies of appearance and disappearance in performative representation. The task of navigating the complexities of climate change is fraught with difficulty; consequently, the argument here is not about political efficacy, yet it remains open to the promise of such projects to present alternative propositions, worldviews, and future visions that emerge from the vantage of the Pacific region. These projects also shed light on how contemporary contingencies stimulate new experiments with aesthetic form and function, raising the question not only of what art might do for climate-change discourses, but also what climate-change discourses might do for art. Ultimately, these works indicate how new concerns, collaborations, and artistic and commercial circuits create new conditions for the development and dissemination of Oceanian cultural production, a phenomenon I examine from a different angle in regard to transnational Samoan performance in the next chapter.

FOUR

Performing Transnational Samoa:
Remittance, Resistance, Community

For the 2016 Festival of Pacific Arts and Culture (FestPac) held in Guam
(Guåhan) in Micronesia, the government of the Independent State of Samoa
broke with tradition and invited the London-based GAFA Arts Collective
to help represent the nation. Under the creative directorship of Sani
Muliaumaseali'i, GAFA (meaning "genealogy") proudly advertises itself
as "London and Europe's FIRST Samoan Arts Collective,"[1] and comprises
an intercultural and interdisciplinary cohort of creative and performing
artists of Samoan heritage along with antipodean, British, and European
collaborators. The company's work focuses on Samoan art practice and culture that reflects ancestral roots, and since 2011 its members have developed an innovative body of work in theater, dance, cabaret, opera, and art
and design. The work featured at FestPac was *A Family Called Sāmoa* (2012),
which combined many of these genres to offer a layered meditation on
Samoan cultural history, and was first performed in London to commemo-
rate the fiftieth anniversary of Samoan national independence. Its title and
production circumstances are particularly apt for thinking about a global
Samoan "family" manifested through migration, and for the ways in which
the performing arts are meaningful in expressing, maintaining, and developing those transnational connections. As the "UK contingent of the
Samoan delegation,"[2] GAFA appeared at FestPac as both a Samoan envoy
and a European company and foreign nation. This choice is significant in
the context of FestPac, a traveling two-week festival held every four years
among twenty-seven Pacific constituents with an emphasis on sharing and
exchanging culture to prevent the erosion of customary practices, because
it highlights how the festival functions as a barometer for gauging changing notions of identity in Pacific Island nations. GAFA's inclusion illustrates how Samoa is progressively fashioning and representing itself via its
transnational resources, presenting itself as a site where national and cultural identity are increasingly off-island and hybridized through the multisited, multistepped, and multidirectional traffic of population movement.

These dynamics, which are accelerating and proliferating within the globalizing Pacific, and their relay through the performing arts, are the topics I take up in this chapter.

The previous two chapters of *Moving Islands* have emphasized oceanic imaginaries in considering how performance evinces and advances intricate, mobile modes of interrelation across and beyond the Pacific Ocean world. Chapter 2 tracked the voyages of the transpacific vaka and its (re)crossing of various jurisdictional boundaries to reveal the complex translocal circuitries of the "Brown Pacific." Chapter 3 explored the performative collaborations and negotiations between Pasifika artists and a range of international partners, stakeholders, and audiences in the fight against climate change and sea-level rise, tracing voluntary and temporary movement in the present primarily designed to prevent forced and permanent movement in the future. This chapter signals a turn away from a preoccupation with the ocean as sovereign highway or existential threat toward a concentration in the remainder of the book on migration, border-crossing, and urbanization. Here I access a body of work that focuses directly on the experience of contemporary, transnational Pacific migration and on performance's operative role in that phenomenon. I examine the work of Samoan practitioners as the most prominent demographic of diasporic Pacific Islanders with the most visible and varied artistic output. Samoa has a vibrant tradition of precolonial theater in *fale aitu* ("house of spirits"), a form of subversive comic performance, as well as strong contexts for performance and theatrical events in ceremonial, church, and village settings, which has likely encouraged gravitation toward, and development of, that medium in the urban diaspora.[3] In a circumstance that has become common in the wake of the postwar Pacific diaspora, although each artist or company claims Samoan heritage, none is actually resident in the Samoan Islands but is located in/between the chief Pacific Rim nations to which many Pacific Islanders have migrated: Australia, New Zealand, and the United States. Inflected uniquely by their particular cultural contexts, the works demonstrate how performance's expressive vocabularies enable variable iterations of Samoan identity as it has evolved among multiple linked locales. A transpasifika paradigm that breaks down island-rim binaries here accentuates the notion of transformation, the dynamics that morph culture as it is transferred and proliferated and takes root in new spaces and through new intercultural engagements. It also privileges *trans* in the ways that these influences are relayed reciprocally and laterally among different communities, including the home site, pointing to a Samoan culture that comes, through its multilateral geographical reach, to encompass an increasingly heterogeneous range of concerns and aesthetic forms.

This chapter provides alternative ways of thinking about, in Ferrari's words, how "interculturalism and transnationalism are engaged as relational paradigms that can apprehend the mechanics of intercultural collaboration in circumstances of transnational mobility."[4] Developing a dialogic relationship between Western and Indigenous theory, I suggest that theatrical performance can be understood as a form of "social remittance" or "cultural remittance" that activates reciprocal relationships between communities in the diaspora. This approach prompts a more nuanced and holistic apprehension of how theatrical performance operates as an active agent in transnational processes by building solidarity and mediating between local concerns and global forces. With this I pair the Samoan concept of *vā*, the relational space between people, places, and things, as a way to situate the social and aesthetic processes of remittance as they are parlayed through Samoan frames. This discussion addresses the contours of an important body of Pasifika work that is still to be comprehensively examined from a multipolar transnational perspective, while developing new models for reading interculturalism and performance that are applicable in the wider Pacific and internationally.

PACIFIC TRANSNATIONALISM AND THE SAMOAN DIASPORA

The Samoan Islands currently comprise two adjacent South Pacific territories in central Polynesia. Once a single archipelago and sociocultural unit, the eleven volcanic islands were settled about thirty-five hundred years ago. Samoa is unusual in that, unlike many Pacific societies, its origin story is not a story of migration, yet the whole group was named the Navigators' Islands by eighteenth-century European explorers because of the islanders' seafaring abilities, recognizing an extant history of travel and transculturation. Damon Salesa explains that long before the first landing of *papālagi* (foreigners) in Samoa in 1789,[5] Samoans continually moved through, reenacted, and recreated an entity understood as *Sāmoa 'uma* (all Samoa), part of a circuitry that extended beyond Samoa to other parts of the Pacific.[6] Deeply entangled in multiple networks of the Brown Pacific and other foreign communities, Samoans' historical mobilities find continuity in their post-1950s migrations. In addition to missionary, whaling, and commercial shipping routes that took Samoans around the Pacific world and to New

England and Europe during the nineteenth century, a fundamental feature of Samoan life was *malaga*, "customary visits to relatives and villages throughout Samoa and perhaps even as far away as Fiji and Tonga."[7] Central to Samoan politics and involving critical exchanges and alliances, *malaga* was a dynamic practice that actively incorporated new things, people, and approaches. Although the practice became subject to restriction and regulation by colonial governments as they sought to discipline Samoan customs and politics,[8] the "travel[ing] back and forth" connoted by *malaga*, with its reciprocity between dwelling and reaching, visiting and returning, continues to provide a powerful model for purposeful Samoan movement and migration in the present.[9]

Following the Tripartite Convention of 1899,[10] the islands were divided between the colonial powers of Germany and the United States; while most Samoan family groups stretch across both territories, the partitioned areas retain two distinct national affiliations, currencies, laws, and time zones. Independent (formerly Western) Samoa[11] was administered by Germany until the outbreak of World War I in 1914, and subsequently by New Zealand until it reestablished independence in 1962. Although it is an autonomous nation, Samoa is a MIRAB state—dependent on Migration, Remittances, Aid, and Bureaucracy to augment its local industries[12]—and maintains many British- and New Zealand–derived customs and cultural inflections. American Samoa (formerly Eastern Samoa) encompasses the smaller group of islands and since 1951 has been an "unincorporated and unorganized territory" of the United States.[13] Even though, as in independent Samoa, American Samoans have retained land rights and the observance of *fa'a Sāmoa* (Samoan worldview and way of life), US commercial culture has permeated local lifestyles. Colonial heritage is also reflected in the places to which Samoan Islanders migrate, with American Samoans often moving initially to Hawai'i and the US mainland, and independent Samoans primarily to Australia and New Zealand and, via step migration, to the United Kingdom, although long-term movements are often more fluid. These divisions became more acute in 2011 when the independent Samoan government engineered a shift in the International Dateline to position it between the two island groups, overlaying a geopolitical border with a spatiotemporal one. The brief journey between the capitals of Apia and Pago Pago now flips travelers back an entire day, aligning American Samoa with the western boundaries of the United States, and independent Samoa with its major trading partners and expatriate communities in New Zealand and Australia.

Islander migration has become a key feature of the regional culture of the postwar Pacific, as the quickening pace of economic growth in larger countries around the Pacific Rim has impacted island states.[14] As John Connell notes, citizens of "tiny nations" often perceived as being "on the extreme periphery of the global economic system" are moving with new velocity and numbers between the islands and, especially, to the larger cities of the Pacific Rim and beyond, stimulated by social, financial, military, family, educational, and other contemporary exigencies.[15] This phenomenon has become so extensive that the greatest concentrations of Pacific Islanders are now in cities such as Auckland, Honolulu, Los Angeles, San Francisco, Seattle, Vancouver, Brisbane, and Salt Lake City rather than in the island Pacific, generating major social and political impacts at home and in their overseas communities.[16] Samoans comprise the principal component of this Pacific diaspora, forming the largest Pacific Island migrant populations in New Zealand and the United States, and the second largest in Australia;[17] there are now more Samoans living in the United States and New Zealand than in the Samoan islands themselves.[18] (Western) Samoan movement to Aotearoa New Zealand accelerated in the 1950s when the New Zealand government began recruiting Pacific Islanders to work in its rapidly developing industrial and agricultural sectors, encouraging immigration with schemes such as the Samoan Access Quota (1970). Samoan migration to Australia has been mainly via New Zealand citizenship and thence through the Trans-Tasman Travel Arrangement (1973), which allows Australians and New Zealanders to pass freely between the two countries to live, visit, and work.[19] American Samoan migration to the United States was stimulated by the impact of World War II when Pago Pago became a major military installation after the Japanese attack on Pearl Harbor. The wave of movement was triggered after 1951 when the navy terminated operations in Pago Pago and transferred its personnel stateside; this coincided with American Samoa's territory status, which made American Samoans US nationals with free access to the United States.[20] Western/independent Samoans who migrate to the United States typically come through American Samoa or Hawai'i or via the green-card lottery.[21]

Over several decades, this phenomenon has given rise to a multisited transpacific web of personal, political, economic, and cultural interconnections. As Paul Spickard et al. point out, for example, "Samoan migrants to Seattle are likely to have relatives on the north shore of the island of O'ahu in Hawai'i, Pago Pago in American Samoa, Apia in Western Samoa, Auckland, and Sydney."[22] Mixed ancestries through intermarriage are common, as is the process of individuals and families moving through multiple nodes over a lifetime. The transnationalization of Samoan culture has become intensified as overseas migrant enclaves have eventually become permanent expatriate settlements and demographic centers where Samoan social customs and institutions are replicated in the context of new reference communities and are modified and enacted differently to varying degrees, especially by subsequent generations.[23] Cluny Macpherson describes how "Auckland-based Samoans who returned from visits with Samoan relatives in Los Angeles would comment on the differences in the *fa'asamoa* they had seen in the United States and vice versa. Samoans from Carson in California would, in turn, comment on the differences between their practices and those of Samoan communities that had formed around military communities in Seattle," which were different again from "Samoans in the community that had formed around the Pearl Harbor naval base in Hawai'i."[24] As this chapter will show, this diversifying of Samoan culture has had a central impact on artistic expression.

Camille Nakhid rightly argues that since many practices of Pacific "transmigrants" are unique in their links to the customs and traditions of the Pacific, any explanation of Pacific transnationalism "requires its own specifically Pacific perspectives, research and framework."[25] A central feature is the practice of reciprocity, which "distinguishes Pacific transnationalism from other classifications involving negotiations across boundaries such as migration and globalisation, and highlights what is expected of a Pacific 'transnational.'"[26] This should not suggest that other diasporic or transmigrant populations do not engage reciprocally, but rather that Pacific transnationalism rests on vital in/formal customs of exchange that are socially and culturally specific and need to be taken into consideration in its analysis. Scholars of Pacific transnationalism have identified a wide range of reciprocal practices carried out by people at home and away, but the examples and critical frameworks remain largely social scientific. Usefully, literary scholar Paul Lyons has acknowledged how such reciprocity "creates and sustains forms of circulation commensurate with the mobility of the global system itself, that enables supporting local struggles while thinking beyond the level of national boundaries," and suggests that much of Oceania's art "is a way of affirming such networks, linking up localities, and creating and maintaining alternative spaces."[27] Nevertheless, there is still a general lack of attention paid to how cultural traditions and transitions, social practices, and reflections on and interventions into lived experience are developed in and through theatrical performance as a particular medium of cultural exchange.

THE INTANGIBLE ECONOMIES OF PERFORMANCE:
RETHINKING RECIPROCITY AND REMITTANCE

How might we talk about how genres of theatrical performance operate within these multiply networked social matrices? What models might be productive for discussing and analyzing their transnational creation and circulation? A significant preoccupation in transnational scholarly discourse is the subject of remittances. Defined broadly as "a sum of money or (formerly) a quantity of an item transferred from one place or person to another," and "the action of transferring money, etc., to another place or person,"[28] remittances are evoked predominantly in transnational literature to refer to monies or goods sent home by migrant labor forces to their countries of origin. According to World Bank estimates, official global remittances hit a record high of $714 billion in 2019;[29] they are therefore an important feature of worldwide economic processes and are especially relevant to the Pacific Islands, which contain several of the top remittance-earning countries in the world per share of GDP. Consequently, a great deal of scholarship in Pacific and transpacific studies has tended to privilege financial remittances in studies of translocal transactions. This is certainly pertinent to Samoa (independent Samoa, especially), which is bound inextricably to these economic circumstances as one of the world's most remittance-dependent developing countries. By far the biggest changes to contemporary culture in the Samoan islands have come from the vast volume of remittances—cash, commodities, and material goods—through which local family support, village development, national infrastructure, and social and political advancement are facilitated. Indeed, as Paul Shankman argues, "People have become Samoa's most valuable export,"[30] as migration has become an end in itself whereby ever larger numbers of people are sent overseas to satisfy escalating family needs and obligations in the islands.[31]

Here, however, I want to parse the variable dynamics of transnational experience in a different way with reference to "social remittances" and "cultural remittances," a less tangible economy of ideas, behaviors, narratives, values, and social capital that flows reciprocally between the homeland and the diaspora. Sociologist Peggy Levitt, the seminal theorist on the topic, coined the term "social remittances" to explain how people at the grassroots level form cultural connections and transmit and receive culture in ways that contribute to a transnational collectivity.[32] Rather than focusing on the assimilation that a migrant might undergo in a host country, Levitt's model emphasizes the ideas and values from the adopted culture that the migrant sends or brings home with them and that affect the home culture. She further examines how cultural formations from both places continue to circulate reciprocally in a process of adaptation and creolization.[33] In contrast to the "world-level diffusion of institutions, cultures, and styles that arise from economic and political globalization," social remittances function as a "migration driven, local-level form of cultural diffusion."[34] They usually travel via more localized and identifiable pathways, are more systematic and intentional than global flows, and are activated through mutual social ties.[35] These remittances may not all be accepted or necessarily change culture, but they might introduce new ideas or open up space for commentary or debate about existing or potential practices.

Whereas Levitt's concept of culture is a broadly sociological one, centering mainly on sport, politics, community organization initiatives, religious affairs, and general social norms, subsequent scholars, especially in the fields of Latin American, circum-Atlantic, and European studies, have augmented her ideas to consider how diasporic culture mutually influences home and host communities through more varied forms of cultural and artistic engagement. Juan Flores, notably, proposed the term "cultural remittances" to supplement "social remittances"[36] as "a more accurate and challenging way of describing the content of the counterstreams that are catalyzing and accompanying change in many parts of the world. . . . It is, after all, in language, music, literature, painting, and other expressive genres that the values and lifestyles remitted from the diaspora to the homeland become manifest in the most tangible and salient ways."[37] I propose that we could usefully understand certain kinds of theatrical performances as cultural remittances (my preferred term). This topic has rarely been taken up by scholars,[38] but I posit that remittance theory provides a rich avenue for examining how theater and performance in the Samoan diaspora carries ideas, practices, and identities, both affirmative and subversive: transcending borders but maintaining cultural ties, creating and transferring cultural adaptations, reinforcing connections between established communities in various diasporic sites, and forging networks between new forms of contact culture.

To pursue these ideas, I want to make an intervention in terms of genre and also geography. This approach necessitates a more flexible definition of remittance to elucidate theater's particular modes of transmission within a context of Pacific transnationalism. Whereas the experience of return migration does feature centrally in some of my case studies, and some works do travel back to the islands, curate collaborations between island and off-island artists, or send back income generated from theatrical enterprise, a more nuanced investigation of theater's role requires a fuller appreciation of the ways that "new concepts and practices are not transferred just between host countries and countries of origin"[39] but flow in "transnational social spaces" that encompass both migrants and nonmigrants with connections to several nation-states.[40] As Sa'iliemanu Lilomaiava-Doktor's research on social remittances in the Samoan diaspora has found, these transactions are not "purely bilateral between the island home and one or another rim country. Rather, Samoa, New Zealand, the United States and Australia are sites of transnational, triangular, and circular exchange."[41]

Here, Pacific anthropologist Helen Lee's more finely tuned declensions of transnationalism present a useful vocabulary for describing how identities are negotiated across multiple sites and in symbolic and emotional ways in addition to material and interpersonal praxis. Lee proposes the term "intradiasporic transnationalism" for situations where "transnational ties can continue across the diaspora even if ties to the homeland diminish."[42] These intradiasporic ties are often far more reciprocal than ties to the homeland, Lee argues,[43] and thus are potentially more revealing of forms of cultural circulation among off-island Pacific Islanders. Moreover, I suggest, theater can still undertake reciprocal cultural work while operating locally within communities in particular host sites via a process that Lee terms "indirect transnationalism"; that is, "transnational ties that are maintained through others, but which nevertheless have a tangible quality that constitutes a significant connection."[44] This form of transnationalism is especially relevant to subsequent-generation migrants: "If migrants or their children retain any involvement with members of their ethnic group in the host nation they are likely to be part of a web of transnational ties even without direct involvement in the home nation."[45] These activities might include participation in ceremonial events, support of sports teams, being present at social events in which monies are donated, and indeed participation in theatrical productions and/or attending performances.

These more indirect connections, which cultivate a transnational sensibility from afar, highlight the role of emotional transmissions and labor. The notion that long-distance engagements are affective conduits that accompany capital flows taps into the increasing scholarly interest in the role of emotions and affect in our understanding of human mobility and the constitution of transnational communities and identities.[46] It is particularly relevant to theatrical performance as both a tangible and an intangible product, and as an imaginative, aesthetic, and embodied practice that represents or otherwise evokes reflexive encounters with the world. In this regard, it is helpful to refer to cultural theorist Jenny Burman, who makes the case for "an expanded use of the concept of remittance in interdisciplinary scholarship on diasporic discourses and conditions,"[47] which takes up its role in an "economy of sentiment."[48] For Burman, the "term's affective content is implied by the extended definition of 'remit,' with its many nuances exceeding the act of sending: to surrender, to withdraw, to set free, to relieve from tension. . . . [R]emittance is treated as an investment in the fullest sense of the word,"[49] which includes emotive investments. In her schema, cultural remittances can likewise operate from the diasporic dwelling-place without necessarily needing to travel "home," referencing the homeland but being transmitted to the diasporic city and/or beyond. This approach foregrounds "the idea of cultural remittance as public address: poetry and other forms of cultural expression that pay tribute to people and places left behind but also address a wider . . . audience."[50] These gestures are not merely nostalgic, but express more agential forms of desire (which Burman calls "yearning") that keep connections alive and changing, and that advance a set of potentially transformative possibilities that might shift the asymmetrical power relations that underlie globalization processes.[51]

These applications rescue the concept of remittances from its primary associations with island economic dependency and route it toward other productive questions of cultural maintenance and transition. Viewing performance from the Samoan diaspora in this way encourages consideration of one means by which performance functions as a cultural intervention, attending to the broader transactions that arise from the audience/performer reciprocity so central to theater's interactive dynamism, and highlighting the role of theatrical performance in creating and sustaining transnational networks as well as providing artistic reflections of its processes and effects. Part of this, as Camilla Stevens has observed, is to think of theater as "a multi-sited transnational practice in which authors, actors, and audiences make temporary homes for displaying bodies and discourses not always recognized by the majoritarian culture of the nation-state,"[52] and to consider the grassroots performance event as "a unique setting where new styles and ideologies are 'rehearsed' in front of a collective body of people who may identify or disidentify with them."[53] In the Samoan case, however, these aspects need to be augmented with reference to Indigenous understandings of sociospatial relations that make Samoan connections meaningful.

I explore various ways that diasporic Samoan performance engages the core concept of vā, a transactional space of relation or space of negotiation between places, people, and things. Vā is a complex philosophy with many cultural variations and applications, and is understood and expressed differently by the artists featured here. A concept with "economic, political, spiritual, cultural, and social dimensions,"[54] vā is a space formed through mutual relations, exchanges, or intersections between persons, objects, or social groups and is also an indicator of the quality of the relationship.[55] Vā is, as Samoan writer Albert Wendt describes it, "the space between, the betweenness, not empty space, not space that separates, but space that relates, that holds separate entities and things together in the Unity-that-is-All, the space that is context, giving meaning to things. The meanings change as the relationships and the contexts change."[56] Based on a relational or distributed rather than an individual or discrete sense of self, vā traditionally characterizes respect relationships and informs culturally proper and improper behaviors, as captured in the expressions *tausi le vā* or *teu le vā* (to care for, nurture, decorate, or embellish the social space).[57] Vā has a profoundly temporal aspect as well. Understood within a nonlinear and more circular or coeval arrangement of time-space (*tā-vā*), vā traverses genealogical as well as geographical space, activating history and memory, and linking the past and the present, the living and the dead.[58]

Samoan theorist Albert Refiti explains that since the 1990s, scholars have advanced new understandings of vā-space to analyze the ways that transnational relations reaffirm connected social spaces in the diaspora, and to relate vā to new diasporic constructions of Samoan identity.[59] For Lilomaiava-Doktor, in the migrant context vā drives acts of reciprocity between movers and stayers, including the sending of remittances and other acts, obligations, and gestures that enhance the home site.[60] Vā also conditions the search for new community as identity is transformed in the diaspora. Removed from the Samoan village setting that historically anchored the conceptualization and practice of vā,[61] vā has accordingly been reconstituted as a means of relationship-building that encourages a growing intradiasporic Pasifika identity, as well as a strategy for negotiating and maintaining mutual respect between the migrant Samoan community and people of the new land.[62]

The reciprocal energies of vā resonate richly with cultural remittances and provide philosophical nuance for their enactment in Samoan performance contexts. In essence, vā might be understood as the concept, philosophy, or faculty that drives and conditions remittances. In terms of remittances, we can read the performer/audience interface as facilitating a shared space of articulation where people "come together to debate their common affairs, contest meanings, and negotiate claims,"[63] affirming certain experiences and cultural mores and challenging others. Attention to vā, however, reveals the more specific and expansive ways in which these dynamics operate. Vā is a space that can be aesthetically transformed;[64] in an artistic context, vā can be a way of activating the space (between performers, the performers and the audience, and the world) to create a social commonality for all participants.[65] For Rosanna Raymond, the spatiotemporal dimensions of vā coalesce in and through the performer's body, which acts as a "genealogical vessel that collapses time and space, allowing our ancestors and atua [gods] to have a presence in the Now,"[66] living through the performer at the point of performance in charged exchanges between human and material audiences.[67] Within such a shared time-space, but from a different perspective, Sitiveni Halapua identifies *talanoa* (face-to-face storytelling, dialogue) as an important cultural tool for exploring the nature of the vā between people and resolving political conflicts through people's dialogic rights and exchange obligations to speak, to hear, and to speak in return.[68] Likewise, Caroline Sinavaiana Gabbard argues that genres of creative cultural production can enact the ideal of *teu le vā* by marshaling an assemblage of people to search for truth and the right solution;[69] in some cases, such work also seeks to cultivate and reconstruct vā relationships in social and spiritual dimensions by exposing abusive behaviors and bearing witness to the effects of cultural dissonance.[70]

I analyze these dynamics through a constellation of performances that chart artistic and social relationships between multiply situated nodes of the Samoan diaspora, and that directly engage issues of Samoan culture and identity in various transnational contexts. Beginning with relationships to independent Samoa, I consider the solo and ensemble stage performances of Tusiata Avia's *Wild Dogs under My Skirt* (New Zealand, 2002, 2019); then *Teuila Postcards* (2006–9) by the Australian dance/theater collective Polytoxic; and Michel Tuffery's *Siamani Samoa* (*German Samoa*, 2011, 2015), a community performance art project that uncovers Samoa's colonial relationship with Germany. I then turn to affiliations with American Samoa as they are expressed in two plays: Dan Taulapapa McMullin's *Pink Heaven* (2000), written from the continental United States, and *The Holiday of Rain* (2011) by Victoria Nalani Kneubuhl from Hawai'i. In taking this approach, I practice what Barbara Burns McGrath calls "ethnographies of the particular"[71]—something that performance analysis is admirably equipped to accomplish—which "encourages the writer to move beyond generalizations that construct cultural difference"[72] and that smooth over contradictions and conflicts of interest, and to focus instead on more individual, specific narratives in particular times and places that allow for insights into various local and global interactions, multiple ideas, differential experiences and imaginings, and an understanding of culture as heterogenous.[73] This stance also supports April K. Henderson's prompt for scholars to pay closer attention to how Samoans negotiate between individuality and collectivity, especially through their artistic works.[74]

This is not a reception study. I do not survey or interview spectators or facilitate talkbacks, nor do the case studies assess the social impact of cultural remittances beyond the theater—such a project is far beyond the scope of this single chapter. But through close readings, conversations with the artists, and personal experience of the performances (acknowledging that in many cases I am not the target audience, although not a wholly unintended one), I begin this process by looking at the performance event as a site of transmission that activates multivalent modes of exchange between Samoan communities in the diaspora, and that operates in complex intercultural negotiation with various host societies and colonial powers. Because theater is ideational as well as representational, it has the capacity to envisage beyond quotidian scenarios and to create richly textured presentations that are densely layered and critically self-reflexive. Consequently, whereas some artists have chosen a more documentary approach to bearing witness to life in the diaspora, detailing the realities of sociocultural adjustment and the changing nature of the fa'a Sāmoa in a quasi-ethnographic mode, other works are fashioned in a subversive, satirical, or fantastic manner, intervening imaginatively and unexpectedly in established accounts of transnational migration, colonialism, and globalization, as well as tourism, Christianity, sociosexual stereotypes of Polynesia, and economic development and foreign investment. Read together, the works testify to evolving forms of Samoan interculturalism as ideas and practices move ever more freely between Samoan societies in different parts of the world, contributing to the vā of transnational Samoa. As Cluny and La'avasa Macpherson observe, "Migrant enclaves do not constitute discrete, distant communities but rather sites in which modification and experimentation are legitimated by the necessity of finding solutions to new social, economic, and political realities. These modifications that seem to meet new needs can find their way back into Samoan 'traditional' forms, and in the *social space between* these two settlements a meta-culture emerges which is neither a 'migrant' nor a 'traditional' culture but a contemporary Samoan one."[75]

"N IS FOR NIU SILA": TUSIATA AVIA'S *WILD DOGS UNDER MY SKIRT*

"The reason corned beef is so popular in the islands is because it so closely resembles the taste of human flesh. Our cannibalism is canned, and Pacific

Brand® adds extra fat and salt to Polynesian tastes."[76] This declaration is delivered with disarming charm by our interlocutor, who sways her hips languidly and smiles sweetly at her Auckland audience as she cradles the machete she's just plunged into a large tin of *pisupo* (corned beef),[77] peeling open the metal edge "like a jagged scream" to expose the glistening pink meat, and sucking on her fingers with devilish pleasure. So begins Tusiata Avia's solo performance piece *Wild Dogs under My Skirt*, a punchy and pointed testament to Samoan culture and its often uneasy collisions with Niu Sila (New Zealand). Avia's opening provocation—we laugh, but are we entirely sure she's joking?—musters its transnational social network through its simultaneous address to independent Samoa, diasporic Samoa, and New Zealand, gesturing to how these communities are differently implicated in and affected by the same entwined tendrils of colonialism, consumption, and globalization.

Of all the sites in the contemporary Pacific, Aotearoa New Zealand has become the most significant destination for Pacific migration. From the early twentieth century, New Zealand (then a British dominion) exercised a special duty of kinship with its South Pacific neighbors; after the status of New Zealand citizenship was established in 1949, New Zealand extended citizenship entitlement to its colonies of the Cook Islands, Niue, and Tokelau.[78] In 2002, Immigration New Zealand launched the Pacific Access Category, a residency ballot open to limited numbers of people from Kiribati, Tonga, Tuvalu, and Fiji. Although New Zealand did not extend citizenship entitlement to Western Samoa (which it colonially administered from 1914 to 1961), agricultural schemes established in the 1950s, work permit schemes instituted in the 1970s, and the Samoan Quota residency ballot (1970) have opened certain pathways, as has Samoan eligibility for special New Zealand citizenship grants. The upshot has been the rapid growth of New Zealand's Pacific population, including the emergence of the northern city of Auckland as the world's largest Polynesian center.[79] These demographic shifts have had a marked impact on art, music, literature, theater, and fashion since the 1980s. The evolution of a new, urban Pasifika style, alongside (and sometimes in collaboration with) Indigenous Māori cultural production has, in relative terms, been supported by official arts policy, with targeted funding for creative development and programming.[80] Within this milieu, Samoans have emerged as the dominant artistic voice. In their volume *Floating Islanders: Pasifika Theatre in Aotearoa*, Lisa Warrington and David O'Donnell catalog nearly five hundred Pasifika productions staged in New Zealand between 1981 and 2016, the majority of which are by Samoan practitioners.[81]

From this embarrassment of riches, I have chosen Avia's performance because it offers particularly apt examples of the relationships between vā and cultural remittances, demonstrating how vā drives acts of reciprocity, including the sending of affective gestures to Samoa and to the diasporic city; and, through its sometimes controversial provocations, negotiating changing relationships between island Samoans and migrant Samoans, between migrant Samoans and people of the new land, and between New Zealand and Samoa itself. Avia was born in Christchurch, New Zealand, the daughter of a Pākehā mother and a Samoan migrant father. The recipient of multiple awards and residencies, in 2020 Avia was appointed a Member of the New Zealand Order of Merit for her services to poetry and the arts. *Wild Dogs* is one of New Zealand's best-known and enduring Samoan productions and has been presented regularly in different versions since its debut in 2002. Avia toured the piece as a one-woman show around New Zealand, Australia, Hawai'i, Europe, Africa, and the Middle East from 2002 to 2008, and it was published as a collection of poetry in 2004. In 2016, *Wild Dogs* was converted into a six-woman play directed by Samoan-born, New Zealand–based theater-maker Anapela Polata'ivao, and evolved through several iterations, including for the 2019 Auckland Arts Festival, where I saw it. It had its overseas premiere at the SoHo Playhouse in New York City in 2020. I will be focusing primarily on the solo performance, but with reference to key moments from the ensemble version by way of comparison and elaboration.

Avia embodies several female-identified characters, moving fluidly back and forth between personal and external narratives, between New Zealand and Samoan geographies and subject positions, and between the village and the urban milieus of Apia and Auckland. Her solo performance, drawing upon *fale aitu*, *fāgogo* (performative storytelling), and different Samoan and English dialects, activates relational space between herself and these others; she enacts vā through her genealogical body, channeling different characters through the condensation of time and space in the heterotopic, spatiotemporal realm of the stage, and relating them within an urban, cosmopolitan realm. It is not only localities but the characters themselves who are "in between," including migrants, adolescents, *fa'afāfine*,[82] *afakasi* (mixed race),[83] *aitu* (spirits), prostitutes, and a mongrel dog; throughout, Avia exhibits an empathetic engagement with the abused, the marginalized, and the outcast caught up in the turbulence of larger transnational social processes. These vā-poetics provide the framework and vehicle for the cultural remittance sent via *Wild Dogs*, which, as Stevens rightly argues, "is not the nostalgic return to the homeland; rather, it is a transnational lens through which to view the island *and* the . . . community abroad."[84] Avia's meditation on the contradictions, histories, and cultural changes taking place between Samoa and New Zealand highlights how theater's cultural remittances can curate a democratic space of solidarity that promotes consensus about the past and the present, but can at the same time create a crucial forum for expressing conflictual opinions that are also vital for community building. These permutations of local culture are indicative of changing Samoan norms and protocols as they take root in new social geographies and as a younger, overseas-born generation, less served by the culture of their parents' generation and less bound by the strictures of Samoan hierarchies, is encouraged to reflect on, question, and critique aspects of the *fa'a Sāmoa* and to treat sensitive and taboo issues.[85]

The violence of food colonialism—the fatty, salty, overprocessed *pisupo* and its enthusiastic integration into the local Samoan exchange economy at the expense of Indigenous foods, or the globalizing lines of flight that connect McDonald's Apia and McDonald's Otara[86]—is shown to be well sedimented within home and diasporic Samoan culture. Yet this twisting of tradition and modernity braids forward into Avia's reminder that "we are direct descendants of flesh-eaters,"[87] a reiteration of her prior warning that foreign consumption of Polynesia may be countered by a resurgence of ancient appetites that threaten to consume the consumer. Early in the show, Avia places these themes in dialogue with her consideration of how Samoa's contemporary diasporic relationship with New Zealand has been occasioned in part by its previous colonial relationship. The scratchy strains of the New Zealand national anthem give way to an aural recording of former New Zealand prime minister Helen Clark's formal apology to Samoa on the fortieth anniversary of independence in 2002. Clark expressed regret for the injustices of New Zealand's "inept and incompetent" military and civil administration of the country, including the 1918 docking of the ship *Talune* carrying passengers with influenza, which resulted in the deaths of over 20 percent of the Samoan population; the 1929 shooting of nonviolent protesters by New Zealand police (Black Saturday); and the banishment of Samoan leaders and the stripping of their chiefly titles.[88] Avia channels the ambivalent Samoan response to Clark's apology through ironic recourse to precolonial custom, declaring: "In the old days, Helen / you would have presented yourself trussed // like a pig / ready for umu,"[89] holding her joints stiff, suffering for hours in the sun, while the Samoans went about their business:

then, Helen
if we decided

not to kill
you, cook

you
then

you could consider yourself
forgiven.[90]

If Avia expresses skepticism about the perlocutionary effect of Clark's
political plea, then the ensemble performance—staged after, not during,
Clark's term in office (1999–2008)—presented a more strident rejection.
Under red and blue downspots evoking the colors of the New Zealand flag,
the cast of women sit on a row of chairs oriented upstage, backs facing us.
After listening to Clark (who is not actually Clark this time but, in a parodic
queering, a male voice impersonating her characteristic baritone), the
women rise, and the loud sound of flushing toilets floods the soundscape.
Having evacuated the excreta of apologies for New Zealand's colonial
damages, the women come forward as a group; one of them delivers the
address to Clark and, at the close, they lift both fists aloft in unison, middle
fingers defiantly raised.

The response of a woman (or a group of women) to a female political
leader—who, to be sure, is attempting to make amends for a male administration (what sort of apologist is she?)—centers the gendered lens through
which life between Niu Sila and Samoa is examined in *Wild Dogs*. The performance's cultural remittances focus largely on women's social roles and
sexualities—including those of transnational *fa'afāfine*—exploring how
these dimensions of the *fa'a Sāmoa* change in New Zealand, but, due to the
intense reciprocity between the locales, are also changing culture in Samoa.
One example of this counterstream occurs in the vignette "Ode to da life,"
in which a visiting return migrant not only tells Samoan girls about the
good life overseas, but in the process, actively performs this acculturated
identity to her rapt audience. New Zealand is a paradise of leisure and
plenty: "All da Palagi[91] dey very happy to us / Dey say Hey come over here
to Niu Sila / Come an live wif us an eat da ice cream / An watch TV2 evry
day."[92] But New Zealand also promises social and sexual liberties, free
from the strictures of patriarchal violence, village prohibitions, and Chris-

Figure 17. The ensemble expresses contempt for New Zealand's postcolonial apologies in Tusiata Avia's *Wild Dogs under My Skirt*, directed by Anapela Polata'ivao and produced by Victor Rodger. Hannah Playhouse, Wellington, for the New Zealand Festival, 2018. The cast featured Nora Aati (Aunty Avai), Petmal Lam (Aunty Fale), Saane Vaipulu (Manila), Stacey Leilua (Tusiata), Katerina Fatupaito (Dusky Maiden), and Anapela Polata'ivao (Teine Sā). Photograph by, and courtesy of, Matt Grace.

tian religious mores: Jesus "say to us Now you can / Do anyfing you like / Have da boyfrien, drink da beer / Anyfing, even in front your fadda / An never ever get da hiding."[93]

These idealized enticements to the urban environment are complicated in the show's other narratives, in which imported gender expectations, compulsory churchgoing, and parental beatings, as well as low-level jobs, racism, and poverty are rife for Samoan migrants. As one young immigrant testifies, "Our house doesn't need a lawn mower. Our house doesn't need a can opener. Our house has six cousins living in the garage and a machete." But Avia's dual perspective casts a diasporic eye back on Samoa itself to uncover women's experiences of physical and sexual abuse, and the shameful consequences for those who act out transgressively. Men move around the edges of these testimonies: Samoans in the authoritarian form of fathers and ministers, *papālagi* in the transient capacities of tourists, visitors, and disengaged lovers. The most resonant emphasis, however, is how women condition the behavior of other women in both social and spiritual realms, not only or necessarily as a repressive force, but as a way to maintain heritage and identity. In the segment "Fings da kirls should know," set in Samoa, Avia adopts the forbidding persona of Aunty Fale to tutor her young female listeners via a list of instructions that interweave Christianity with Indigenous Samoan beliefs. Prohibitions like "Don comb your hair in da night-time," "Don forget to cover da mirror at da night-time," and "Don kafaovale [go partying]—don make aroun"[94] are calculated to avoid the wrath of the Tele Sā, the beautiful spirit women, neither humans nor ghosts, who wander the villages of Samoa, functioning as guardians and protectors. Charming, seductive, and jealous, they keep pretty young women in line, making sure they behave appropriately and conform to the community's norms.[95] In their role as internal mechanisms by which Indigenous traditions are maintained, Tele Sā represent another strand of feminine identity that must be negotiated in the diaspora.

Wild Dogs locates its most potent and poignant symbol of women's identity and possibility in the *malu*, the Samoan female tattoo, which is the desired rite of passage that Avia anticipates at the end of her performance: "I want my legs as sharp as dogs' teeth / wild dogs / wild Samoan dogs / the mangy kind that bite strangers," like the black octopuses "that catch rats and eat them," like black centipedes "that sting and swell for weeks."[96] A counterpart to the male *tatau* (*pe'a*), the *malu*'s more subtle, angular markings that circle the thighs, delicate yet formidable, lend the performance its title while opening to the "unlimited power that exists across the spectrum of womanhood."[97] For Wendt, *tatau* exemplifies vā networks by activating dense social and sacred relationships: "Tatauing is part of everything else that is the people, the *aiga* [family], the village, the community, the environment, the atua [gods], the cosmos."[98] Tatau designs are "scripts-texts-testimonies"[99] that translate the body into a spatiotemporal matrix of historical, cosmological, and kinship relations, between interior and exterior, self and other, individual and community, past and present, living and dead. To receive *tatau* is to undergo an act of metamorphosis that invests the body, making it more than it was, inscribing it with lines of descent and ascent that have profound political and spiritual implications and that remake the person as a living archive.[100]

Tatau has an important role in diasporic and transnational complexes, marking connections between cultures and locations, which corresponds with *tatau*'s own long history of migration and exchange. Juniper Ellis explains that "even traditional tattoos embody the cross-cultural traveling of signs, making visible and material the process by which culture moves both within and beyond the Pacific."[101] Samoa's *tatau* origin story tells of the art form being brought to Samoa from Fiji by the legendary twin sisters Ta'emā and Tilafaigā, "express[ing] a practice of borrowing from 'elsewhere' in order to designate the bearer's home place."[102] In this version of the myth, *tatau* is itself a cultural remittance, a practice encountered and incorporated abroad, brought back by traveling Samoans and adapted in the process of transfer.[103] As Ellis writes, "The patterns at once promise that the bearer will be at home—by bearing marks of belonging, meaning, and identity—and inaugurate a redoubled journey toward creating meaning from elsewhere. This apparently most fixed sign proclaims that the subject is as much an itinerary as an identity, that location is as much a passage as a place."[104] As a New Zealand–born Samoan and self-identified *afakasi*,[105] Avia's relationship to the *malu* thus registers her transnational belonging and becoming, and activates her genealogical body, her "responsibility to the *va*, her induction into *va*-consciousness, *va*-time, *va*-space,"[106] all the things she is constituted by but also responsible for. The subject-becoming implied by the act of tattooing also has a vital link to sexuality;[107] as Samoan women's sexuality is often more closely observed and regulated than men's, here Avia expresses the desire to have it on her own terms, even as the *malu* inscribes her social obligations. In the final lines, Avia articulates her wish to break from the *tufuga ta tatau* (*tatau* master) to claim fuller sexual and self-independence: "I want to frighten my lovers / let them sit across from me / and whistle through their teeth."[108]

The various thematic strands introduced in this discussion—migration, female sexuality, *tatau*, religion, and colonialism—are entangled in the show's finale. Whereas Avia's solo performance ended with an intimate admission, the Auckland Festival version marshaled the full dynamism of its group of women on a larger stage[109] to deliver a more spectacular reflection on the complexities and contradictions of transnational identity. The ensemble performance changed the order of Avia's poems so that the finale segued from Polata'ivao's powerful, threatening monologue of the "devil pa'umuku girl" (the prostitute) in her role as Teine Sā, the human incarnation of Tele Sā. She embodies the emblem of roving sexuality that is both the network that sustains the community and the threat to it: "We will go to da house of Pulotu [the underworld] we will go wif our black arses flashing."[110] As she speaks, the other women start to move forward out of the shadows on all fours, their fervor stirring, energy rising. They shout out the words to "Wild Dogs," shifting the lines among them in increasing intensity: now they have *become* the dogs—teeth bared, eyes rolling, they bark, growl, drool, and slide forward with their fearful power barely tethered. As they become unleashed, their choreography incorporates the form of Māori haka—*toa wāhine!* As a group force they are stunning; their *malu* shorts—white on black in relief—flash before us. But just when it seems as if it will end triumphantly, with these sexy, intimidating women owning the stage—they falter. Uncertainty and grief grip them—it's over—behind them, rays of golden light from the fretworked slats of the set break through, simultaneously evoking the church windows of orthodox Christianity and customary patterns of Samoan design as the operatic strains of soprano Aivale Cole's "Telesa" crowd out the sonic space. The women stand, cowed, in tears, and then walk back and offstage in single file, casting reproachful glances at us as they exit.

This sequence—overwhelming, breathtaking, heartbreaking—reveals the theater as a vā-vortex that captures the competing forces acting on Samoan women's identities in the islands and in the diaspora. This ending of *Wild Dogs* figures the diasporic city as a location where new desires and freedoms can be explored and exercised, but it is weighted by the impress of colonial religion that continues to tame sexuality and social behavior, while the Tele Sā offer a cautionary reminder of the need to remember and respect traditional Samoa, lest one get carried away by Niu Sila and forget. Both versions of *Wild Dogs under My Skirt*—solo and ensemble—are fruitful illustrations of how the diasporic stage enables candid, and often troubling, examinations of a range of sensitive issues that speak to the metaculture evolving in the space between Samoa and New Zealand. In this regard, I suggest that the "indirect transnationalism" in operation here has, potentially, a more visceral and immediate effect on participants in the theatrical event compared to those experiencing other activities whereby transnational ties are maintained through others. Even if physical travel is not involved in the production and its cultural remittances, theater's heterotopic possibility, its strategic evocation of other people, places, and situations, and its modes of autopoiesis between spectators and performers[111] creates a particularly compelling site for the visible, public constitution of transnational community.

OH TIKI, YOU'RE SO FINE: POLYTOXIC AND POLYNESIAN POP CRITIQUE IN AUSTRALIA

Despite their dense transnational social field and their long association of making and remaking a "Tasman World" within Oceania, New Zealand

and Australia are distinguished by their divergent logics of territorial nationalism and their attitudes to their respective managerial roles in the Pacific. Although these approaches are, as Nicola Baker points out, more sophisticated than the common "notion of New Zealand playing 'good cop' to Australia's 'bad cop' in the region,"[112] one of the biggest differences and points of contention between the two countries is the position on Pacific Islander immigration. As we have seen, while acknowledging New Zealand's colonial and neocolonial heavy-handedness and expressions of racism, its sense of identification with the region and its immigration policies have contributed to a one-fifth Polynesian population whose presence and energetic cultural production have become a reckoning force of contemporary urban New Zealand life. By contrast, Australia has no special relationships with its Pacific Island neighbors; despite heavy reliance on Melanesian labor during the nineteenth century, immigration in the period since federation was restricted by the White Australia Policy (1901–73). This was followed by a policy of official multiculturalism from the 1970s, yet this policy extends no singular immigration privileges to any international country except for New Zealand.

Most Samoan immigrants to Australia have come via step migration from New Zealand under the Trans-Tasman Travel Arrangement (which minimizes reciprocal entry formalities for Australian and New Zealand citizens), although this has been increasingly tempered with social restrictions as a result of Australia's mounting fears about "back door" entry from the Asia-Pacific.[113] At thirty times the size of New Zealand, Australia occupies a different insular identity as the "island continent," historically constructed as a bounded and unitary geo-body.[114] Australia's bureaucratic interests have typically extended northward to Asia, but in the early 2000s the Pacific was cast, in the words of former prime minister John Howard, as "our patch,"[115] a self-imposed shouldering of a regional burden that enables and justifies imperialist acts of control of the area. Amid a twenty-first-century climate of national securitization, Australia's sovereign territory has both contracted through excision (to stymie asylum seekers) and expanded through annexation and intervention, including the 2015 "takeover" of Norfolk Island, offshore detention centers in Papua New Guinea and Nauru as part of Australia's "Pacific Solution" for refugees (2001–7, 2012–13), and military operations in so-called failed states like the Solomon Islands.[116]

These circumstances have shaped the creative industries in Australia. Whereas New Zealand has well-established funding and creative development infrastructures to directly support Māori and Pasifika work, Australia lacks such targeted institutional frameworks. Pasifika performance, while visible, is more sporadic and less recognizable as a key facet of the performing arts ecology; Australia is still more likely to play host to Pacific work from abroad than to feature "homegrown" production. This is the local context from which Polytoxic performance ensemble proceeds. Established in 2000 to respond to the absence of a Pacific Islander performance scene in Australia,[117] the company, based in Brisbane, has developed a repertoire of theatrical performances that mix drama and a fusion of Polynesian, contemporary, and street dance styles, along with Suzuki-inspired physical theater and circus. Its six Samoan and *papālagi* performers have become recognized for their intercultural collaborations with a range of Pasifika and Australian creative companies and communities, touring throughout Australia and to the Pacific Islands and Canada, and establishing a reputation as "ambassadors for a new generation of artists working across cultures."[118] The culture of Western/independent Samoa is central to Polytoxic's work, with its founding members comprising second-generation migrants raised in Australia. Company cofounder Efeso Fa'anana was born in New Zealand, and his family migrated to Australia in the early 1980s, spending time in Samoa every second year; as he recalls, "I grew up in both cultures—Samoan and Australian—and my parents gave us a good balance between the two."[119]

These transnational dynamics are prominent in the company's first full-length production, *Teuila Postcards*. While privileging Samoa, Polytoxic's oeuvre enlists a wider transpasifika element. Albert Refiti observes that vā-space has become linked with new identity and community constructions in the diaspora;[120] namely, vā "as an idea intending to unify many Pacific nations into a single Pasifika identity."[121] Likewise, Kirsten McGavin has revealed how diasporic Pacific Islander identity in Australia is often predicated on a panethnicity and an appropriation of broader Pacific culture. In addition to their own specific island heritage, people adopt more layered and hybrid positions, often identifying as "Pasifika," "Islander," or "Nesian" as a way to affirm a distinct culture within Australia, assert the commonalities of Islander cultures and traditions, and reinforce Islanders' connections to each other.[122] Polytoxic's cultural remittances thus open up relational spaces that connect several social groups beyond the Samoa/Anglo-Australia dyad, connecting Pasifika audiences but also incorporating a critical address to "multicultural Australia."

Polytoxic develop local forms of solidarity through their active deconstruction of regional stereotypes wrought by Western modernity. A notable strategy is their profound reliance on intertextuality, especially the ironic sampling, recycling, and redeployment of the pop-cult detritus of Western representations of the South Pacific: films, musicals, ethnographies, visual art, artifacts, tourist brochures, and television advertisements. These are expressed via the integral aesthetic of "neo-tiki," a postcolonial reclamation of the midcentury "tiki" cult of Polynesian Americana with its appropriative mishmash of psychedelic *primitiva*, priapic effigies, exotic cocktails, and ersatz island havens for the urban beachcomber, born in California, brushing Asia, and then exported (back) to Oceania.[123] These cited texts are parodied, recontextualized, and reperformed in ways that both register and resist the pervasive infiltration and impact of displacing foreign cultural flows. By placing the vigorous and critical Pacific Islander body back centrally within the tiki frame[124] and splicing the more transpacific vocabularies of tiki with specifically Samoan references, the performers create empowering spaces of Samoan and associated Pacific identity within the diaspora. Significantly, this device also enables Polytoxic to comment on the host nation, as the reappropriation of US tiki culture flexes back across the Pacific Ocean to critique Australia's regional presence and policies.

Teuila Postcards, which debuted at Brisbane's Afrika Pasifika Festival in 2006 and was performed until 2009,[125] was devised, directed, and presented by three core artists, Lisa Fa'alafi, Efeso (Fez) Fa'anana, and Leah Shelton. Subtitled "A tongue in cheek look at the oppression and evolution of an island," the show is a politically charged comedic cabaret that draws on a subversive antiauthoritarianism found in both Samoan comic performance like *fale aitu* and the "Aussie sense of humour."[126] As one of the first theatrical works that sought to connect with a diasporic Samoan audience in Australia, the performance was created deliberately for that demographic; Shelton recollects that during the show's Sydney run the audience was 90 percent Samoan. At the same time, she explains, Polytoxic wanted to create an accessible work that would also be educational for a non-Samoan audience, that would entertain but would also probe more challenging issues of the tourist gaze, Australia's history of colonization, and the contradictions in the nation's avowed "multicultural" policy.[127] *Teuila Postcards* is framed loosely as a travelogue, with the three performers playing tourists who journey from Australia (although their archetypal portrayal might suggest any wealthy Western country) to Samoa and back. Their clichéd expectations of idyllic beaches, swaying coconut palms, and happy natives are subverted and recalibrated though a nonlinear series of vignettes in a range of choreographic and theatrical styles that deconstruct a conspectus of Western fantasies from the past and the present, juxtaposing them with more nuanced depictions of Samoan culture.

Figure 18. Leah Shelton and Efeso (Fez) Fa'anana in *Teuila Postcards* by Polytoxic at the Cremorne Theatre, QPAC, Brisbane, 2009. Photograph by Cloé
Veryard, courtesy of the photographer and Polytoxic.

The vibrant, hyperrealist aesthetic of *Teuila Postcards* bathes its lavishly
costumed performers in glorious Technicolor à la the garish filters of
Logan's *South Pacific*, backed by nightclub soundtracks that segue from sul-
try steel guitar rhythms to contemporary rave to the Elvis-style retro-pop
of *Blue Hawaii*.[128] The performers switch roles swiftly between episodes,
supported by a malleable set of five flats placed end-to-end and bookended
by intaglio palm trees, featuring smaller removable inserts through which
actors or objects can be seen or transferred as the performance requires,
variously creating airplane windows, a dressing room, a bar, or a village
dwelling. Augmenting the live action, media projections superimpose
images, video, and text (suggesting, perhaps, our own "projections").
While the "tourists" are caught in their own play of desire, ending their
vacation sun-saturated, hungover, with cameras full of photos of locals
crystallized forever in fetishized frames, the performance offers more to its
spectators. Displacing the primacy of the tourist gaze, the show's dance-
theater format offers a fluid and dynamic performative space for experimentation with Polynesian identities, presenting scenes in which characters provide candid representations of life in Samoa, as well as nondialogic
displays of the Polynesian body that evoke predominantly visual and
embodied practices and stereotypes in a variety of critical modes.

The performative dismantling of stereotypes is a key tactic for building solidarity with Pacific audiences, and broadens the critical frame of *Teuila Postcards* beyond sole inscriptions of "Samoanness" to address a wider Pasifika community based on shared histories of oppression and commoditized representation. One of Polytoxic's projects is to demonstrate how Western fantasies are historically inscribed. Taut with repressed desire within her corseted black carapace, the Victorian Pālagi Missionary Lady's prurient fascination with the Samoans' "wicked" *pōula* ("night dances") reveals how the association of Samoans with sexual license long predates Margaret Mead's ethnofantasy,[129] and exposes the hypocrisy of the missionaries and their suppression of Samoan customs based on cultural misunderstandings and preconceptions. Correspondingly, key targets for revision are the "dusky maiden" and the "noble savage": well-worn metonyms for the Pacific Islands as a "leisure-pleasure" zone, and continually repackaged along a continuum from eroticized exoticism to commercial kitsch. In one vignette, "beauties" and "warriors" are wanted for a television advertisement for "Island Splash" soda: the Polytoxic performers audition and are made over as hyperexoticized clichés, with grass skirts, coconut bras, and wooden tiki masks, cavorting among the tropical flora and worshipping the giant Island Splash bottle as it rises monumentally from their reverential circle. Through neo-tiki, to borrow from Katrin Sieg, the Polynesian actors' exaggerated impersonation of whites' impersonations of Polynesians enlists the Brechtian paradigm of drag, which "entails the insertion of critical (and comic) distance between the actor and her roles in order to denaturalize and historicize them."[130]

Teuila Postcards performs other important forms of reciprocity within its transnational matrix. As reviewer Mary Ann Hunter notes, "Polytoxic happily take the piss out of the touristic and exoticising impulse but crucially give us something in return—providing insight into the realities behind the postcard grin."[131] Polytoxic uses its position between Samoan and Australian cultures to provide a pedagogical view of a complex milieu distinct from homogenizing and infantilizing visions, presenting audiences with information about Samoan etiquette, language, the *fa'a Sāmoa*, the drudgery of village women's labor, *fa'afāfine*, and the central place of Christianity in Samoan social life. At the same time, these travelers' views of Samoa raise critical questions about Australia as the host nation. The foregrounding of Samoan performers as tourists who travel and consume island experience with celebratory ease at once references a reality (a younger, more affluent generation of off-island Samoans visiting the "homeland"), but also points implicitly to other Pacific Islander border crossings that are, for many, a more fraught and difficult experience. The performance thus prompts audiences to consider

Australia's own history of racist immigration policies and the contradictions inherent in its official "multicultural" status. With an awareness that stereotypes of island-based peoples emerge alongside and inform stereotypes of the Islander immigrant, Polytoxic's critical revisions urge rethinking not only of Polynesians in the South Pacific, but (other) (non)citizens within Australia's migrant enclaves. These overtones are reinforced by historical scenes in *Teuila Postcards* in which *papālagi*[132] colonists speak pejoratively about the subservient and unruly "natives" in need of policing and protection. Although Australia did not have a colonial presence in Samoa, these vignettes nevertheless resonate with Indigenous Australians' own excision from sovereignty, as well as reminding us of the troubling parallels between the settler-custodian state's dislocation and dispossession of unwelcome migrants, and its related characterizations of dysfunctional Aboriginal communities at home and of "at-risk" Pacific nations abroad.[133]

Polytoxic's gift to us, then is complicated, enfolded within and reaching out to multiple communities and histories. It accrues extra layers in light of the ways that the concept of "paradise" itself is remitted. Although Polytoxic gamely ironizes tired Pacific clichés and points to Samoa's penetration by colonialism and globalization, they do not dismiss the notion of the island paradise but retain a strategic investment in it (Samoa is still a welcoming, friendly, and beautiful place). If, for McMullin, postwar American tiki culture represented the inner decay and the abject (justifiable) fall of the Polynesian,[134] then Polytoxic's neo-tiki approach recuperates the vibrant Polynesian body and co-opts the paradisal resonances that ghost tiki escapism. From this perspective, one might argue that for white/Australian audiences, at least, Polytoxic treads a fine line regarding their own commodification, embodying the contradictions of Polynesian representation embedded in practices of Western looking. The dual invitation and challenge to audiences through the heightened, self-conscious displays of attractive Samoan dancing bodies—highlighting our complicity and daring us to indulge our fantasies—has dangerous implications. As Sieg suggests of similar Indigenous displays, this strategy "also courts essentialist readings," for how are spectators to distinguish between actor and role if the role is in such close correspondence to prevailing assumptions about (Polynesian) authenticity? "Does not the actor's body," she asks, "risk lending corporeal proof to images believed to be accurate?"[135] Thus, the performers' flirtation with their audiences might be understood to create ambivalent reciprocal transactions that register, simultaneously, a web of colonial signification that proves difficult to escape.

For certain Samoan / Pacific Islander audiences, however, the deployment of paradise may have a very different valence. As Kalissa Alexeyeff's research has revealed, images and imaginaries of a Pacific paradise, especially via the material culture of tourism, are not just components of a European mythos but have been adapted by locals across transnational Pacific communities as an "affective geography"[136] that expresses personal and community desires and attachments to homeland and heritage.[137] This "repurposing"[138] of paradise (which does not forget its gendered, colonialist, and capitalist legacies) frequently finds generic images of paradise layered alongside photos of people and gifted objects in people's homes and personal spaces[139] to express nostalgia and future longing, and to offer a salve for the truncated socioeconomic realities that Pacific Islander migrants often experience in host nations.[140] From this angle, *Teuila Postcards'* activation and montaging of common Pacific images of paradise alongside portrayals of quotidian Samoan life are expressions of vā relationality, linked to poignant acts of memorialization and aspiration for the Samoan/Pasifika patrons they engage.

Yet there is a more critical upshot to speaking through this trope in the Australian context. Given that "paradise discourse" operates through the dichotomy of Eden and the apocalypse,[141] we can read the performance's investment in a Pacific paradise as a politicized, resistant response to bureaucratic Australian representations of the South Pacific, which are frequently wrought in negative terms as "doomsday" or "nightmare" scenarios of failure in socioeconomic development, overcrowding and poverty, impending environmental disaster, and corrupt and incompetent leadership. Such depictions provide a governmental rationale for the Australian right to manage Pacific affairs and to shape regional agendas on Australian terms.[142] Paradise is therefore an empowering counterdiscourse that insists on pride in home and heritage and emphasizes Islander self-determination regarding their future outcomes. The remittance-work of *Teuila Postcards* sustains affirming ties to a cultural heritage and local concerns while reflecting a broader postcolonial and intradiasporic Pacific consciousness that might buckle the armature of "fortress Australia." In so doing, the performance marks a shift from performing *island* Australia (that is, as a terrestrial, self-enclosed, and self-sufficient entity) to performing *archipelagic* Australia, an oceanic approach that views Australia as part of a larger island region including maritime Southeast Asia and the Pacific, and that traces and activates their connections.[143] The work, in effect, abjures the notion of the Pacific becoming an Australian space and suggests, through the permeable flows of peoples and cultural forms, how Australia might also be productively understood as a Pacific space.

"DIE PERLE DER SÜDSEE": REVISITING GERMAN SAMOA

From the perspective of colonial history, compared to other imperial powers such as Britain, France, and the United States, Germany came belatedly to the Pacific, due in large part to the country's late unification and emergence as an international player, and the "Iron Chancellor" Otto von Bismarck's antipathy to colonization, which he maintained until the 1880s.[144] Although that colonial period is the focus here, it is also important to recognize—as transnational and global historians have done—a longer and deeper history of engagement and entanglement between German and Pacific worlds, including Germans' complex and sustained presence in the region in nonimperial roles prior to the late nineteenth century.[145] Between 1884 and 1900, Germany used its existing trade and plantation holdings to annex Pacific colonies in Samoa (the two main islands of Upolu and Savai'i); New Guinea, the Bismarck Archipelago, and Nauru; and the Caroline, Mariana, Palau, and Marshall Islands. The short-lived German colonial empire fell to Allied forces during the onset of World War I in 1914; following the Treaty of Versailles, German Samoa was transferred to New Zealand, while New Guinea and the western Pacific colonies went to Australia, and the Micronesian territories came under a Japanese mandate. In contrast to Germany's African colonies, the expanse, remoteness, and comparative insignificance of the German Pacific meant that there was no large military support and no standardized pattern of local administration.[146] Germany justified its possession of relatively nonlucrative colonies in *cultural* terms—of self-fashioning, prestige, aesthetics, and civilizing missions—especially in Samoa, which was touted as "Die Perle der Südsee" ("the Pacific Pearl") and held special affection for Kaiser Wilhelm II, for whom the Samoan people were "kindred spirits" with Germans[147] and Samoa a place of romantic longing and cultural exoticism.[148]

The Reich's attitudes to Samoa, according to Christopher Balme, manifested in an uncharacteristically "protective attitude towards inhabitants of the islands" that "surpassed mere paternalism and took on occasional traits of a kind of mythic affinity" with Samoans that intensified after annexation.[149] Governor Wilhelm Solf and his successor, Erich Schultz-Ewerth, practiced sensitivity to the history and ethics of Samoan society and were committed to preserving integrity while cultivating the people.[150] Yet this period was characterized by continual Indigenous movements against Solf's politics, complicated by settler opposition and internecine Samoan rivalries. As historian Peter Hempenstall sees it, Solf's governorship from 1900 to 1910 "can be read as a continuing contest between his attempts to insert German legal and bureaucratic structures into Samoan society and the Samoans' proto-nationalist struggle to retain their traditional political culture,"[151] punctuated by sometimes violent resistance, uprisings, and Solf's exile of several dissident chiefs to Saipan in 1909. Nevertheless, there remains a prevailing sense that compared to the blunter instrument of New Zealand colonialism, with its more robust military presence and concerted efforts to erode the *fa'a Sāmoa*, the German tenure represented a relative era of cultural openness, exchange, and administrative moderation.

For contemporary theater-makers and performance artists, what is at stake in returning to this era, especially so long after national independence? What forms of (transnational) community are memorialized and activated, and how and why are they significant? What values and practices are remitted? Unsurprisingly, given the brief influential yet ambivalent term of German rule, diasporan Samoan artists have exhibited a variety of responses to the Siamani-Samoa period and its legacies. Identifying the German administration as the start of systematized colonial oppression in Samoa, Tusiata Avia's adaptation of Spanish dramatist Frederico García Lorca's *The House of Bernarda Alba* (in development) transposes the play's setting to 1910 Samoa under German occupation and uses Lorca's pre-civil war indictment of Spanish society to draw out the culture shock of colonization and the Catholic Church's repression of the *fa'a Sāmoa*. Rosanna Raymond's *Acti.VA.tion* ceremonies in the South Seas collection at the Berlin Ethnological Museum (2014) revived and reinvigorated human-material vā relationships between the performer and Pacific *taonga* (treasured ancestral objects) brought to Germany in the late nineteenth and early twentieth centuries. Prominent interdisciplinary artist Yuki Kihara has developed several video, installation, and performance works that explore and critique relations between Germany and Samoa as part of her broader interventions into debates about gender, race, culture, and politics in the Pacific undertaken from her position between cultures (Samoan and Japanese) and genders (*fa'afafine*). Projects such as *Culture for Sale* (2012), *Them and Us* (2015), and *Der Papālagi* (*The White Man*, 2016) investigate how Samoan identity was contextualized and, in some cases, appropriated under German rule, tracing connections between the historical colonial gaze and contemporary tourist dispositions.[152]

I want to look differently at how transnational relationships between Germany and Samoa have been activated performatively by concentrating on Michel Tuffery's *Siamani Samoa* (*German Samoa*) series. Born in Wellington, New Zealand, of Samoan, Rarotongan (Cook Island), and Tahitian ancestry, Michel Tuffery is one of Oceania's most significant artists and was made a member of the New Zealand Order of Merit in 2008 for his services to art. Tuffery emerged as one of a new generation of Pasifika artists in the 1990s who were radically reforging and redefining contemporary Pacific art with new media and styles beyond adherence to customary forms or the Western art canon. Over the past thirty years, he has developed an increasingly multidimensional and influential oeuvre that has been exhibited worldwide, encompassing not only painting, printmaking, and sculpture, but also public events, performance art, VJ-ing, and other genres of time-based media. Tuffery's projects often take the form of "series" undertaken over several years and in multiple stages, with performance usually coming later and representing a sampling, synthesis, and extension of the work produced in previous phases.

Although performance has always been a significant component of Tuffery's art practice, dating back at least to his collaborations with the New Zealand performance collective Pacific Underground in the 1990s, disciplinary blind spots among theater and performance studies scholars and art historians have led to his visual and plastic artworks being far more well known than his performance output (an omission that this chapter seeks to rectify). In part, this is possibly because Tuffery rarely centers himself as an embodied performer or subject but rather functions as a director, mediator, and facilitator, activating the various social groups and components of his projects in ways that nurture vā relationality; as he describes it, "My kaupapa [purpose, mission] within my art practice is the role of working 'in between' as a connector."[153] Deeply imbued with the protocols of Pacific Island ceremony, Tuffery's performance work treats key themes of genealogy, historiography, and the multivalent impacts of Western colonization and globalization on human and environmental domains in the Pacific Islands. The method that increasingly binds together much of this production is his social engagement, "collaborating with a wide range of communities to produce art together."[154] Based on his belief in art's capacity to stimulate conversation and to connect disparate or disenfranchised groups with their own histories in playful and unlikely ways, Tuffery's relational practices work to strengthen social bonds, with the artist operating as a bridge between community and audience.[155]

Siamani Samoa cites the rich and sometimes troubling cultural, material, and affective traffic between Samoa and Germany, principally during the period from Germany's annexation of Samoa in 1900 to its cession to New Zealand in 1914. Tuffery treats this legacy, however, as an enduring one, highlighting relationships that persist to the present day. The project had its genesis in the late 1990s when Tuffery was conducting research at the

Canterbury Museum in Christchurch and encountered the museum's collection of Samoan *selu pa'u* (*selu la'au*), women's ornate wooden hair combs crafted from the late 1800s. He was fascinated by the intercultural exchanges in the artifacts' intricate design[156] as well as their visual resonances with the architectural fretwork on German colonial-era buildings in Apia. These links, together with Tuffery's discovery of his own German heritage, led to his extensive research in public and private archives in New Zealand, Germany, and Samoa, including gathering oral histories from Deutschspeaking elders in Samoa.[157] The series consists of paintings that cite and modify historical photographs, a digital montage that creates a multimedia performance when projected with live music and dance, and laser-cut acrylic versions of the *selu pa'u* that operate as artworks in their own right as well as potent accessories when worn by the dancers. These elements are densely textured with visual, aural, political, historical, and gestural symbolism, taking up a plethora of entwined themes, including imperial allegories, memories of German personalities in Samoa, the impact of plantation culture, recollections of old buildings, music, foodstuffs, intermarriages, and the visits of Samoans to Germany for diplomatic, educational, and entertainment purposes.

Tuffery's emphasis throughout is on the reciprocal exchange between the two places rather than a one-way trajectory of colonial dominance, proving that "we Samoans were actually interacting more actively with Germany, before New Zealand took control in Samoa . . . we were meeting intellectually and in the same way."[158] Art and performance serve as a vehicle for prompting local Samoans to think about what they have been exposed to, to open up community dialogue on this long-repressed topic, and to reawaken a relationship with Germany in the present.[159] Central to this approach, Tuffery explains, is taking pride in being Samoan and creating "a space of good energy" among audiences.[160] In adopting a more positive approach to the historical record, Tuffery contests the notion of Samoans as "victims" of German colonization, and points to the more complexly motivated, multidirectional journeys and dignity of Samoan travelers, recalling Samoans who gained medical degrees in Germany, who brokered political transactions at the highest levels, and who influenced German fashions.[161] *Siamani Samoa* has been presented as an integrated performance event in three phases: Apia, Samoa, in 2011; Porirua, New Zealand, in 2011–12; and Sydney, Australia, in 2015. For the purposes of this discussion I concentrate on the Apia and Sydney iterations because they illuminate two different views of Tuffery's relationship to the audience (as an "outsider" and as a fellow diasporan, respectively), and offer contrasting exam-

ples of how staging conditions (the urban mise-en-scène versus an experimental theater venue) affect how the performance event creates a sense of
community "at home" and in the diaspora. Moreover, the Apia and Sydney
shows enable a comparison of how, and to what ends, the memory of the
German Samoa period is evoked strategically as a conduit for cultural
remittances that relay and endorse narratives, practices, and values in contexts of direct transnationalism and intradiasporic transnationalism.

In Samoa, Tuffery directed three multimedia performances as free public events that took place in and around Apia.[162] Each featured an architectural projection installation where a giant digital montage was superim-
posed on the exterior facades of historical buildings, such as the German-era
Old Courthouse. The one-hour display of static and moving images,
including video footage and samplings from Tuffery's visual art pieces for
the project, was accompanied by live music from the Royal Samoa Police
Band. A local institution, the Police Band plays a form of Viennese brass
band music; every morning, they parade through central Apia from the
police headquarters to Government House, where they perform the
national anthem and raise the Samoan flag. While the band serenaded the
buildings and audiences with a repertoire of customary Samoan music and
old-time German songs, interspersed with their own singing in polyphonic
harmony, female dancers ("all of German descent")[163] from Le Taupou
Manaia dance group performed their *siva fa'a-taupou* (princess dance) in
synchronization with the band. Each dancer wore one of Tuffery's large,
ornamental hair combs, produced by the artist in hot pink (red) acrylic,
black acrylic, and (white) rimu wood (*Dacrydium cupressinum*) to reference
the tricolor standard of the German Samoan colony. The flag was never
flown due to the outbreak of World War I, but it still has pride of place
today in some Samoan homes.[164] As is typical of Tuffery's work, each comb
represents a retooling and elaborating of its already intercultural design to
create synthesized vignettes that encode and condense elements of the
complex crossings between the two nations.

This multisensory experience was designed to provoke an affective
response, stirring memories among an older generation of Samoans and
educating a younger generation about a legacy rapidly disappearing from
sight and living memory. As the first type of large-scale media installation
art in public spaces in Samoa, Tuffery's work employed an innovative diasporic art form to reroute and return Samoa's transnational archives with a
difference. Specifically, it cultivated a critical poetics of nostalgia to encourage local modes of historical consciousness that reflect the artist's own values and concerns about changes to Samoan society occasioned both by the

Figure 19. Michel Tuffery, *Tava'e ma le lua Solofanua at Brandenburg Gate Berlin* (*Tropicbird and Two Horses at Brandenburg Gate Berlin*), 2011. H. 290 × L. 270 × W. 3 mm. Laser-cut comb in black acrylic worn by female dancers in the Apia, Porirua, and Sydney performances of *Siamani Samoa*. Based on Samoan *selu pa'u/selu la'au*, the intricate design echoes the fretwork on German-era colonial buildings; the three holes at the base reference German coconut plantations in Samoa. Depicting two horses from the Berlin Quadriga with a Samoan tropic-bird (instead of the Prussian eagle), the comb recalls the presence of Samoa in Germany, alluding to Tupua Tamasese Lealofi II's visit to Berlin in 1910. Photograph by Diana Looser; personal collection of the author, gift of the artist.

absence of a migrant middle generation and by the impact of foreign development on the self-governing microstate.[165] Tuffery's counterstream tackled the problem of the number of German-era historical structures in Apia and Samoa being demolished without record and replaced with modern edifices funded by East Asian (especially Chinese) compensatory development. In contrast to Tuvalu, which, as noted in chapter 3, recognizes Taiwan as a diplomatic partner, Samoa was one of the first Pacific nations to cement diplomatic relations with China in 1975, and the government has actively used this partnership to further its own development agendas.[166] These infrastructural gains, however, are sustained in light of increasing local anxieties about Chinese domination of the business sector, limited sovereignty through debt and dependence on foreign assistance, and recent legislation in favor of Chinese investors that undermines safeguards for Samoans' customary land rights.[167]

Civic landmarks that were depicted or that performed in *Siamani Samoa* included the original Fale Fono (Parliament House, 1916) and the first hospital at Moto'otua (1912), both replaced by Chinese aid projects. The old Apia Courthouse (1902), still standing for the performance, was superseded in 2010 by a Chinese-sponsored Courts Administration Building and was demolished in 2020 to make way for a hotel. *Siamani Samoa*'s cultural remittances, then, attempted to change local Samoan culture (or at least to encourage debate) by sending back principles of heritage conservation modeled in New Zealand. As Tuffery put it in a Radio New Zealand interview, "I was explaining [to the Samoans] that Wellington was a really successful city as far as maintaining historical buildings . . . I feel we've got it right here in Wellington and it's just trying to share that over in Samoa, the importance of these buildings, because these buildings are like visual diaries."[168] Tuffery's project was thus situated within a multilateral transnational matrix, whereby German colonial memory was activated via New Zealand's neoliberal notions of urban preservation and regeneration, and deployed in part as a means to balance Samoa's national identity with its MIRAB state aspirations by combating Asian donor neocolonialism in the globalizing Pacific Century.

The architectural projection installation on the facade of the Old Courthouse offers a finer view of how these effects were worked out in the performance. The building was enlivened with animated forms, transforming into a dynamic construction that opened out its accreted affective, historical, and political content. This imagery, together with the live musicians and dancers, encouraged meaningful relationships between the spectators and the architecture, defamiliarizing the structure and encouraging the community to view it anew in ways that might aid its preservation. Akin to Rosanna Raymond's performative activations, which *teu le vā* in their ceremonial relation between the human and the material artifact, Tuffery invigorated the neglected Courthouse structure, reinvesting it with potent animacy. The Courthouse was suffused with kaleidoscopic patterns—symmetrical and repeating—that bled into one another with stained-glass vividness, melting into abstraction and then congealing, revealing with startling clarity a place or object, a face, or a video sequence before fading like ghosts. The projected images diversified, multiplied, came into convergence, transformed again, then reappeared. Spectators saw, variously, black-and-white photos of colonial Apia, studio portraits of *taupou* (whose memory was echoed by the dancers),[169] and Tuffery's paintings of Solf and of paramount chief Tupua Tamasese Lealofi II. This latter portrait referenced Tamasese's visit to Berlin in 1910. Despite being displayed in several German zoos as part of a *völkerschau* (ethnographic show), he saw himself as an ambassador on a diplomatic mission and met with Kaiser Wilhelm; images of the Kaiser's watch, gifted to Tamasese, acknowledged this recognition and reciprocity. Elsewhere, inter alia, people were confronted with images of the German Parliament Building, the beloved Mulivai Cathedral in graduated states of demolition, and the German coconut plantations that transformed Samoa's landscape. This copious cultural archive, playing out across the Courthouse's two-story timber frame, interspersed with the built structure, foregrounding the building's own role as a backdrop to this era, while at the same time stimulating memories of its important subsequent role in Samoa's modern history and road to independence; for example, as the site for the lowering of German flag and the raising of the British one in 1914, and as the place where Mau resistance leader Tupua Tamasese Lealofi III was fatally shot by New Zealand police in 1929.[170]

Albert Refiti's theories of Samoan cosmogony, space, and architecture provide useful ways of interpreting the significance of the arrangement of Tuffery's digital montage. Refiti discusses the complementary and oscillating concepts of *mavae*, how things "grow, extend, proliferate and circulate outwards by finding new pathways and connections," and *tofiga*, which "locates, gathers, corrals and appoints things and people to places" by providing them with a foothold.[171] *Mavae* and *tofiga* alternate to form the world,[172] with their alternation built into the form of genealogy (*gafa*), whereby the unfolding "process of becoming is interspersed with moments of refolding, redistribution and recombining."[173] A relationship to the past eschews the Western linear narrative of progressive history in favor of the Polynesian concept of tā/vā (time-space) that suggests movement toward a future in which one's being is oriented to a dynamic past, an "ever-moving ancestor-duration"[174] in which past, present, and future revolve together, rather than being treated as separate.[175] Within this genealogical schema, different generations and events, rather than starting or finishing, are understood as "comings and goings," as patterns "that are diffracted, diffused, obviated and converged at different stages,"[176] a processual, transforming sequence of events "which also suggests . . . the idea of a chain of images mixing or separating."[177] This dynamic of diversification and convergence, comprising many parts that are all part of one another, is linked to the Samoan idea of personhood as an interconnected matrix, a sum of many parts in a connected vā system, extending out and feeding back in.[178]

From this point of view, it is possible to see Tuffery's nonlinear interlacing of abstract and documentary elements that expand, contract, morph, multiply, and converge as visualizing an Indigenous Samoan genealogy. What this accomplishes in the local Samoan context is to enfold Wilhelminian *Weltpolitik* and its vestiges into a dominant process of Samoan becoming rather than understanding it as an alien and alienating imposition, and allows one to reflect on history as the work's transtemporal scheme constantly translates the past into the present. In so doing, the project's form and content constitutes a vā negotiation, evoking a web of constitutive lines of equal relationship between Samoa and Germany. Tuffery's cultural remittance to Apia, in the form of diasporic art that combines foreign aesthetics and Indigenous principles, urges a community rethinking of the German period to nurture Samoan pride in ways that resist the developmental telos of Asia-Pacific modernity.

The Sydney show in 2015, which I attended as an invited guest of the artist, added Australia to the Samoa–Germany–New Zealand triangulation.[179] It was a more mature performance that integrated material from earlier phases of the *Siamani Samoa* series, including new additions drawn from Tuffery's research and exhibition in Germany in 2014 to mark the centenary of German cession. The biggest shift in focus was that the performance was not a "homecoming" to Samoa remitted by a diasporic artist, but operated intradiasporically, with Tuffery reaching out from New Zealand to connect with Samoan church and cultural groups in the Sydney area, and "exporting" Samoa via the seventeen members of the Royal Samoa Police Band on their first international tour. The Australian setting also modified the performance's cultural remittance work, demonstrating its operations beyond a homeland-hostland binary. In this case, information about the German Samoan period that had been accumulated throughout the project was remitted via New Zealand to an Australian Samoan community in order to cultivate offshore relationships with Samoa from new perspectives. To achieve this effect, whereas the Apia show depended on a site-specific, urban mise-en-scène, the Sydney show transformed Carriageworks, an experimental theater venue, into a "Samoa space" that temporarily grounded its moving audiences. Refiti observes that *mavae* and *tofiga* have accrued new diasporic meanings, connoting a spreading out from a compressed community to encompass multiple worlds, and then becoming knotted, finding a fixed position in the diaspora. When social gatherings are no longer connected to traditional ancestral places in the *nu'u* (village), *tofiga* becomes a "mobile concept" that "appoints identity within the community rather than tangibly connecting people to place."[180] For Refiti, the *fale* (meeting house) offers a quintessential "image of an affective structure of belonging that Samoans actively use to signal the weaving and fortifying of relations gathered under one roof."[181] In the diaspora, it signals "the collective binding of communities on the move" without ancestral ties to their new home;[182] significantly, it is possible for a building without a traditional *fale* architecture to gather and combine a new community in this way.[183]

Accordingly, the makeover of the high proscenium theater of Carriageworks' Bay 17 created what I'll call a "virtual *fale*" to corral and bind its audiences. In addition to the large pieces of decorated *siapo* (barkcloth) and *i'e tōga* (fine mats) that framed the proscenium and the raised stage, which functioned as a *paepae*, or elevated platform in a *fale* that acts as a threshold between the mundane world below and the divine realm above,[184] a huge projection screen behind the stage presented the close-up image of the trussed interior roof structure of a village *fale*. As Refiti notes of the symbolism of the lashings, "The fale with its woven roof is concerned with fixing, binding and knotting people together."[185] To the audience's right were displayed nineteen of Tuffery's laser-cut combs. This artwork component, Refiti contends, fills a gap in the absence of traditional ritual attractors in the *fale*; in the diaspora, the work of the *tufuga-fautele* (housebuilder) has been transferred to the artist in the development of contemporary Pacific art.[186] All this, together with the *umu* meal, the opening *'ava* ceremony,[187] and the speeches delivered by a *tulāfale* (orator chief), created a charged vā-space between people and locations, the past and the present.

Within this milieu, the Police Band performed their repertoire alongside dancers from the Sydney community. The first act, as in Apia, concentrated on projected archival imagery from the German colonial period backed by German and Viennese tunes. The second act, however, changed tack to cultivate affective relationships with Samoa from Australia. After standing for

Figure 20. The Royal Samoa Police Band perform to a backdrop of Michel Tuffery's photographic montages and video art combining German and Samoan imagery, in *Siamani Samoa* at Carriageworks, Sydney, 2015. Photograph by, and courtesy of, Susannah Wimberley.

the Samoan national anthem, we were serenaded with sentimental Samoan numbers like "I Left My Heart in Samoa," "Samoa Matalasi," and "Sei Oriana," which resonated with pleasing images of Samoan towns and landscapes, flora and fauna, and smiling locals. Female dancers, wearing the combs, approached the forestage and danced along with the brass band, followed by young boys performing an energetic *fa'ataupati* (slap dance) to live Samoan drumming against a backdrop of footage of a *siva afi* (fire dance). The act culminated in the *taualuga* (customarily, the final dance at a Samoan event), and everyone present was invited to join the dance "in the spirit of one country, one team, one Samoa."[188]

For Tuffery, the "performance" does not reside in the action on stage, but rather in the interactions between the audience members, and he gauges its success according to the conversations that people are compelled to begin.[189] The audiences for the performances were predominantly Samoan. During the matinee, I sat beside an elderly lady from Savai'i who had left Samoa thirty years before and had since lived in New Zealand and

Australia, making regular trips back to Samoa. She observed that it was unusual for a *pālagi* to be watching the show and asked me if I was German. This lady, like many other older audience members, clapped, laughed, and called out throughout the show, and approached the stage to donate money for the band. She and her friends sang along to all the songs in the second half of the performance; as we snacked on peanuts, she volunteered memories and told me about the different Samoan songs and their significance. I watched the evening performance with a German man of about my age from the Sydney Goethe-Institut, one of the show's sponsors. His response was very different. He was particularly discomfited by the first act of the performance, especially the Samoans' singing of the German national anthem. As a self-identified member of Germany's second postwar generation, he evinced anxiety about avowals of German nationalism and what he perceived to be a valorization of Germany's erstwhile imperial ambitions, and found the experience alienating. These dissensual reactions, while individual rather than representative, shed light on the complex cultural work of *Siamani Samoa*. Beyond its direct transnational and intradiasporic transnational connections between Samoans on-island and abroad, the project's remittances travel out to Germans and Germany, forcing a reconsideration of that historical relationship and the terms on which it might be reactivated. The work, furthermore, suggests how an Indigenous response to the Germans in Samoa might complicate postcolonial theorizations of the dynamics between colonizer and colonized. The patterns of identification and disidentification that course through and help construct the performance event speak to the dense layerings of Indigeneity, diaspora, and colonialism that constitute the region, and are worked out differently in the following section across the American Pacific.

AMERICA'S TROPICAL FRONTIER? AMERIKA SĀMOA IN THE DIASPORIC IMAGINATION

The United States' interest in Samoa in the late nineteenth century was driven by naval and commercial ambitions. The deepwater harbor of Pago Pago offered a safe stopping point and potential coal depot for the transpacific steamers that would help America pursue its "New Manifest Destiny" in the form of lucrative Asian markets. Yet the 1899 partition, which ceded the islands of Tutuila, Manu'a, and Aunu'u to the United States, came just after the Spanish-American War, during which the United States gained new Pacific Island possessions that opened a northern route to Asia. Almost overnight, eastern Samoa went from being a focus of desire to being largely irrelevant to US interests, and was placed under a protective but loose naval administration that generally left the Samoan population alone to maintain their customary lifestyles on their own lands. This situation transformed suddenly, profoundly, and permanently with the onset of World War II, when the neglected South Pacific colony became a strategic linchpin in the United States' conflict with Japan. The massive influx of marines, munitions, and material goods, as well as the injection of cash into a subsistence economy, irrevocably changed Samoan tastes, lifestyles, and ambitions, and set in motion the mechanisms for postwar migration.[190] The first major exodus was military, and took place when the navy handed over administration of American Samoa to the US Department of the Interior in 1951 and transferred its operations to bases in Hawai'i and California. Military and nonmilitary migration accelerated, especially with the advent of a commercial air service to Hawai'i in 1959,[191] and by the 1960s it had become "institutionalized as a rite-of-passage for young Samoans."[192]

As US nationals (but not US citizens), American Samoans can hold US passports and live and work freely in the United States, yet despite the large numbers of off-island Samoans, including those from independent Samoa, they make up only a tiny proportion (less than 0.5%) of America's overall population. Demographically, Samoans are lumped into the amorphous "Pacific Islander American" category, or formerly, the more problematic "Asian Pacific American" conglomerate. On the mainland, there is little visibility or support for creative Pacific work, although there is more infrastructure and recognition in Hawai'i. These theater voices, however, are significant aspects of this transpacific sociospatial network, and are important for evaluating and imagining Samoan experience in the context of America's enduring colonial entanglements in Oceania. Here, I discuss two contrasting takes: Dan Taulapapa McMullin's *Pink Heaven*, written from California, and Victoria Nalani Kneubuhl's *The Holiday of Rain*, produced in Hawai'i. If Polytoxic encouraged the concept of an archipelagic Australian theater, then these American Samoan works might similarly be understood to promote an archipelagic American theater from the Pacific.

Pink Heaven received a staged reading at the Asian American Theatre Company in San Francisco in 2000, directed by Māori film and theater artist Rena Owen. The child of Samoan parents who met in San Francisco, with a father in the US Army, Taulapapa was born in Sendai, Japan, and spent his early years on military bases in Europe, the continental United States, and Hawai'i, before moving to American Samoa with his mother to live with relatives while his father served in Vietnam. Later, Taulapapa's immediate family relocated to San Pedro, California, where he grew up, trained as a visual artist, and spent several years working in the television industry in Los Angeles. During the 1990s, Taulapapa, who identifies as *fa'afafine*, expanded his art practice to incorporate prose writing, poetry, and performance work, as well as filmmaking and painting, developing a diverse body of work that explores critical—sometimes controversial—views of migration, queer sexuality, and colonialism in a transnational Samoan context.[193] Taulapapa's work as a transnational artist manifests not only in the content of his art pieces but also in their production across multiple geopolitical spaces; his artistic period of the past generation has been characterized by a consistent movement between independent and American Samoa and the US mainland, spending several months at a time in each place. He notes, "Everything, from my first story, was about Samoa. I have a life here in America, I'm an American, but everything I've ever written has been about Samoa. I guess that's the part of my life that has defined me, but has also defined my difference here in the United States."[194]

As a Samoan artist in the United States, Taulapapa maintains a transnational and mutually influential artistic circle of Samoan and other Pacific Islander colleagues that spans the United States and Hawai'i, New Zealand, Australia, and the Samoas. Yet he also speaks to a different dynamic that arises from the United States' ongoing colonial relationship with Samoa, the status of American Samoans as an ethnic minority within an expansive and largely apathetic nation-state, and the relative lack of a Pasifika artistic community in contrast to sites such as New Zealand. He admits, "Sometimes I used to envy my friends in New Zealand so much because they're so supported by the culture, compared to trying to be a Polynesian in the United States as a minority group. Pacific Islander culture within the structure of the United States doesn't receive the same kind of support for the arts. I don't know if that's good or bad. I used to think it was a bad thing, and now, aesthetically, I think I do some things that are different from artists in New Zealand."[195] Arguably, these include greater independence to remit more challenging interpretations of contemporary American Samoa under US control, and greater impetus to bear witness to the breakdown of vā relationality between Samoans under this form of modernity. Taulapapa's work also interrogates the nature of the vā relationship between Samoa and America, drawing attention to how the absorption of the islands by a major world power has long been met with administrative deferral and arm's-length assistance that continues to withhold the full benefits and privileges of American belonging.

Pink Heaven, which the playwright describes as "my most personal and most painful work,"[196] is a domestic realist play that employs the scenario of return migration to foreground Taulapapa's concern about the ways American Samoa has deteriorated under the aegis of the US government's military and civil bureaucracies. The action takes place in a house in the fictional Lealataua village on the western side of Tutuila in the early twenty-first century. Loto, an affluent and recently widowed woman who left American Samoa as a young postwar migrant, returns home after fifty years in San Francisco, bringing her younger son, Lele, a queer poet. Loto's plan is to enjoy her final years in her childhood village, build a beautiful "white house with electric lights and swans,"[197] and spend time with her eldest son, Pai, her daughter-in-law, Peti, and their children, who now occupy the old family home. But the homecoming is a nightmare: Pai remains mysteriously sequestered in his room, leaving Loto in the hands of Peti, a disturbed cocaine addict with a history of sexual abuse. Peti is also a return migrant raised in Wilmington, California, who fled back to Samoa after she and Pai killed an elderly man in a hit-and-run car accident. Harboring a deep resentment and paranoia toward Loto, whom she sees as a threat to her imagined paradise and unfettered route to material assets, Peti systematically dispossesses and isolates her mother-in-law while putting regular doses of rat poison into Loto's ice water, eventually killing the old woman.

As an affective gesture and "imaginative return"[198] sent back to American Samoa and to the wider United States, Taulapapa's play resonates with Kezia Page's concept of the "remittance text"; that is, the text sent from the diaspora that highlights the inequalities of the exchange between "denizens of the metropolitan diaspora" and "people who live in the region, traditionally separated as 'First' and 'Third' world spaces respectively."[199] Even though all the characters in the play are both diasporic and local, both First and Third World, and their space holds qualities of the rural and of the metropolitan that they bring with them, the remittance text usefully takes a critical-ethical position on the relationship between the homeland and the diaspora, directing attention to relations between those at home and those away, including inequalities between members of the same diasporic community. It furthermore takes on issues of power inherent in the monetary remittance transfers that frequently accompany cultural transactions. Taulapapa's remittance text figures American Samoa as a kind of "fallen Eden." Although this is a recurrent trope in Western literature about the Pacific, persisting through Jack London, Somerset Maugham, and Paul Theroux,[200] these writers, as Paul Lyons notes, usually undergird their critiques with "a sense of imperial nostalgia in the face of an Oceania in the process of being contaminated."[201] Taulapapa stages his anticolonial and antitouristic account from a Polynesian perspective, lamenting the deleterious impacts on a culture propped up by American monetary largesse, especially the dissolution of cultural practices and heritage, family ties, and respect for elders. Taulapapa's critique addresses Samoan complicity in this process, particularly through the counterstreams remitted via migration circuits. The play questions the implications of these easy-access routes to and from the States, asking whether they improve people's lives or simply generate a set of new problems.

The homestead in *Pink Heaven* serves as a metaphor for the family's disintegrated state as well as for broader cultural corrosion. The "old American house," built in "South Pacific colonial (military/missionary) style,"[202] has "tropical decay everywhere. Lizards on the ceiling. Termite infested wood. . . . Rusted appliances and broken, cloth-covered furniture,"[203] while tire tracks plow up the once-meticulous lawn and Pai's wreck of a truck litters the front yard. The house exists in uneasy tension with its lush environs of green mountains, palms, breadfruit, and plumeria trees, an odd foreign import that probably fit its setting better in the past than it does today. In this regard, the neglected house becomes symbolic not only of a compromised Samoan culture but also of a degraded US one: Loto's comment "So much money from the States on this island, and the island looks worse every day"[204] speaks to how the earlier colonial order has given rise to the apathy of contemporary US territorial management, which has undermined Samoan indigeneity while at the same time opening doors for large numbers of emigrants who leave things to rot at home.

The battle between Loto and Peti epitomizes this clash of values and aspirations. From one perspective, theirs is a personal struggle whereby Taulapapa adumbrates subtler contours of Samoan migrant experiences through attention to the stratifications of race and class that diversify and divide members of migrant groups. The pictures of Samoan and American ancestors that line the walls of the family home adduce a history of intermarriage: we learn that "because of [Loto's] mixed heritage, she could pass as white in some places,"[205] an asset that has almost certainly smoothed her passage when navigating the racial hierarchies of the US mainland. Classy and impeccably groomed, she has lived a comfortable life in her "big house in San Francisco."[206] Peti, in contrast, is "big, dark, angry but empty,"[207] brought up in a "shack"[208] in a working-class suburb of Los Angeles and raped daily by her father while her mother worked as a prostitute at the east end of the Carson Mall. Peti's victimization of Loto emerges as an act of revenge born of class and racial jealousy, as well as an avaricious desire to absorb Loto's considerable material wealth, taking advantage of the breakdown of the customary social order to effect this goal:

> LOTO: In old Samoa you would not even sit in the same room as me and when you brought me tea you would slide across the floor.
> PETI: That was then, this is now.[209]

Peti's ambition to realize her version of the American Dream denied to her on the mainland is, ironically, only possible in the quasi United States of American Samoa, where federal appropriations and generous welfare checks help finance her junk-food binges, her drug-fueled lunch dates with the governor's daughter, her new cars, and her gaggle of Western Samoan maids. Foreign cultural norms that privilege individual capital accumulation lead Peti to violate protocols of the *fa'a Sāmoa*, such as her habit of taking all the food, wreaths, and fine mats after *fa'alavelave*[210] and having her maids sell them at the market.[211] Here, central symbols of reciprocity and harmonious vā relations that lie at the heart of local and transnational Samoan exchanges are traded in for cash, registering the impact of crass commercial values on long-held, holistic systems of community cohesion.

That the "empty" Peti has become a receptacle for the worst excesses of contemporary American culture encourages a reading of the women's relationship as an analogy for the multivalent ways in which US globalization saps the energy and agency of Samoan lifeways. As a remnant of the "old Samoa," Loto, "once very fit and now frail,"[212] is cowed into submission by the bigger, brasher, younger, and more cunning woman; Loto is being consumed in her own space, while Peti's legal maneuvering questions even that status. But Taulapapa's remittance text does not pitch Samoa and the United States solely against each other, but uses two *totolua* (mixed-race)[213] characters who have lived in both worlds to construct a more nuanced thesis about the mutual, multigenerational imbrication of the two spaces. Loto's recalled Samoa is also a colonial one, of neat lawns cut with metal knives, starched and ironed pinafores, and missionary schooling, and then "American Marines crying like babies on the operating tables," heralding the moment "when everything changed in Samoa."[214] If Loto's homecoming is a (futile) quest to recapture a nostalgically rendered era of Samoan familial respect, order, and loyalty that still persisted under prewar naval rule, then US-born Peti's migration to contemporary Samoa is a quest for a place where she can be truly American. As she tells Loto, "You should go live in the so-called independent nation of Western Samoa. You're in the eastern islands: American Samoa. We live like Californians here."[215]

The most visceral symbol of decay and contamination is the mostly absent character of Pai. Hidden in his room for the majority of the play, pounding periodically on the wall, he emerges at the close of the final scene and shuffles agonizingly to the door of his dead mother's room, "leprous, skin covered with sores and swollen. Face sunken."[216] In presenting the abject body of the once star surfer and footballer as a metaphor for colonial degradation and loss of spirit in the territory of American Samoa,[217] Taulapapa places his work within the counternarrative of a diseased Pacific that has long been part of Pacific discourse. As Rod Edmond observes, during the nineteenth century especially, leprosy was moralized as "a just punishment for a corrupt and diseased society,"[218] with numerous writers employing the leprosy trope "as an image of the dismembering and putrefying effects of colonialism,"[219] particularly to comment on the parlous cultural condition of US territories. In Polynesian culture, Edmond explains, leprosy figures as the opposite of *tatau*: whereas *tatau* inscribes and builds up genealogical stories, social and cultural histories, and kinship relations on the skin, strengthening the individual's ties to community, leprosy attacks and destroys the skin, impairing its protecting and mediating functions, and its boundary relations between self and other, individual and society.[220] Instead of Pai's virile masculinity and social networks finding expression in the *pe'a*, his corporeal corruption presents a decrepit and disturbing image of a dislocated and corrupted community in the wake of Loto's death.

What room is there for redemption, then, in this toxic tale of anomie and cultural evacuation? The play finds hope in the return encounter of Lele (the character with whom Taulapapa identifies most strongly). As a counter to heteronormative masculinity, which finds its dissolution in Pai, Lele's processes of transculturation as a queer subject allow the play to explore alternative facets of Samoan sexuality and their relationship to migrant experiences. Lele's early childhood in Samoa was characterized by *fa'afafine* culture, where a broader spectrum of identities was permissible. He relates the brutal culture shock of attending school in California with "my face made up and wearing a girl's blouse" and being "beaten," "kicked," and "spit on,"[221] and his painful adjustment to performing an "appropriate" gay identity in the United States.[222] Lele's return to Samoa is similarly difficult: doing menial labor on the floor of the fish cannery, he is sexually harassed by his workmates and victimized by Peti over the erotic content of his published volume of poetry. Using the otherwise disenfranchising US administrative system to drive a wedge between Samoans themselves, Peti declares, "I took a copy to the Governor. He called the U.S. Department of the Interior. They said it's salacious and seditious. Lele is . . . a fag trai-torer."[223] When Peti tries the homophobic gambit of stealing Lele's clothes and forcing him to wear a dress, Lele is initially horrified: "I can't walk around like this. . . . I don't choose to be a fa'afafine,"[224] but to Peti's cha-grin, he discovers new freedoms, privileges, and social acceptance in this embodied role—"Now, people seem to have different expectations of me. And I feel comfortable with them"[225]—and lands a good job as secretary to the local tuna company officials. Ultimately, Lele's renewed identification as a *fa'afafine* stimulates his shift from wanting to "leave and go home to San Francisco"[226] to claiming that Samoa "is my homeland."[227]

Lele's geographic, emotional, and sexual journeys therefore complicate the emplotment of queer migration "as a movement toward a 'liberated' gay or lesbian identity and the corollary implication that queer migrants would thus find a return to their more 'repressive' countries of origin undesirable."[228] They also challenge the attendant assumption that queer subjects who choose to return "would also transmit or directly bring back—as a form of social remittance—their new-found conceptions of sex-ual identity and, perhaps, would encourage or even impel the social and political processes and formations that enable public expressions of lesbian and gay identities in countries in the global north."[229] Maja Horn argues, as *Pink Heaven* does implicitly, for a critical interrogation of the "modernity-tradition divide" and the "chronopolitics of development"[230] that under-write much international LGBTQ discourse, and to think in more complex ways about how migratory queer ideas and practices travel and the "queer 'homework'"[231] that they enact, beyond simply imposing new ideas "brought home." Lele's adaptation to the continuing possibilities of the *fa'a Sāmoa* represents a productive alternative to the limiting categories of US queer culture, offering ways of relating to his homeland that are generative and more expansive, and that exceed the distortions of Peti's constructed world. Indeed, it is Lele's newfound social status that proves to be Peti's downfall when Lele makes it known to the community that Peti murdered his mother. After Peti devolves into madness and is overcome by the villag-ers as she attempts to drown Pai's illegitimate newborn (whom she believes is possessed by Loto's vengeful spirit), we sense that Lele will occupy the family home and begin a process of social and cultural regeneration medi-ated through his creative role as artist.

This returns us to the figure of the artist and to Taulapapa as author of the remittance text, an emotive investment in American Samoa that spans two spaces and reaches toward potentially transformative possibilities. The critical-ethical attention to the social conditions of colonialism and globalization can be discomfiting for diasporic and homeland audiences. Taula-papa's work has often caused controversy in Samoan communities in the United States and Samoa; although he is a major artist whose work has received international critical acclaim, in American Samoa he has had projects banned or defunded on the grounds of being too sexual or political. This is to the extent that when he comes back, Taulapapa admits, it has often been easier for him to live in independent Samoa than in American Samoa.[232] The artist's own homecomings, then, are laced with difficulty, lending an exilic quality to his diasporan experience: "back and forth throughout my life, like a seabird in the north, like a seabird in the south."[233] Yet, as Sinavaiana Gabbard reminds us, Samoan writers working with confronting material (abuse, violence, broken families, and cultural dislocation) testify to the violation of vā among characters due to colonialism and cultural dissonance, and symbolize vā by showing empathy for their suffering. In this context, Taulapapa's *Pink Heaven* tries to cultivate and reconstruct vā relationships in social and spiritual dimensions, opening up spaces in the vā of this vexing historical moment.[234]

• • •

A very different formal and thematic take on American Samoa's relations with the United States and the Pacific is presented in *The Holiday of Rain* by Victoria Nalani Kneubuhl, one of Oceania's foremost dramatists. Of Samoan and Native Hawaiian descent and raised in Samoa and Hawai'i, Kneubuhl, based in Honolulu, has written numerous plays based on her Samoan and Hawaiian heritage that have been produced extensively throughout the Pacific, the United States, and Europe. Kneubuhl's Hawaiian works are predominantly historical dramas that treat critical issues in Hawai'i's colonial past;[235] her plays set in Samoa—while also frequently historiographic—tend to have a lighter tone and a heightened sense of metatheatricality. Key characteristics of her work include a temporal fluidity between the past and the present, the incursion of the numinous into the mundane world, and an interrogation of limiting depictions of women and Pacific Islanders. *The Holiday of Rain* shifts focus from Taulapapa's realist aesthetic to consider how farce and fantasy can be vectors for cultural remittances; it also broadens the geographical frame by tying American Samoan concerns to wider Hawaiian and transpacific ones.

The Holiday of Rain, commissioned in 2011 for the fortieth anniversary season of Honolulu's Kumu Kahua Theatre, is set in the transpacific nexus of Pago Pago in the 1910s and the 2010s. Through a mélange of history, myth, speculative fiction, and postcolonial critique, Kneubuhl redresses the racist and misogynist framings of modernist literary representations of the Pacific with a comic, cross-temporal repositioning of Somerset Maugham's short story "Rain." "Rain" (1921) was one of a series of "South Seas" narratives penned by the British writer and dramatist during his Pacific travels, and became his most famous, reprinted and replayed on page, stage, and screen throughout the twentieth century. Describing the battle of fire-and-brimstone missionary Reverend Davidson for the soul of prostitute Sadie Thompson, and ending with Davidson's suicide after he succumbs to his desire for Sadie, the story had its inception during a voyage that Maugham took with his secretary and lover, Gerald Haxton, from Hawai'i to Tahiti in December 1916. Quarantined en route in the newly acquired US naval outpost of Pago Pago, Maugham took notes on the township and its locals, the boarding house, the missionary couple on board the steamer, and "Miss Thompson" from Honolulu's notorious Iwilei red-light district; and later, in a conflation of travel ethnography and fiction, transposed the descriptions almost verbatim into his tale, along with the same supercilious tone.[236]

What Kneubuhl describes as a "screwball play" was inspired by her childhood in American Samoa: "When I was a girl, my parents moved to Samoa in 1962 and lived not far from the house where Somerset Maugham, Gerald Haxton and Miss Thompson stayed. My grandfather remembered their visit."[237] Although Kneubuhl notes that "'Rain' is probably the piece of Western Literature most associated with Pago Pago,"[238] she is alert to the broader regional remit of Maugham's disparaging stereotypes: "As a Pacific Island writer, it is hard to resist wanting to comment on one of the Western writers who first wrote about the Pacific and contributed to so many images the Western world would come to hold about islanders."[239] Taking advantage of the autobiographical correlations between Maugham's own journey and "Rain," in Kneubuhl's play Maugham and Haxton become subject to a spell cast by the notorious early-twentieth-century occultist Aleister Crowley (as vengeance for Maugham's—historically accurate—plagiarism of Crowley in his 1908 novel, *The Magician*), and all three are accidentally transported to present-day American Samoa. At the Sadie Thompson Bed & Breakfast (named for its famous forebear),[240] staff and locals run "fantasy visits" based on a scripted "Rain" scenario for wealthy gay couples from the US mainland who want to role-play as Maugham and Haxton, an enterprise that, as proprietor Tinamoni admits, is "so much work—hiding the electrical outlets and the overhead lights, hours of research."[241] Complicit in their tourist commodification, costumed actors who are mostly *afakasi* and look to varying degrees Samoan or *pālagi* take the roles of the David-

Figure 21. Eleanor Svaton as Effie Von Elsner in her role as Sadie Thompson and Tyler Tanabe as Gerald Haxton in Kumu Kahua's production of *The Holiday of Rain* (2011), by Victoria Nalani Kneubuhl. Directed by Harry Wong. Photograph courtesy of Kumu Kahua Theatre, Honolulu, Hawai'i.

sons, Sadie, Dr. Macphail and his wife, and the local "natives," and perform a heavily ironic and kitschy replaying of old South Seas stereotypes.
Maugham and Haxton are mistaken for a visiting couple and—with Crowley co-opted as a last-minute replacement for the actor playing Davidson—
are incorporated into a self-reflexive scenario that is at once a politically
loaded farce and, inevitably, the "historical" basis for Maugham's influential story.

Christopher Balme interprets the Broadway version of "Rain" as one of
several mid-twentieth-century representations of the Pacific that (after
Freud) he terms "dramas of displacement," where "displacement" is
understood as "a dramaturgical and theatrical strategy whereby local
issues are played out in remote milieus whose existence is only possible
because of colonial projects." Both "microcosms of the colonising power
and liminal spaces where Western patterns of behaviour and control never
fully pertain," these colonial settings enable the reexamination of (Western)
cultural questions.[242] In Maugham's narrative, the local Samoans are back-
ground scenery, while the European characters are the "displaced
people"—quarantined travelers or military personnel. The battle of wills
enacted in the outpost between two American citizens, culminating in
Sadie's triumph (and the completion of her own transpacific crossing from
San Francisco, Honolulu, Pago Pago, Apia, and finally—victoriously—to
Sydney), on the American stage becomes the ground for a Western cultural
struggle, representing the freedom of a younger US generation from older
Calvinist mores.[243]

In bringing temporal dislocation to bear on geographical transposition,
and having Samoans play *papālagi* and an occultist play a missionary,
Kneubuhl stages a new drama of displacement that sets the stage for examining Pacific cultural questions instead. These questions primarily involve
competing matters of Pacific Islander agency and representation in the
wake of colonialism that cut across racial, gendered, and religious lines,
and, as in Polytoxic's work, are at once locally specific and applicable
across a broader regional matrix. However, the remittance work undertaken by *The Holiday of Rain* differs from the other examples in this chapter
in that the sending place or host site is not only a destination for Samoan
migration but also a Pacific Island under colonial control,[244] and Kneubuhl
addresses her audience as both a Samoan and a Native Hawaiian: a traveling Pacific Islander and an Indigenous inhabitant of that colonized site.
Routed through Kumu Kahua Theatre, an articulating joint between
regional American theater and Pasifika performance cultures, Kneubuhl's
remittances treat common concerns among the Indigenous peoples of the

region, nurturing and embellishing the vā-space between linked communities across Polynesia. At the same time, her work is particularly attentive to the resonances between Hawai'i and American Samoa as Polynesian entities under the colonial aegis of the United States, as well as the dialectic between indigeneity and migration that underpins Pasifika identity.

The play interrogates and refigures Maugham's underlying assumptions about the Pacific and its peoples; however, its metatheatrical take on role-playing centralizes issues of mimesis, alterity, and dis/identification that lie at the heart of colonial discourse, bearing witness to the intransigence of these views and their supporting structures. *The Holiday of Rain* resists conceptualizations of the Pacific as a mise-en-scène for predominantly Western social dramas, placing center stage Samoan characters with complicated lives who are themselves transnational subjects. Reed Edmond (Dr. Macphail) is a businessman traveling regularly between Apia and the United States, Theo Von Elsner (Mrs. Davidson) is an artist whose work is exhibited in San Francisco, while Charmian Drake (Mrs. Macphail) is a professor of Pacific literature on sabbatical from her US university and considers Maugham "one of the crowned pricks of the colonial canon."[245] These cosmopolitan professionals stand in positive contrast to the bounded natives who form a shadowy, menacing backdrop to Maugham's depiction of a deidealized Pacific: casual actors in a local tourist enterprise, performing (at least to begin with) with ironic distance between character and role, and dismantling the dynamics of their clichéd characterizations in between scenes.

Kneubuhl's drama foregrounds the constructed nature of Western imaginings of the Pacific; the fantasy folds in on itself as the very performances carried out by the actors expose the fiction of Maugham's recordings, especially his determination to perceive the Pacific as a fallen Eden and to cater to his readership's desire for the "dangerous" and "exotic locations that they would never dare visit."[246] Maugham, for instance, admires the inn, "But no-one would believe it could be this nice or this clean, and that's not what the public wants in a Pacific scenario. People want grit, flies, and heat. Yes, that's it, a worn bed, a ragged mosquito net, a rickety washstand, and rain, endless rain."[247] Likewise, Maugham decides, Effie's Sadie is "much too appealing. I'll have to make her more whore like,"[248] while Tinamoni's portrayal of innkeeper Mrs. Horn (a twenty-first-century version of Maugham's Mr. Horn) will "have to go. Too intelligent, too refined to be a native wife. She's probably horribly unstable, and we just haven't seen it yet. . . . Native women, mixed-blood women, just aren't like her!"[249] The veracity of Maugham's own performance threatens the critical distance enjoyed by some of the other participants; whereas Charmian is convinced that Maugham is a brilliant actor and scholar, and hopes that he will visit her university class to "do his little act" as "a living deconstruction of everything Maugham was,"[250] hotelier Blake Von Elsner, playing Sefo the "native helper," finds it hard to deal with Maugham's condescension and racist comments, performing his social role with increasing rebelliousness:

> MAUGHAM: *(To Blake)* Boy, coffee if you please.
> BLAKE *pours a cup, hands it to MAUGHAM.*
> BLAKE: Ua ou fiamimilo lou ua (*I want to twist your neck*).
> *TINA gives BLAKE "the eye" as he EXITS.*
> MAUGHAM: What does that mean?
> TINA: Oh, it means good day—only in *his* village, nowhere else.[251]

Similarly, as the fiction is sustained, other performers also find their typecast roles burdensome—even traumatic—as with the female characters playing Sadie Thompson (Effie Von Elsner) and Mrs. Davidson (Theo), who feel entrapped within the demeaning confines of the island-hopping prostitute and the repressed missionary wife.

That the narrow parameters of Maugham's imagination feed the characters' insecurities signals the other drama that accompanies and intersects with the "Rain" scenario. Part of appreciating the Samoa-based characters as complex, modern subjects is to acknowledge their pain, challenges, and failures: Blake's struggle to carry on after his parents' deaths, Charmian's history of drug and alcohol addiction, Theo's self-loathing and anger after her car crash that killed her former lover, Effie's unhappy marriage to a chronically unfaithful older man, and Reed's thwarted attempts to find redemption for the faults of his youth. In a move typical of Kneubuhl's dramaturgy, which infuses the supernatural and the quotidian, we learn that Tinamoni is a "holy guardian angel,"[252] an immortal being sent to guide, encourage, and spiritually uplift these "souls in [her] little circle."[253] This circumstance adds a different inflection to Tina's "Rain" redux beyond profitable tourist performance: through playing these assigned roles, the characters are given an opportunity to face up to, work through, and transcend the repressions, traumas, and crises analogized in the stereotypes they act out and to achieve personal growth. This subplot thus inscribes a further appropriation of Maugham's narrative, whereby critical, embodied scrutiny turns commercial clichés into forms of therapy for Pasifika characters.

Tina's ability to effect these conversions, however, is threatened by Crowley, who, doubling as Reverend Davidson, runs amok in the hotel, attempting various pseudo-Christian conversions on various characters—the gay Maugham included—fueling their sense of sin and guilt. It is this manifestation of Crowley as an avatar of colonial repression and division, which erupts from the past into the present, that the play is ultimately set to overcome. Here Hawaiian references that resonate for the play's Honolulu audiences overlay the Samoan setting. Although European missionaries had a tremendous influence in Samoa, they had not the same complicity in colonial annexation as in Hawai'i, where New England–driven conversion was figured as Americanization, and missionary-descendant oligarchs helped overthrow the Hawaiian monarchy. As Rob Wilson puts it, "These postcolonial days in Hawai'i, Christianity seems all but a cover story for settler colonialism, haole domination, and the master narrative of service to the macroforces of sugar, real estate, Polynesian tourism, and U.S. statehood."[254] While acknowledging this reality, Kneubuhl's own previous work (her 1988 play *The Conversion of Ka'ahumanu*, for example), has been more open to the transformative possibilities of conversion for women and the marginalized. In *The Holiday of Rain*, Kneubuhl resists the fatal contact narrative and gestures toward ways in which new acts of conversion might advance postcolonial subject formation and generative world-making.

In this respect, Kneubuhl's dramaturgy hews to Wilson's concept of "counter-conversion":[255] rewriting narratives of conversion and evangelical Christianity and putting them to "neonative usages" and "diasporic counterpurposes"[256] to chart "alternative visions of identity and transpacific maps" to new destinations.[257] Counterconversion here denotes a "becoming-in-reverse" away from demoralizing and pacifying developmentalist doxa and toward oceanic conceptions of place, space, and transnational community.[258] Wilson sees this approach exemplified in the work of Epeli Hau'ofa, both in his new paradigm for Oceania spawned from his epiphany in Hawai'i, where the expanding island world and its encircling firmament inspired a vision of new forms of Pacific Islander consciousness in a holistic ecumene of transnational mobility and social networks; and in his bawdy, raucous, Rabelaisian fiction, which undoes the indoctrinations of the Pacific Century. In consonance with Hau'ofa, Kneubuhl's work draws on the affirmative power of laughter, on a long history of clowning as critical commentary in the Pacific, to eschew stultifying and restrictive attitudes and to embrace the copresence of alternative paradigms that reveal the potential of the Indigenous sacred in the profane: where gods are found in Samoan housekeepers and help Pacific Islanders work at their personal and geographical trajectories within transnational modernity.

Nevertheless, as critics of Hau'ofa have warned, Oceania is beset by neocolonial and globalizing influences that make this work arduous and ongoing. In *The Holiday of Rain*, these obdurate forces are indicated by the play's temporal displacement, as old-fashioned attitudes are relocated to the present and subjected to postcolonial interrogation—a move that simultaneously registers their present-day persistence. Whereas the debunking of South Seas clichés has the potential to create empowering spaces for characters and audience members, Kneubuhl's play-within-a-play is deeply ambivalent, with its unwitting accomplices engendering the very discourse that they seek both to capitalize on and to critique. The denouement presents the illusion of order reestablished: Crowley's perverse ministrations are arraigned, the time-travelers are retemporalized, and Tina's crew sits down to cake and tea in a final scene reminiscent of a Maughamesque comedy of manners. But is it so easy? Can one simply wear (out) a role and then "toss it off . . . Like a worn out dress"?[259] The play's structures subvert the contemporary characters' assumptions of ironic detachment: Maugham and Haxton return to 1916, and via the chicken-and-egg problem occasioned by the time-travel trope, the fiction Maugham constructs from the adaptation of his own scenario becomes the "reality" penned and published in the 1920s. That the participants in the latter-day "Rain" show are trapped by these ideological and transtemporal impasses might record *The Holiday of Rain*'s acknowledgment that the work of dismantling entrenched stereotypes is not a straightforward process of sloughing off a foreclosed past, but entails grappling with a pervasive feedback loop of colonial discourse from which the characters are still struggling to emerge. This shared awareness that Kneubuhl's drama of displacement seeks to remit to her audiences is not wholly pessimistic but operates in a mode of transnational yearning; by critically activating the relational space between American Samoa, Hawai'i, and the United States, Kneubuhl draws a Pacific community into a conversation about the difficulty, but also the hope, of living in a contested contemporary milieu.

METACULTURES: SAMOAN THEATER IN THE SPACE BETWEEN

Samoan theatrical practice in the contemporary Pacific must be understood as a component and exponent of a transnational world "tied together by flows of people, money, tangibles . . . and intangible cultural properties."[260] Throughout this chapter, I have overlaid another network of relationships across this oceanic domain, constelling several examples of transnational performance that pursue various political, cultural, personal, and historical engagements with the Samoan Islands while treating pressing issues of migration, colonialism, globalization, tourism, Christianity, sex and gender stereotypes, and foreign development. The case studies demonstrate how Samoa is linked multiply and reciprocally with other Pacific Islands, and with the industrialized nations of New Zealand, Australia, and the United States. They also reveal a more global outreach to Asia and to connections reemerging and newly emerging with Germany and the United Kingdom. Although the Samoan case is an exemplary one, the general approaches I have taken in this chapter are applicable to other Pacific Island communities whose cultural production is increasingly being figured in off-island, multisited, and reticulated terms. The transpasifika perspective I have adopted enables close readings of relations between different Pacific communities, and well as relationships between Pacific Islanders and those from beyond the region; it also emphasizes processes of change and transformation that occur between various "home" and "host" communities, paying attention to reciprocal forms of adaptation and creolization that affect transmigrants as well as those who stay put. The framework of cultural remittances provides a productive means of tracing the grassroots transmission and reception of culture through theatrical performance. When considered in terms of not only direct transnationalism but also intradiasporic transnationalism and indirect transnationalism, we see how remittances move beyond the dual territorial logic of the homeland-hostland dyad to embrace a more multipolar, networked series of lived relationships. The Indigenous epistemology of the vā helps theorize the relay of affect, narratives, practices, and identities in the transnational Samoan context. The relational space between elements of the onstage world, between performers and human and material audiences, and between the performance and the wider world entwines genealogy and geography and centers Samoan protocols while offering a multiscalar model for linking the minutiae of the performance event with the evolving macrostructures of the Pacific Century.

The examples discussed here extend the notion of intercultural performance beyond minoritarian collaborations or theatrical experiments in blending or interweaving two or more performance cultures to pursue a more sophisticated analysis of the ways that performance expresses and contributes to a Samoan "meta-culture," a contemporary Samoan identity that emerges in the social space between "traditional" and "migrant" Samoan cultures,[261] and that is developing in diverse forms in different locations alongside new community formations and coalitions. Ultimately, an island-centered view of the Pacific Ocean world makes clear that Samoans are not passive recipients of the changes wrought by globalization but are active participants in world-historical processes. Indeed, the findings of this chapter support Fepulea'i Micah Van der Ryn's argument that to place Samoa at the center of a transpacific network productively reverses Immanuel Wallerstein's world systems model;[262] instead of the islands being positioned on the global periphery, the heretofore "core" countries of New Zealand, Australia, and the United States become the peripheries from which money, goods, and cultural capital are extracted in the manufacture of Samoan prestige.[263]

Chapter 5 continues my focus on the urban percolations of Pasifika cultures by turning to artists from other Pacific communities who have taken on the city as a creative stage. It further considers the imbrication of urbanization, militarization, and nuclearization in the postwar Pacific, and analyzes performative responses to those legacies in the present.

| Destination Urbanesia:
Cityscapes, Militarization,
and Islander Identities

At the Fine Arts Theatre of the University of Guam for FestPac 2016, members of the New Zealand delegation delivered an "Urbanesian political presentation."[1] The bracket of three linked performances began with the stand-up comedy routine *So-So Gangsta* by charismatic Samoan/Welsh comedian James Nokise, which used self-deprecating humor and trenchant political insight to probe New Zealand's gang culture, including Nokise's own experience of joining the youth gang The Bloods, while challenging us to acknowledge racial tensions, notions of criminality, and social preconceptions and prejudices. Next, Māori slam poet Te Kahu Rolleston's impassioned, rhythmic outpouring of narratives of Aotearoa in *te reo* Māori and English articulated a powerful indictment of the impact of colonization on contemporary Indigenous life and issued a call for the decolonization of knowledge. The deracinating experience of urban drift that infused Rolleston's performance was echoed in Fiji / New Zealand artist Jahra "Rager" Wasasala's compelling and disturbing multidisciplinary work *godd-less*, which confronted the global epidemic of missing and murdered Indigenous women. Merging contemporary dance, ritualistic imagery, and spoken-word poetry, Wasasala painfully expressed the violence of these losses, her choreographed body gyrating, convulsing, manipulated seemingly to the point of breaking; gagging, gasping, words threatening to fail. This triptych by three millennial performers contributed something new and significant to the regional conversation at FestPac by locating Pasifika identity squarely within the realm of the urban.[2] The performers' subjectivities and the content and form of their pieces were expressly shaped by their urban roots and by the dis/identifications forged in and through the spaces of the city, pointing to the emerging cultural geographies and new social and generational forces changing the face of the contemporary Pacific world.

This chapter investigates "Urbanesia" as a spatial configuration, creative arena, and mode of lived experience. Coined by New Zealand–based Samoan / Cook Islander poet and performance artist Courtney Sina Meredith, the term "Urbanesia" ("city islands") describes the new physical mappings and social formations that emerge from the energetic polyglot Pasifika cultures of contemporary metropolises, where island and city come into profound collision and act as the crucible of fresh global identities. Chapter 5 thus builds on the discussions of urban migration introduced in chapter 2 and developed more fully in chapter 4, but shifts the focus from diasporic critical frameworks to concentrate on aesthetic genres and approaches informed by urban logics and structures of feeling, taking the city itself as a complex performing entity. It investigates what Pasifika creative production might tell us about the dynamics and challenges of cities and related urban infrastructures, exploring how performance produces, negotiates, and resists forms of urban experience. As an elastic cartography that takes the modern city as its common ground, Urbanesia emphasizes Pasifika identities shaped by expansive, mobile cultural fields and counters the artificially imposed and colonially restrictive geocultural categories of Polynesia, Melanesia, and Micronesia. At present, Urbanesia is associated mainly with Auckland, New Zealand, as the world's largest Pasifika node, and in addition to a new category at FestPac, has served as the title for a New Zealand play anthology and a contemporary Auckland arts and culture festival.[3] However, Urbanesian cultural production can, I argue, be fruitfully extended to encompass a broader range of sites and situations: beyond New Zealand, "Urbanesia" or "being Urbanesian" can name a disposition and a strategy that helps to illuminate and connect modes of Islander selfhood in cityscapes elsewhere, such as Sydney, Honolulu, Los Angeles, San Francisco, Tokyo, and London. Moreover, an Urbanesian optic can serve as a powerful analytic for examining how Pacific artists frame coalitions with different communities across global, urban spaces to interrogate shared genealogies and conditions of mobility and immobility conditioned by and worked out across frameworks of citizenship, race, (neo)colonialism, and militarization.

These considerations indicate how and why cities are an important topic or frame of reference for Oceania. Unlike in other parts of the world where major cities, stretching back centuries or millennia, have long been defining features of their societies, urbanization in Oceania is almost exclusively a post-nineteenth-century phenomenon, occasioned by foreign colonialism and its capitalist and militarist adjuncts. Oceania has been notably absent from much significant work on urban theory; as we have seen,

Figure 22. Promotional still for the solo stand-up comedy show *So So Gangsta* (2013) by Samoan/Welsh comic James Nokise. Photograph by, and courtesy of, Matt Grace.

Islander lifeways have frequently been framed in pastoral terms through ties to ancestral lands and seas. From the outside, there is a tendency not to think of the Pacific Islands as sites for these forms of modernity, nor of Pasifika peoples as full participants in the new global urban reality—still less, perhaps, as *influencers* of urban cultures though their creative output. On the contrary, however, as the FestPac presentation affirmed and as this chapter will show, the regime of urban life is increasingly important to understanding Pasifika cultural production, not only in the burgeoning "rim" cities (whose resources, Hau'ofa stated, must be measured in any assessment of Oceania) or other metropolises worldwide, but also within the globalizing islands themselves.

In this regard, the discussions and case studies advance new perspectives in the discourse of "urban performance studies," which has come into prominence since the 2010s. In particular, I take up calls by scholars in this subfield to pay attention to how distinct cities are produced across the globe via the specificities of local cultures, and to move beyond Western theory and Euro-American perspectives toward new definitions of cities and urban areas, and toward more varied forms and experiences of urbanization.[4] This necessary diversification, as Nicolas Whybrow suggests, helps avoid the assumption of a "universal we" when talking about cities,[5] and diverges from hierarchies of prominent northern metropoles and canonical itineraries of "cities that matter" to privilege alternative kinds of urban spaces and the performances they generate. Usefully, D. J. Hopkins and Kim Solga advocate going beyond binaries, as I do, to construct networks of linked performance, mapping across multiple urban landscapes in a "relational geography"[6]—an approach that supports the transpasifika connections that energize the concept of Urbanesia.

I explore what an Urbanesian optic might contribute through a constellation of case studies arranged within a bifold structure. The chapter makes two key moves. The first part traces the urbanization of the Pacific through internal and transnational migration, making the argument that the connected urban milieu is increasingly the marker of contemporary Islander identities. I analyze the cross-disciplinary development of an urban Pasifika aesthetic in Aotearoa New Zealand and chart the aspirational possibilities of a new Urbanesian identity in Courtney Sina Meredith's germinal play *Rushing Dolls* (2011), which expresses worldly, utopian desires for its female protagonists who hail from an ascendant Pasifika creative class. I place this work alongside a more problematic imagining of urban indigeneity in Māori / Cook Islander playwright Mīria George's *and what remains* (2005). George's dystopian scenario of ethnic cleansing in multicultural

Aotearoa, set in the capital city's international airport as the last Māori prepares to leave the country, reconfigures discourses of migration and moving islands, and foregrounds the charged intersection of place and nonplace. Subsequently, I shift attention from works that stage the city in artistic performance venues to works that take the city itself as a stage, addressing the city's uneven distribution of wealth and opportunity, and highlighting those *citadins*[7] who are often rendered invisible or disappear into the cityscape. My primary focus here is Tongan performance artist John Vea and his performative placement of "urban taros" in sites around the Auckland central business district to comment on migration, gentrification, and Pasifika manual labor.

Moving out to other locales, the linchpin of the chapter concerns a trilogy of cinematic artworks by London-based Fijian New Zealander Luke Willis Thompson (2018), connecting urbanization and militarized violence toward Black bodies across three sites in Fiji, the United Kingdom, and the United States, and linking discourses of the Black Pacific to the globalizing movement of Black Lives Matter. Thompson's work cues the second major move in the chapter, which attends to other ways in which island spaces become urbanized through the webs of foreign militarization that course through the Pacific, spawning bases and military cities that trade on the islands' strategic geographies. This take on Urbanesia emphasizes practices and legacies that are urgent for understanding both the region and the world, especially in light of the neo–Cold War security tensions that undergird the Pacific Century. After discussing militarized (im)mobilities across the long arm of the American Pacific—Guam and the Marshall Islands—including the atrocities of nuclear militarism, the final section of the chapter elaborates the concept of "nuclear performativity" with reference to France's extensive and long-term bomb-testing campaign in its Pacific colonies. The Tahitian play *Les Champignons de Paris / Te mau tuputupuā a Paris* (2017) by Emilie Génaédig and La Compagnie du Caméléon draws explicit connections between the Parisian metropole and the French Pacific to expose the urban logic that effaces "remote" island worlds in order to hone weapons that ostensibly protect northern cities. The play also reveals how the military's radical infrastructural refashioning of French Polynesia—in addition to the environmental tragedy—has left unresolved social and economic problems in its wake.

Taken together, these works enable a variegated analysis of how Pacific peoples have deployed intercultural performance techniques to articulate ground-level experiences of globalism; to resist hegemonic notions of national identity; and to negotiate the often-entwined coils of imperialism, militarism, and neoliberalism that infiltrate and bind the region. Revealing how urbanism in Oceania derives from specific geographies, Indigenous histories, colonial enterprises, and patterns of migration, the following discussion illuminates how performance can rethink and reconfigure forms of urban space to facilitate greater participation and social justice.

THEORIZING URBANESIA

It isn't like an Island nipple, nup,
no breezing trees and caramel sand

no coconut truths spilling over woven fans
no plans of making love to the land.

. . .

Way South

where the beast sleeps

Way South

with its mean streets
and ciggy-stained teeth.
  —Courtney Sina Meredith, *Rushing Dolls*

Rural-urban migration within the island Pacific and international migration to metropolises around the Pacific Rim have influenced identity, nationality, and sovereignty throughout the region.[8] Although circumstances and prospects vary widely across Oceania, John Connell and John Lea affirm that "in an island region, the image of which is all too often that of a place of palm-fringed lagoons populated with rural people whose traditional cultures are intact and whose diet is based on local products, reality has become rather different."[9] Urbanization in the Pacific is a colonial phenomenon: the nineteenth-century coastal communities and trading posts on the selvage edge of empire that eventually evolved into administrative centers and more diversified loci for agricultural processing, mining, and fishing were expatriate creations populated by migrants from metropolitan powers. Typically, they maintained rigid colonial hierarchies and unequal social divisions through forms of "urban apartheid,"[10] whereby Indigenous peoples were made unwelcome or discouraged through restrictions, curfews, and menial employment options. The construction of airstrips from the early twentieth century, like railway stations in Australia or the United States, advanced urban development by connecting the region.[11] World War II brought thousands of Pasifika people into contact with urban life for the first time, while independence in many Pacific Island nations during the 1960s and 1970s resulted in rapid urbanization and massive rural-urban migrations for bureaucratic, educational, social, and employment opportunities.[12] These demographic shifts led to an indigenizing of urban centers, which were no longer forbidden or alien, but places "where national identities might be forged in place of parochial ethnicities."[13] Beyond the bounds of formal regulated planning, the dominant form of urban growth has been "urban villages" or "village cities," informal and squatter settlements anchored on kin-based place relationships, which dominate the physical space of the city.[14] Moreover, as I have established, international migration to the industrialized cities of the Pacific periphery has become a rite of passage in many island nations, leading to permanent, off-island urban communities.

The primary node of Urbanesian cultural production, as theorized by Meredith, is New Zealand as a liminal island/rimland zone. Pacific Islanders have been contributing to New Zealand's art since the first waves of modern migration in the 1940s and 1950s, but the current phenomenon, according to Tokelauan curator and scholar Fulimalo Pereira, reflects the increasing number of "second- or third-generation New Zealanders whose parents had largely been estranged from their homeland cultures and educated, socialised and politicised during the turbulent 1960s and 1970s."[15] During the same period, intensive rural-urban Māori migration caused significant structural changes to Māori social networks, institutions, and cultural expression.[16] For these urban-born generations, the city, rather than the village, rural community, or tribal structure, provides the impetus and common ground. In an echo of the vā-space discussed in the previous chapter, these people—frequently of mixed ancestry and negotiating multiple cultures, backgrounds, and sites—inhabit, in Pereira's words, "a unique locale that is often expressed as a liminal space: the space between."[17] This position generates its own freedoms beyond a sense of deracination, itinerancy, or fragmentation, whereby artistic expression is developed through a process of intercultural translation, inventing new forms, reinterpreting old ones, and appropriating and reproducing elements from the surrounding milieu.[18] In the 1990s, these new expressions were exemplified by the Pacific Sisters, a pioneering ensemble of Māori and Pasifika transmedia creative artists. Devising groundbreaking works in a wide

Figure 23. *21st Sentry Cyber Sister* (1997). Wearable art piece made up of twenty-seven parts, each created by one of the members of the Pacific Sisters art collective: Rosanna Raymond (Samoa), Ani O'Neill (Cook Islands), and two of the founding members, Suzanne Tamaki (Te Arawa, Ngāi Tūhoe, Ngāti Maniapoto) and Niwhai Tupaea (Ngāti Katoa). Tapa, feathers, bone, *harakeke*, nylon, shells, seeds, coconut shell, videotape, plastic. A guardian figure who protects the museum's collections, the *21st Sentry Cyber Sister* wards off racism and signifies the contemporary presence of Māori and Pacific cultures and their drive toward self-determination. In the Pacific Cultures Collection of Te Papa Tongarewa | Museum of New Zealand, courtesy of Te Papa and the Pacific Sisters.

range of genres, including visual art, film, music, and fashion, the Pacific Sisters combine natural and processed materials, and draw together influences from ancestral pasts and contemporary settings to visualize forms of future self-determination. As Rosanna Raymond, member of the collective, explains, "We get our inspiration from our immediate urban/media environment. We don't stare at coconut trees—we stare at motorways,"[19] and the innovative, transgressive genres and identities produced as a result "express our uniqueness as an urban tribe."[20]

These new ideas and trends, starting on the street, began to come of age at the turn of the twenty-first century. When the Wellington-based magazine *Loop* published its special issue "Polifusion" in 2000, it announced the mainstream recognition of a phenomenon that had been brewing for at least the previous decade across the full artistic spectrum.[21] The transpasifika energies that have emerged from these dense urban entanglements also involve local permutations of global cultural flows, especially the African-Caribbean modalities of reggae, rap, and hip-hop (and associated cultural forms like DJ-ing, breakdancing, MC-ing, and graffiti), which have provided a social consciousness and artistic vocabulary to express resistance to oppression, feelings of disaffection and marginalization, as well as home-grown avenues of empowerment and pride.[22] Samoan/Japanese performance artist Yuki Kihara elaborates: "With energy similar to youth cultures such as hip-hop in Black America and the punk movement in the United Kingdom, Urban Pacific in New Zealand is pro-Pacific in thinking and is reflected in their everyday living. Urban Pacific in its own anarchistic way refuses to conform."[23] An urban Pasifika aesthetic reconfigures relationships to elders, customary practices, and church and community mores, as well as to the often exclusionary and racist Pākehā establishment. It thus opens space for emergent identities, expressive styles, and perspectives that are hopeful, aspirational, and imagine new ways of being in the world, but that also critique, in often abrasive and discomfiting ways, the manifold social, economic, and ethnic problems of the urban. Urbanesia(n) as space, condition, and habitus provides a grounding yet accommodating framework for the multiplex cultural identities of Pacific Islanders on the move. In turn, these flourishing enunciations reinscribe and modify the fluctuating assemblage of the city itself, reshaping national and regional identity.

As an example, I turn to a work that directly expresses and advances the potential of evolving forms of Urbanesian selfhood, and which contains the first use of the term itself: Courtney Sina Meredith's *Rushing Dolls*. Meredith (b. 1986), of Samoan, Mangaian (Cook Islands) and Irish descent, has gained an impressive international profile for her poetry and prose writing, which has featured in festivals and residencies in Asia, Australia, and Europe. She is currently the director of Tautai, Aotearoa's leading Pacific arts organization, where she continues to "bring Urbanesia to life" by elevating the Pacific community and their role in contemporary arts practice.[24] Meredith describes her work as "an ongoing discussion of contemporary urban life with an underlying Pacific politique."[25] *Rushing Dolls*, her first play, won two Adam New Zealand Play Awards in 2011, and excerpts were subsequently broadcast to a worldwide audience of forty million listeners on the BBC World Service. The full script received a public, staged reading at Auckland's Herald Theatre in 2015. The play is a semiautobiographical experiment that seeks to instantiate and subject to aesthetic analysis the young, Pasifika creatives currently reinventing Auckland, the sprawling, ethnically diverse conurbation in New Zealand's upper North Island that is home to 35 percent of the country's population. In writing the piece, Meredith explains: "I wanted to create a little world, based on my life, that could hold the truths and hopes of the community to which I belong. I could not find myself or my peers online, on TV, in books, in history or in the backyard. There was nowhere in the world to turn and see my people shine—my burgeoning order of ambitious young Pacific and Maori women, born to realise the dreams of our ancestors while honouring our own contemporary will."[26]

The protagonists of *Rushing Dolls* are Cleopatra Felise and Sialei Felise, two multiethnic, urban-born Pasifika women in their early to mid-twenties. Cleo (like Meredith) is Samoan, Mangaian, and Irish; her cousin and best friend Sia is Māori, Samoan, and Tongan. Cleo is a queer performance poet with "a strong urban following"[27] and is also a trailblazing events manager with an enviable clientele. Sia is a graduate of the nation's premier fine arts program and is a successful multimedia artist. Less a narrative-driven drama than a series of snapshots into the lives and ambitions of the new Urbanesian generation, the play clicks between tight scenes in sassy dialogue and Cleo's performance poetry—Pacific orality morphed into urban form—the prismatic imagery of which offers fragmented, vivid, and fleeting insights into her personal map of her world. "I walked my soul," she says, "it was a city,"[28] and throughout we track the young women's adventures across the heterotopic[29] sites and spaces of Auckland, following Cleo's preparations to land her dream job with the international company World Class and to begin a new phase of her career in Berlin. In a more profound sense, however, the piece is a statement that lays claim to an idea of the city, one that understands Auckland as a proudly Pasifika space. Its treatise on Urbanesian becoming does not simply demonstrate how the city produces new Pasifika realities, but emphasizes how this demographic is reproducing the city and determining its future direction.

In an opening scene from the play, Cleo's and Sia's modes of being in the world are distinguished from derogatory racialized stereotypes of urban poverty when they attend a launch at a hip art gallery on K-Road.[30] One of the exhibits is a Māori fiberglass doll made by a white-appearing artist with the accompanying statement: "Girl, sixteen, pregnant, lives in south Auckland, has no prospects, likes to tag dairy walls."[31] As both art critics and social critics, Cleo and Sia anatomize not only the racial and gendered politics of the "Girl" doll's production but also its socioeconomics, making reference to the impacts of New Zealand's vehement neoliberal turn in the 1980s, with the privatization and social welfare rollbacks that have contributed to acute inequalities within New Zealand cities. In contrast to "Girl," Cleo and Sia are restless, articulate, gifted, entrepreneurial, and brimming with personal, professional, and sexual confidence. As Cleo defines herself: "My unique Pacific perspective, it's intrinsic to who I am, which is ambitious, educated, passionate, Urbanesian, a new breed."[32] Likewise, Sia is "fearless and babyless. No jail time and no hand-outs. No fucking excuses."[33] They are, instead, rushing dolls: on the move, on the go, enlisting urban tropes of mobility and speed. Like the Russian nesting dolls that the quasi-homonym suggests, their subjectivity is multifaceted and complex, indicating the different personae, obligations, and expectations that they need to manage; in Cleo's words: "I'm a girl in a girl in a girl in a girl / I'm a Rushing Doll."[34] A new phenomenon, they emerge from working-class origins to take their place in the creative class, understood in Richard Florida's terms as people who "engage in work whose function is to *create meaningful new forms*,"[35] and whose transferable, useful creativity is the principal driving force in the growth and development of cities, regions, and nations.[36] *Rushing Dolls* does not ignore the precarities routinely experienced by creative workers under neoliberalism, but deliberately chooses a more optimistic focus, accentuating the role of Pasifika innovation in this trend; Meredith's characters are not merely consumers of culture but producers of it, social influencers actively changing the urban status quo.

In terms of female Pasifika aesthetic representation, it is instructive to think about *Rushing Dolls* alongside New Zealand's first Pasifika play to feature an all-female cast, *Frangipani Perfume* (1997) by Samoan playwright Makerita Urale.[37] In Urale's play, the three sisters who work as night-shift cleaners in the city tell an important truth about the poor, exhausted migrant workers whom mainstream citizens rarely see. Whereas these sisters retreat into a "dusky maiden" island fantasy as a salve for their menial existence, Cleo and Sia declare that they are "what dusky maidens wish they could be"[38] and express a bold coming-of-age that insists on a very different gendered habitation and utilization of urban space: "We're leaders. This is our moment."[39] While the women in *Frangipani Perfume* survive in the city's interstices, Cleo and Sia demand full and free access to the streets, chasing the burning potential of "brown girls in bright red lipstick."[40] The two cousins assertively traverse the city from K-Road to Grey Lynn, from the upscale Quay to South Auckland, attending fashionable parties, luxury cinemas, classy restaurants with prominent politicians, gallery openings, and strip clubs; negotiating high-profile business deals; delivering inspirational invited lectures to school leavers; and being interviewed for an *Arts Pacific* segment on television. Their active self-fashioning through beautiful clothes, chic apartments, gourmet food, coveted guest lists, and circulation of their own art-making partakes of the consumer fantasies of Auckland as a routing-point for Asia-Pacific capital, and evinces a cosmopolitan disposition that links Auckland to a network of global cities and international itineraries of desire; as Sia enthuses: "Today it's Auckland, tomorrow Tokyo, next week the BBC, then Dubai, American boys, hard candy and shiny cars."[41]

Given these heady possibilities, one might reasonably wonder what prevents *Rushing Dolls* from ultimately celebrating neoliberal lifeways. How might we understand Cleo's and Sia's achievements as something more or other than having won the rat race on Pākehā terms? Meredith remains alert to these questions, threading the tension between personal ambition and more traditional cultural responsibilities throughout the fabric of her play. One of the more thoughtful moments in the piece transpires in Sia's choice not to accompany Cleo to Germany and to continue her career in New Zealand while supporting their extended family. This decision is not presented as a compromise but as a different measure of success whereby Sia's creative contributions are shown to draw inspiration from these blended influences. Even Cleo's staunch determination to make it in the wider world relies on a different grammar that is less concerned with replicating Pākehā privileges than recasting them in Pasifika terms.

In this regard, we might consider how Meredith's Urbanesian disposition intersects with and nuances Henri Lefebvre's oft-cited notion of the "right to the city." For Lefebvre, the right to the city does not refer to simple visiting rights, but "can only be reformulated as a transformed and renewed *right to urban life*."[42] He imagines this right, somewhat amorphously, in the form of a new urban politics: "In the most 'positive' of terms it signifies the right of citizens and city-dwellers, and of groups they (on the basis of social relations) constitute, to appear on the networks and circuits of communication, information and exchange."[43] The right to the city "legitimates the refusal to allow oneself to be removed from urban reality by a discriminative and segregative organization," and advocates that *citadins* resist the thrust of the city to "reject towards peripheral spaces all those who do not participate in political privileges."[44] Importantly, Lefebvre's concept does not just involve the right to occupy already-produced space, but extends to the right to produce urban space so that it meets its inhabitants' needs.[45] Moreover, and significantly for Pasifika populations in New Zealand, whereas conventional enfranchisement empowers national citizens, the right to the city empowers urban inhabitants, who, regardless of nationality, earn their membership in that community by living out the routines of everyday life in the city.[46]

Lefebvre's theory has been widely adopted by researchers interested in progressive responses to disenfranchisement in cities engendered by the restructurings of neoliberal urbanism, especially those responses that move beyond state policy to give urban dwellers a greater say in decisions that shape the city.[47] Although *Rushing Dolls* does not approach the radical transformations that full implementation of Lefebvre's ideas would incur, its concept of the Urbanesian nevertheless rests on the right of Māori and Pasifika peoples—so often marginalized in urban and national discourse—to participate equally in decisions that affect the urban region, and to contribute toward a refashioning of the city and nation-state. Accordingly, Meredith's formulation puts pressure on Lefebvre's class bias and preoccupation with confronting the capitalist city. Lefebvre argues that "only the working class can become the agent, the social carrier or support of this realization,"[48] and consequently, the subsequent critical uptake has paid particular attention to how cities can become the focus for anticapitalist resistance.[49] Cleo and Sia, however, exercise a right to the city in different classed, gendered, and racialized ways that encourage an ethnic reworking of Auckland in contrast to its dominant Pākehā histories. Although Cleo admits that "I brave seas of white faces!"[50] they are peripheral to the world that Meredith's characters inhabit, which is replete with networks of people who comprise the urban Pasifika beat. *Rushing Dolls* not only describes but actively reclaims and renames the space of Auckland, foregrounding Pasifika characters who no longer reside in the margins but take center stage in a new culture that they are in the process of creating. In the end, Cleo's imminent departure from New Zealand holds out the promise of forging new spaces of Urbanesian identity in cities elsewhere:

Take me Vegas, New York
I run my talk
Seattle, Chicago
I fly my talk

Take me LA, DC, LSD, Jersey, Ecstasy–
take me![51]

TERMINAL EXILE: MĪRIA GEORGE, *AND WHAT REMAINS*

Rushing Dolls, then, is an aspirant, idealistic celebration of Urbanesian potential and self-actualization, stemming from the multicultural Pacific fusion of Auckland and Aotearoa and closing on the cusp of Cleo's adventure to seek fulfillment overseas. Mīria George's play *and what remains* is also centrally concerned with the departure of young people from Aotearoa, but turns the trope on its head to expose the raw fissures in the national imaginary that reveal the conflicts and exclusions of the Urbanesian, especially the ruptures between immigrant (including Pasifika) and *tangata whenua* (Māori) imaginaries and experiences. To a large extent, George's work strives toward the same notion of democratic participation that Meredith's work advocates, but goes about it in a strikingly different manner. Whereas Meredith's play situates evolving Urbanesian identities within what José Esteban Muñoz calls a "brown commons,"[52] figured here as a relational matrix that bypasses a primary relationship with the official nation-state, George's drama, located in the capital city of Wellington and the seat of the nation's political economy, is profoundly haunted by the specter of the state and its power to embrace or exile. Set in the International Departures Lounge at Wellington Airport in the (then) near future of 2010, *and what remains* hinges on Mary, the last Māori to leave Aotearoa in the wake of the draconian conservative government's program of Indigenous ethnic cleansing and enforced relocation to make way for a fresh nation of immigrants.

Mīria George (b. 1980) is a poet and writer for theater, film, and television, of New Zealand Māori (Te Arawa, Ngāti Awa) and Cook Islands Māori (Tumutevarovaro, Enua Manu, Ngāti Kuki 'Ārani) ancestry. Cofounder of Tawata Productions and Tawata Press, her award-winning work has toured New Zealand, Australia, Hawai'i, Canada, and the United Kingdom. George's plays underscore New Zealand's place in the wider Asia-Pacific complex, frequently drawing together Māori, Pacific, and

Asian characters into plots that include crises of urban youth and neoliberal governmentality (*Urban Hymns*, 2009) and the state-sponsored capitalist abrogation of Indigenous natural resources (*The Night Mechanics*, 2017). Transpacific currents, Indigenous politics, and urbanism coalesce in *and what remains*, arguably George's most controversial work, which scandalized the Pākehā critical and theatergoing establishment when it was first staged at the City Gallery in Wellington in 2005 and remounted at downtown BATS Theatre in 2006. David O'Donnell credits George's play with helping spark a "renaissance of political themes in Maori theatre"[53] after the more narrative, mythically oriented mainstream work of the 1990s. A decade after its premiere, critic Adam Goodall affirmed that "the mark left by *and what remains* on Māori theatre—the community, the work, the whakapapa—is still felt to this day, laying the groundwork [for] a new generation of bold, political indigenous writers and makers."[54] George's turn to speculative realism marks a subtrend in contemporary Māori theater, especially by young women playwrights (see Aroha White's *2080* [2015], for instance, and Whiti Hereaka's *Te Kaupoi* [2010]). Rather than looking to the historical past to delineate and address social and racial schisms, human rights breaches, and rifts in the national narrative that condition the present, these dramatists pivot to the future, unfolding Orwellian dystopias of radical social and urban reorganization, the disciplining of racially marked bodies, and sexualized violence, where the festering threats and problematic political proclivities of the current moment are pursued to their acute ends.

The airport lounge in George's play serves as the gathering space for a group of characters that represent a microcosm of New Zealand's multicultural milieu; all are in their late twenties and most are city-dwellers. Cosmopolitan Ila is a wealthy executive of Gujarati Indian heritage, an experienced traveler on her way to visit family and friends in London. Solomon, a New Zealand–born Samoan graphic designer, is about to head off on his Big OE,[55] while Anna, an Iban Malaysian janitor in International Departures, cleans the bathrooms and dreams of traveling herself. Peter, a Pākehā dairy farmer, arrives later in the play to try to find his long-term partner, Mary, a Māori health worker facing the terrible choice between leaving her homeland forever or suffering mandatory sterilization if she stays. The production's symbolic all-white set and costumes reinforce the disturbing themes of cleansing, tabula rasa, the whitewashing of history, and the imperatives of a white supremacist governmental logic, while the soundscape's recurrent roaring of jet planes taking off confers an atmosphere of menace and impending disaster. The dialogue has a repetitive, circular

Figure 24. From left: Erina Daniels (Mary), Simon Vincent (Peter), Rina Patel (Ila), Semu Filipo (Solomon), and Sam Selliman (Anna) in *and what remains* by Miria George, directed by Hone Kouka. Tawata Productions, City Gallery, Wellington, 2005. Photograph by, and courtesy of, Matt Grace.

quality that reflects both the temporal abeyance—exacerbated by the announcement that all flights are delayed—and the inability of any of the characters to truly relate to or connect with one another. These happenstance and transient meetings between strangers highlight a world in which there is little empathy, organic society, or link to heritage; no one is able to help Mary, and the only decisive action that the immigrant/settler characters take is not to leave after all: in the end, only Mary departs.

So, what does this bleak drama present us with? How does its take on the Urbanesian reconceptualize intercultural issues and urban sensibilities in Aotearoa New Zealand? I want to begin by parsing the dynamics of the play's airport setting. Airports are key components of urban infrastructure in the globalizing world. The reality of accelerated "aerial mobility"[56] has reshaped concepts of urbanity and has affected how the contemporary city is organized spatially and socially. As urban sites "emerge as staging posts on internationally organised flows of goods, people, signs, images, commodities and information,"[57] they create a situation in which, for Manuel Castells, "The space of flows has taken over the logic of the space of places,"[58] constituting the "dominant urban landscapes" of the contemporary world.[59] Airports are concentrations of networked infrastructures that support these supermodern spaces of flow, themselves "generic cities"[60] of mobility and of perpetually migratory populations. As proximity to the network becomes more important than downtown, we are witnessing the development of "airport cities,"[61] the "aviopolis"[62] or the "aerotropolis,"[63] where the airport directs everyday life and determines the city's design, location, and rationale. Although Wellington Airport may not represent the same kind of global megaproject as other Pacific world hubs like Beijing, Changi, or LAX, the transnational movements of ordinary Oceanians speak to Max Hirsh's theory of *airport urbanism*, which bids us pay attention to how quotidian members of the flying public—what Hirsh calls the *nouveaux globalisés*—not just the managerial elites, are plugged into the infrastructure of international aviation.[64] This viewpoint, moreover, usefully illustrates "how small-scale urban infrastructure systems support complex socioeconomic interdependencies across international frontiers."[65]

Famously, French anthropologist Marc Augé categorized the airport, like similar installations produced by supermodernity, as a *non-lieu* ("nonplace"). In contrast to what Augé calls a sociological or anthropological notion of place, associated with "the idea of a culture localized in time and space,"[66] shot through with identity, relations, and history, and informed by local references and living know-how,[67] "a space which cannot be designated as relational, or historical, or concerned with identity will be a nonplace."[68] For Augé, nonplaces create the shared identity of the people who pass through them, generating experiences of solitude and similitude, and are lived through in the present moment.[69] This doesn't mean, however, that nonplaces are vacant or devoid of signification. Places and nonplaces are not divorced from one another but function as polarities that "intertwine and tangle together"; never entirely erased or completed, "they are like palimpsests on which the scrambled game of identity and relations is ceaselessly rewritten."[70] By extension, "Non-places mediate a whole mass of relations, with the self and with others, which are only indirectly connected with their purposes."[71]

Indeed, in *The Textual Life of Airports*, Christopher Schaberg attends to the imbricated or oscillating quality of the place and the nonplace to make the case for the airport as something more than just a generic zone of transit, reading it as replete with affects, moods, signs, energies, and heightened daily performances. As Schaberg argues, airports constitute a charged backdrop as "sites where identity is confirmed or questioned; they are spaces of public display; they are contested zones where privacy and national security vie for priority; they are complex factories for the production of patriotism and the privilege of mobility."[72] Helpfully, Schaberg draws a connection between the postmodern airport—the departure lounge, in particular—and Lefebvre's description of the modern city street in terms of the way it "publishes" the workings of the "social text,"[73] becoming, in Lefebvre's words, "the mirror image of the things it connects," and "a microcosm of modern life" that "plucks from obscurity all that is hidden."[74] For Schaberg, "Whole systems of cultural production and social classification are consolidated in the departure gate," which "becomes a stage" that casts into relief the social dynamics that unfold between people as they wait for their flights.[75] These social dynamics index the wider world more pointedly when they are redoubled through the reflecting mirror of the theater itself. Consequently, it is productive to acknowledge Schaberg's concept of *terminal immaterial* in relation to George's play; that is, when literary representations of airports are put to use in such a way as actual operations of flight vanish, and the airport creates a flattened, open space for other observations and reflections, usually grim ones.[76]

In *and what remains*, while the airport backdrop amplifies and ironizes the play's central, reflexive discourse on "flight," the departure lounge's theatrical intersection of place and nonplace functions as a critical platform for examining identity politics, anatomizing civic and national inequalities, and assessing legitimacy and belonging, where the personal and cultural histories galvanized by the chance meeting of the characters' temporarily convergent itineraries are revealed and debated. The play contrasts the experiences of global transit, flows, transience, displacement, and migration with Indigenous place and belonging made utterly precarious under a genocidal regime, setting the stage for alternative tactics of localized resistance that attempt to stymie the logic of the nonplace. With the characters locked in carceral limbo as disruptions to the city's infrastructure cause seemingly endless delays, the drama fleshes out the vision of a nightmarish prospective New Zealand that has seen neoliberal conservative policies taken to their extremes.

In a ghosting of New Zealand's Liberal Era (1890–1912) when Māori were presumed to be a dying race, Māori are here revealed to have been subject to a barrage of twenty-first-century rollbacks on cultural and political gains made since the 1970s, especially since the 1975 Waitangi Tribunal, which was established in order to address claims and reparations arising from Crown breaches of the Treaty of Waitangi, the nation's founding document, signed between Māori and British representatives in 1840. Notably, as Māori scholar Brendan Hokowhitu argues, this resistance movement and especially the "Treaty's promotion as the pre-eminent conduit for colonial redress was the direct result of a developing urban Indigenous subjectivity."[77] The real-world political climate in which *and what remains* was nurtured was stirred by reactionary public comments by conservative National Party politician Don Brash, leader of the opposition during Helen Clark's Labour government. In his now infamous Orewa[78] speech in 2004, Brash vowed to address what he viewed as "the dangerous drift toward racial separatism in New Zealand" caused by "the entrenched Treaty grievance industry."[79] He characterized the Treaty process as a threat to the nation's future and concluded that "the Treaty of Waitangi should not be used as the basis for giving greater civil, political or democratic rights to any particular ethnic group."[80] By erroneously positing Māori as an unfairly privileged group and stoking Pākehā fears about the implications of biculturalism, Brash effectively sought to undermine Māori sovereignty, announcing his intention to remove "divisive" race-based features from governmental legislation, to abolish Māori seats in parliament, and to refuse customary title for the foreshore and seabed.

Although Brash was not elected, in George's play-world, Brash's vision has become the dominant paradigm for a uniform New Zealand society: the foreshore and seabed title has been denied, a members' bill has revoked all references to the Treaty of Waitangi in legislation, and a subsequent bill has deleted all references to *tangata whenua* (Indigenous people, people of the land) in government legislation; as Ila says, "Their culture was effectively written out of New Zealand history."[81] These erasures have led to a demonizing of urban Māori in particular, who, Hokowhitu notes, have posed "the greatest threat to the neocolonial state, spatially, politically, and temporally,"[82] and who, in an ugly refraction of Meredith's "Girl" doll, are reductively defined in the play by "teen pregnancy, domestic violence, child abuse, unemployment."[83] There is no place for Māori in this brave new world of immigrant New Zealanders; as Solomon declares, "The country was calling for something to be done!"[84] The solution is a birth control program that Mary initially helped to implement as a health worker. Originally carried out to prevent teenage pregnancy, she notices the age-limit gradually rising:

> I worked in cities, throughout the length of the country.
> *Beat*
> The places changed, the people never changed. Always, always Maori women . . . now twenty-one, twenty-two . . . to twenty-five years of age.[85]

Finally realizing that this is in fact a targeted sterilization program to which she herself will be subject, Mary is given the option to avoid it by taking free passage out of the country. As Solomon remarks coldly, "Sixteen percent of this country was a problem that we were forced to solve. And we did."[86]

The Samoan character Solomon's antipathy toward the idea of Mary foregrounds tensions between Pasifika and Māori communities in New Zealand and breaks open the politics of the Urbanesian as conceived by Meredith. Rather than avow affiliations between Pasifika and Māori based on shared genealogies and related experiences of historical migration, modern displacement, and urban adjustment, George's *terminal immaterial* centralizes the role of Māori as *tangata whenua* and their complicated relationship to certain Pacific Islanders as both descendants and as those who preceded the postwar migrations. If *Rushing Dolls* largely avoided the settler-colonial nation-state as a determining factor in Māori-Pasifika relations, then George's play demonstrates how the neocolonial state centrally mediates Solomon's interactions with Mary, inhibiting connection. Brash's emphatic statement in his 2005 Wanganui speech, that "New Zealand is a nation of immigrants and the descendants of immigrants,"[87] as Alice Te Punga Somerville has argued, problematically diverts and undermines Indigenous self-determination efforts by privileging shared experiences of mobility rather than common connections to place, a move that places the settler at the center of the national narrative and suggests that the difference between first occupants and later arrivals is merely a matter of timing.[88] Brash's sentiments are echoed by Solomon, who espouses conservative values that align him with the state's dominant "we," declaring that Māori "were from somewhere else! Just like the rest of us."[89] Here, voyaging histories, rather than providing a point of Oceanian attachment, serve as the schism sundering Māori from an autochthonous affinity with place and from others' sympathetic identification with their plight. Solomon says as much: "What's happened to Mary, is Mary's problem. . . . I don't give a shit that she's leaving. I don't give a shit why she's leaving."[90]

What, then, of Mary in all of this? A largely silent character, people talk about her and around her; George's commentary, perhaps, on how the national discourse about Māori often excludes Māori voices. Mary's potential to intervene, consequently, emerges through symbolic actions, resistant tactics that draw on the airport's charged valences between place and nonplace to make a stand for home, locality, and history in ways that challenge, if only temporarily, the airport's systemic logic and its irrevocable push to departure. In a deeply poignant moment late in the play, Mary stands alone in the sterile airport bathroom. We discover that the suitcase she has guarded protectively throughout the previous scenes is full of soil from her ancestral land in the rural Bay of Plenty. As the roar of an airplane signals the resumption of departing flights, Mary kneels wearily before her suitcase and unlatches it: "Mary smiles sadly at the dark earth inside. She rises gently and, with one step, she stands in the earth. As Mary sinks into the mound, she closes her eyes."[91] In her attempt to reinstate *tūrangawaewae* (home ground; literally, a place to stand), Mary stakes a claim in the fertile genealogical and spiritual resonances of Papatūānuku, the earth mother, to inject a poetics of dwelling, a historical rootedness, into the airport's milieu of transit, transience, and accelerated time, and into its physical structure built on reclaimed land and driven by the imperatives of global capital instead of *iwi* (tribal) priorities. Mary's relocation of the soil itself, packaged for transport, recalls ancient Pacific practices of taking material from the ancestral homeland to furnish the new one, thus investing contemporary exile with the protocols of precolonial voyaging.

Yet the soil is never intact: created from the breakdown and recombination of many different elements, eroded, redistributed, augmented, cultivated, transferred, and shot through with multiple claims, it indexes a more complicated and contentious relationship between place and nonplace, and between groundedness and movement, which Mary's act is not able to fully reconcile. The inherently contested nature of the soil is spotlighted after Peter's arrival. The Pākehā farmer refuses to leave with Mary, asserting, "Our blood is in that land! I can't walk away, I can't leave it behind me!"[92] Just before Mary's boarding call is announced, they struggle: "The momentum of the struggle knocks them both to the floor. The suitcase lies between them."[93] In its symbolic encapsulation of New Zealand history, this brief scene exemplifies the role of the departure gate as a stage for the social microcosm and for Augé's palimpsestic inscriptions of "the scrambled game of identity and relations." In this Māori-Pākehā rupture over the land, George's future haunts the past, gesturing to tensions that root back to the nineteenth century and are enfolded in the Treaty of Waitangi itself. Ultimately, the two sides remain at an impasse, the bicultural relationship enacted as a failed romance.

According to Hokowhitu, "The continuing aspiration of the neocolonial project is to produce an Indigenous subject concurrent with its discourses, whether through necropolitics or biopolitics: to kill or make live, both symbolically and materially."[94] George's futuristic, dystopian modernity envisages an Indigenous subject that conforms via removal and erasure, painfully ironizing the notion of moving islands and presenting us with a discomfiting cautionary tale—one refracted in Ila's recurring question, "Who's gonna be next?"[95] In leaving us to ponder what remains, George's scenario of precarious belonging anticipates the nation itself as a nonplace, evacuated of history, identity, and organic sociality. In so doing, her work provokes audiences to take heed of the unresolved political and historical claims that must be addressed before a truly inclusive, democratic New Zealand can be realized.

URBAN HARVEST: JOHN VEA'S *CULTIVATE* SERIES

From July to October 2012, Auckland Art Gallery Toi o Tāmaki hosted the *Home AKL* exhibition, which featured the work of three generations of Pasifika artists who call Auckland home.[96] According to Pākehā art critic Anthony Byrt, the exhibition addressed "all the themes you'd expect: diaspora, disconnection, celebration of homeland, the slippages that occur when one culture collides with another."[97] Although *Home AKL* made Pasifika art visible and confronted stereotypes, Byrt posits that "it was, ultimately, a show about belonging."[98] For Byrt, the show was "missing a genuinely critical reflection on the contemporary economic and cultural contradictions for Pasifika communities in Auckland."[99] He acknowledges the work of two young performance artists of Pacific heritage not included in the exhibition, who, in contrast, "weren't asking questions about belonging. Instead, they were presenting quietly confrontational views of what the inter-related issues of race, class and poverty look like in New Zealand's biggest city."[100]

These young artists were both finalists for the prestigious 2014 Walters Prize: Luke Willis Thompson's piece *inthisholeonthisislandwhereiam* had participants take a meandering taxi ride from the gallery to a suburban villa, which turned out to be the artist's own home; and Kalisolaite 'Uhila's durational performance *Mo'ui tukuhausia* presented a Pasifika parallel to Taiwanese performance artist Tehching Hsieh's *One Year Performance 1981–1982* ("Outdoor Piece") in New York City, in which the artist lived for three months as a homeless man in Auckland's central business district. Although Byrt does not mention him, I will add John Vea to this brace of artists invested in situated responses to urban survival and the precarity of city living. Through their orchestrated encounters that probe not what home *is* but what home *does*, Byrt argues, these artists examine the contemporary conditions in which we live, "moving us through a city we thought we knew and thought we belonged to, tearing it open to show us what's really inside."[101] This section of the chapter shifts its approach to the Urbanesian to consider works that tackle the economic disparities and violences of the city by using the city itself as a backdrop and/or complicating the boundary between the cityscape and the gallery. I begin with a discussion of primary interventions by Vea before embarking on an analysis of Thompson's oeuvre.

A New Zealand–based mixed-media artist of Tongan descent, John Vea (b. 1985) works with sculpture, moving image, and performance, with a key focus on the impacts of Pacific migration and gentrification in urban New Zealand, drawing attention to the experiences and contributions of the country's Pacific underclass. He has staged numerous performances and exhibitions in sites and galleries around New Zealand, and developed a more international profile with his participation in the 2017 Honolulu Biennale and a solo exhibition at Sydney's Centre for Contemporary Asian Art in 2019. Vea's pieces make visible the implications of being a laborer in the agricultural, marine, and construction sectors, often by embodying the act of physical labor itself. Employing an ethnographic methodology based in *talanoa*, Vea gleans his material from dialogues with the Pasifika community, enacting these narratives with himself as the subject and using objects or mundane actions as metonyms for broader labor processes.[102] For example, in the video installation *Finish this week off, and that's it!* (2009, remade 2014), Vea critiqued the circumstance whereby laborers with physically demanding jobs in the construction industry have to survive on a minimal budget. Five life-size projections filmed one week apart depict Vea holding a large rock for as long as he can. During the filming period, Vea ate below the poverty line; the images and the impact on his endurance register the detrimental effect on his body and strength. In his 2018 work, *You kids should only experience this for a moment—don't be here for life like me,* Vea created a walk-through installation where video-projected workers and industrial machinery turning plaster potatoes evoked menial Pacific Islander labor in a potato chip factory, cautioning against the trap of being confined to a life of drudgery. Vea amends the blind spots in our perception of urban workers; as curator and critic Ioana Gordon-Smith writes, "Without any end product or service, it is labour in and of itself that we encounter, and the person who enacts it that we are forced to see."[103]

It is, however, Vea's ongoing installation and performance work with "urban taros"[104] that particularly interests me here. A recurrent motif in Vea's oeuvre, they are simplified, stylized renderings of the taro root vegetable ubiquitous throughout the tropical Pacific, created from plaster cast in road cones. Vea first cast the taros in 2008 and continues to use these original objects alongside new ones, with the taros becoming invested with the stories that they accrue from project to project. Vea's early installation *Import/Export* (2008) featured the taros packed into wooden pallets, each hand-marked with the name of the twelve Pacific Forum countries participating in the New Zealand government's Recognised Seasonal Employer Scheme (RSE). The alien taros, packaged for transport, attend to how RSE workers, while indispensable to New Zealand's agriculture industries as well as to the economies of their home nations, are profoundly *un*recognized: paid minimum wage, tied to their employers in a relation of dependence and potential exploitation, and promptly repatriated at the end of their tenure with little to show for their labor. As Scott Hamilton notes, like their nineteenth-century predecessors who followed (indentured) labor routes to the mills and plantations of the Pacific, these transient migrant workers are difficult to conceptualize, unassimilated into modern Australasian capitalist systems and occupying a "twilight space between economies and cultural codes."[105]

Vea intends to create and perform with the urban taros for as long as the government's RSE scheme is in operation.[106] The urban taros have subsequently been activated in several performances in which Vea and fellow artists from the HEPT (Help Everyone Pass Together) Collective[107] "plant" the urban taros in sites throughout the city. In an early iteration of his series *Cultivate*, begun in 2008, Vea and his co-artists transported the urban taros

Figure 25. An installation of urban taros remains after a performance of *Cultivate* (2015) by John Vea and HEPT Collective at Auckland's Wynyard Quarter, the site of one of New Zealand's largest urban regeneration projects. Photograph courtesy of John Vea.

in supermarket trolleys from Vea's downtown studio to plant them in Auckland's Myers Park, enacting the process of workers migrating from one site to another. More recently, the performance was presented as part of "Tidelines" (2015), a series of artist installations sponsored by the Auckland Council organization Panuku Development Auckland, charged with transforming the Wynyard Quarter of Auckland's central business district in an ambitious thirty-year project that constitutes one of the largest urban regenerations in New Zealand.[108] In staging this version of *Cultivate*, Vea observed: "The Wynyard Quarter is occupied by both present and past migrant workers who either work in marine and fishing industries or on the recent re-development of the Quarter. But their stories are not told or reflected here. This new crop of 'urban taros' will not be a permanent or elaborate memorial, but will act as a reminder of what is missing."[109]

Gordon-Smith views the taros as "multiples [that] can also be understood as generic units typical of capitalism; cheaply made, easily reproducible and entirely divorced from the people who made them."[110] Granted, but might the taros, through their fusion, dense cultural signifiers, and accreted narratives, suggest something more or other than loss, evacuation, or alienation? Might the reciprocal performance of planting invest something of the richness of the biological taro—its fecund exchange relations and histories of connection—into the urban, rather than rendering them void in plaster?

Colocasia esculenta (*taro*, Aotearoa, Tahiti; *talo*, Samoa, Tonga; *ndalo*, Fiji; *kalo*, Hawai'i) is one of the most important cultigens in the Asia-Pacific region and is a staple food and vital part of the agricultural and sociocultural traditions of Pacific peoples. Although taro was domesticated in Asia as well as the Pacific, the different strains mean that taro can be considered a native plant of the Pacific.[111] Like the canoe, the woven mat, warrior traditions, tapa cloth, and *tatau*, the taro is a transpasifika icon (in Pearson's sense), connecting the cultures and histories of many communities across the region. Replete with social, spiritual, and economic resonances, taro features prominently in myths, legends, and oral traditions throughout Oceania, as well as in cultural festivals.[112] As a valuable item of wealth, exchange, and sustenance, the taro connotes life, growth, community, prestige, and the fulfillment of social obligations. Juliana Flinn observes that actions involving sharing taro, presenting it at feasts, and offering it to visitors "communicate kinship, respect, prosperity, strength of character, commitment to generosity, and a concern for the well-being of others. As such, these activities shape the reputation of the individual, kin group, village, and sometimes the entire island community."[113] As a symbol of the kinship ties between people and land, taro binds concepts of past heritage and future development. In certain Pacific sites, such as Hawai'i, the cultivation of taro by historic methods is a powerful expression of Indigenous cultural revitalization following displacement by foreign peoples and techniques.[114] Taro also speaks to Pacific Islander migrations in the present; recall how, in Hawai'i, the taro corm and its offshoot is a metaphor for a diasporic subjectivity (chapter 2)—exemplary of Oceania's rhizomatic potential—and in a more material sense, taro consumption is a means of maintaining homeland connections when abroad. Inno Onwueme explains that the "socio-cultural attachment to taro has meant that taro itself has become a totem of cultural identification. People of Pacific Island origin continue to consume taro wherever they may live in the world, not so much because there are no substitute food items, but mainly as a means of maintaining links with their culture."[115] This attachment has made taro a lucrative export commodity to diasporic Pacific Islanders, augmenting its role in generating economic by-products from alcohol fuel and animal feed to cosmetics and plastic production.[116]

To render this fruitful, networked, and historied object in plaster, a putatively alien, inorganic, inedible, and non-Pacific material, might indeed, prima facie, reference the disconnection of migrant workers from their home environment and the displacement of traditional economies of exchange within neoliberal systems of production. Yet the re-formed taro, I contend, does not negate or forget the taro's prior resonances so much as recombine and remobilize them to index and instigate new kinds of relationships and to take on the urban in a more active and reciprocal fashion. This approach begs us to consider Vea's further intercultural layering upon the already intercultural taro, enlisting the broader meaning of transpasifika in the sense of Pacific and non-Pacific interactions. The interface between taro and plaster is not unidirectional: taro is turned into plaster (the urban), but in the same process, plaster is turned into taro, whereby the symbolic urban is remolded and resignified through Pacific form. These dynamics are enfolded and extended through the road cone used as a mold. If the road cone is centrally implicated in remaking space in the city and affecting its transits and flows—redirecting traffic, temporarily demarcating areas undergoing fluctuation and change—then the taro / road cone amalgam creates room for pondering how Pasifika energies have a role in reshaping and redirecting urban space and experience. At the same time, this referent is ambivalent: do we pay more attention to the vibrant orange road cones than the Māori and Pasifika construction workers laboring within their boundaries? By materializing Pasifika forms in hybrid states that accentuate their confluences and contradictions, Vea instantiates the labor networks that make possible these intercultural situations,[117] while pushing members of Auckland's mainstream society to change their relation to the urban.

I'll analyze these dynamics through a reading of the 2013 version of *Cultivate*, a street performance of the placement of the urban taros outside the Papakura Art Gallery as part of Vea's exhibition *Homage to hoi polloi*. On the broad, paved sidewalk, against a backdrop of traffic, parking lots, a supermarket, and other commercial buildings, a crowd of passersby has congregated. Five burly Pasifika men line up on the roadside, clad in laborer's outfits of black singlets and T-shirts, cargo pants, and loose denim shorts. A couple of them have broad-brimmed woven sunhats. All the men wear black balaclavas, showing only the eyes, rendering them anonymous and indistinguishable. Before three of them lie hessian sacks; one man has a wheelbarrow, the central man (Vea) holds a hoe. Walking forward, Vea takes handfuls of dirt from his pocket and scatters them purposefully over the cultivation area of concrete paving stones. Back in line, standing upright with the hoe, he begins to sing softly, while the other men take the urban taros from the sacks and wheelbarrow and "plant" them on the concrete in five rows resembling the arrangement of taros in a Tongan village plantation. Their simple, repeated motions of placing the plaster forms upright on the pavement are businesslike, almost automatic. When they're finished, they return to their line. Vea rearranges a couple of the taros, makes a few symbolic digs with the hoe among the patch, sounding the dull clang of metal against concrete, and the men file off, leaving us with the urban taro plot and disappearing into the cityscape.[118]

This pop-up, ritual intervention, lasting only a few minutes, is deeply inflected with poignant resonances. Although visually, the work appears to be a masculine performance of physical labor, the piece also embeds recognition of women migrant workers' experiences of struggle and loss. The song that Vea sings is a Tongan lullaby, "'Ana Lātū," which is a lament for a child who has passed away.[119] Here, Vea weaves the song into a story told to him by a fellow HEPT member about migrant Pacific women hiding their pregnancies (especially if they are out of wedlock) because of cultural pressures, and suffering miscarriages alone and in secret; the concern also extends to pregnant female workers pushed to their physical limits in fields and factories and surviving on poverty-level subsistence, and losing their babies because of the stress on their bodies.[120] Singing as the men plant "fertilizes" the urban taros with these stories, adding to their signifying and testifying power. Like the soil that Vea scatters to prepare the ground — taken from Myers Park to connect the 2008 and 2013 performances of *Cultivate* — reminding us of what is below the concrete, the urban taros prompt us to look beneath the surface. Temporarily claiming urban space, the taro plot credits the contributions of Pasifika laborers in making and remaking the city of Auckland by bolstering its infrastructure and feeding its citizens, while bearing witness to the sacrifices sustained in the process.

By replicating the protocols of Tongan gardening on the urban street, *Cultivate* brings the island and the city into rich imbrication. Rather than registering a sterile yield, the piece calls upon the city to perform, and makes the concrete itself fertile by opening up its many histories, both manifest and latent, suggesting how the Pasifika labor that went into constructing the street connects it to wider genealogies. The urban taro planted in pavement remembers histories of indenture, suffering, and endurance, but it also calls up linked narratives of migration, exchange, and social prestige, pointing to the pride, solidarity, and community that sustain Pacific peoples as they navigate the give and take of Urbanesian life. At the end of the performance, the urban taros are left for people to harvest, leaving ghostly, residual traces from the plaster. By taking them home, audiences separate the worker-performers from their labor,[121] but — significantly — in so doing, they also redistribute the taros throughout the city in ways that gesture to the possibilities of these storied, fusion objects passing through and becoming embedded within the wider cityscape (Vea frequently receives photographs of the taros installed in houses and gardens throughout Auckland).[122] In its astute response to the socioeconomic exigencies of Pasifika laborers and its complex interface between the Pacific and the urban, Vea's art practice attempts to shift public attitudes toward the city, and to encourage a more capacious, inclusive acknowledgment of what might grow therein.

FROM THE BLACK PACIFIC TO BLACK LIVES MATTER: LUKE WILLIS THOMPSON

Educated in Auckland and Frankfurt, Fijian New Zealander artist Luke Willis Thompson (b. 1988) has gained recent and rapid critical acclaim for a body of work in readymade sculpture, film, and live performance that attends to traumatic legacies of racial discrimination, institutional violence, and coerced migration, frequently working out these themes across urban contexts. Thompson's work is a documentation less of acts of violence than of their aftermaths, sedimented in sites and spaces, haunting objects, held in the body, and arcing across intergenerational memory. Thompson challenges us to recall or otherwise encounter the conflicts and clashes of the recent and historical past, and their seepage, residue, and invocation in images, bodies, names, things, places, and texts, leaving open the difficult question of what we are to do with these memorial traces. In *Untitled* (Te Tuhi gallery, 2012), Thompson installed three garage roller doors belonging to Pākehā businessman Bruce Emery, who in 2006 stabbed Māori teenager Pihema Cameron to death after he caught Cameron tagging the doors. Thompson's relocation and repurposing of the physical object, containing the partially erased vestiges of Cameron's final scriptural act, testify to the social injustice of the event (Emery served only eleven months in prison for the killing) and attempt to rehumanize the young Māori man. As Thompson's international profile has expanded, he has moved beyond New Zealand as site and subject while retaining similar themes and approaches. In *eventually they introduced me to the people i immediately recognised as those who would take me out anyway* for the 2015 New Museum Triennial in New York City, gallery patrons participated in a psychogeographical performance in which they followed a Black performer, in silence, on one of several previously undisclosed routes around the city. Traversing sites of memorial and homage—some racially charged—the walks, playing on the uncomfortable connotation of "take me out," echoed the format of the police pursuit and acknowledged the current conversation on "walking while Black."[123]

Currently based in London, Thompson forms part of a loose cohort of Pasifika solo artists and performance companies (predominantly expatriate Australians and New Zealanders) making a marked impact on the cultural and diplomatic life of the British capital. Thompson's Urbanesian aesthetic manifests in the ways that his art projects frame coalitions among Pacific peoples and other communities of color in urban spaces worldwide, drawing on Blackness (rather than Indigeneity) as a differently positioned stance to explore potentially affiliated identities and experiences. This approach was highlighted in Thompson's first solo New Zealand exhibition in 2018 at the Adam Art Gallery | Te Pātaka Toi in Wellington for the biennial New Zealand Festival.[124] Curated by Stephen Cleland, the exhibition was the first to bring together Thompson's three filmic artworks, all with allusions to real-life violence, sites of conflict, and the loss of loved ones. It featured the debut of a new, Pacific work, *How Long?* (2018), about Fiji's involvement in international military combat, and two works previously commissioned and presented separately overseas. *Cemetery of Uniforms and Liveries* (2016), first exhibited at the Institute of Modern Art in Brisbane, shows two Black British men whose maternal forebears were the victims of police violence; and *autoportrait* (2017), which premiered at London's Chisenhale Gallery, depicts Diamond Reynolds, who came to social media prominence in 2016 after she live-streamed the police shooting of her boyfriend Philando Castile at a traffic stop in Minnesota.

Although Thompson's work has garnered international praise, it has also proven contentious; when *autoportrait* was nominated for the prestigious Turner Prize in 2018, it caused a social media controversy, with some commentators criticizing Thompson's success in the elite, white art world based on what they perceived to be a relentless focus on Black suffering and death; and members of the collective BBZ London staged a protest at Tate Britain, wearing T-shirts emblazoned with the slogan: BLACK PAIN IS NOT FOR PROFIT.[125] My discussion does not weigh in on this particular debate (the artist provided his own articulate rejoinder in his 2019 artwork *Black Leadership*), but seeks rather to pursue a more generous and complex reading of Thompson's work that attends to the performative dynamics of encounter between viewer and subject and the larger relations they indicate and sustain. In taking this approach, I am drawn to Tina Campt's elegant conceptualization of the *Black gaze*, which she recognizes in Thompson's oeuvre. A leading scholar on encounters with Blackness in contemporary art, Campt defines the Black gaze as "a particularly challenging point of view that confronts us with the precarious state of black life in the twenty-first century" and that "transforms this precarity into creative forms of affirmation."[126] For Campt, the Black gaze is not empathic, in that it does not invite the viewer to put themselves in the subject's place or to presume to share their experiences; instead, it encourages to viewer to recognize disparity and to feel across that difference, "shift[ing] the optics of 'looking at' to an intentional practice of *looking with and alongside*."[127] The Black gaze thus "demands the affective labor of *adjacency*," by which we "feel beyond the security of our own situation to cultivate instead an ability to confront the precarity of less-valued or actively devalued individuals, and doing the ongoing work of sustaining a relationship to those imperiled and precarious bodies."[128]

Campt sees Thompson, a Pacific artist who identifies as Black, as occupying a position of adjacency (rather than identity) with the forms of violence against African American and Black British subjects that his works have addressed. Given that Thompson's work with Fijian subjects inscribes these relationships more directly, I want to examine the effect of bringing his different works into mutual conversation, as took place in Thompson's 2018 Te Pātaka Toi exhibition. In linking the Pacific Islands to broader contexts of Black identity and cultural expression, Thompson's exhibition contributes to a significant transpacific history of African and African diasporic influence that—beyond general shared experiences of imperial and colonial violence—has shaped Asian/American and Oceanian configurations of the "Black Pacific."[129] The Black Pacific represents a counterpoint to Gilroy's Black Atlantic and an alternative matrix to the Brown Pacific. In the nineteenth century, for example, Africans from the United States and the Caribbean traversed Oceania as sailors and whalers, and a Black community had established itself in Honolulu by the 1830s;[130] during the twentieth-century interwar years, African American narratives of the internationalized Pacific extended the reach of Black internationalism and emphasized affinities with foreign nationals and colonial subjects in the Pacific Rim as a counterdiscourse to US imperialism.[131] Other confluences include the cultural impacts of Black US military servicemen in the region during World War II; the vital importance of Nigerian governmental and artistic models, as well as the Negritude literary movement, on anticolonial cultural production in Papua New Guinea in the 1960s and 1970s; the significant engagement with work by African, Papua New Guinean, African American, and Caribbean writers as models for a Pasifika theater praxis in New Zealand; and the reggae, hip-hop, and associated flows that comprise one significant characteristic of the Urbanesian. The Black Pacific also manifests through the many ways that political struggles of the African diaspora have resonated with South Pacific struggles against colonial rule and racism. A recent expression of solidarity occurred with the Māori and Pasifika Black Lives Matter demonstrators who performed haka outside the US consulate in Auckland to protest the callous police murder of George Floyd in Minneapolis in May 2020. Thus, I am interested in what new perspectives and conversations on Thompson's work might be opened up by reading the 2018 exhibition as an integrated experience.

Arranged over three levels in Te Pātaka Toi, *How Long?*, *Cemetery of Uniforms and Liveries*, and *autoportrait* were positioned at the farthest reaches of the gallery's labyrinthine architecture; corridors and stairwells opened into angular presentation spaces never visible all at once, requiring us to venture through the space in a process of discovery and encounter. Thompson heightened the serendipitous nature of these encounters, and the theatricality of the experience, by darkening the gallery completely and sealing off all sources of natural light: upon entering the exhibition, I was given a small flashlight to guide my way around. These tactics produced an immersive conceptual space and the sense that, while each element offered distinctive subjects and situations, we had entered one artwork rather than three. In suturing the sites of Fiji, London, and Saint Paul, the triptych links the operations of militarization in the Pacific and the militaristic structures of urban police brutality. By registering performances of militarized violence on Black bodies across Pacific Island (Fijian/Melanesian), Black British, and African American contexts, Thompson's work extends the contours of the Urbanesian by yoking evolving discourses on the Black Pacific with the globalizing movement of Black Lives Matter.

Militarization, writes Jodi Kim, has become "a way of life" across the Pacific. It "exceeds the temporal parameters of war, the spatial demarcation of military bases, the functional ends of military institutions, and the enlistment of military personnel."[132] In addition to the chain of military bases that form a violent interconnectedness across the region—highlighting the Pacific as an arena of geostrategic locations and an extraction zone for deployable bodies—the effects of militarization permeate more profusely, arising from "the colonial and neocolonial nexus of state and capital that generates a proliferation of military logics beyond formal military institutions and sites, and beyond the war-making, peace-keeping, and security functions of the military itself. Regimes of militarism pervade the ideological and institutional, the material and discursive, the global and local, and act as a structuring force and logic not only in international geopolitical relations but also in the daily and intimate lives of (neo)colonized and gendered racial subjects."[133] One such extension, Kim points out, is law enforcement's targeting of people within the nation-state via a "domestic militarized immobilization."[134]

Thompson's *How Long?* testifies to Fiji's imbrication in this nexus, gesturing to the global mobilization of its citizens driven by US and British economies of war. Filmed in several towns and villages in Fiji, the piece comprises four silent cinematic portraits in color, which distinguishes it from the other two works shot in black and white. Yet all of the portraits exhibited here—hybrid genres in which film, photography, and performance coalesce—inhabit a similar aesthetic and encourage a similar viewing disposition, with all subjects arranged in a three- or four-minute static pose for the camera in an appropriation of the format of Andy Warhol's *Screen Tests* (1964–66). In this case, we encounter four Fijian individuals from different families: an adult man, an adult woman, a boy, and a baby. Each bears the name of a contested nation or territory from the past four decades: Jone Lebanon (born 1979), Rosi Lebanon (born 1984), Rupeni Iraq (born 2011), and Inia Sinai (born 2017). These appellations derive from Fijian naming traditions whereby names don't necessarily follow maternal or paternal lines or necessarily require antecedents. A child can be given new first names or surnames if an event or relation is deemed significant enough; hence, a child born while their parent is serving or killed overseas could end up being named after that war zone.[135]

Collectively, the portraits construct an "embodied timeline"[136] that registers the impact of the privatization of war on communities in Fiji, as well as the problematic ways that Fijian bodies have become a valuable commodity in the postmodern military context. Fijian Australian artist and scholar Torika Bolatagici observes the long history of Fijian recruitment: by foreign armies in both world wars, as UN peacekeepers in Lebanon and Sinai since the 1970s, and, since the twenty-first century, via aggressive enlistment by British, American, and Kuwait-based private security military companies to the extent that security work now brings in more money than Fiji's other major industries of tourism, sugar, and clothing production.[137] That these high-risk activities are often unregulated, Bolatagici argues, speaks to a neocolonial commodification whereby the agentive structures of Fijian indigeneity are "stripped bare and re-inscribed with notions of an essential universal 'blackness.'"[138] Histories of race and representation converge to perpetuate colonial stereotypes (warrior, criminal, athlete) that construct Black bodies as cheap, exploitable, and expendable. At the same time, Fiji's recent history of coup-related instability speaks to how these foreign deployments have exacerbated the country's own

Figure 26. Above: Luke Willis Thompson, *How Long?* (2018), 16 mm color negative film transferred to digital video, silent. Below: Luke Willis Thompson, *Autoportrait* (2017), 35 mm, black and white, silent. Installation view at Adam Art Gallery Te Pātaka Toi, Victoria University of Wellington, 21 February–15 April 2018, curated by Stephen Cleland. Photograph by Shaun Waugh.

domestic militarism, given that the individuals who instigated Fiji's coups d'état in 1987, 2000, and 2006 were enabled by their experience of serving in overseas conflicts.[139]

Thompson's portraits reveal to us the afterlives of performance: they do not portray direct scenes of violence but gesture to its genealogies and persistent workings, evoking past perpetrations deferred and transferred, and inscribed upon and embedded in descendants. Although, for some Fijians, openly carrying a family history of military service is a source of pride and affirmative identity, this emotion is harder for me to access in these works, confronted as I am with the silent bearing of individual witness mediated by slowness (silent film projection speed) and enforced stillness. These techniques invite reflection on how the precarities and im/mobilities of life under regimes of militarism are intensified representationally through the particular filmic medium. Although the human subjects are composed for the camera, they do not all exhibit *composure*: most exude discomfiture as they struggle with the glare of the apparatus during the unedited take. The *Screen Tests* (or "stillies") were a special mode of experimental portraiture determined by Warhol's exacting rules: tightly framed, harshly lit, with bare scenography and in a fixed frontal position, sitters had to maintain a sustained pose for the entire one-hundred-foot roll of film, with no talking, smiling, or blinking. Although ostensibly a collaborative filmmaking exercise, requiring the willing participation of the sitter, these diabolically challenging performance conditions turn the screen test into the singular human subject's struggle to survive the confrontation with the camera. Divorced from its industry purpose (to try out an actor for a cinematic role), the screen test is displaced onto a different sphere of social being, generalizing the condition of being tested such that it becomes an *existential predicament*:[140] as Noa Steimatsky argues, "*Being* is staged and its performance put to the test"; thus, the screen-test situation gives rise to the struggle for subjecthood.[141]

In the context of Thompson's exhibition, the notion of the nonactor being required to sustain or wrestle with a certain kind of performance of self, effectively, the challenge of appearing as themselves—a performance that, framed by logics of authority and surveillance, reverberates with coerced performances beyond the camera—is profound. As Harvey Young has perceptively remarked of associated instances of compulsory motionlessness in portraiture, Black subjects' active performance of stillness constitutes "an enactment of arrest that resonates with their daily, lived embodied experiences."[142] This is especially so with Thompson's two other works, *Cemetery of Uniforms and Liveries* and *autoportrait*, both of which take up the discourse of domestic militarization to expose how the expendability of Black life is carried over perniciously into practices of policing. To juxtapose international warfare with the increased militarization of the police force in (this case) the United Kingdom and the United States is not analogous but causal; rather than viewing foreign and domestic policy as separate, it is precisely though foreign policy—wars overseas and a state of permanent international military preparedness—that quotidian militarization and domestic acts of state violence are justified and exercised upon the community. This situation, which urban theorist Stephen Graham labels the "new military urbanism," posits that "the key 'security' challenges of our age now centre on the everyday sites, spaces and circulations of cities,"[143] involving the local deployment of military technologies, increased surveillance tactics, a militarized visual culture, and more punitive criminology. In Britain, public concerns continue about the influx of firearms, coercive devices, and combat-training techniques, as well as police chiefs' recent announcements of a more aggressive policy on the use of lethal force. In the United States, this trend is far more pronounced: the war on terror has encouraged federal programs that supply officers with equipment and tactics designed for the battlefield. The Department of Defense's 1033 Program and the Department of Homeland Security have so far handed out over $40 billion in military-grade weaponry to law enforcement.[144] In light of the alarming increase of execution-style deaths of young Black men by police, Kashif Jerome Powell is clear about how "the logics of militarization operate through sociopolitical performatives that not only dehumanize black bodies, but also creates [sic] the conditions for their elision."[145]

Cemetery of Uniforms and Liveries (which takes its title from a section of Marcel Duchamp's glass painting *The Large Glass*, 1912–23) mimics Warhol's medium and method directly by using the same Kodak Tri-X 16 mm film stock, composition, and lighting effects. We are presented with two silent, black-and-white portraits, both of Londoners of Jamaican heritage. The first shows "Brandon," grandson of Dorothy "Cherry" Groce, who was shot by police in her home in Brixton in 1985, an event that helped to spark the Brixton riots, which became a case study for debates about the paramilitarization of policing. The second portrait is of "Graeme," the son of Joy Gardner, who suffered asphyxia and subsequent cardiac arrest when she was restrained and gagged by police during an immigration raid on her home in Crouch End in 1993. Entering the darkened room, as I inevitably do, in medias res, it's hard to know who is Brandon and who is Graeme. One man is more slenderly built, his eyes more widely open; he appears, perhaps, more nervous (he swallows a couple of times). The other man is stockier, more impassive, possibly more defiant before the camera. But then, it's almost impossible to tell what he feels, because the exigencies of the screen-test format so limit personal expression that they tend to reduce each individual to a problematic sameness. This effect is likely the point: moving against the overtly white context of the *Screen Tests* (of the 472 that Warhol made, only 5 were of people of color), Thompson forces us to confront how Black subjects bear up in regard to what Steimatsky calls the "oppressive anthropometric-criminological iconography" that subtended the *Screen Tests*,[146] conceptualized as they were as cinematic versions of mug shots, ID photographs, or passports, and having their closest precedent in Warhol's 1964 mural portrait *Thirteen Most Wanted Men* after the police brochure of the same name.[147]

Freeze! Framed, exposed, captured, shot: these are the violent regulatory undercurrents that the medium invokes, and that indeed enlist our own projections. *Cemetery* bids us to recall brutality against Black women through the men who have suffered these tragic family losses, but the Warholesque mug shot poses of Graeme and Brandon simultaneously confront us with uncomfortable racist assumptions about the a priori criminality of young Black men. In this uneasy encounter, spectators themselves are being tested, and some may fail. Indeed, there seems (to me, at least, as a Pākehā woman) something voyeuristic, almost predatory, about all this hunting in the dark in pursuit of an encounter that feels like an invasion of privacy. But is there an alternative? Recalling the challenge and promise of Campt's Black gaze, if we take the time to sit or stand with each individual as the film spools, to confront and feel beyond our own discomfort, how might we work toward creating a more genuine and generative connection? Of the extended sitting posture, the sustained control for the camera, Steimatsky writes: "It is as if a cumulative inter-subjectivity, effected by the face-to-face of apparatus and sitter, is deposited in the portrait—pictorial, sculptural, photographic—and comes to stand, indeed, for the longer biographical and historical time, for the experience, the life of the person that has brought him or her hither."[148] This might encourage us to think about the greater depth and span of the subject's life that cannot be encompassed, and that can never be wholly known, speaking to Amelia Jones's admission of "the inexorable failure of representation to offer up the self as a coherent knowable entity." "Something always escapes the image," she remarks: it is *"never enough* to contain the bodies it renders."[149] Together with the equivocal visuality of the face—both a nuanced register of an inner life but also a barrier, opaque—this interaction recognizes the complexity of the person portrayed.

In her book *Precarious Life*, Judith Butler discusses Emmanuel Levinas's ethic of nonviolence grounded in the moral claim of the "face" of the "Other." Although we should not take Levinas's face to mean a literal or even a human face, his duty of responsibility to the Other is relevant to the viewer-subject dynamic in Thompson's portraits. Butler writes, "The face, strictly speaking, does not speak, but what the face means is nevertheless conveyed by the commandment, 'Thou shalt not kill.'"[150] Levinas's ethical injunction issues from "the constant tension between the fear of undergoing violence and the fear of instigating violence,"[151] and thus, Butler argues, "The face makes various utterances at once: it bespeaks an agony, an injurability, at the same time that it bespeaks a divine prohibition against killing."[152] Levinas's value here is in helping think through the complicated relationship between representation and humanization.[153] Given the dehumanization that can take place when the literal face is "captured" by the image, effacing the face in the Levinasian sense, Butler contends, "The human is indirectly affirmed in that very disjunction that makes representation impossible." Thus, "For representation to convey the human, then, representation must not only fail, but it must *show* its failure."[154] Consequently, perhaps it is precisely in the *limits* of capture in the screen-test format, our constant confrontation with what exceeds seizure and representation in the images of the Fijian descendants of war or the Black British descendants of police violence—that which cannot be reduced to personification or diminished to the already known—that we become aware of the face through the face, and aware of the precariousness of life itself, opening the possibility for humanization.[155]

This holds true for the potential recuperation of subjects for whom the violent actions of others have defined them in the public eye, as in Diamond Reynolds's portrayal in *autoportrait*. The two four-minute takes present a "sister image" or "counter image" to Reynolds's own horrific, frenetic video that caromed through cyberspace, circulating out of her ambit, in the moments after Castile's murder. Framed in three-quarter profile, like some subjects of Warhol's later screen tests, she exhibits a calmness lacking in the other portraits. Eyes downcast, her only movement her lips as if in song or prayer, shot from below and lit from above, Reynolds offers an image beatific, devotional, and enigmatic; our eyes don't meet—she occupies, it seems, a private world of her own. The piece seeks a curative function in silence, stasis, and control, including the circumstances of the work's exhibition: it exists offline and without a digital equivalent, and can only be viewed in a darkened room that requires the spectator's entire attention, a cinematic portrait staged as a live event. Sitting alone with Reynolds's giant image to the whirring purr of the projection device, and with the Facebook video in mind, I experience a shuttling between chaos and calm. Thompson's piece ironizes the glamour of Warhol's *Screen Tests*, synching its industrial and existential elements to provide a critique of the ways in which traumatized citizens are turned into celebrities while injustices remain unredressed.[156] There is a reflexive poignancy to the function of media, too, given that despite Reynolds' traumatic and apodictic evidence—of violence, but not necessarily of guilt—the officer who fired at Castile seven times at point-blank range was ultimately acquitted. In response to the harrowing spectacle of the witness video, *autoportrait* creates space for a more meditative, humanizing connection with Reynolds that never lets us forget the nexus of racist violence that led to officer Jeronimo Yanez's decision to shoot Castile, but points to her identity beyond that event.

To think about Jone Lebanon, Rosi Lebanon, Rupeni Iraq, and Inia Sinai in relation to Brandon, Graeme, and Diamond Reynolds—and all the others we think about through them—enlists Fijian identity into global flows of Black identities, while emphasizing how local police violence is implicated in the operations of foreign militarization and security. Thompson's Urbanesian documentary project extends transpasifika networks by testing the possibilities of a political Blackness that highlights solidarities across Pacific/Melanesian, Black British, and African American domains, exposing, disrupting, and resisting the oppressive, militarized calculus that undergirds the foreign and domestic regulation of Black lives. In this respect, his triptych is sympathetic to the mission of the Black Lives Matter Global Network, which is "to build local power and to intervene in violence inflicted on Black communities by the state and vigilantes."[157] I have suggested here how Thompson's performative use of film portraiture supports Campt's notion of the Black gaze, whereby our affective labor undertaken through active, participatory acts of witnessing might prompt us to address the disparity between self and other, thereby repurposing vulnerability into something more affirmative and regenerative. Accordingly, Thompson's exhibition provides one possible response to Powell's question: "Given the violent ghosts of the black past that materialize through acts of militarization, how do we reach back towards this history of violence and death, while simultaneously stretching forward to (re)shape future instantiations of blackness?"[158] On these grounds, we might then consider anew the open question encoded in Thompson's experimental appropriation of the screen test aesthetic: what future roles might his subjects inhabit?

MILITARY BASES AND NUCLEAR TOWNS: OTHER URBANESIAS

After Manila in the Philippines, the most densely populated place on earth is not in South Asia, China, Central Africa, or South America. It is, in fact, in Oceania, on Ebeye (Epjā) atoll in the Marshall Islands. How did this situation come to be? Ebeye sits adjacent to Kwajalein Atoll, which since World War II has served as a base for US military operations. Kwajalein currently hosts the Ronald Reagan Ballistic Missile Defense Test Site, which primarily carries out long-range intercontinental ballistic missile interception tests and numerous other "space-surveillance and launch projects for government agencies and private corporations."[159] The exceptionally rapid and intense urbanization on "supersaturated" Ebeye[160] — fifteen thousand people crammed onto eighty acres of land — has been caused by labor demand for base construction, the job opportunities and conveniences of the nearby installation, as well as an influx of migrants relocated from the irradiated northern atolls of the Marshalls in the wake of US nuclear weapons testing. In what Connell and Lea describe as "an extreme and belated example of urban apartheid,"[161] the Marshallese are concentrated on Ebeye while the Americans live on Kwajalein. The US Army provided the educated, middle-class American residents on Kwajalein (military personnel but mainly civilians working for defense contractors) with "comfortable living quarters, recreation facilities, a fully functional school system, a hospital, shops, and many other amenities" in the hope of creating "a 'quality of life' on par with a small American town."[162] Pacific historian Greg Dvorak, who spent his childhood on "Kwaj," explains that the urban planners, engineers from the defense contractor Bell Laboratories, based "their designs roughly on their hometowns in suburban New Jersey" to overlay an "image of transplanted American suburbia" in the middle of the Pacific.[163]

The contrast with Ebeye is dramatic. Reporting on his visit in the 1980s, US congressman John F. Seiberling likened Kwajalein's tropical American setup to "Fort Lauderdale or one of our Miami resort areas, with palm tree-lined beaches, swimming pools, a golf course, people bicycling everywhere." Ebeye, on the other hand, "is an island slum, overpopulated, treeless, filthy lagoon, littered beaches, a dilapidated hospital, and contaminated water supply."[164] Despite subsequent capital works projects funded by Marshallese and foreign governments (spurred in part by protests by Marshallese landowners over the military occupation of their ancestral lands and the unequal distribution of money and resources), Ebeye is still known as the "slum of the Pacific,"[165] suffering from power and water shortages, junk heaps, almost exclusive reliance on imported foods, and social problems affecting the atoll's youth. Robert Barclay's *Meḷaḷ: A Novel of the Pacific* (2002) opens with the vivid firsthand impressions of Rujen Keju, a Marshallese worker at the Kwajalein sewage plant, and his sons, Jebro and Nuke. They evoke life on Ebeye in an army-built, concrete block-house, jam-packed with family and clan members and beset by foul plumbing, roaches, and rats; in the long room are "a bald and armless Black Barbie, and sleeping flies upside-down on the stalks of plastic flowers in Pepsi-can vases."[166] As the characters make their way to their ferry-boat commute to Kwajalein, where their access is restricted and closely monitored, Barclay describes how "beyond the dump's smoldering mounds of trash the reef lay strewn with rusting twisted piles of cars and trucks and heavy machinery . . . all of it blistered and fusing together in different shades of orange and black."[167] Military-led urbanization high-lights how the Marshallese have been displaced in their own country, and signals more broadly how transpacific militarization has prompted mas-sive societal changes in islands across the region. It is the performative confluence of the urban, neocolonial, military, and nuclear in the Pacific that I want to untangle in the remainder of this chapter.

In this second section of the chapter, I focus on how militarization has created different kinds of urban spaces and experiences across the Pacific world, framing an alternative way of exploring the forms and implications of Urbanesia and its attendant cultural production. To expand the thinking around "Urbanesia" and the "Urbanesian" does not detract from their meanings and identities as Meredith and others have conceived them. Rather, the framework draws attention to differentiated sites, modes, and experiences of transpacific urbanism throughout the region; furthermore, in prompting us to ponder other ways in which island spaces become urbanized, it helps avoid what Max Hirsh calls the "ideological rut" expressed as the "reductive tendency to subsume all dimensions of urban change under a critique of neoliberalism."[168] Keith L. Camacho and Laurel A. Monnig acknowledge that "a majority of Pacific Islanders dwell in areas not directly affected by militarist policies and practices,"[169] and—with the exception of Fiji—this situation describes most of the communities and art-ists discussed so far who have contributed to an urban Pasifika aesthetic in New Zealand and its offshoots in Australasia and the United Kingdom. Yet, they argue, "For colonial powers, nevertheless, the Pacific remains a critical area for the implementation of various military agendas" and is a highly militarized part of the world, especially for those living under the aegis of the "American Pacific."[170] As the situation on Ebeye demonstrates—and it is hardly unique—militarization is a "*structuring force* of (im)migrations, displacements, and diasporas" and "operates as a specific modality of neo-colonialism."[171] Thus, as Victor Bascara, Keith L. Camacho, and Elizabeth DeLoughrey point out, if the Pacific is "on the move," the fact is that "much of that mobility and exchange arises from the structures of militariza-tion."[172] In turn, resistance and demilitarization movements have engen-dered some of the region's most widespread transpasifika connections through what Sasha Davis terms "affinity geopolitics": cross-ocean link-ages of solidarity that frame and practice nonhegemonic agendas for inter-national security.[173]

Consequently, the following discussion not only responds to urban per-formance studies but also joins forces with recent calls for a "critical milita-rization studies" that, as Bascara et al. explain, "weaves the complex histo-ries of state violence in the region in relation to issues of ethnicity, indigeneity, gender and sexuality," and "entails a strategic centring of alternative communities and epistemologies that apprehend and engage with the legacies and currency of Pacific Island militarisation."[174] This approach is especially important because, as I established in chapter 1, the military presence in the Pacific (especially that of the United States) and the resultant military-industrial-academic complex has been responsible in no small measure for the erasure of the Pacific Islands in Cold War area stud-ies paradigms, with persistent implications for theater and performance studies. A long history of militarism has thus "made the entire region of the Pacific Rim both hotly contested and curiously underexamined,"[175] placing the Pacific Islands "at both the centre and the margins of any reckoning with the colonial and neocolonial history of state violence in the region."[176] In a period of tenacious and increasing militarization in the Pacific, part and parcel with the Obama administration's "Pacific pivot," Obama's self-billing as "America's first Pacific president,"[177] Hillary Clinton's articula-tion of "America's Pacific Century," and Trump's neo–Cold War belliger-ence toward China and North Korea, it is ever more pressing to analyze these workings. In so doing, such analysis also connects to other sites and regimes, tracing new networks and offering remappings of the region that revise disciplinary boundaries and that cross and contest established state formations and linguistic, political, and colonial histories.[178]

Those of us who gathered for FestPac 2016 in Guam/Guåhan could not fail to be aware of the significance of Indigenous cultural expressions of Pacific Islander identity taking place on an island of which one-third is covered and controlled by US military bases. As the "tip of America's spear" that provides a security buffer with Asia and that helps protect US interests in a critical regional system of transnational capital that represents the new fulcrum of the global economy,[179] the colonized territory of Guam is a nucleus in the massive US military complex that Walden Bello describes as a "transnational garrison state."[180] Millions of people in the Asia-Pacific region live with the impacts of plans devised at the US Pacific Command, headquartered in Hawai'i, the largest unified military operation in the world, with an "area of responsibility" that stretches over half the planet's surface, from Alaska to Antarctica, and from the west coast of North America across the Indian Ocean to Africa's east coast, encompassing forty-three countries, twenty territories and possessions, and 60 percent of the world's population.[181] This network has engendered a "base-produced modernity"[182] with its own subeconomy and subculture[183] that functions materially and discursively, embedding US troops in other nations and territories and conscripting the labor of marginalized ethnic groups, while pursuing rhetorical and performative strategies that submerge violent histories and Indigenous decolonization efforts, and depict the military presence as natural, benevolent, and desirable.

According to Davis, the US "Baseworld" follows a similar design the world over, conforming to "a general plan that is easily legible to the people who often shuffle from one base to another."[184] This unfolding and bifurcating across the Pacific serves as a version of Antonio Benítez-Rojo's concept of a "repeating island," "an island that proliferates endlessly, each copy a different one";[185] in this case, the extension of a template established in the 1890s for taking over and changing the landscapes of the islands that the United States came to control.[186] B. A. Harmon, W. D. Goran, and R. S. Harmon affirm that "urbanized military bases have many similarities to cities";[187] in addition to the urbanized nonbase communities that bases propagate, bases have "housing, retail, office, recreational and industrial spaces, just like other urban areas," and have significant populations and huge payrolls.[188] Military bases have their own rhythms and circulations like other kinds of cities, but their mobile populations and dynamic patterns are largely dictated by external factors (such as troop deployments) and by top-down command.[189] Militarized urbanism may therefore be motivated by a different logic from that of urban villages and commercial cities in the Pacific, but it similarly involves the appropriation of native land, while the bases' highly secured boundaries and access restrictions represent a particularly uncompromising latter-day echo of the Indigenous segregations and curfews of erstwhile colonial towns.

Inevitably, Islander subjectivities have been shaped by these Urbanesian experiences of the militarized Pacific, even if they do not serve in the armed forces. In her prose piece "Inside Out," reminiscent of the inequities between Ebeye and Kwajalein, Indigenous Chamorro author C. T. Perez writes about "the feeling of exclusion" created by the "seemingly endless fence" that separated the Naval Air Station (NAS) on Guam from the world outside.[190] "Inside" contained "spectacular, cliff-line views and expansive, well-manicured fields . . . an orderly world of tidy streets and neatly kept lawns, showcasing houses straight out of the home section of a Sears catalogue." "Outside," in contrast, represented "an uncivilized world" of rented Quonset huts, "pothole-ridden, mud-lined roadways, undecipherable landmarks, [and] nameless streets rampant with loose dogs."[191] Perez grapples with how to negotiate her relation to the inside/outside and to the land and the changing landscape, and with how to transcend her anger over Guam's stolen treasures and the "mental bondage of our colonial existence."[192] Similar dynamics of inclusion and exclusion, support and alienation, are shown to operate even when one is ostensibly on the "inside." Chamorro poet Jan Furukawa's "Local" expresses an Urbanesian subjectivity derived from the way that the military base supplies and determines one's whole life experience:

Call me Navy brat,
born at the military hospital, . . .
Kindergarten at Naval Station's Monkey Tree,
shopping at the ship office, commissary, base exchange,
furniture, automotive, outdoor, and hobby shops,
and bookstore and toy store.
Took in the latest out of Hollywood at NAS amphitheater,
took out pins at any of the base bowling alleys,
took special occasion suppers at the Fiddler's Green.
Took Military Airlift Command flights out of Andersen[193]
to visit family in Hawai'i, into the college years,
still "dependents."[194]

However, divorced from her military husband and no longer a dependent, she and her daughter are "turned away at Big Navy front gate / base inaccessible without a sponsor."[195] As she reflects, "We are now relics of a naval experience on Guam— / brat, wife, and finally, ex- or widow. / We are 'local.'"[196] Furukawa's poem is thus a painful, complicated, and gendered revelation of how US military infrastructures both constitute and disavow Indigenous identity on Guam. Perez's and Furukawa's reflections on inside and outside indicate, after Giorgio Agamben, how colonized subjects are reduced to "bare life" under military regimes. Excised from the colonizer's body politic and its protections, they are cast into the category of those who, beyond "them" and "us," simply do not matter.[197]

The most pernicious reductions to "bare life" and the *homo sacer* (sacrificial person)[198] have derived from the Cold War legacy of nuclear militarism in the Pacific and its violent, ongoing effects for peoples of the region. For fifty years, from 1946 to 1996, Western powers used Oceania as a laboratory for nuclear testing. The United States' dramatic and destructive end to the war with Japan by means of the atom bomb created the idea of using the Pacific for vital military experiments.[199] The operation traded on colonial dominance, taking advantage of the fact that, by the twentieth century, virtually all of the Pacific Islands had become dependencies of US and European empires, and deploying those colonies (or, as in Australia, the colonial mentality of government ministers) to test the bomb and enhance their own "Great Power" status. From 1946 to 1958, the United States detonated sixty-seven atomic and hydrogen bombs at Bikini and Enewetak atolls in the Marshall Islands, in 1962 a further twenty-four tests at Christmas Island in what is now Kiribati, as well as fourteen atmospheric airbursts and high-altitude nuclear tests. Britain undertook twelve atomic tests on the Monte Bello Islands in Western Australia and at Emu Fields and Maralinga in South Australia from 1952 to 1958, and carried out nine hydrogen and atomic tests on Christmas and Malden Islands in 1957–58. France tested its nuclear weapons in the Sahara until Algeria gained its independence; the French then turned to their Polynesian territories, launching the most sustained and prolonged program of nuclear testing, with 193 atmospheric and underground tests at Moruroa and Fangataufa atolls from 1966 to 1996.[200]

These desert and ocean sites were consciously and deliberately constructed as vast, empty, disposable spaces, depopulated and isolated, and divested of their relationality, networks, and prior histories.[201] At the same time as nuclear powers worked to make vacant their proving grounds, they radically transformed these spaces with tens of thousands of tons of equipment in a massive refashioning of infrastructure and development that irrevocably changed the Pacific and inducted its peoples into a nuclear modernity. In what will now seem a familiar narrative, Stewart Firth explains how "nuclear towns"[202] sprang up across the Pacific, homes away from home for task force personnel. In the Marshalls during the 1950s, for instance, "Enewetak and Medren Islands . . . became American towns in the middle of the ocean complete with recreation fields, barber shops, chapels, theatres and networks of residential streets with barracks and mess halls. Airstrips, wharves, laboratories, administration buildings and stores covered the remaining surface area of the islands. Anything less like the Enewetak of traditional times, with coconut palms and thatched houses, is hard to imagine."[203] These global powers evinced little concern for the Indigenous peoples who occupied these areas, nor indeed for the civilian and military personnel who staffed the nuclear sites (often drawn from local laborers and the regional military, not just from the colonizing powers). Inhabitants suffered forcible displacement and exile from their homelands and reserves, and exposure to hazards and long-term illnesses from radiation and fallout. Although, after the collapse of the Soviet Union and the end of nuclear testing in 1996, international organizations were mainly diverted toward other issues, for people living near the "nuclear sacrifice" zones that have been rendered interminably toxic (the half-life of the radioactive element plutonium-239 is twenty-five thousand years), the battle for cleanup, restitution, repatriation, and compensation is just beginning.[204]

To focus on the Urbanesian aspect of this phenomenon highlights how the testing programs left *social and economic* legacies as well as environmental and corporeal ones. Noting a tension in terms of how Oceanians responded to the tests, Nic Maclellan acknowledges the significant and widespread antinuclear protests that took place from the 1950s onward, but recognizes that "many people welcomed the development of nuclear infrastructure across the region, for the jobs and financial opportunities created by an influx of military personnel." Pacific Islanders certainly bore the brunt of US, British, and French nuclear weapons, yet "some benefited from employment or seized the opportunity for adventure."[205] To admit these varying experiences enables a more complex picture of this era, demonstrating how Pacific Islanders were not simply victims but were also participants in these operations.[206]

How have Pacific Islanders responded performatively to these traumatic and contradictory experiences? And how might a focus on performance and performativity enable a revelatory critical analysis of international nuclear discourse? I approach these questions through the lens of what I will call *nuclear performativity*, a whole register of entwined technoscientific, material, rhetorical, and ritual actions, taking place from the macrostructural geopolitical level to the molecular conditionings of everyday social relations, via which the nuclear program was justified, carried out, and continues to make manifest its effects. As an expression of hegemonic power, nuclear performativity is characterized by its tension between spectacle and secrecy, display and deterrence, demonstration and denial or deferral; and between its sudden, immediate violence and its slow onset, revealed in bodies and lands obliquely and over generations. In his ethnography of a US weapons laboratory, *Nuclear Rites*, Hugh Guster-son speaks to this inherent tension by acknowledging the "complex and ambiguous relationship between nuclear weapons, weapons scientists, and the body":[207] nuclear nations developed a spectacular new means of dis-membering bodies and edifices in the service of power, but they under-mined the exercise and display of that power by claiming that weapons exist to prevent rather than facilitate human dismemberment.[208] Gusterson argues, therefore, that "the discourse on the effects of nuclear weapons is perched on a razor's edge between the bomb's need for bodies to display its power and society's need to conceal and transmogrify the bodies of victims and executioners if that power is to be stable. In the end, the relationship between bodies and weapons is such that the human body is simultane-ously present and absent, so that even in its presence it is in the midst of a figurative disappearance that both presages and retrospectively erases its literal disappearance."[209]

To draw attention to nuclear performativity (in its senses of display, something subject to evaluation, and bringing something about) enables interrogation of the strategic duplicity of the dominant discourse on ulti-mate weapons, including scrutiny of what it occludes and effaces. The Atomic Age ushered in an entirely new paradigm of world-making (or unmaking) with what Gusterson refers to as "the scientific drama of bring-ing something fundamentally new into the world."[210] The awesome yield of the bomb and its terrifying destructive power—both a rehearsal and a cautionary performance in itself—which caused men watching from miles away to vomit and urinate, annihilated the staged naval fleets, and often obliterated the island on which it was detonated, inaugurated a new global regime in a manner that was overtly theatrical and exhaustively docu-mented (the United States' Operation Crossroads test at Bikini Atoll in 1946 is claimed to be the most photographed event in history).[211] Yet this play of exemplary empire among established and emerging superpowers, in which Indigenous peoples have largely been props, foils, experiments, or collateral damage, might be understood less as a novel phenomenon and more as an extension of imperial theater in Oceania reaching back to at least the eighteenth century. To scrutinize nuclear performativity, as a branch of critical militarization studies, means attending to such histories. It likewise means examining the propaganda, speech acts, and other rhe-torical performances that publicly naturalized and legitimated this new weapon of mass destruction by excising all references to death and empha-sizing metaphors of birth, the sun's radiance, divinity, and world peace; and that performed acts of substitution and deferral, such as the slippage of "bikini" from connoting an irradiated atoll to conjuring the allure of the two-piece swimsuit.[212]

Nuclear performativity also manifests in the way that civilian audiences in the Global North were trained to respond to the threat of Cold War–era nuclear destruction. Tracy C. Davis's meticulous analysis in her book *Stages of Emergency* leaves us in no doubt about the theatrical and dramaturgical nature of nuclear civil defense exercises in Britain, the United States, and Canada, and of the usefulness of reading those exercises from that perspective. But whereas Davis's case studies are predicated on "coordinated campaigns of rehearsal," motivated by a "what if?" that "anticipate[d] an eventual—though perhaps perpetually deferred—performance,"[213] the fundamental difference for Oceanians affected by the tests is that exile and evacuation from homelands, loss of liberty and community, contamination from fallout, environmental toxicity, and death have already occurred; as Firth, writing in the mid-1980s, put it, they "have already lived in what might be our common future."[214]

It is from this standpoint that Oceanian artists and activists have critiqued the logic of nuclear performativity and have framed their own, counterhegemonic versions that perform alternative experiences of nuclearization (recall *Masters of the Currents* in chapter 2). In the Marshallese context, Kathy Jetñil-Kijiner's spoken-word piece *History Project* (2012) testifies to the injustice of US testing as that which has been and which continues to unfold, staking a claim in her urgent, embodied presence and the impassioned delivery of her solo performance to resist the effacement of the nuclearized body and its histories. The piece begins with a teenage Jetñil-Kijiner (b. 1987) researching the history of the US tests on Enewetak and Bikini atolls, especially the disastrous performance of the 1954 Castle Bravo test, a "runaway" fifteen-megaton thermonuclear device that showered radioactive fallout onto the nearby inhabited atolls of Utirik and Rongelap.[215] She files through books, articles, and websites, but ultimately, she declares, "this / is not new information // i knew all this already."[216] Her knowledge emerges through lived experience, from her parents' bitter stories, firsthand accounts "of what / we call jelly babies / tiny beings with no bones / skin red tomatoes / the miscarriages unspoken"[217] and from the shriveling death that "i watched happen / to my grandfather / and my cousin."[218] Exposing the duplicitous nature of nuclear rhetoric, she expresses anger over

> my islander ancestors
> cross-legged before a general

listening to his fairy tale
bout how it's
    for the good of mankind
to hand over our islands
let them blast radioactive energy
into our lazy limbed coconut trees
our sagging breadfruit trees
our busy fishes that sparkle like new sun
into the coral reef[219]

Jetñil-Kijiner's testimony also addresses the social and economic fallout from this era: the loss of ancestral land and customary social relations, urban migration, and the cultural fracturing due to US financial compensation: "all of the thousands of dollars / funneled across the pacific / exploding like a second sun / and sprinkling over us in the form of / cans of spam, ramen, and diabetes."[220] This brief account of Jetñil-Kijiner's piece indicates how performance can powerfully rehabilitate a history "faded into shadows / into murmurs of a people a home / the world has forgotten and ignored,"[221] both revealing and repudiating the diminishment of the Marshallese to the sacrificial bodies of empire's others. Whereas *History Project* tabulates the violence against the Marshallese as victims of American geopolitical maneuvering, related performance works further probe the contradictions caused by the appeal of nuclear development and urban modernity, and explore the complicated ways in which Pacific Islanders were made complicit in the nuclear program. It is to a fuller analysis of one such work, *Les Champignons de Paris*, that I now turn.

NUCLEAR PERFORMATIVITY: *LES CHAMPIGNONS DE PARIS*

Do you know what makes the ocean glow
When unwelcome guests are making nuclear tests
   —Herbs, "French Letter," from *Light of the Pacific*[222]

Although the United States' military imprint in the Pacific has been the most extensive and pervasive, growing up in New Zealand in the 1980s, I was not aware of American military operations as having the deepest impact on our national and regional policies, but rather those of the French. I vividly remember the bombing of the *Rainbow Warrior*, the flagship of the activist environmental organization Greenpeace, in Auckland Harbor on

July 10, 1985, carried out by French agents sent by their government. The *Rainbow Warrior* had sailed to New Zealand after helping relocate the population of Rongelap to Kwajalein for "decontamination" in spring of that year, and was preparing to sail to French Polynesia for action against an upcoming nuclear test at Moruroa atoll.[223] Our country's first experience of state-sponsored international terrorism spurred worldwide condemnation and local anti-French sentiment, which was particularly resonant for my own family, especially my mother, who at the time was working as a French teacher in a local school. Circulating jokes ("What piece of the rainbow don't the French like?" "The Greenpeace") served as coping strategies for graver concerns about the transnational and neocolonial machinations of the nuclearized Pacific, with the pernicious reach of radioactive fallout now buttressed by espionage and sabotage; and about the stakes of New Zealand's evolving antinuclear platform following Prime Minister David Lange's declaration of New Zealand as a nuclear-free zone in 1984.[224]

The French attack on the *Rainbow Warrior* strengthened New Zealand's opposition to nuclear arms and oriented its foreign and defense policy to cultivate closer relations with South Pacific nations combating the same issues. The South Pacific Nuclear-Free Zone Treaty signed in Rarotonga in August 1985, while not unilateral, galvanized numerous antinuclear initiatives and lent significant impetus to the Nuclear Free and Independent Pacific movement, which, since the 1970s, had linked antinuclear activism with independence and sovereignty struggles.[225] The Pacific antinuclear movement is notable in itself, and in the context of this book, because of the way it mobilized so many heterogenous constituencies around a common cause, moving upward from grassroots activism and the interests of Pacific peoples to work in parallel with state policies and actions.[226] The movement was not only instrumental in advancing a cooperative politics of Pacific regionalism, but it also forged affiliations with nations beyond the region and between Pacific Islanders and non-Pacific Islanders, weaving a transpasifika matrix that indexes the global Pacific.

The antinuclear movement in Oceania has generated a great deal of Indigenous and non-Indigenous cultural production, from performative protests and cultural activism to songs, films, poetry and prose, and visual art.[227] Theatrical performance has also had a notable role: in addition to Jetñil-Kijiner's works, the legacy of US nuclear testing is treated in Dan Taulapapa McMullin's play *Bikini Boy* (2004), while the multimodal performance *The Career Highlights of the MAMU* (2002), by Trevor Jamieson and Scott Rankin, tells stories of the Spinifex people (Pila Nguru) of the Great Victoria Desert in Western Australia, including their experiences of the

British-led nuclear tests. My discussion takes up the intercultural French/ Tahitian play *Les Champignons de Paris / Te mau tuputupuā a Paris* (2017), a compelling and uncompromising documentation of over three decades of near-continuous bombing in French Polynesia and its widespread fallout across social, environmental, physical, cultural, political, and economic domains. The play reveals how France, in its effort to maintain a nuclear footing with Britain and the United States, exposed Tahiti to five hundred times the maximum safe level of plutonium,[228] and drastically ruptured Mā'ohi culture and lifeways. Given France's firm colonial hold on its Polynesian territory, perpetuated by the situation of economic dependence and investment in what Teresia Teaiwa calls "militourism" ("a phenomenon by which a military or paramilitary force ensures the running of a tourist industry, and that same tourist industry masks the military force behind it"),[229] entrenched in large part by this very nuclear legacy, a public performance on this topic in either Tahiti or France is particularly noteworthy.

Authored by French playwright Emilie Génaédig and directed by François Bourcier, the play was created by Compagnie du Caméléon, a socially conscious French Polynesian theater company founded in 2005, and features three male actors, European Guillaume Gay, and two Mā'ohi performers, Tepa Teuru and Tuarii Tracqui. Recipient of the Prix Beaumarchais in 2016, the full production premiered in Tahiti in 2017 and was subsequently performed in France, including at the Avignon Festival, where it was awarded the 2018 Grand Prix Tournesol for live performance addressing social, political, and ecological issues. It was remounted in Tahiti in 2019 at La Maison de la Culture | Te Fare Tauhiti Nui in Pape'ete, where I saw it.[230] The play was published in a bilingual French/Tahitian edition in 2017;[231] my discussion of the play, which I present here in English translation, contributes to growing efforts by Pacific scholars to bridge linguistic schisms in Oceania and open up important work to wider readerships.

Les Champignons de Paris covers a period from 1956 to the present day, offering a kaleidoscope of perspectives on the world's longest and most continual nuclear testing campaign in sites ranging across France, Algeria, New Caledonia, Tahiti, and the French Polynesian atolls of Mangareva, Moruroa, Hao, and Tureia. Drawing from letters, testimonies, archival film footage, political reportage, poetry, and dramatized vignettes, the play concatenates the voices of soldiers, technicians, military wives, Polynesian workers at the nuclear bases, and inhabitants of the militarized atolls, together with those of politicians in Paris and Pape'ete, journalists, military brass, and scientists. An important figure who appears as a character and whose poetry in French and *te reo* Tahiti is interwoven throughout the performance is the late Mā'ohi artist and activist Henri Hiro (1944–1990), who grounds the play's anticolonial and antinuclear stance and reinforces its reach toward greater Mā'ohi self-determination. Energized by public debates after each performance, *Champignons* interrogates the necropolitical logic of France's nuclear performativity in its exposé of how, per Achille Mbembe, "Civil peace in the West . . . depends in large part on inflicting violence far away,"[232] and rests on an expression of sovereignty understood as "the capacity to define who matters and who does not, who is *disposable* and who is not."[233] As the play's title makes clear (punning on the world-famous portobello or button mushrooms first cultivated in the French capital), these mushroom clouds are *of Paris*, deadly alien exports spreading poisonous spores, thus highlighting the power structures whereby colonized islands are effaced and reproduced as toxic experimentation zones or spaces of touristic fantasy in order to maintain French security and global status. While refuting the specious French rhetoric about the harmless nature of the tests, *Champignons* also addresses a central contradiction of nuclear development: the desire for jobs and financial opportunities, and for new amenities and technologies from Europe. Consequently, the play offers insights into the implications of the massive social, economic, and infrastructural changes and schisms wrought by urban military investment in French Polynesia.

The notion of a military program shrouded in secrecy from the Mā'ohi people is potently materialized in the production's mise-en-scène. Translucent plastic sheeting drapes the entire set of the intimate Petit Théâtre, hanging from the walls, swathing the floor, and covering the table and two chairs on stage. Enveloping the set in inorganic material, which separates the actors from their natural environment, serves as an abundant metaphor for the foreign infrastructural overlay on to Mā'ohi *fenua* (land), as well as the restrictive rewriting of spatial relations due to military occupation and contamination, and, most obviously, the French nuclear campaign in the Pacific as a gigantic cover-up (it should not escape us that "Moruroa" translates as "big lies").[234] The performers convey this process of retrieving fragments of a willfully obscured and classified history by rummaging among the folds of plastic on the stage floor to discover various hidden objects—a pair of spectacles, a letter, a hat, a radiation mask—scattered detritus that they piece together into narrative in the vignettes. The plastic sheeting enables another central device, simple but highly effective, of using theater's materiality to tackle the problem of how to represent the often-intangible "slow violence" of radioactive contamination.[235] Michelle Keown has criticized scholars' "often uncritical enlistment of abstraction and meta-

Figure 27. *Les Champignons de Paris* uses the device of fluorescent paint to indicate the elusive yet inescapable effects of radioactive contamination. Play written by Emilie Génaédig and presented by La Compagnie du Caméléon, directed by François Bourcier. Le Petit Théâtre, La Maison de la Culture | Te Fare Tauhiti Nui, Pape'ete, Tahiti, 2017. Photograph by, and courtesy of, Stéphane Sayeb and Victoire Brotherson, Tahiti Zoom.

phor" in discussing the effects of nuclear contamination as an unspeakable force, carried in the body but invisible to narrative and to history.[236] The performance makes tangible these abstractions when, periodically, actors appear in a full radiation suit and mask, bearing a paint roller and a container of fluorescent green paint marked with the trefoil radiation hazard symbol. Gradually and methodically, as the scenes progress, they mark the other characters and parts of the set with stripes of paint. Visible under some lights but not under others, the paint provides a compelling visual signal of the evasive yet pervasive infiltration of nuclear poisoning. While still, arguably, a metaphor, it is a critical one that refuses the literal and figurative disappearance of the body that is both crux and paradox of atomic discourse and the centrifuge in which nuclear performativity garners its hegemonic force.

Throughout, *Champignons* probes the hierarchical relationship between the metropole and the colony, revealing how Mā'ohi have been exploited in service to a nation-state of which they are never fully able to partake. Chief politicians and high-ranking military officials from the Parisian center appear on the upstage projection screen much larger than life, with Māʻohi surveilled and controlled but unable to return the gaze fully. This effect of French militarism as an unstoppable force is epitomized in the scene where Territorial Assemblyman John Teariki presents his passionate 1966 submission before General Charles de Gaulle, imploring him to stop the impending nuclear tests on Moruroa and Fangataufa. De Gaulle does not appear on stage, but as a giant face looming hugely on the screen in grotesque slow motion, evoking the inexorable power of the state. Teariki's realization, "Democracy explodes in the face of nuclear divinity,"[237] cues the alarming advent of nuclear violence, as the European actor, in military uniform, dons sunglasses and watches proudly as an atomic detonation on screen blinds us all while the *Marseillaise* booms through the theater. In an arresting move, a Polynesian character turns and walks upstage "into" the burgeoning explosion: he is immersed by the bomb, becomes the bomb, in a moment of rending annihilation.

The necropolitical dimension of nuclear imperialism is a key throughline of the production, making clear, in Mbembe's words, how the colony is "the site par excellence where controls and guarantees of judicial order can be suspended,"[238] thus subjecting colonial populations "to living conditions that confer upon them the status of the *living dead*,"[239] as well as a site for exposing its own citizens to war—the French soldiers and workers who must die in service of France's desire to defend itself. Early scenes set in the Sahara Desert that enact nuclear accidents and their subsequent cover-ups prove that France was well aware of the dangers of nuclear testing before it moved its operation to French Polynesia after Algerian independence. This posture is reiterated from the very first Pacific test, when France's ailing science and de Gaulle's impatience to see a bomb in action cause a nuclear disaster on Moruroa; the wind causes the mushroom cloud to bifurcate, showering the atoll of Mangareva with toxic rain:[240]

POLICEMAN: The rain is radioactive. We must assemble the
   population at the hospital to give them iodine.
SOLDIER: Don't do that: you'll just fuck it up. We must minimize the
   contamination figures so that the Polynesians don't suspect
   anything!
POLICEMAN: But why?
SOLDIER: Don't you get it? At the slightest fallout, we are supposed
   to stop the tests. But we are not going to stop at the first test . . .
   So, we say nothing![241]

Speaking to the dissolution of humanity that is an expression of the "violence of the state of exception,"[242] Mangarevan schoolteacher Jacqueline suggests, "Perhaps they take us for guinea pigs."[243] This deceptive discrepancy between military and civilian care and amenities is carried over to the construction of atomic shelters. A French solider boasts to a Mangarevan man and his elderly father about all the modern conveniences they can expect at the fallout shelter, declaring, "We cannot do enough for you!"[244] The Mangarevan's subsequent testimony, however, takes place against a backdrop of juxtaposed images of the French and Polynesian shelters as he tells us: "I go around the island, I go to Taku, which is a small town where there is a military unit. There, there is the military shelter. It is a bunker. With walls twenty-six centimeters thick. Covered with protective metal sheeting. When you see that with your own eyes . . . Why, me, little Mangarevan, did they put me with my family in an atomic shelter that does not offer the same guarantees as a military bunker?"[245]

A primary goal of *Champignons* is to show how the exercise of necropower extended to the military urbanization and industrialization of French Polynesia, and to delineate the irrevocable social and economic impacts on Islander lives. Pape'ete, initially a missionary enclave, was remade as a colonial city in parallel with the renovation of Paris in the mid-nineteenth century, and was radically remade again in the 1960s as a militarized city to support the bases on the outer atolls, resulting in an extreme spatial reorganization of the islands. During this period, huge changes were made to the airport, harbor, and docks; and there was a massive influx of French troops and of "metropolitans" (people from mainland France), as well as a mass migration of Polynesians from outer islands who flocked to Pape'ete in search of jobs and money.[246] Tahiti-based anthropologists Bengt and Marie-Thérèse Danielsson argue that the "sudden flooding of the beautiful and peaceful islands of French Polynesia by twenty thousand foreign troops and merciless profiteers in the 1960s . . . is fully comparable, in both its swiftness and magnitude, to the destruction wrought by a tsunami."[247] Tahiti experienced incredibly rapid change: the population soared, and along with the injection of new, foreign goods and amenities, integration into a cash economy, and huge housing projects, came concerns about traffic jams, waste, large urban slums, social problems, and alienation from traditional foodstuffs, lands, and lifeways. How these social changes complicated protests against the tests are shown in a scene set on Bruat Avenue in downtown Pape'ete in 1980, with Henri Hiro leading a protest march to a soundtrack of dissent and people hurling insults. A young Tahitian man, Terai, joins the small band of walkers and admits, "My parents are ashamed of me, that I want to participate in this march, they don't understand."[248]

Although, later, when the French resumed their tests in 1995, there was widespread urban rioting and violence that shattered the postcard image of Tahiti that the French were so anxious to project, Henri's response acknowledges a reality of this new modernity: "There are lots of people who are very happy that the tests are happening here. It creates work and good salaries."[249]

These tensions between the immediate material benefits and veiled dangers of military urbanization are dramatized in a series of scenes between two Tahitian friends, Tihoti and Moerani. Moerani, who has a new job at the Centre d'Expérimentation du Pacifique (CEP)[250] on Moruroa, tries to persuade Tihoti to give up his traditional job as a fisherman and join him at the urbanized base. Lauding the displays of French largesse, he tells Tihoti: "There are trees, coconut palms, restaurants, terraces . . . Someone takes care of your bedroom and your laundry, it's like you're in a four-star hotel. You can do all kinds of sports activities, there are many things to do. And all that without spending a dime, since almost everything is free. . . . And every two weeks I take the plane back here to Pape'ete: it's covered."[251] While remaining cagey about the precise nature of his work with the bomb, Moerani enthuses about his fabulous salary and his "access to incredible things . . . Do you realize, I have eaten an apple! . . . Because even imported products become accessible! Seriously, with what you can earn over there, you could save your money, buy a house for your family, a car, a moped for your *vahine* [woman], pay for your children's education . . . You would be recognized, you would be one of those who have succeeded . . . Job, money, what more do you want?"[252] Persuaded that "nuclear energy is the new economic engine" and that "Mururoa[253] has become the place where every real man should be,"[254] Tihoti joins up, but learns quickly that the trade-off is a divorce from Indigenous life under French colonial dominance at the base. He must abandon fishing, dance, and customary clothing, and is forbidden from speaking Tahitian, his friendly "'Ia orana" replaced with a curt "Bonjour."

Champignons exposes the ever-widening gulf between French attempts to control the narrative of benign testing and the perceived effects on bodies and environments that the Polynesians cannot fail to notice. Drawing on testimonies still largely kept secret in the present day, characters speak out against the military smokescreen. When things pall for Tihoti on Moruroa, he berates Moerani (who is visibly sick and coughing) for refusing to talk about the dangers so that he can keep his job and continue to take advantage of the military infrastructure, and calls out the hazards:

Look at the fish that are dying. They are everywhere after the deto-nations; it stinks. . . . Matau and Pierre are gravely ill. The military have repatriated Serge, and we don't know if he is still alive. And Teriitaria? He was a stevedore here. One day, he sees blue patches breaking out all over his body and growing steadily as the hours go by. We take him to hospital and, three days later, we call his wife to tell her that he has died. Don't tell me that he caught this disease while working on the dock in Pape'ete in the sun! Stories abound of comrades taken from Moruroa in sealed lead boxes . . . Is it strange to be worried?[255]

Addressing the audience directly, Tihoti asks: "Hey, Farāni [France], if your nuclear tests are harmless, why don't you do them at home? Here you are: this pebble, it comes from Moruroa. If I offer it to you, could you put it under your children's pillow every night?"[256]

The parlous effects of thirty years of nuclear colonialism are cataloged in a gripping late scene in which France's 210 atomic and thermonuclear explosions—listing the names of the bombs and their kiloton measurements—scroll on the projection screen; it's visually overwhelming as the list becomes dizzying to comprehend. As the register of nuclear violence rolls doggedly upward, the three actors enter in their radiation suits and masks and progressively cover the entire set with "radioactive" paint. When the scrolling finally ceases, we are presented with footage from former French president Jacques Chirac's announcement of the cessation of the nuclear tests on 29 January 1996. In contrast to his smiling face and magnanimous disposition, our confrontation with the slathered stage, glowing sickly, purulently, in the blue light, testifies to the impossibility of understanding this history as a foreclosed past, and only as a condition that is just beginning. In the words of one Polynesian character: "They want to urge us to forget a period, oh, so tragic for us! To start a new one, no longer with the threatening noises of nuclear tests, but with—beneath our feet—the deadly silence of 147 wells of radioactive waste."[257]

Indeed, the final scenes of *Champignons*, set in the present day, bear wit-ness to these still-emerging reckonings and dispossessions. We are reminded of the appalling statistics of health problems and cancer deaths suffered by former soldiers and CEP workers, the lack of medical follow-ups, and the unheeded calls for compensation, in addition to the legacy of economic dependency, the Urbanesian reality of 23 percent unemploy-ment, and the infrastructural problems caused by demilitarization, espe-

Figure 28. Wearing radiation suits, actors in *Les Champignons de Paris* (Guillaume Gay, Tuarii Tracqui, and Tepa Teuru) watch archival footage of former French president Jacques Chirac announcing the end of nuclear testing in French Polynesia in 1996. Play written by Emilie Génaédig and presented by La Compagnie du Caméléon, directed by François Bourcier. Le Petit Théâtre, La Maison de la Culture | Te Fare Tauhiti Nui, Pape'ete, Tahiti, 2016. Photograph by, and courtesy of, Emilie Génaédig.

cially on the outer islands.[258] We meet the Tureian man who cannot get a bank loan because of the terrifying risk of a fatal tidal wave from the collapse of nearby Moruroa, reduced to a lethal wasteland and perilously destabilized by the subterranean tests. His painful lament speaks to the deep betrayal of Mā'ohi existence by the French regime: "These islands, the Earth, it's our Nourishing Mother. We fucked her with a bomb. . . . Magnificent, said General de Gaulle. Is it magnificent today? What did they do to my Land? *Ua ha'avi'ivi'i rātou i to'u fenua*. They have contaminated my country."[259] Ultimately, the play's counterhegemonic nuclear performativity encourages the possibility of rapprochement between the colony and the metropole. In the closing scene between two Polynesians and a metropolitan, the actors appeal to the foundational principles of the French Republic in which they all stake a claim, asserting that "the future lies in dialogue, in the upheaval of relations between our peoples, where there will be no question of policy-makers and implementers, the strong and the weak . . . but fraternity rediscovered."[260]

• • •

This chapter has gathered together and extended discussions in several disciplines to make the case for the urban as an intrinsic category not only for understanding significant, emerging ways of life, identities, and forms of intercultural production in Oceania, but also for investigating major modalities of settlement and unsettlement in the region brokered by the colonial past and by the unfurling geopolitical, economic, and military forces of the Pacific Century. By constellating several works by young visual and performing artists (most born after 1980)—Samoan, Cook Islander, Māori, Tongan, Fijian, Chamorro, Marshallese, and Mā'ohi—I have explored the potential of "Urbanesia" as physical space, creative arena, mode of lived experience, and intervention; the flexible, networked capacities of which add additional dimensions to the transpasifika mappings traced throughout this book. The chapter's bipartite arrangement enables discussions in urban performance studies to be excavated and linked to critical militarization studies, opening up ways of thinking about how the urban is constituted and reconstituted in different contexts throughout the region, and shedding light on the Pacific's unique geographies, Indigenous histories, and patterns of mobility and globalization. Ultimately, the chapter is vested in how performance, with its embodied materiality, provocative spectator-subject relations, and experiments with spatiotemporality, is a potent medium for reflecting on, producing, and negotiating the urban experiences of Pasifika peoples. Whether celebrating aspiration, hope, and success, or redressing the violence and dispossessions of neoliberal and military hegemony, the case studies present pathways for fostering greater democratic participation and social justice across the Pacific and the wider world.

six

Epilogue: Pacific Futures

Vast and volatile, fractured and frenetic, teeming with activity and innovation, oppression and resistance, secrets and revelations, the merging and
morphing Pacific Ocean world is a far cry from Magellan's peaceful, empty
zone of transit. Myths of the vacant ocean and isolated isle have been convenient fictions for global powers that have made use of the Pacific for a
variety of colonial, military, scientific, and developmental projects, the
effects of which have spilled over into the priorities and methods of academic disciplines, including theater and performance studies. But the
Pacific world of the early twenty-first century is a crucible of dynamic
movement, exchange, and transnational contention in which some of the
world's most significant political, economic, and environmental issues are
being forged and tested. In his sprawlingly ambitious modern history,
Pacific, Simon Winchester says as much when he writes:

> For all its apparent placidity, the Pacific seems today to be posi-
> tioned at the leading edge of any number of political challenges and
> crises. . . . The future, in short, is what the Pacific Ocean is now com-
> ing to symbolize. If one accepts that the Mediterranean was once the
> inland sea of the Ancient World; and further, that the Atlantic Ocean
> was, and to some people still remains, the inland sea of the Modern
> World; then surely it can be argued that the Pacific Ocean is the
> inland sea of Tomorrow's World. What transpires across these sixty-
> four million square miles of ultramarine ocean matters, and to all of
> us. Hence the need to write about it.[1]

But *how* to write about what Winchester accurately deems "an oceanic
behemoth of eye-watering complexity" and staggering dimensions,
embracing an "immense spectrum of happenings and behaviors and people and geographies and biologies," presents a daunting authorial challenge: the Pacific world can seem "too overwhelmingly confusing—the

body of water too monstrous, its narrative too insuperably challenging in its variety and vastness."[2]

Moving Islands has approached the task selectively, by exploring contemporary cultural and artistic performances that speak to the region's unfolding exigencies, privileging intercultural projects inaugurated by artists and communities within and from the Pacific Islands. Throughout, I have emphasized the value of performance's capacity to materialize larger, abstract forces and flows, and to provide a site for urgent and immediate human and more-than-human expression, connection, and collaboration. I have similarly highlighted the potential of performance to test and trouble ideological and epistemic positions, and to imagine other possibilities for being in the world. In focusing on island cultures from a networked and relational perspective, one of my underlying premises has been that if the Pacific is indeed the sea of Tomorrow's World, then we must pay attention to how islands, as routing points, linchpins, proving grounds, storied sites, and spaces of experimentation, have often been positioned, for better or worse, at the forefront of its various forms of modernity and futurity. Even if the conditions brewing in the Pacific world have assumed a particular force and urgency since the millennium, invocations of Winchester's sort are hardly new; as Chris Ballard reminds us, "Projections in which the Pacific serves as a kind of future for the globe at large have a long genealogy," with pronouncements of the Pacific Age or Pacific Century stretching back to the late 1800s.[3] But what has often been missing from such past and present prognostications, Ballard observes, is a determined concern for the ways that these futures "might find distinctive form or articulation in a Pacific context,"[4] hence the necessity of paying attention to specific sites and communities within Oceania. In related fashion, Viet Thanh Nguyen and Janet Hoskins wonder if scholars of the twenty-second century will speak of a "transpacific world."[5] I see no compelling reason why we shouldn't speak of one now, but we must remain critically attuned to the scope and terms of that world-making. It is vitally important that we continue to expand and reconfigure the rubric of the transpacific. To prioritize Pacific Islander interventions is not merely an additive project, providing new examples for an extant archive, but also involves a reconceptualization of dominant notions of the region and of what a transpacific optic might be able to elucidate.

Erin Suzuki's notion of "several alternative transpacifics"[6] that are not always congruent or reconcilable is, in my view, the most suitable way to understand a region so resolutely resistant to homogenous characterization. The transpasifika perspective that I have adopted is one way (but only one) of reading cultural production from this area. Taking the Pacific's inherent complexity as a point of embarkation rather than a destination, I have found *etak* to be an apt metaphor and design for this book, whose chapters chart multiple voyages across and beyond the Pacific by following different constellations of case studies, pursuing varied arguments to their different ends. This doesn't mean, however, that no common themes, strategies, or lessons emerge from the study. Together, the performances profiled throughout this book have emphasized the imbrication and significance of small island societies within larger social operations, drawing attention to the centrality and plentitude of the ocean as a relational medium. The works have highlighted the intrinsic simultaneity of indigeneity and diaspora, roots and routes, groundedness and movement, in understanding the dynamics of Islander lives and identities, and have insisted on their articulations with migration and imperialism in apprehending transpacific currents. Across the book, artists have acknowledged and experimented with shared practices and tropes that connect peoples across the Pacific, such as the vaka, tapa cloth, taro, *tatau*, warrior traditions, and woven mats. The artistic and cultural performances have likewise shown how artists have drawn upon genealogy and tradition, and local concepts of time and space, reworking them in new forms, contexts, and collaborations to frame alternatives to imposed narratives and remit more affirmative and subversive stories of being and becoming. These tactics continue to adapt to the ever-changing circumstances of the region. Poised at this moment of writing, when the world remains assailed by the rampant spread of COVID-19, it remains to be seen how the new social and economic challenges, interpersonal strictures, and technological practices brought about by the coronavirus pandemic will impact the performance collaborations and trends that have taken shape since the twenty-first century, and in what new ways we might make and receive performance from Pacific worlds.

In its methods and approaches, this book's contributions can be understood as part of a series of paradigm-shifting turns in our field over the past generation: the circum-Atlantic turn of the 1990s, the hemispheric turn of the 2000s, and what I see as the transpacific turn of the 2010s, which has been fomenting in pockets of our discipline and is now coming into greater clarity. This claim orients us to the question of what this book's insights might hold for the field at large, and what difference Oceania might make to the practices of theater and performance studies, particularly in the US academy. To consider how Pacific theories and praxes might productively impact aspects of our discipline makes me think about my place here in

Figure 29. *Protect Our Aiga, Samoa* (2020), pictorial image from Michel Tuffery's *Handle with Care* series, an ongoing project begun in March 2020 in consultation with Pacific Health Plus, Porirua, that responds to the COVID-19 global pandemic. The campaign was designed to convey simple messaging directly to Māori and Pasifika communities, which have been disproportionately impacted by the pandemic. The images, which were displayed as posters in different public spaces, adapt vintage postage stamps from Aotearoa New Zealand and other Pacific Islands. While encouraging community members to "stamp out" coronavirus by staying home, washing hands, and wearing masks, the posters emphasize ties to ancestry and culture as part of a holistic approach to healthcare and urge particular care for elders. This poster is based on a Western Samoan postage stamp, "Samoan Girl and Kava Bowl," issued in 1935. Courtesy of Michel Tuffery, MNZM, and Jayne Tuffery, with special thanks to Lee Pearce.

California, where I am composing these closing lines. California, we shouldn't forget, was for centuries rendered by mapmakers—wonderfully, stubbornly—as an island, broken off from the continent and floating in the Pacific Ocean.[7] If Vicente M. Diaz noted the institutional "West Coast hegemony" of Asian American studies and Pacific studies within the American academy,[8] what potential might there be in these West Coast influences, these seismic ripples from California, to unsettle the East Coast hegemony of US performance studies?

To begin with, this project's informing frameworks may help to recast some of the debates about performance studies' "internationalism" that have surfaced periodically since the millennium. Responding to charges of Anglo-American "imperialism" stemming from the discipline's broad intercultural experiments as well as the consolidation of a US academic paradigm "going global," scholars have acknowledged ongoing issues of social, economic, linguistic, and institutional inequality in the field, as well as dynamics of power and privilege that elevate certain voices while denying others a place at the academic table, and have evinced a desire to address them.[9] Nevertheless, discussions of this sort (which have also occurred in theater studies) have largely sidestepped rigorous engagement with area studies legacies and related geopolitical paradigms that invest disciplinary histories and influence disciplinary constructions and methods. As a result, such conversations, while well intentioned, have a certain circularity and tend toward an additive model of inclusion that fails to examine (and thus replicates) familiar assumptions and blind spots. My work highlights the need to reexamine these premises and calls for greater scrutiny of the spatial imaginaries and geographies of power that underpin disciplinary methods. How can we reinvigorate conversations about global theater and performance studies through a more determined analysis of the political economy of knowledge-making and its attendant assumptions about how and what we see? We might, then, reposition how our discipline understands the relationships between performance, people, culture, and place, with implications for how people and their worlds are represented in our scholarship.

Relatedly, attending to Oceanian performance might usefully reinforce performance studies' interdisciplinary commitments. This book has shown how performance intersects crucially with a range of other discourses; among them, geography, historiography, environmental humanities, digital humanities, Indigenous studies, transnational migration studies, urban studies, and militarization studies. The arguments contained here prompt us to further consider not only, as Diana Taylor has suggested, how an inter- or transdisciplinary approach might enable us to envision different, more complex objects of analysis,[10] but also—reciprocally and significantly—how thinking in terms of performance helps advance these interdisciplinary dialogues. Furthermore, the scalar dynamics of the Pacific Ocean world encourage a reorientation of the relationship between micro and macro scales of action. The Pacific's geographic expanse and diversity, together with consideration of how the local and particular interfaces with regional and global forces and flows prompt us to conceive differently our objects of study and shift current ways of thinking about how comparative, interdisciplinary analyses of embodied arts practices might be undertaken across different scales.

A key contribution of this study has been to enhance conversations about the "new intercultural turn" in theater and performance studies. There are rich possibilities for Pacific work to inform future research projects on contemporary and historical subjects alike that, as Charlotte McIvor and Justine Nakase put it, "approach interculturalism as fluid, ephemeral, multi-modal, and minoritarian,"[11] and that privilege local, vernacular modes of exchange and dialogue, the processual and transformational capacities of performance projects, multiple identity positions, and intersectional analyses.[12] Methodologically, the projects examined in this book are instructive for thinking beyond aesthetic experiments in blending or interweaving different performance cultures to also consider how intercultural formations emerge though complex, unfolding genealogies, and to acknowledge the multiplicities that inhere *within* cultures. They moreover encourage us to analyze more finely the performative dimensions of *how* cultural forms are changed, transferred, proliferate, and take root in new spaces, including how ideas and influences are relayed reciprocally and laterally among cultural contexts. This approach requires that we trace varied intercultural dynamics not just on the stage or within the performance area but also among performers and audiences, and in/through the socioeconomic, political, and institutional structures that make performance possible.

The methods pursued in *Moving Islands*, similarly, might serve as an instructive reminder to take seriously theater and performance studies' historic concerns with what D. Soyini Madison has termed "theories of the flesh"; that is, "the distinctive interpretations of the world carved out of the material realities of a group's life experiences."[13] Madison frames her thoughts within a Black feminist context, but her ideas resonate strongly with calls made by Oceanian and other Indigenous scholars in adjacent disciplines. Madison points to the importance of specialized knowledges, including Indigenous thought and practice, to guide, adjust, and alter our dominant analyses and to direct the authority and knowledge/power of the critic.[14] We must attend anew to the revelatory capacity of Indigenous thought and intellectual traditions for our work—on their own and/or as complementary discursive strands—in order to counterbalance the thrall to Western theory and Eurocentric strategies of reading that still hold sway in our field. By extension, the drive of such theory to attend to performance's relationships with poeisis and kinesis (rather than just mimesis) proves valuable for reaching beyond nonrepresentational modes of interpretation.[15]

What next, then, for research on performance from Pacific worlds? How might our field move forward in response to the current and ongoing upheavals of the Pacific Century? Although the project I've pursued here might appear to be widely encompassing, it is only one of myriad stories, patterns, and pathways that might be traced across this huge terraqueous domain. Inevitably, these journeys have been shaped by my own position as a Pākehā scholar who has lived mainly within a transpacific world, and by the privileges and pitfalls of that perspective. The Pacific holds, and needs, many stories told about it from all kinds of positions and points of view. This means that some readers will naturally take another angle on my ideas and interpretations, bring alternative insights, or see or feel differently. On this, I am with Dwight Conquergood, who observes that performance, as an essentially contested subject, "locates disagreement and difference as generative points of departure and coalition for its unfolding meanings and affiliations."[16] Disagreement is thus inevitable and healthy; what is important is the ongoing, evolving dialogue.

With that in mind, I venture some thoughts for ways in which this dialogue could continue. The field could benefit from further work that connects Oceania with broader transpacific and global matrices. This would take place in a mode of productive engagement, acknowledging differences and disjunctions but exploring expanded frameworks for understanding Pacific Islander lives within broader realms of experience, especially as they are relayed through performance. It likewise responds to Chadwick Allen's call for more cosmopolitan analyses that situate Indigenous cultural production within broader multicultural, transnational, and global contexts.[17] Much of the research emerging in transpacific performance studies today still tends to fall into a focus on Pacific Islands or a focus on countries and territories of the "rim." Exciting and inspiring as this work is, by breaking down these geocultural boundaries we stand to gain a more sophisticated picture of how Pacific worlds are constituted through various cultural transactions. A significant part of this is a clearer understanding of the ways that Asia, Australia, and the Americas have also been molded by their ambitions and imprints in the island Pacific, revealing engagements that frequently remain disavowed on their mainlands. This networked research approach in no way dismisses the benefit of close, detailed investigations of specific sites; these situated studies are essential for understanding the region in its depth as well as its breadth. But this locally focused scholarship needs to be balanced with wider, multisited, and transmedial studies, especially if we want to examine how the microstructures of performance interface with macro-level forces, past and present.

We need to repair the postwar breakdown that has occurred between Pacific studies and wider studies of the humanities. As *Moving Islands* has demonstrated, it is not just that our field stands to benefit from Oceanic insights; Pacific studies, in return, has much to gain from the frameworks and methods of theater and performance studies. Many research projects would benefit from more sustained dialogues between theater/performance scholars, literary scholars, art historians, historians, ethnomusicologists, and anthropologists working with Pacific topics (and, more broadly, climate scientists, geographers, and political economists). A plurality of voices is necessary to engage the region's heterogeneity, but it is also vital to bring those voices into conversation. While I recognize the value of both the long-form monograph and the essay collection, when it comes to performance our field's engagement with Pacific research could be even more creative, and push further beyond Western humanistic scholarly models. How can we continue to experiment with inventive platforms and venues for dialogue, ones that affirm alternative modes of knowledge and expression and that support respectful, mutually beneficial collaborations between academics and artists?

Realistically, however, none of this research about or in relation to the Pacific is going to flourish unless students in our discipline get trained in its objects and methods. We need better infrastructures for making this work intelligible within larger scholarly frames, especially in the US academy. One obvious step is simply to start teaching more of this material, including Indigenous and non-Indigenous cultural production in our university curricula. We should read the writing of scholars from the region, and invite them as well as practitioners into our conversations in classrooms and at conferences. It is neither sufficient nor appropriate to view the island world of the Pacific as too remote, too narrow, too different, too marginal, or too hard (or not hard enough) for serious consideration by our field. The more that we can cultivate a nuanced awareness of our many existing and potential connections to the Pacific area, the more capacity we will have to move forward generatively together.

I would like to give the final words to Teresia Teaiwa. A pioneering scholar and artist of African American and i-Kiribati heritage, she was, until her untimely passing in 2017, one of the most astute and eloquent commentators on topics in Pacific studies. Her famous poem "AmneSia" offers an apt and elegant summation of the feeling and purpose of this book, as she tells us:

> get real
> we were always
> just stepping stones
> erich von daniken
> saw the footprints of the gods
> chris connery
> saw the trademarks of capitalism
> who's gonna give a damn if they don't/can't remember
> that the whole of the donut is filled with coconuts
> they're after american pie in the east
> and some kind of zen in the west
> east and west are of course relative
> the rim of our basin
> is overflowing with kava
> but the basin of their rim
> is empty
> they take their kava in capsules
> so it's easy to forget
> that there's life and love and learning
> between
> asia and america
> between
> asia and america
> there's an ocean
> and in this ocean
> the stepping stones
> are
> getting real[18]

Notes

EPIGRAPHS

Epigraph sources: Henry David Thoreau, *A Week on the Concord and Merrimack Rivers* (1849; New York: Thomas Y. Crowell, 1911), 303–4; John Hay, quoted in Barbara K. Bundy, Stephen D. Burns, and Kimberly V. Weichel, eds., *The Future of the Pacific Rim: Scenarios for Regional Cooperation* (Westport, CT: Greenwood, 1994), 60; and Teresia Teaiwa, "AmneSia," in *Terenesia: Amplified Poetry and Songs by Teresia Teaiwa and Sia Figiel*, Hawaii Dub Machine, 2000, CD.

CHAPTER 1

1. O. H. K. Spate, *The Spanish Lake* (Minneapolis: University of Minnesota Press, 1979), ix.

2. Christopher B. Balme, *Pacific Performances: Theatricality and Cross-Cultural Encounter in the South Seas* (New York: Palgrave Macmillan, 2007); Margaret Werry, *The Tourist State: Performing Leisure, Liberalism, and Race in New Zealand* (Minneapolis: University of Minnesota Press, 2011); Marianne Schultz, *Indigenous Culture on Stage and Screen: A Harmony of Frenzy* (Houndmills, UK: Palgrave Macmillan, 2016); James Wenley, *Aotearoa New Zealand in the Global Theatre Marketplace: Travelling Theatre* (New York: Routledge, 2021); and Adria L. Imada, *Aloha America: Hula Circuits through the U.S. Empire* (Durham, NC: Duke University Press, 2012).

3. For more information on the development, form, and concerns of this post-1960s dramatic output, see my previous book, *Remaking Pacific Pasts: History, Memory, and Identity in Contemporary Theater from Oceania* (Honolulu: University of Hawai'i Press, 2014), especially chaps. 1 and 2.

4. Thomas Gladwin, *East Is a Big Bird: Navigation and Logic on Puluwat Atoll* (Cambridge, MA: Harvard University Press, 1970), 182–83.

5. Gladwin, *East*, 183.

6. David Lewis, *We, the Navigators: The Ancient Art of Landfinding in the Pacific*, 2nd ed. (Honolulu: University of Hawai'i Press, 1994), 184.

7. Renee Pualani Louis with Moana Kahele, *Kanaka Hawai'i Cartography: Hula, Navigation, and Oratory* (Corvallis: Oregon State University Press, 2017), xvi.

8. Elizabeth DeLoughrey, *Routes and Roots: Navigating Caribbean and Pacific*

Island Literatures (Honolulu: University of Hawai'i Press, 2007), 3; Vicente M. Diaz and J. Kēhaulani Kauanui, "Native Pacific Cultural Studies on the Edge," *Contemporary Pacific* 13, no. 2 (2001): 315–17; Amy Ku'uleialoha Stillman, "Pacific-ing Asian Pacific American History," *Journal of Asian American Studies* 7, no. 3 (October 2004): 245.

9. Diaz and Kauanui, "Native Pacific Cultural Studies," 317.

10. Gary Y. Okihiro, *Island World: A History of Hawai'i and the United States* (Berkeley: University of California Press, 2008), 2.

11. Paul Gilroy, *The Black Atlantic: Modernity and Double Consciousness* (London: Verso, 1993), 15.

12. Joseph Roach, *Cities of the Dead: Circum-Atlantic Performance* (New York: Columbia University Press, 1996).

13. See David Armitage, "Three Concepts of Atlantic History," in *The British Atlantic World, 1500–1800*, 2nd ed., ed. David Armitage and Michael J. Braddock (New York: Palgrave Macmillan, 2009), 13–29. The past generation has seen a flourishing of scholarship that rethinks the Atlantic world according to different priorities and migratory trajectories, that shifts the regional frame beyond the northern hemisphere, and that draws the Atlantic into more extensive global circulations. For an example of the last, see Sean Metzger, *The Chinese Atlantic: Seascapes and the Theatricality of Globalization* (Bloomington: Indiana University Press, 2020).

14. Roach, *Cities of the Dead*, 144, 165, 173.

15. Roach, *Cities of the Dead*, 30.

16. Roach, *Cities of the Dead*, 30.

17. John Carlos Rowe, "Transpacific Studies and the Cultures of U.S. Imperialism," in *Transpacific Studies: Framing an Emerging Field*, ed. Janet Hoskins and Viet Thanh Nguyen (Honolulu: University of Hawai'i Press, 2014), 136.

18. See T. Damon I. Salesa, "'Travel-Happy Samoa': Colonialism, Samoan Migration and a 'Brown Pacific,'" *New Zealand Journal of History* 37, no. 2 (2003): 186 n. 20.

19. In his monograph *Brown Boys and Rice Queens: Spellbinding Performance in the Asias* (New York: NYU Press, 2014), Eng-Beng Lim does use the term "circum-Pacific performance" (8) to describe his configuration of Bali, Singapore, and the United States (Asian America). Although this matrix enables a compelling transnational and transcolonial analysis of queer Asian performance, it is, to my mind, insufficient to encompass the diverse inter/cultures of the Pacific Rim; moreover—and perhaps most significantly—it points to the inadequacy of a single circum-Pacific imaginary to grasp the complexity of the islands that populate the ocean itself. Perhaps it is fair to view the Pacific world as comprising many different circum-Pacific networks (of which Lim's example is one) linking a variety of translocal communities, as I shall explain below.

20. See Fernand Braudel, *The Mediterranean and the Mediterranean World in the Age of Philip II*, trans. Siân Reynolds, 2 vols. (1949; London: Collins, 1972); Peregrine Hordern and Nicholas Purcell, *The Corrupting Sea: A Study of Mediterranean History* (Malden, MA: Blackwell, 2000); and Michael Pearson, *The Indian Ocean* (New York: Routledge, 2003).

21. Rob Wilson and Arif Dirlik, "Introduction: Asia/Pacific as Space of Cul-

tural Production," in *Asia/Pacific as Space of Cultural Production*, ed. Rob Wilson and Arif Dirlik (Durham, NC: Duke University Press, 1995), 1.

22. Martin W. Lewis, "Locating Asia Pacific: The Politics and Practices of Global Division," in *Remaking Area Studies: Teaching and Learning across Asia and the Pacific*, ed. Terence Wesley-Smith and Jon Goss (Honolulu: University of Hawai'i Press, 2010), 53–54. Clearly, in physical terms, the earth is encompassed by one single oceanic realm, but I am discussing geocultural conceptions.

23. Arif Dirlik, "Introduction: Pacific Contradictions," in *What Is in a Rim? Critical Perspectives on the Pacific Region Idea*, ed. Arif Dirlik (Lanham, MD: Rowman and Littlefield, 1998), 3.

24. Dirlik, "Introduction," 3.

25. R. Gerard Ward, "Earth's Empty Quarter? The Pacific Islands in a Pacific Century," *Geographical Journal* 155, no. 2 (July 1989): 235.

26. Stillman, "Pacific-ing," 245.

27. Richard Lansdown, ed., *Strangers in the South Seas: The Idea of the Pacific in Western Thought* (Honolulu: University of Hawai'i Press, 2006), 4–6.

28. See Paul Sharrad, "Imagining the Pacific," *Meanjin* 49, no. 4 (1990): 596–606.

29. B. Pualani Lincoln Maielua, "Moanaākea," in *The Space Between: Negotiating Culture, Place, and Identity in the Pacific*, ed. A. Mārata Tamaira (Honolulu: Center for Pacific Island Studies, University of Hawai'i at Mānoa, 2009), 142–43.

30. Alice Te Punga Somerville, "Where Oceans Come From," *Comparative Literature* 69, no. 1 (2017): 27.

31. Te Punga Somerville, "Where Oceans Come From," 28.

32. At present, Fiji, Kiribati, Nauru, Palau/Belau, Vanuatu, and the Marshall Islands are independent republics; Papua New Guinea (which includes the Autonomous Region of Bougainville), Aotearoa New Zealand, Tuvalu, Solomon Islands, and (Western) Samoa are likewise independent/sovereign states, although American Samoa is an unincorporated and unorganized territory of the United States. Hawai'i is a US state, the Northern Mariana Islands are a commonwealth of the United States, while Guam/Guåhan is an unincorporated and organized US territory, and the Federated States of Micronesia constitute a sovereign/independent nation and also a US associated state. Rapa Nui (Easter Island / Isla de Pascua) is a special territory of Chile, Pitcairn Island is a British overseas territory, and Norfolk Island is an external territory of Australia. Tonga is an independent monarchy. The Cook Islands and Niue are self-governing states in free association with New Zealand, while Tokelau is a dependent territory of New Zealand. French Polynesia is an autonomous overseas territory of France, whereas Wallis and Futuna is a French overseas collectivity, and New Caledonia / Kanaky is a special collectivity of France. The Torres Strait Islands are annexed to Australia. When diasporic communities are taken into consideration (e.g., Australian South Sea Islanders), then the frame grows even bigger and becomes more complex. This diversity is likewise true of socioeconomic statuses, with polities ranging from new metropoles to MIRAB microstates.

33. In 1832, French explorer Dumont d'Urville classified Pacific Islands and

Islanders according to the culture areas of Polynesia, Melanesia, and Micronesia (along with an original fourth category, Malaysia, now much of island Southeast Asia). These subregional designations, while based on a problematic conflation of race and culture, have been tremendously influential for conceptions of the Pacific area. See Paul D'Arcy, "Cultural Divisions and Island Environments since the Time of Dumont d'Urville," *Journal of Pacific History* 38, no. 2 (2003): 217–35.

34. Recent scholarship has also acknowledged the pivotal role of islands in the Indian Ocean complex. See Burkhard Schnepel and Edward A. Alpers, eds., *Connectivity in Motion: Island Hubs in the Indian Ocean World* (Cham, Switzerland: Palgrave Macmillan, 2018).

35. Lewis, "Locating Asia Pacific," 56.

36. Greg Fry, "The South Pacific 'Experiment': Reflections on the Origins of Regional Identity," *Journal of Pacific History* 32, no. 2 (1997): 180, 186.

37. Fry, "South Pacific Experiment," 196.

38. Fry, "South Pacific Experiment," 200.

39. Fry, "South Pacific Experiment," 193.

40. Teresia Teaiwa, "For or *Before* an Asian Pacific Studies Agenda? Specifying Pacific Studies," in Wesley-Smith and Goss, *Remaking Area Studies*, 120.

41. Fry, "South Pacific Experiment," 201.

42. Ron G. Crocombe, *Asia in the Pacific Islands: Replacing the West* (Suva, Fiji: IPS Publications, University of the South Pacific, 2007), 3–15.

43. DeLoughrey, *Routes and Roots*, 104.

44. Wilson and Dirlik, "Introduction," 3.

45. Quoted in Wilson and Dirlik, "Introduction," 3.

46. Wilson and Dirlik, "Introduction," 2.

47. Hillary Clinton, "America's Pacific Century," *Foreign Policy* 189 (November 2011): 56–63.

48. Clinton, "America's Pacific Century," 57.

49. Clinton, "America's Pacific Century," 58.

50. Clinton, "America's Pacific Century," 58.

51. Clinton, "America's Pacific Century," 62.

52. Matthew Farish, "Archiving Areas: The Ethnogeographic Board and the Second World War," *Annals of the Association of American Geographers* 95, no. 3 (September 2005): 663.

53. Martin W. Lewis and Kären Wigen, *The Myth of Continents: A Critique of Metageography* (Berkeley: University of California Press, 1997), 167.

54. Terence Wesley-Smith and Jon Goss, "Introduction: Remaking Area Studies," in Wesley-Smith and Goss, *Remaking Area Studies*, ix–x.

55. Lewis and Wigen, *Myth of Continents*, 167.

56. Teaiwa, "For or *Before*," 110.

57. Teaiwa, "For or *Before*," 111.

58. Keith L. Camacho, "Transoceanic Flows: Pacific Islander Interventions across the American Empire," *Amerasia Journal* 37, no. 3 (2011): xix.

59. Camacho, "Transoceanic Flows," xx.

60. Oscar G. Brockett and Franklin J. Hildy, *History of the Theatre*, 10th ed. (London: Pearson, 2008).

61. Bruce McConachie, Tobin Nellhaus, Carol Fisher Sorgenfrei, and Tamara Underiner, eds., *Theatre Histories: An Introduction*, 3rd ed. (New York: Routledge, 2016); see the section "Oceania" in James Brandon, ed., *The Cambridge Guide to Asian Theatre* (Cambridge: Cambridge University Press, 1997). See also Marvin Carlson, "Reflections on a Global Theatre History," in *The Cambridge Companion to Theatre History*, ed. David Wiles and Christine Dymkowski (Cambridge: Cambridge University Press, 2013), 149–61.

62. Marvin Carlson, "Performance Studies and the Enhancement of Theatre Studies," in *The Rise of Performance Studies: Richard Schechner's Broad Spectrum*, ed. James Harding and Cindy Rosenthal (Houndmills, UK: Palgrave Macmillan, 2011), 18–19.

63. Steve Tillis, "Conceptualizing Space: The Geographic Dimension of World Theatre," *Theatre Survey* 52, no. 2 (November 2011): 301–2.

64. Tillis, "Conceptualizing Space," 302.

65. Edmund B. Lingan, "The Contested Maps, Multiple Worlds, and Negotiable Borders of Theatre," in *Mapping across Academia*, ed. Stanley D. Brunn and Martin Dodge (Dordrecht: Springer, 2017), 377–79.

66. Lewis and Wigen, *Myth of Continents*, 186.

67. Tillis, "Conceptualizing Space," 306.

68. Nancy C. Lutkehaus, "Miguel Covarrubias and the Pageant of the Pacific: The Golden Gate International Exposition and the Idea of the Transpacific, 1939–1940," in Hoskins and Nguyen, *Transpacific Studies*, 124–25. To clarify: these were not the first physical maps of the Pacific Ocean per se. Indigenous maps of parts of the Pacific, such as Marshallese "stick charts" (*meddo*, *rebbelib*) are ancient. Dutch cartographer Jan Jansson's map of 1650 was the first to depict the whole ocean, and the interior was fairly well mapped by the end of the eighteenth century. The IPR's and GGIE's maps, however, were the first to centralize the Pacific Islands within a broader regional space that emphasized their part of and contribution to a larger world system.

69. See Paul F. Hooper, "The Institute of Pacific Relations and the Origins of Asian and Pacific Studies," *Pacific Affairs* 61, no. 1 (1988): 98–121.

70. Etsuko Taketani, *The Black Pacific Narrative: Geographic Imaginings of Race and Empire between the World Wars* (Hanover, NH: Dartmouth College Press, 2014), 9.

71. Taketani, *Black Pacific Narrative*, 9.

72. Andrew M. Shanken, *Into the Void Pacific: Building the 1939 San Francisco World's Fair* (Oakland, CA: University of California Press, 2014), 11.

73. Miguel Covarrubias, *Pageant of the Pacific*, pamphlet to accompany map lithographs (1940; San Francisco: Pacific House, 1943), n.p.

74. The official guidebooks make clear the commercial, continental, East-West focus of the exposition. See, for instance, Golden Gate International Exposition, *A Pageant of the Pacific: Official De Luxe Views* (San Francisco: H. S. Crocker, 1939), n.p.

75. Shanken, *Into the Void Pacific*, 97.

76. For an excellent discussion of Covarrubias's approach and aesthetic in this project, see Alicia Inez Guzmán, "Miguel Covarrubias's World: Remaking Global Space at the 1939 Golden Gate International Exposition," in *Miguel*

Covarrubias: Drawing a Cosmopolitan Line, ed. Carolyn Kastner (Austin, TX: Georgia O'Keeffe Museum, 2014), 23, 30–31.

77. Matt K. Matsuda, *Pacific Worlds: A History of Seas, Peoples, and Cultures* (Cambridge: Cambridge University Press, 2012), 2.

78. Matsuda, *Pacific Worlds*, 2.

79. Matsuda, *Pacific Worlds*, 2–3. Here and throughout, I use "assemblage" in Gilles Deleuze and Félix Guattari's sense of a rhizomatic collection of relations between heterogenous entities. *A Thousand Plateaus: Capitalism and Schizophrenia*, trans. Brian Massumi (Minneapolis: University of Minnesota Press, 1987).

80. Matsuda, *Pacific Worlds*, 5.

81. Covarrubias, *Pageant of the Pacific*, n.p.

82. James Clifford, "Hau'ofa's Hope," in *Returns: Becoming Indigenous in the Twenty-First Century* (Cambridge, MA: Harvard University Press, 2013), 201. Elizabeth DeLoughrey fleshes out this concept impressively in her book *Routes and Roots*.

83. The China Clipper aircraft inaugurated transpacific airmail and commercial air travel with its journey from San Francisco to Manila in November 1935.

84. Covarrubias, *Pageant of the Pacific*, n.p.

85. Rob Sullivan, *Geography Speaks: Performative Aspects of Geography* (Farnham, UK: Ashgate, 2011), 102.

86. Epeli Hau'ofa, "Our Sea of Islands" [1993], in *We Are the Ocean: Selected Works* (Honolulu: University of Hawai'i Press, 2008), 31.

87. Hau'ofa, "Our Sea of Islands," 31.

88. Epeli Hau'ofa, "The Ocean in Us," in *We Are the Ocean*, 42.

89. Wesley-Smith and Goss, *Remaking Area Studies*, xvi.

90. Wilson and Dirlik, "Introduction," 4.

91. Wilson and Dirlik, "Introduction," 6, 11.

92. Wilson and Dirlik, "Introduction," 5.

93. Wilson and Dirlik, "Introduction," 12.

94. Scholars spell "transpacific" as a single, nonhyphenated word to differentiate it from the economic priorities of the Trans-Pacific Partnership trade agreements.

95. Viet Thanh Nguyen and Janet Hoskins, "Introduction: Transpacific Studies. Critical Perspectives on an Emerging Field," in Hoskins and Nguyen, *Transpacific Studies*, 7.

96. Erin Suzuki, "Transpacific," in *The Routledge Companion to Asian American and Pacific Islander Literature*, ed. Rachel C. Lee (New York: Routledge, 2014), 352.

97. Suzuki, "Transpacific," 352.

98. Lisa Yoneyama, "Toward a Decolonial Genealogy of the Transpacific," *American Quarterly* 69, no. 3 (September 2017): 471.

99. Yuan Shu and Donald E. Pease, "Introduction: Transnational American Studies and the Transpacific Imaginary," in *American Studies as Transnational Practice: Turning toward the Transpacific*, ed. Yuan Shu and Donald E. Pease (Hanover, NH: Dartmouth College Press, 2015), 7. Also Hoskins and Nguyen, *Transpacific Studies*, 9.

100. Shu and Pease, "Introduction," 3.

101. Yoneyama, "Toward a Decolonial Genealogy," 472, 475.

102. Hoskins and Nguyen, *Transpacific Studies*, 25, 27; Suzuki, "Transpacific," 352.

103. Hoskins and Nguyen, *Transpacific Studies*, 8, 27; Shu and Pease, "Introduction," 20.

104. Yoneyama, "Toward a Decolonial Genealogy," 472.

105. Yoneyama, "Toward a Decolonial Genealogy," 477.

106. Yoneyama, "Toward a Decolonial Genealogy," 479–80.

107. Yoneyama, "Toward a Decolonial Genealogy," 479.

108. Hoskins and Nguyen, *Transpacific Studies*, 33; Shu and Pease, "Introduction," 20–21.

109. Tina Chen, "(The) Transpacific Turns," in *Oxford Research Encyclopedia of Literature*, posted online 30 January 2020, https://doi.org/10.1093/acrefore/97801 90201098.013.782

110. Erin Suzuki, *Ocean Passages: Navigating Pacific Islander and Asian American Literatures* (Philadelphia: Temple University Press, 2021), 8.

111. Yuan Shu, Otto Heim, and Kendall Johnson, eds., *Oceanic Archives, Indigenous Epistemologies, and Transpacific American Studies* (Hong Kong: Hong Kong University Press, 2019).

112. See the watershed collection *Archipelagic American Studies*, ed. Brian Russell Roberts and Michelle Ann Stephens (Durham, NC: Duke University Press, 2017); also Brian Russell Roberts, *Borderwaters: Amid the Archipelagic States of America* (Durham, NC: Duke University Press, 2021).

113. Suzuki, "Transpacific," 353.

114. Paul Giles, "Antipodean Transnationalism: The Empire Lies Athwart," in Shu and Pease, *American Studies*, 240.

115. Giles, "Antipodean Transnationalism," 240.

116. Eveline Dürr and Philipp Schorch, eds., *Transpacific Americas: Encounters and Engagements between the Americas and the South Pacific* (New York: Routledge, 2016).

117. Prue Ahrens and Chris Dixon, eds., *Coast to Coast: Case Histories of Modern Pacific Crossings* (Newcastle upon Tyne: Cambridge Scholars Publishing, 2010).

118. A case in point is *Theatre and Performance in the Asia-Pacific: Regional Modernities in the Global Era* (New York: Palgrave Macmillan, 2013) by Australian academics Denise Varney, Peter Eckersall, Chris Hudson, and Barbara Hatley, which deals with theater and performance from Australia, Japan, Indonesia, and Singapore. Similarly, *Touring Variety in the Asia-Pacific Region, 1946–1975* (Cham: Palgrave Macmillan, 2020) by Australian scholar Jonathan Bollen maps commercial entertainment circuits across Hong Kong, Manila, Melbourne, Singapore, Sydney, Tokyo, and Taipei.

119. Greg Fry, "Framing the Islands: Knowledge and Power in Changing Australian Images of 'the South Pacific,'" *Contemporary Pacific* 9, no. 2 (Fall 1997): 305.

120. Fry, "Framing the Islands," 332.

121. See, inter alia, Lee and Francis, *Migration and Transnationalism: Pacific Perspectives* (Canberra: ANU E-Press, 2009); Paul Spickard, Joanne Rondilla,

and Debbie H. Wright, eds., *Pacific Diaspora: Island Peoples in the United States and across the Pacific* (Honolulu: University of Hawai'i Press, 2002); Elfriede Hermann, Wolfgang Kempf, and Toon van Meijl, eds., *Belonging in Oceania: Movement, Place-Making and Multiple Identifications* (New York: Berghahn, 2014).

122. Teaiwa, "For or *Before*," 113.

123. Vicente M. Diaz, "'To "P"' or not to "P"?' Marking the Territory between Pacific Islander and Asian American Studies," *Journal of Asian American Studies* 7, no. 3 (October 2004): 184.

124. Diaz, "To P," 186.

125. J. Kēhaulani Kauanui, "Asian American Studies and the 'Pacific Question,'" *Asian American Studies after Critical Mass*, ed. Kent A. Ono (Malden, MA: Blackwell, 2005), 124.

126. Kauanui, "Asian American Studies," 124, 133.

127. Diaz and Kauanui, "Native Pacific Cultural Studies," 316.

128. Diaz and Kauanui, "Native Pacific Cultural Studies," 315.

129. Diaz, "To P," 190; Konai Helu Thaman, "Decolonizing Pacific Studies: Indigenous Perspectives, Knowledge, and Wisdom in Higher Education," *Contemporary Pacific* 15, no. 1 (2003): 2.

130. See Albert Wendt, "Towards a New Oceania" (1976) in *Readings in Pacific Literature*, ed. Paul Sharrad (Wollongong, NSW: New Literatures Research Centre, University of Wollongong, 1993), 9–19; and Rob Wilson, "Introduction: Toward Imagining a New Pacific," in *Inside Out: Literature, Cultural Politics, and Identity in the New Pacific*, ed. Vilsoni Hereniko and Rob Wilson (Lanham, MD: Rowman and Littlefield, 1999), 1–14.

131. Diaz, "To P," 192; Thaman, "Decolonizing Pacific Studies," 2, 14.

132. Hau'ofa, "The Ocean in Us," 50–51.

133. Susan Y. Najita, "Oceania," in Lee, *Routledge Companion*, 167, 168, 173.

134. Elizabeth McMahon, Carol Farbotko, Godfrey Baldacchino, Andrew Harwood, and Elaine Stratford, "Envisioning the Archipelago," *Island Studies Journal* 6, no. 2 (2011): 124. A foundational inspiration for this mode of thinking remains Martinican writer Édouard Glissant's *Poetics of Relation*, trans. Betsy Wing (Ann Arbor: University of Michigan Press, 1997).

135. McMahon et al., "Envisioning the Archipelago," 114. DeLoughrey, for instance, argues that her concept of *archipelagraphy*—"that is, a historiography that considers chains of islands in fluctuating relationship to their surrounding seas, islands and continents—provides a more appropriate metaphor for reading island cultures" (23). See Elizabeth DeLoughrey, "'The Litany of Islands, the Rosary of Archipelagoes': Caribbean and Pacific Archipelagraphy," *ARIEL* 32, no. 1 (2001): 21–51.

136. Chris Ballard, "Oceanic Historicities," *Contemporary Pacific* 26, no. 1 (2014): 112.

137. Schorch and Dürr, "Transpacific Americas as Relational Space," in Dürr and Schorch, *Transpacific Americas*, xv.

138. Hau'ofa, "The Ocean in Us," 41.

139. Quoted in Geoffrey White, "Foreword," in Hau'ofa, *We Are the Ocean*, xx.

140. Hau'ofa, "Our Sea of Islands," 36.

141. More work of this sort is emerging. The Transpacific Dis/Positions interdisciplinary working group funded by the University of California Humanities Research Institute takes its cue from Hau'ofa's "sea of islands," focusing on "island worlds that have been intimately connected within a vast relational network" (1) to read the transpacific mobilities occasioned in recent history by a range of colonial, Indigenous, military, and touristic forces. This project (in which I have participated) likewise calls for new regional theoretical and methodological perspectives for understanding human experiences and agency in the Pacific. See "Transpacific Dis/Positions: Crosscurrents in Indigenous, Diasporic, and Colonial Histories of Oceania," project summary, University of California, Santa Cruz, May 2018; and the UCHRI Pacific Worlds Initiative: https://uchri.org/awardees/pacific-worlds-initiative/

142. There are, of course, notable exceptions: Stephanie Nohelani Teves's *Defiant Indigeneity: The Politics of Hawaiian Performance* (Chapel Hill: University of North Carolina Press, 2018) is one such. While more locally focused, it forms a valuable complement to more multisited studies.

143. As in Greg Dening, *Performances* (Chicago: University of Chicago Press, 1996).

144. See, for instance, Richard Schechner, "Intercultural Performance: 'An Introduction,'" *TDR* 26, no. 2 (Summer 1982): 3–4; Schechner, *Between Theatre and Anthropology* (Philadelphia: University of Pennsylvania Press, 1985); and Victor Turner, *The Anthropology of Performance* (New York: PAJ Publications, 1988).

145. Daphne Lei, "Interruption, Intervention, Interculturalism: Robert Wilson's HIT Productions in Taiwan," *Theatre Journal* 63, no. 4, special issue, "Rethinking Intercultural Performance" (December 2011): 571.

146. See, inter alia, Daphne P. Lei and Charlotte McIvor, eds., *The Methuen Drama Handbook of Interculturalism and Performance* (London: Methuen, 2020); Charlotte McIvor and Jason King, eds., *Interculturalism and Performance Now: New Directions?* (Houndmills, UK: Palgrave Macmillan, 2019); Ric Knowles, *Performing the Intercultural City* (Ann Arbor: University of Michigan Press, 2017); Charlotte McIvor, *Migration and Performance in Contemporary Ireland: Towards a New Interculturalism* (London: Palgrave Macmillan, 2016); Leo Cabranes-Grant, *From Scenarios to Networks: Performing the Intercultural in Colonial Mexico* (Evanston, IL: Northwestern University Press, 2016); Royona Mitra, *Akram Khan: Dancing New Interculturalism* (Houndmills, UK: Palgrave Macmillan, 2015); Erika Fischer-Lichte, Torsten Jost, and Saskya Iris Jain, eds., *The Politics of Interweaving Performance Cultures: Beyond Postcolonialism* (New York: Routledge, 2014); Marcus Chen Chye Tan, *Acoustic Interculturalism: Listening to Performance* (Houndmills, UK: Palgrave Macmillan, 2012); and Ric Knowles, *Theatre and Interculturalism* (Houndmills, UK: Palgrave Macmillan, 2010).

147. Key texts here include Bonnie Marranca and Gautam Dasgupta, eds., *Interculturalism and Performance: Writings from PAJ* (New York: PAJ Press, 1991); Rustom Bharucha, *Theatre and the World: Performance and the Politics of Culture* (1990; New York: Routledge, 1993); Patrice Pavis, ed., *The Intercultural Performance Reader* (New York: Routledge, 1996); Julie Holledge and Joanne Tompkins, *Women's Intercultural Performance* (New York: Routledge, 2000); Coco

Fusco, *English Is Broken Here: Notes on Cultural Fusion in the Americas* (New York: New Press, 1995); Christopher Balme, *Decolonizing the Stage: Theatrical Syncretism and Post-colonial Drama* (New York: Oxford University Press, 1999); Una Chaudhuri, "Beyond a 'Taxonomic Theatre': Interculturalism after Postcolonialism and Globalization," *Theater* 32, no. 1 (2002): 33–47; and Helen Gilbert and Jacqueline Lo, "Toward a Topography of Cross-Cultural Theatre Praxis," *TDR* 46, no. 3 (Fall 2002): 31–53. Curiously, this genealogy often excludes works that are determinedly intercultural, such as Roach's *Cities of the Dead*, as well as Latin American texts that have not had much truck with the "intercultural" but nonetheless address similar questions and subjects, such as Alicia Arrizón's *Queering Mestizaje: Transculturation and Performance* (Ann Arbor: University of Michigan Press, 2006).

148. Knowles, *Theatre and Interculturalism*, 3.

149. Knowles, *Theatre and Interculturalism*, 43.

150. Knowles, *Theatre and Interculturalism*, 59.

151. Knowles, *Performing the Intercultural City*, 1.

152. Knowles, *Theatre and Interculturalism*, 59.

153. Knowles, *Theatre and Interculturalism*, 59.

154. Cabranes-Grant, *From Scenarios to Networks*, 5.

155. Erika Fischer-Lichte, "Introduction: Interweaving Performance Cultures—Rethinking 'Intercultural' Theatre: Toward an Experience and Theory of Performance beyond Postcolonialism," in Fischer-Lichte, Jost, and Jain, *The Politics of Interweaving*, 17.

156. Suzuki, "Transpacific," 352.

157. "About the Artist: Sue Pearson," *Contemporary Pacific* 22, no. 1 (Spring 2010): vii.

158. That language is Norfolk (or Norf'k, descended from Pitkern), a creole forged from eighteenth-century English and Tahitian dialects. Michael Ritzau, "'Indigenous' Sense of Place and Community in a Small Island: Norfolk Island and the Pitcairn-Descendant Population" (Honors thesis, School of Geography and Environmental Studies, University of Tasmania, 2006), iii.

159. Ritzau, "Indigenous Sense of Place," 33–34.

160. See Melissa Davey, "'We're Not Australian': Norfolk Islanders Adjust to Shock of Takeover by Mainland," *The Guardian*, 21 May 2015, https://www.theguardian.com/australia-news/2015/may/21/were-not-australian-norfolk-islanders-adjust-to-shock-of-takeover-by-mainland; and Melissa Davey, "Norfolk Islanders Go to UN to Fight Australia over Right to Self-Govern," *The Guardian*, 12 March 2018, https://www.theguardian.com/australia-news/2018/mar/13/norfolk-islanders-go-to-un-to-fight-australia-over-right-to-self-govern

161. I spell "transpasifika" as one single, unhyphenated word to speak back directly to the discourse of transpacific studies. This spelling also distinguishes the term from other usages such as "Trans Pasifika" (that is, queer and transgender Pacific Islanders). As a point of contrast, researcher Graham Webster's "Transpacifica" website and blog discusses trilateral relations between Japan, China, and the United States, https://transpacifica.net

162. In New Zealand, it has also come to describe a genre of theatrical production by creative artists of Pacific Islander descent, as documented in Lisa

Warrington and David O'Donnell's *Floating Islanders: Pasifika Theatre in Aotearoa* (Dunedin: Otago University Press, 2017).

163. Broadly, the term connotes sovereignty or self-determination.

164. While acknowledging this congruence, *transpasifika* tries to accommodate those creative artists who identify as ethnic Pacific Islanders but who, for various reasons, are reticent about identifying as "Indigenous."

165. Chadwick Allen, *Trans-Indigenous: Methodologies for Global Native Literary Studies* (Minneapolis: University of Minnesota Press, 2012), xiv–xv.

166. Chadwick Allen, "Performing Serpent Mound: A Trans-Indigenous Meditation," *Theatre Journal* 67, no. 3 (2015): 411.

167. Allen, "Performing Serpent Mound," 411.

168. Rossella Ferrari, *Transnational Chinese Theatres: Intercultural Performance Networks in East Asia* (Cham: Palgrave Macmillan, 2020), 8.

169. Amelia Jones, "Introduction: *Trans-ing* Performance," *Performance Research* 21, no. 5 (2016), 2, 1.

170. Diaz, "To P," 185.

171. Kauanui, "Native Pacific Cultural Studies," 129.

172. Rowe, "Transpacific Studies," 147.

173. See Peggy Fairbairn-Dunlop and Eve Coxon, eds., *Talanoa: Building a Pasifika Research Culture* (Auckland: Dunmore Publishing, 2014); also consult Vilsoni Hereniko, "Indigenous Knowledge and Academic Imperialism," in *Remembrance of Pacific Pasts: An Invitation to Remake History*, ed. Robert Borofsky (Honolulu: University of Hawai'i Press, 2000), 78–91.

174. Teaiwa, "For or *Before*," 117.

175. Teaiwa, "For or *Before*," 118.

176. Rowe, "Transpacific Studies," 143.

177. Louis and Kahele, *Kanaka Hawai'i Cartography*, xviii, 3.

178. Louis and Kahele, *Kanaka Hawai'i Cartography*, 165.

179. Most of these "lines" are not strictly linear, but involve curves and other geometric shapes. Thompson's four star lines are "Ke Kā o Makali'i" (The Canoe-Bailer of Makali'i), "Iwikuamo'o" (Backbone), "Manaiakalani" (The Chief's Fishline), and "Ka Lupe o Kawelo" (The Kite of Kawelo). See Nainoa Thompson, "Hawaiian Voyaging Traditions: Hawaiian Star Lines and Names for Stars," http://archive.hokulea.com/ike/hookele/hawaiian_star_lines.html

180. Pauline Wakeham, "Beyond Comparison: Reading Relations between Indigenous Nations," *Canadian Literature* 230–31 (2016): 130.

181. Wakeham, "Beyond Comparison," 130.

182. Wakeham, "Beyond Comparison," 132.

CHAPTER 2

1. For a version of the myth, see Te Rangihiroa / Peter Buck, *Ethnology of Manihiki and Rakahanga* (Honolulu: Bishop Museum, 1932), 14–20; for the full account of the play, see 198–202. A shorter, lay version can be found in Te Rangihiroa / Buck, *Vikings of the Sunrise* (New York: Frederick A. Stokes, 1938), 53–56.

2. Hawaiki (Havaiki, Havai'i, 'Avaiki) is a sacred place of origin and return for many cultures across Polynesia. Its location varies depending on the mythic source, but it is generally considered to be the departing point for the ancestral migrations and the final destination for the soul after death.

3. This legend has genealogical similarities to origin myths from Aotearoa New Zealand, in which Māui hooks up the North Island (Te Ika a Māui / The Fish of Māui). The island on which I was born and grew up, Te Waka a Māui (South Island / Te Waipounamu) is Māui's canoe.

4. Te Rangihiroa, *Ethnology*, 203. For performances on Aitutaki, see Te Rangihiroa, *Vikings of the Sunrise*, 97–99; and *The Material Culture of the Cook Islands* (New Plymouth, NZ: Thomas Avery and Sons, 1927), xxi, 296. For performances on Manihiki and Rakahanga, consult Te Rangihiroa, *Ethnology*, 202–3. See also H. M. Chadwick and N. K. Chadwick, *The Growth of Literature*, vol. 3 (Cambridge: Cambridge University Press, 1940), 377, 382.

5. Te Rangihiroa, *Material Culture of the Cook Islands*, xxi.

6. Te Rangihiroa does surmise that the number of voyages was "probably exaggerated" (*Ethnology*, 19), but the narrative structure of the performance is still significant in this regard.

7. Te Rangihiroa, *Ethnology*, 199. Other nuku took different approaches to portraying voyaging canoes. In *The Voyage of Ru* (Aitutaki, 1926), Ru-enua's vessel *Ngapua-Ariki* was represented by a substantial length of coconut leaves tied end to end, carried in by the actors. The canoe remained stationary within the playing space, while the characters' paddling motions, gestures, and dialogue illustrated the progress and perils of the voyage.

8. See Margaret Werry, "Interdisciplinary Objects, Oceanic Insights: Performance and the New Materialism," in *Theater Historiography: Critical Interventions*, ed. Henry Bial and Scott Magelssen (Ann Arbor: University of Michigan Press, 2010), 222.

9. Te Rangihiroa, *Ethnology*, 10. The Cook Islands became a British protectorate in 1888 and were subsequently included within the boundaries of the Colony of New Zealand in 1901. They were administered as a New Zealand dependent territory until independence in 1965.

10. The evangelical influence has been pervasive. Nuku continue to be performed in the Cook Islands, but Vilsoni Hereniko notes that "Although the nuku began as historical enactments [. . .] it has now become synonymous with biblical pageants." *Woven Gods: Female Clowns and Power in Rotuma* (Honolulu: University of Hawai'i Press, 1995), 147. It must be noted, however, that more recent examples of nuku based on legendary topics (*peu tupuna*) have been documented, suggesting a continuity of transmission and a generative synthesis of old and new elements. See Marivee McMath and Teaea Parima, "Winged Tangi'ia: A Mangaian Dramatic Performance," in *South Pacific Oral Traditions*, ed. Ruth Finnegan and Margaret Orbell (Bloomington: Indiana University Press, 1995), 215–55.

11. Te Rangihiroa's theory of Polynesian origins is understandable, perhaps, in the context of the racial prejudice he encountered as an Indigenous scholar in a white academic world. His scholarship carefully disavowed any association between Polynesians and "dark-skinned" inhabitants of Melanesia

(characterized in the early twentieth century as "Oceanic Negroids"), claiming instead that the "master mariners of the Pacific must be Europoid" (*Vikings of the Sunrise*, 16), and charting a migration route—now debunked—through Micronesia instead of Melanesia. See Patrick Vinton Kirch, *On the Road of the Winds: An Archaeological History of the Pacific Islands before European Contact* (Berkeley: University of California Press, 2002), 24–27.

12. Te Rangihiroa, *Vikings of the Sunrise*, 317.

13. Paul D'Arcy, *The People of the Sea: Environment, Identity, and History in Oceania* (Honolulu: University of Hawai'i Press, 2006), 4.

14. D'Arcy, *People of the Sea*, 13.

15. "Remote Oceania" refers to the area that lies east of the Solomon Islands, the Bismarck Archipelago (Papua New Guinea), and the Philippines, and that is characterized by island clusters separated by more than 215 miles of ocean (D'Arcy, *People of the Sea*, 9–10).

16. K. R. Howe, "Introduction," in *Vaka Moana, Voyages of the Ancestors: The Discovery and Settlement of the Pacific*, ed. K. R. Howe (Auckland: David Bateman, 2006), 11.

17. This might be taken broadly to refer not only to Pacific Islanders traveling mercantile sea courses during the colonial period, but also to the many diasporic routes taken by Islanders on ships or airplanes in the post–World War II era.

18. Richard Feinberg, "Introduction: Theme and Variation in Pacific Island Seafaring," in *Seafaring in the Contemporary Pacific Islands: Studies in Continuity and Change*, ed. Richard Feinberg (DeKalb: Northern Illinois University Press, 1995), 4, 5.

19. Feinberg, "Introduction," 4.

20. Mainly in parts of Micronesia, where customary navigation systems were still in use.

21. Lewis, *We, the Navigators*, 307.

22. Lewis, *We, the Navigators*, 12, 15.

23. Satawal is an atoll in the Caroline Islands, part of the Federated States of Micronesia.

24. Paul Sharrad, "Pathways in the Sea: A Pelagic Post-colonialism?," in *Literary Archipelagoes / Archipels littéraires*, ed. Jean-Pierre Durix (Dijon: Centre de recherches "Image/Texte/Langage," University of Dijon, 1998), 95–107. For a further useful survey on this topic, see Michelle Keown, "Our Sea of Islands: Migration and *Métissage* in Contemporary Polynesian Writing," *International Journal of Francophone Studies* 11, no. 4 (2008): 503–22.

25. *Moana*, animated feature film, dir. John Musker and Ron Clements, Walt Disney Pictures, 2016. I could spend considerable time and energy unpacking the politics of this film, along with my view that it problematically elides Indigenous voyaging histories into a hegemonic American progress narrative. However, suffice it to say here that the film has been polarizing for Pacific Islander audiences. For a discussion, see A. Mārata Ketekiri Tamaira and Dionne Fonoti, "Beyond Paradise? Retelling Pacific Stories in Disney's *Moana*," *Contemporary Pacific* 30, no. 2 (2018): 297–327.

26. Hau'ofa, "Our Sea of Islands," 27–40.

27. Ben Finney, "Renaissance," in Howe, *Vaka Moana*, 332.

28. Finney, "Renaissance," 332.

29. Teves, *Defiant Indigeneity*, 10.

30. Louis and Kahele, *Kanaka Hawai'i Cartography*, 86–87.

31. For a detailed and erudite discussion of vaka symbolism in the past and present, see Elizabeth DeLoughrey's chapter "Vessels of the Pacific: An Ocean in the Blood," in *Routes and Roots*, 96–157.

32. Peter Nuttall, Paul D'Arcy, and Colin Philp, "Waqa Tabu—Sacred Ships: The Fijian Drua," *International Journal of Maritime History* 26, no. 3 (2014): 428–29.

33. Nuttall, D'Arcy, and Philp, "Waqa Tabu," 428.

34. Allen, *Trans-Indigenous*, xv.

35. Allen, *Trans-Indigenous*, xiv.

36. Allen, *Trans-Indigenous*, xiv–xxxiii, *passim*.

37. I acknowledge that the subregional division of Oceania into Melanesia, Micronesia, and Polynesia imposes concrete boundaries and ethnological typifications that are, in reality, far more porous and complex. I use these terms here because of their ubiquity in discussions of the Pacific and as categories for critical analysis.

38. Allen, *Trans-Indigenous*, xxviii.

39. For a discussion of this issue, see D'Arcy, *People of the Sea*, 5.

40. In his 1949 volume *The Coming of the Maori*, Te Rangihiroa lamented the typical lack of detail about sailing techniques in customary narratives, but noted how this apparently casual approach to recording voyaging accomplishments contrasted with the concern expressed by European writers on that topic, including their tendency to exaggerate the difficulty of surviving long voyages (Wellington, NZ: Whitcombe and Tombs, 1950), 46, 49. For a critical reexamination of early twentieth-century narratives of Māori origins, see David Simmons, "A New Zealand Myth: Kupe, Toi and the 'Fleet,'" *New Zealand Journal of History* 3, no. 1 (1969): 14–31; for a famous (and now much criticized) refutation of voyaging accomplishments, refer to Andrew Sharp's *Ancient Voyagers in the Pacific* (Harmondsworth: Penguin, 1957).

41. Christine Riding, "Shipwreck in French and British Visual Art, 1700–1842: Vernet, Northcote, Géricault, and Turner," in *Shipwreck in Art and Literature: Images and Interpretations from Antiquity to the Present Day*, ed. Carl Thompson (New York: Routledge, 2013), 124–25.

42. Leonard Bell, *Colonial Constructs: European Images of Māori, 1840–1914* (Auckland: Auckland University Press, 1992), 166–67, 152. For an excellent discussion of attitudes to, and cultural appropriations of, Māori during the Liberal era, consult Werry, *Tourist State*.

43. Bell, *Colonial Constructs*, 168, 170–71.

44. Author's conversation with Greg Semu, Zoom, 4 May 2020.

45. Judith Ryan, "Greg Semu: *The Raft of the Tagata Pasifika (People of the Pacific)*, 2014–16," 10 June 2016, National Gallery of Victoria, Australia, https://www.ngv.vic.gov.au/essay/greg-semu-the-raft-of-the-tagata-pasifika-people-of-the-pacific-2014-16/

46. Semu, conversation with author.

47. Greg Semu, *The Raft of the Tagata Pasifika (People of the Pacific)*, solo exhibition, world premiere, viewed at the National Gallery of Victoria, Melbourne, Australia, 9 July 2016.

48. Rebecca Schneider, *Performing Remains: Art and War in Times of Theatrical Reenactment* (New York: Routledge, 2011), 10.

49. Schneider, *Performing Remains*, 2.

50. Author's interview with Michel Tuffery, 28 August 2016.

51. *Tagata Pasifika* (television program), "Greg Semu—Raft of the Tagata Pasifika," 7 March 2017, https://www.youtube.com/watch?v=Bd2veLStlqc

52. Alice Te Punga Somerville, *Once Were Pacific: Māori Connections to Oceania* (Minneapolis: University of Minnesota Press, 2012), 205.

53. Te Punga Somerville, *Once Were Pacific*, xxiii.

54. Te Punga Somerville, *Once Were Pacific*, 3, xxi.

55. Te Punga Somerville, *Once Were Pacific*, xxiii.

56. Albert Wendt, "Afterword: Tatauing the Post-colonial Body," in Hereniko and Wilson, *Inside Out*, 405.

57. Bill Viola, *The Raft*, 2004, color high-definition video projection on wall in darkened space, 5.1 ch. surround sound, Projected image size 156 × 88 in., 10:33 minutes.

58. Neil Ieremia and Black Grace, *Waka*, performance program, 2012, courtesy of Black Grace, Auckland, New Zealand.

59. Analysis based on my viewing of an archival DVD recording of *Vaka* (2012), courtesy of Black Grace, Auckland, New Zealand; as well as my conversations with Neil Ieremia (Stanford, California, 19 March 2017) and Abby Ieremia (Auckland, New Zealand, 27 March 2017).

60. Auckland is New Zealand's major city, containing the world's largest Polynesian population.

61. Michael Fried, "Géricault's Romanticism," in *Another Light: Jacques-Louis David to Thomas Demand* (New Haven: Yale University Press, 2014), 98–99.

62. Quoted in Warrington and O'Donnell, *Floating Islanders*, 10.

63. I take this term from Rebecca Schneider, following Fred Moten and John Donne.

64. Anna Marbrook, Hoturoa Barclay-Kerr, and Kasia Pol, in collaboration with the New Zealand Festival and Te Āti Awa and other Taranaki Whānui iwi, *A Waka Odyssey*, Wellington, for the New Zealand Festival, 23 February 2018.

65. "Mālama Honua Worldwide Voyage—Island Wisdom, Ocean Connections, Global Lessons," YouTube video, 5:47, posted by ʻŌiwi TV, 2 May 2014, available at https://www.youtube.com/watch?v=ytq6d0D4oE4. See also "Worldwide Voyage Highlight Video," 30:08, posted by the Polynesian Voyaging Society, 30 June 2017, available at http://www.hokulea.com/worldwide-voyage-highlights/; and also Jennifer Allen, *Mālama Honua: Hōkūleʻa—A Voyage of Hope* (Ventura, CA: Patagonia, 2017).

66. Polynesian Voyaging Society, "*Waʻa Kaulua*—Our Canoes" (n.d.), available at www.hokulea.com/vessels/

67. Polynesian Voyaging Society, "Join the Education Voyage" (n.d.), available at http://www.hokulea.com/get-involved/join-the-education-voyage/

68. Polynesian Voyaging Society, "The Mālama Honua Worldwide Voyage

Continues into 2018" (n.d.), available at http://www.hokulea.com/worldwide
-voyage/

69. James Cook, in James Cook and James King, *A Voyage to the Pacific Ocean;
Undertaken, by the Command of His Majesty, for Making Discoveries in the Northern
Hemisphere*, 3 vols. (Dublin, 1784), 2:250–51.

70. Polynesian Voyaging Society, "World Voyage Highlight Video."

71. One who has been initiated as a master navigator according to a customary process from the Caroline Islands in Micronesia. The recent resurrection of
the Pwo ceremony, including the induction of navigators from elsewhere in
Oceania, can also be understood as part of the broader voyaging revival.

72. Polynesian Voyaging Society, 'Ōiwi TV, and Hawaii News Now,
"Mālama Honua: 'Ohana Hōkūle'a, Episode 2," video, 25:20, 11 November 2014,
available at http://www.hokulea.com/malama-honua-ohana-hokulea-episode
-2/. The other most important voyage was presumably the return leg from
Tahiti to Hawai'i that marked the completion of the global circumnavigation.

73. For a detailed account of these tensions, see Ben Finney, *Hokule'a: The
Way to Tahiti* (New York: Dodd, Mead, 1979). For another perspective, see Sam
Low, *Hawaiki Rising: Hōkūle'a, Nainoa Thompson, and the Hawaiian Renaissance*
(Waipahu, HI: Island Heritage Publishing, 2013). Thompson's 1980 voyage to
Tahiti was also a significant step forward in this regard.

74. See, for example, the 1985–87 Voyage of Rediscovery, the gathering
prior to the 1992 Festival of Pacific Arts ("Seafaring Pacific Islanders") in Rarotonga, the 1995 convocation at Taputapuātea Marae on Ra'iātea (Nā 'Ohana
Holo Moana), and the 2010 Blue Canoes project.

75. I take this term from Albert Wendt's novel *Ola* (Honolulu: University of
Hawai'i Press, 1991): "We are more water than blood. So our water-ties to one
another are more important than our blood-ties! We carry within us the seas
out of which we came" (124).

76. Natacha Gagné, "Brave New Words: The Complexities and Possibilities
of an 'Indigenous' Identity in French Polynesia and New Caledonia," *Contemporary Pacific* 27, no. 2 (2015): 372.

77. Gagné, "Brave New Words," 372, 375, 380.

78. Gagné, "Brave New Words," 380, 382, 386; Mā'ohi refers to the Indigenous people of the entire Society group.

79. Gagné, "Brave New Words," 381.

80. Gagné, "Brave New Words," 375, 385, 386.

81. A *marae* is a place of worship or meeting place.

82. A carved wooden plank erected on a *marae* (usually one of several), possibly representing divinities related to it or functioning as a conduit between
the celestial and terrestrial realms; see Hiriata Millaud, "Unu," flyer distributed
by the Assembly of French Polynesia, Pape'ete (n.d.), available at http://www.as
semblee.pf/_documents/assemblee/APF-DEPLIANT-UNU.pdf.

83. "Tahiti Arrival," Mālama Honua online video archive, 4:14, uploaded by
'Ōiwi TV, 25 June 2014, available at http://www.hokulea.com/tahiti-arrival/.
Thompson spoke in English with a French translator.

84. Finney, *Hokule'a*, 271–72.

85. For footage of these various events and activities, see the posts from

June and July 2014 archived in Polynesian Voyaging Society, "Video Stories," available at http://www.hokulea.com/category/video-stories/

86. Nicholas Thomas, *Entangled Objects: Exchange, Material Culture, and Colonialism in the Pacific* (Cambridge, MA: Harvard University Press, 1991), 7.

87. *Te Feti'a 'Avei'a*, directed by Marguerite Lai, Marae 'Ārahurahu, Paea, Tahiti, 5 July–2 August 2014.

88. An organization dedicated to reviving the cultural traditions of voyaging and raising awareness about environmental sustainability through a partnership of Indigenous knowledge and modern science. In 2010, Pacific Voyagers completed the construction of seven *vaka moana* representing several Pacific nations, which set sail on a series of Pacific voyages during 2011–12 ("Te Mana o Te Moana" Voyage) to promote the organization's aims. See Pacific Voyagers, "History of Pacific Voyagers" (n.d.), available at http://pacificvoyagers.org/hist ory-of-pacific-voyagers/, as well as its two-part television series *Te Mana o Te Moana—The Pacific Voyagers* (2015).

89. Karen Stevenson, "'Heiva': Continuity and Change of a Tahitian Celebration," *Contemporary Pacific* 2, no. 2 (1990): 257, 259.

90. Stevenson, "Heiva," 271–72.

91. Stevenson, "Heiva," 265. The *Heiva* format is also found on other islands in French Polynesia, and it is now international; see, for example, the Heiva i Honolulu and Heiva San Diego.

92. Stevenson, "Heiva," 256.

93. Stevenson, "Heiva," 268–69.

94. Stevenson, "Heiva," 269, 274.

95. Bruno Saura, *Tahiti Mā'ohi: Culture, identité, religion, et nationalisme en Polynésie française* (Pape'ete, Tahiti: Au Vent des Îles, 2008), 384–88.

96. Polyphonic choral songs (cf. "hymn").

97. Hava'i, a variant spelling of Hawai'i, is also the ancient name for Ra'iātea in the Society Islands.

98. O Tahiti E and Le Conservatoire artistique de la Polynésie française, *Te Feti'a 'Avei'a / l'étoile guide*, dossier de presse (Tahiti, 2014), 2, available at http:// media-cache.tahiti-tourisme.pf/fileadmin/user_upload/medias/tahiti/docs/Eve nts_Te_feti_a_Avei_a.pdf

99. Teuira Henry, *Ancient Tahiti* (Honolulu: Bishop Museum, 1928), 569–70; Martha Beckwith, *Hawaiian Mythology* (Honolulu: University of Hawai'i Press, 1970), 370–73; Patrick Vinton Kirch, *Feathered Gods and Fishhooks: An Introduction to Hawaiian Archaeology and Prehistory* (Honolulu: University of Hawai'i Press, 1985), 259. There is also a version of this legend that describes Pa'ao as coming from Upolu in Samoa; see William D. Westervelt, *Hawaiian Historical Legends* (New York: Fleming H. Revell, 1923), 66–78. Although historians and folklorists favor the Tahiti/Kahiki origin, it is interesting to consider how the Samoan connection might have resonated implicitly with the Heiva performance, which took place as *Hōkūle'a* and *Hikianalia* sailed from Tahiti to Samoa.

100. Henry, *Ancient Tahiti*, 179.

101. This bias has long been acknowledged by ethnographers. See, inter alia, S. Percy Smith and H. T. Whatahoro, *The Lore of the Whare Wānanga*, vol. 2 (New

Plymouth, NZ: Thomas Avery, for the Polynesian Society, 1913–15), 153; Te Rangihiroa / Buck, *Coming of the Maori*, 46.

102. Henry, *Ancient Tahiti*, 146–47.

103. Henry, *Ancient Tahiti*, 178–79.

104. "Sculpteurs, graveurs et décorateurs oeuvrent pour *Te Feti'a Avei'a*," *Hiro'a: Journal d'informations culturelles* 82 (30 June 2014), available at http://www.hiroa.pf/2014/06/n-82-sculpteurs-graveurs-et-decorateurs-oeuvrent-pour -te-fetia-aveia/

105. Stevenson, "Heiva," 263; see also the Centre des Métiers d'Art's website, available at http://www.cma.pf/wp2011/

106. "Sculpteurs, graveurs et décorateurs," n.p.

107. James Clifford, "Indigenous Articulations," *Contemporary Pacific* 13, no. 2 (2001): 469.

108. *Te Feti'a 'Avei'a / L'étoile guide*, dossier de presse, 3, 4. My translations.

109. A case in point is the late Mā'ohi playwright Jean-Marc Tera'ituatini Pambrun, whose critical postcolonial dramatic portrayals earned him a troubled reputation with local authorities and led to some of his plays being deprogrammed or banned.

110. Steve Mayer-Miller and Crossroad Arts, *No Two Stones*, 18 November 2006, Lambert's Beach, Mackay, Australia; see http://vimeo.com/37552626

111. Gerald Horne, *The White Pacific: U.S. Imperialism and Black Slavery in the South Seas after the Civil War* (Honolulu: University of Hawai'i Press, 2007), 40.

112. For an analysis of the beach as a zone for varied rites of passage, see Greg Dening, *Beach Crossings: Voyaging across Times, Cultures, and Self* (Philadelphia: University of Pennsylvania Press, 2004).

113. Steve Mayer-Miller and Andrew Satinie, interview with the author, 23 July 2014, Mackay, Australia.

114. For a nuanced and insightful discussion of the deep customary relationships with the sea among people from Australia's northern tropical coasts and islands, see Nonie Sharp, *Saltwater People: The Waves of Memory* (Toronto: University of Toronto Press, 2002).

115. Margaret Jolly, "On the Edge? Deserts, Oceans, Islands," *Contemporary Pacific* 13, no. 2 (2001): 422. One should bear in mind that the peoples of Micronesia and Polynesia comprise only about 12 percent of the overall Pacific Islander population.

116. Jolly, "On the Edge," 423.

117. Jolly, "On the Edge," 425.

118. DeLoughrey, *Routes and Roots*, 133, 134.

119. DeLoughrey, *Routes and Roots*, 134.

120. It is notable that Cook's demarcation of "the most extensive nation upon earth," written fifty years before d'Urville's regional partitions, extends its borders west "to the Hebrides [Vanuatu]" (251), thus incorporating Fiji into this broadly Polynesian culture area.

121. DeLoughrey, *Routes and Roots*, 132, 148.

122. Nuttall, D'Arcy, and Philp, "Waqa Tabu," 428.

123. Nuttall, D'Arcy, and Philp, "Waqa Tabu," 429, 445.

124. A. C. Haddon and James Hornell, *Canoes of Oceania*, vol. 1 (Honolulu: Bishop Museum Press, 1975), 319.

125. Haddon and Hornell, *Canoes of Oceania*, 319; Nuttall, D'Arcy, and Philp, "Waqa Tabu," 428.

126. Peter Nuttall, Kaiafa Ledua, Alison Newell, Peni Vunaki, and Colin Philp, "The Drua Files: A Report on the Collection and Recording of Cultural Knowledge of Drua and Associated Culture," prepared for the Oceania Centre for Arts, Culture and Pacific Studies, University of the South Pacific, by the Fiji Islands Voyaging Society, June 2012, 8; Haddon and Hornell, *Canoes of Oceania*, 326.

127. The label applied by the authors to separate the works from any single Western aesthetic genre. Vilsoni Hereniko, Peter Rockford Espiritu, and Igelese Ete, *Vaka: The Birth of a Seer* and *Drua: The Wave of Fire* (Suva, Fiji: University of the South Pacific, 2013), DVD.

128. Nuttall et al., "The Drua Files," 6. Based on this research, a replica *drua* called *i Vola Sigavou* (the first built in over a century), was completed in 2016. See http://www.druaexperience.com

129. These sites are in other parts of Fiji, as well as in Samoa, Cook Islands, Kiribati, Niue, Tonga, Vanuatu, Marshall Islands, Solomon Islands, Tuvalu, Nauru, and Tokelau.

130. Epeli Hau'ofa, "Our Place Within: Foundations for a Creative Oceania," in *We Are the Ocean*, 80.

131. Hau'ofa, "Our Place Within," 92–93.

132. Rotuma is an island located approximately 290 miles north of Fiji. It has been part of Fiji since 1881, but its people, language, and culture have more in common with Polynesian islands to the east, such as Tonga, Uvea, and Samoa.

133. Vilsoni Hereniko, interview with the author, Honolulu, 28 January 2015; see also Hereniko, "Epeli's Owl," *Contemporary Pacific* 22, no. 1 (2010): 119–22. The guardian owl figure appears as a character in Hereniko, Espiritu, and Ete, *Vaka*.

134. Author's interview with Igelese Ete, Suva, Fiji, 6 February 2016.

135. Nuttall et al., "The Drua Files," 4, 22.

136. Lewis, *We, the Navigators*, 260, 269; Haddon and Hornell, *Canoes of Oceania*, 223, 329–30.

137. Nuttall, D'Arcy, and Philp, "Waqa Tabu," 428.

138. Nuttall, D'Arcy, and Philp, "Waqa Tabu," 444.

139. Conceptualized in 1970, the Pacific Way is a political philosophy that emphasizes regional cooperation among Pacific Island states based on common developmental issues and the islands' distinctiveness from other developing nations worldwide. It galvanized a number of regional arts and cultural initiatives, many centering on the University of the South Pacific.

140. Hau'ofa, "Our Place Within," 82.

141. See, for instance, DeLoughrey, *Routes and Roots*, 133; and Michelle Keown and Stuart Murray, "'Our Sea of Islands': Globalization, Regionalism, and (Trans)Nationalism in the Pacific," in *The Oxford Handbook of Postcolonial Studies*, ed. Graham Huggan (Oxford: Oxford University Press, 2013), 612.

142. DeLoughrey, *Routes and Roots*, 154.

143. Hereniko is open about the fact that his performances at the Oceania Centre, following a trend in his playwriting career since the 1987 coup, frequently draw subtle analogies with Fiji's right-wing political situation, typically critiquing the misplacement and abuse of power. In this regard the center at the University of the South Pacific operates as a "safe space," where political concerns can be aired through artistic means, free from the censorship imposed on most media by the military dictatorship (Hereniko, interview with the author, 28 January 2015).

144. Larry Thomas, *The Visitors* (2008), typescript, courtesy of the playwright.

145. Ian Gaskell, "Truth, Identity and a Sense of 'Pacificness,'" *Australasian Drama Studies* 55 (2009): 143.

146. Gaskell, "Truth, Identity," 145.

147. *Drua* was performed live and *Vaka* was screened as a film.

148. Whereas one might take a more cynical view of this production as an attempt to whitewash a troubling history, a deeper analysis of the contributing institutions and artists questions this interpretation. While the ghosts of the coups must be acknowledged, it is important, I think, not to read Fiji as a homogenous entity defined solely by the ideologies of its military leaders or branded only by its traumas, and to allow room for artists and scholars to chart more reparative courses for its citizenry.

149. Hau'ofa, "Our Sea of Islands," 30.

150. Hau'ofa, "Our Sea of Islands," 34, 35.

151. Paul Spickard, "Introduction: Pacific Diaspora?," in Spickard, Rondilla, and Wright, *Pacific Diaspora*, 8.

152. Hau'ofa, "Our Sea of Islands," 36.

153. D'Arcy, *People of the Sea*, 90. See also Joseph H. Genz, *Breaking the Shell: Voyaging from Nuclear Refugees to People of the Sea in the Marshall Islands* (Honolulu: University of Hawai'i Press, 2018), 14–15.

154. Feinberg, "Introduction," 6.

155. Déwé Gördé, *The Wreck*, trans. Deborah Walker-Morrison and Raylene Ramsay (Auckland, NZ: Little Island Press, 2011). Originally published as *L'épave* (Noumea: Editions Madrépores, 2005).

156. Caroline Sinavaiana and J. Kēhaulani Kauanui, "Introduction," special issue, "Women Writing Oceania: Weaving the Sails of Vaka," *Pacific Studies* 30, nos. 1–2 (March–June 2007): 5.

157. Sinavaiana and Kauanui, "Introduction," 5–6.

158. Sinavaiana and Kauanui, "Introduction," 5. On these points, see also DeLoughrey, *Routes and Roots*, 138–42.

159. Letter, Jane Campbell, HTY, to Gary Caulfield, First Hawaiian Bank, 14 January 1986, p. 2, Honolulu Theatre for Youth Collection, 1955–2001, MSS #190, Series II: Box 3, Folder 56, Child Drama Collection, Arizona State University; Katherine Krzys, oral history with Jane Campbell, Part 10, Kailua, Hawai'i, 15 June 2005, VHS recording, Child Drama Collection, Arizona State University; author's interview with Eric Johnson, artistic director, Honolulu Theatre for Youth, Honolulu, Hawai'i, 27 January 2015.

160. It must be noted here, however, that theater for youth—especially in HTY's case—frequently caters to a broader audience demographic, including adults.

161. Susan Soon He Stanton, *Navigator*, unpublished playscript, Honolulu Theatre for Youth, 2010. All page references are to this manuscript. This analysis also draws from a viewing of the archival video recording of the performance at Tenney Theatre, Honolulu, courtesy of Honolulu Theatre for Youth.

162. John Kauffman, HTY, press release, "Song for the Navigator," 31 March 1986, Honolulu Theatre for Youth Collection, 1955–2001, MSS#190, Series V: Box 39, Folder 3, Child Drama Collection, Arizona State University. The Federated States of Micronesia, the Republic of the Marshall Islands, and the Republic of Palau are in a Compact of Free Association (COFA) with the United States; and the Northern Marianas have a Commonwealth Covenant. Except for Guam, which is a US territory, these states are "regarded as independent despite the fact that their covenant arrangements with the United States may appear to be as weighty as their constitutions." Brij V. Lal and Kate Fortune, eds., *The Pacific Islands: An Encyclopedia* (Honolulu: University of Hawai'i Press, 2000), 314. The nation of Kiribati is a former British colony.

163. Jane Campbell, oral history.

164. Wayne Harada, "Islander Brings Firsthand Experience to Play about Micronesian Navigators," *Honolulu Advertiser*, 20 January 1986.

165. Michael Cowell, *Song for the Navigator* (1986; Woodstock, IL: Dramatic Publishing, 1993), vii. All in-text page references are from this publication. My analysis is also based on a viewing of an archival video recording of the performance held in the Child Drama Collection at Arizona State University.

166. Letter, John Kauffman, Artistic Director, HTY, to Micronesian Contacts, 15 July 1985, p. 1, Honolulu Theatre for Youth Collection, 1955–2001, MSS #190, Series V: Box 39, Folder 2, Child Drama Collection, Arizona State University. See also Laura Gardiner Salazar, "How Did You Know How We Are? A Study in Cross-Cultural Theatre," *Grand Valley Review* 6, no. 2 (1990): 39.

167. Cowell, *Song for the Navigator*.

168. HTY's managing director, Jane Campbell, described *Song* as theatrical depiction and exploration of "a 'Third World' America—where people don't eat hamburgers or drive Fords or worship dollar bills" (1). Letter, Jane Campbell to Gary Caulfield, First Hawaiian Bank, 14 January 1986, Honolulu Theatre for Youth Collection, 1955–2001, MSS#190, Series II: Box 3, Folder 56, Child Drama Collection, Arizona State University.

169. Chad Blair, "An Untold Story of American Immigration." For a useful discussion of related issues, consult Suzanne Falgout, "Pohnpeians in Hawai'i: Refashioning Identity in Diaspora," *Pacific Studies* 35, nos. 1–2 (April–August 2012): 184–202.

170. "Haole" = white person, European.

171. The dialect in these extracts is Hawai'i Pidgin (Hawaiian Creole English).

172. Diaz and Kauanui, "Native Pacific Cultural Studies," 320.

173. Diaz and Kauanui, "Native Pacific Cultural Studies," 320.

174. This is not to suggest that the debt to Micronesian navigational tech-

nologies is not acknowledged in Hawai'i or elsewhere in Oceania—it certainly is: my point is that this particular play advances certain narratives over others.

175. Honolulu Theatre for Youth and TeAda Productions, *Second Stage Study Guide*, October 2017, 7. See also http://www.uscompact.org/about/cofa.php

176. All direct quotations are drawn from the world premiere performance of TeAda Productions' *Masters of the Currents*, Tenney Theatre, Honolulu, 13 and 14 October 2017. Additional insights are drawn from my experience of the continental US premiere at Brava Theater Center, San Francisco, 20 October 2018. I am grateful for the illuminating conversation with Ova Saopeng and Leilani Chan on 28 August 2020.

177. TeAda Productions, *Masters of the Currents*, program, Brava Theater Center, San Francisco, 19–20 October 2018, 1.

178. Honolulu Theatre for Youth in collaboration with TeAda Productions, *Masters of the Currents*, program, Tenney Theatre, Honolulu, 13–21 October 2017, 6. See also www.teada.org

179. New Zealand Festival, "A Waka Odyssey," https://www.festival.co.nz /2018/events/a-waka-odyssey/, 30 October 2018.

180. Salesa, "Travel-Happy Samoa," 172.

181. Rowe, "Transpacific Studies," 273.

182. Description based on my viewing of George Nuku, *Bottled Ocean 2116*, installation artwork, Pātaka Art + Museum, Porirua, for the New Zealand International Arts Festival, 8 March 2016. See also Xavier Dégremont, "Bottled Océan 2115—George Nuku—Muséum de Rouen," interview with George Nuku, 21 May 2015, http://www.dailymotion.com/video/x2r289a

183. Nuku, in an interview with Xavier Dégremont.

184. Reuben Friend, *George Nuku: Bottled Ocean 2116*, Pātaka Art + Museum, Porirua, 21 February–15 May 2016, exhibition pamphlet, n.p.

185. Friend, *George Nuku.*

CHAPTER 3

1. The organizers of 350 Pacific are contracted to the umbrella organization 350.org, a global grassroots climate movement founded in 2008 and active in over 188 countries.

2. Author's interview with Fenton Lutunatabua (Pacific communications coordinator, 350 Pacific) and Koreti Tiumalu (Pacific region coordinator, 350 Pacific), Suva, Fiji, 3 February 2016.

3. See Aaron Packard, "Four Ways the Pacific Climate Warrior Coal Blockade Reshaped the Future," blog post, 5 January 2015, *Huffpost Green*, http://www.huffingtonpost.com/aaron-packard/four-ways-the-pacific-cli_b_6112078 .html

4. Wolfgang Kempf and Elfriede Hermann, "Uncertain Futures of Belonging: Consequences of Climate Change and Sea-Level Rise in Oceania," epilogue to Hermann, Kempf, and van Meijl, *Belonging in Oceania*, 189.

5. Kempf and Hermann, "Uncertain Futures of Belonging," 190.

6. Tony Crook and Peter Rudiak-Gould, "Introduction: Pacific Climate

Cultures," in *Pacific Climate Cultures: Living Climate Change in Oceania*, ed. Tony Crook and Peter Rudiak-Gould (Warsaw: De Gruyter, 2018), 2.

7. Elizabeth Ferris, Michael M. Cernea, and Daniel Petz, *On the Front Line of Climate Change and Displacement: Learning from and with Pacific Island Countries* (London: Brookings Institution, London School of Economics Project on Internal Displacement, 2011), 9.

8. Ferris, Cernea, and Petz, *On the Front Line*. See also L. A. Nurse, R. F. McLean, J. Agard, L. P. Briguglio, V. Duvat-Magnan, N. Pelesikoti, E. Tompkins, and A. Webb, "Small Islands," in *Climate Change 2014: Impacts, Adaptation, and Vulnerability. Part B: Regional Aspects. Contribution of Working Group II to the Fifth Assessment Report of the Intergovernmental Panel on Climate Change*, ed. V. R. Barros, C. B. Field, D. J. Dokken, M. D. Mastrandrea, K. J. Mach, T. E. Bilir, M. Chatterjee, K. L. Ebi, Y. O. Estrada, R. C. Genova, B. Girma, E. S. Kissel, A. N. Levy, S. MacCracken, P. R. Mastrandrea, and L. L. White (Cambridge: Cambridge University Press, 2014), 1613–54.

9. Nurse et al., "Small Islands," 1625.

10. Ferris, Cernea, and Petz, *On the Front Line*, 10. Also, John R. Campbell, "Climate-Change Migration in the Pacific," *Contemporary Pacific* 26, no. 1 (2014): 10.

11. Ferris, Cernea, and Petz, *On the Front Line*, 25–26, 28.

12. Carol Farbotko, "Wishful Sinking: Disappearing Islands, Climate Refugees and Cosmopolitan Experimentation," *Asia Pacific Viewpoint* 51, no. 1 (April 2010): 48.

13. Wolfgang Kempf, "A Sea of Environmental Refugees? Oceania in an Age of Climate Change," in *Form, Macht, Differenz: Motive und Felder ethnologischen Forschens*, ed. Elfriede Hermann, Karin Klenke, and Michael Dickhardt (Göttingen: Universitätsverlag Göttingen, 2009), 195.

14. Ferris, Cernea, and Petz, *On the Front Line*, 1.

15. Carol Farbotko, "Tuvalu and Climate Change: Constructions of Environmental Displacement in the *Sydney Morning Herald*," *Geografiska Annaler (Series B)* 87 (2005): 281.

16. Ferris, Cernea, and Petz, *On the Front Line*, 1.

17. Carol Farbotko and Heather Lazrus, "The First Climate Refugees? Contesting Global Narratives of Climate Change in Tuvalu," *Global Environmental Culture* 22 (2012): 385.

18. Kempf, "Sea of Environmental Refugees," 195.

19. John Connell, "Losing Ground? Tuvalu, the Greenhouse Effect and the Garbage Can," *Asia Pacific Viewpoint* 44, no. 2 (August 2003): 104.

20. Patrick D. Nunn, "The End of the Pacific? Effects of Sea Level Rise on Pacific Island Livelihoods," *Singapore Journal of Tropical Geography* 34, no. 2 (2013): 143.

21. Elizabeth M. DeLoughrey, *Allegories of the Anthropocene* (Durham, NC: Duke University Press, 2019), 170.

22. DeLoughrey, *Allegories of the Anthropocene*, 168–69. For a discussion of how climate-threatened Pacific Islands and Islanders are routinely framed in Western documentary film, see chapter 5, "An Island Is a World," 165–96.

23. Farbotko and Lazrus, "First Climate Refugees," 382.

24. Farbotko and Lazrus, "First Climate Refugees," 385.
25. Farbotko and Lazrus, "First Climate Refugees," 383.
26. Farbotko, "Wishful Sinking," 58.
27. Farbotko and Lazrus, "First Climate Refugees," 386.
28. Farbotko and Lazrus, "First Climate Refugees," 382.
29. Crook and Rudiak-Gould, "Introduction," 9.
30. See Peter Rudiak-Gould, "Promiscuous Corroboration and Climate Change Translation: A Case Study from the Marshall Islands," *Global Environmental Change* 22 (2012): 46–54.
31. Kempf and Hermann, "Uncertain Futures," 197.
32. See Crook and Rudiak-Gould, "Introduction."
33. Elizabeth DeLoughrey, "The Sea Is Rising: Visualising Climate Change in the Pacific Islands," *Pacific Dynamics* 2, no. 2 (November 2018): 192.
34. In *Allegories of the Anthropocene*, DeLoughrey acknowledges that "this [situation] is rapidly changing" (192), mainly with reference to poetry and blogs.
35. From his novel *1984*.
36. In addition, there is a regional body of song and dance performance that is not part of the determinedly "theatrical" framing I am using here but is important to acknowledge.
37. Kempf and Hermann, "Uncertain Futures," 194.
38. Kempf and Hermann, "Uncertain Futures," 194.
39. Kempf and Hermann, "Uncertain Futures," 195.
40. Lisa Woynarski, Adelina Ong, Tanja Beer, Stephanie Beaupark, Jonah Winn-Lenetsky, Rulan Tangen, and Michelle Nicholson-Sanz, "Dossier: Climate Change and the Decolonized Future of Theatre," *Theatre Research International* 45, no. 2 (July 2020): 179.
41. Woynarski et al., "Dossier," 182.
42. "Pacific Climate Warriors—6 Months Video," 350.org, 5 May 2015, 350 .org/pcw6monthsvideo/
43. These are the Federated States of Micronesia, Fiji, Kiribati, Nauru, New Caledonia, Niue, Palau, Papua New Guinea, Republic of the Marshall Islands, Samoa, Solomon Islands, Tokelau, Tonga, Tuvalu, and Vanuatu.
44. Aaron Packard and Koreti Tiumalu, "Koreti Tiumalu: Building a Pacific Climate Movement from New Zealand," posted 25 October 2012, 350.org, http://350.org/koreti-tiumalu-building-pacific-climate-movement-new-zeal and/
45. Lutunatabua, interview; Tiumalu, interview.
46. Jason Titifanue, Romitesh Kant, Glen Finau, and Jope Tarai, "Climate Change Advocacy in the Pacific: The Role of Information and Communication Technologies," *Pacific Journalism Review* 23, no. 1 (2017): 142, 145.
47. Kirsten Harstrup, "Waterworlds: Framing the Question of Social Resilience," in *The Question of Resilience: Social Responses to Climate Change*, ed. Kirsten Harstrup (Copenhagen: Royal Danish Academy of Sciences and Letters, 2009), 27.
48. Harstrup, "Waterworlds," 20.
49. Harstrup, "Waterworlds," 24.

50. Harstrup, "Waterworlds," 27.

51. Jane Bennett, *Vibrant Matter: A Political Ecology of Things* (Durham, NC: Duke University Press, 2010), 9.

52. Bennett, *Vibrant Matter*, xvii.

53. Kyle Whyte, "Critical Investigations of Resilience: A Brief Introduction to Indigenous Environmental Studies & Sciences," *Daedalus* 147, no. 2 (Spring 2018): 137.

54. Whyte, "Critical Investigations of Resilience," 140.

55. Hannah Fair, "Not Drowning but Fighting: Pacific Islands Activists," *Forced Migration Review* 49 (May 2015): 58.

56. 350 Pacific, "350 Pacific—Become a Climate Warrior," http://350pacific .org/our-work/what-does-it-mean-to-be-a-warrior/

57. Karen E. McNamara and Carol Farbotko, "Resisting a 'Doomed' Fate: An Analysis of the Pacific Climate Warriors," *Australian Geographer* 48, no. 1 (2017): 19, 21; see also Candice Steiner, "A Sea of Warriors: Performing an Identity of Resilience and Empowerment in the Face of Climate Change in the Pacific," *Contemporary Pacific* 27, no. 1 (2015): 147–80.

58. Tiumalu, interview.

59. Stephen Carleton, *The Turquoise Elephant* (Sydney: Currency Press, 2016). Although Visi and Vika could be (and have been) played by actors with a different ethnicity, Carleton makes it clear that the sisters are intended to be Pasifika (personal communication, 7 October 2018).

60. Lutunatabua and Tiumalu, interview with author, Suva, Fiji, 3 February 2016.

61. McNamara and Farbotko, "Resisting a Doomed Fate," 24.

62. Noelani Goodyear-Ka'ōpua, "Protectors of the Future, Not Protestors of the Past: Indigenous Pacific Activism and Mauna a Wākea," *South Atlantic Quarterly* 116, no. 1 (2017): 188.

63. Goodyear-Ka'ōpua, "Protectors of the Future," 185.

64. Goodyear-Ka'ōpua, "Protectors of the Future," 186.

65. Lutunatabua and Tiumalu, interview, 3 February 2016; Fenton Lutunatabua, "Pacific Climate Warriors Deliver Plight to Pope Francis," blog post, 8 October 2015, http://350.org/pacific-climate-warriors-deliver-plight-to-pope-fr ancis/

66. Tiumalu, interview.

67. Cecilie Rubow, "Metaphysical Aspects of Resilience: South Pacific Responses to Climate Change," in Harstrup, *Question of Resilience*, 88.

68. Rubow, "Metaphysical Aspects of Resilience," 95.

69. Rubow, "Metaphysical Aspects of Resilience," 99–100. See also here Stephen Daniels and Georgina H. Endfield, "Narratives of Climate Change: Introduction," *Journal of Historical Geography* 25 (2009): 215–22.

70. St. Francis has a special affinity with plants and animals.

71. "Encyclical Letter *Laudato Si'* of the Holy Father Francis on Care for Our Common Home," Vatican City: Vatican Press, 18 June 2015, http://w2.vatican.va /content/dam/francesco/pdf/encyclicals/documents/papa-francesco_20150524 _enciclica-laudato-si_en.pdf, 104

72. "Encyclical Letter *Laudato Si'*," 109–10.

73. "Encyclical Letter *Laudato Si'*," 13.

74. This new stance began with a one-day conference on climate change hosted by the Vatican on 28 April 2015 in anticipation of the encyclical's release.

75. Rubow, "Metaphysical Aspects of Resilience," 105–6.

76. See also Steve Bishop, "Green Theology and Deep Ecology: New Age or New Creation?," *Themelios* 16, no. 3 (1991): 8–14.

77. Pandora Fulimalo Pereira, "Lalaga: Weaving Connections in Pacific Fibre," in *Pacific Art Niu Sila: The Pacific Dimension of Contemporary New Zealand Arts*, ed. Sean Mallon and Pandora Fulimalo Pereira (Wellington: Te Papa Press, 2002), 77–79; Adrienne L. Kaeppler, "*Kie Hingoa*: Mats of Power, Rank, Prestige and History," *Journal of the Polynesian Society* 108, no. 2 (June 1999): 170; Nina Netzler von Reiche, "The Revival of 'Ie Tōga Weaving in Samoa," *Pacific Arts* 23–24 (July 2001): 113–14; Janet D. Keller, "Woven World: Neotraditional Symbols of Unity in Vanuatu," *Mankind* 18, no. 1 (April 1988): 4; "*Jaki-ed*: Marshall Islands Textiles," in *Art in Oceania: A New History*, ed. Peter Brunt and Nicholas Thomas (London: Thames and Hudson, 2012), 490–91. Also consult Te Rangihiroa / Peter Buck, *Samoan Material Culture* (Honolulu: Bishop Museum Press, 1930). Although his ideas have been widely critiqued by subsequent anthropologists, Marcel Mauss cites "the remarkable custom of exchanging emblazoned matting" (8) in the Samoan context as a foundational example of his comparative theory of gift exchange in *The Gift: The Form and Reason for Exchange in Archaic Societies*, trans. W. D. Halls (1950; New York: Norton, 1990).

78. Serge Tcherkézoff, "Subjects and Objects in Samoa: Ceremonial Mats Have a 'Soul,'" in *People and Things: Social Meditations in Oceania*, ed. Monique Jeudy-Ballini and Bernard Juillerat (Durham, NC: Carolina Academic Press, 2002), 37.

79. Lissant Bolton, "Tahigogona's Sisters: Women, Mats, and Landscape on Ambae," in *Arts of Vanuatu*, ed. Joël Bonnemaison et al. (Honolulu: University of Hawai'i Press, 1996), 115.

80. Hereniko, *Woven Gods*, 113–16.

81. *Jaki-Ed Project* (Marshall Islands), Ninth Asia-Pacific Triennial of Contemporary Art, Queensland Art Gallery | Gallery of Modern Art, Brisbane, Australia, 24 November 2018–28 April 2019.

82. It is interesting to witness an outgrowth of the concept of performing with mats in Marshallese Climate Warrior Kathy Jetñil-Kijiner's multistranded performance piece *Lorro: Of Wings and Seas* (2018), commissioned for the Ninth Asia-Pacific Triennial of Contemporary Art in Brisbane, Australia. Working with a *jaki-ed* mat as a prop, Jetñil-Kijiner draws on her experience of the weaving circle to explore how women's roles and identities are influenced by Marshallese culture, the legacy of nuclear testing, and a climate-threatened future. The performance can be viewed here: https://www.youtube.com/watch?v=BN QzCAdc-zg

83. Heather E. Young Leslie, ". . . Like a Mat Being Woven," *Pacific Arts*, New Series 3, no. 5 (2007): 124.

84. Young Leslie, "Like a Mat," 125.

85. In the sense of a source of action that can be human or nonhuman, "something that acts or to which activity is granted by others" (373). Bruno

Latour, "On Actor-Network Theory: A Few Clarifications," *Soziale Welt* 47, no. 4 (1996): 369–81.

86. Phyllis S. Herda, "The Changing Nature of Textiles in Tonga," *Journal of the Polynesian Society* 108, no. 2 (June 1999): 160.

87. Penelope Schoeffel, "Samoan Exchange and 'Fine Mats': An Historical Reconsideration," *Journal of the Polynesian Society* 108, no. 2 (June 1999): 137.

88. Lutunatabua, interview; Tiumalu, interview.

89. Young Leslie, "Like a Mat," 122.

90. "Encyclical Letter *Laudato Si'*," 63.

91. Tcherkézoff, "Subjects and Objects," 29.

92. Thomas, *Entangled Objects*, 4.

93. Thomas, *Entangled Objects*, 7, *passim*.

94. Heather Lazrus, "Sea Change: Island Communities and Climate Change," *Annual Review of Anthropology* 41 (2012): 289.

95. Author's interview with Edvard Hviding, Bergen, Norway, 31 May 2015.

96. Edvard Hviding, "The Making of *Moana* and the European Tour," *Moana: The Rising of the Sea*, devised by Vilsoni Hereniko, Peter Rockford Espiritu, Igelese Ete, Allan Alo, and Edvard Hviding, program, Bergen, Bergen International Festival, 2015, 6.

97. Vilsoni Hereniko, Peter Rockford Espiritu, Igelese Ete, and Allan Alo, *Moana: The Rising of the Sea*, DVD, ECOPAS and USP, 2014; Vilsoni Hereniko, Peter Rockford Espiritu, Igelese Ete, Allan Alo, and Edvard Hviding, *Moana Rua: The Rising of the Sea*, DVD, ECOPAS, University of Bergen and Bergen International Festival, 2015.

98. From Twitter comment posted by *Guardian* columnist Jeremy Leggett, 9 December 2009: https://mobile.twitter.com/JeremyLeggett/status/6501333764

99. On this general topic, see Elfriede Hermann and Wolfgang Kempf, "'Prophecy from the Past': Climate Change Discourse, Song Culture and Emotions in Kiribati," in Crook and Rudiak-Gould, *Pacific Climate Cultures*, 21–33.

100. *Water Is Rising: Music and Dance amid Climate Change*, dir. and prod. Judy Mitoma, UCLA Center for Intercultural Performance, in collaboration with the Foundation for World Arts, Los Angeles, 2011, https://www.youtube.com/watch?v=8O91psfnNMU; www.waterisrising.com. See also Steiner, "A Sea of Warriors."

101. Keren Zaiontz, *Theatre & Festivals* (London: Palgrave Macmillan, 2018), 4, 9.

102. Andy Bennett and Ian Woodward, "Festival Spaces, Identity, Experience and Belonging," in *The Festivalization of Culture*, ed. Andy Bennett, Jodie Taylor, and Ian Woodward (Farnham, UK: Ashgate, 2014), 18.

103. The 2013 *Moana* also included a presentation from the country of Niue.

104. Kathy Jetñil-Kijiner, "Tell Them," in Hereniko et al., *Moana: The Rising of the Sea*, program, Bergen International Festival, 2015, 19.

105. On the possibilities of melodramatic rhetoric in environmental contexts, refer to Steven Schwarze, "Environmental Melodrama," *Quarterly Journal of Speech* 92, no. 3 (2006): 239–61.

106. Shannon Davies Mancus, "Mother Earth Tied to the Train Tracks: The

Scriptive Implications of Melodrama in Climate Change Discourse," *Performing Ethos* 5, nos. 1–2 (2014): 88.

107. Mancus, "Mother Earth," 91.

108. Mancus, "Mother Earth," 89.

109. Mancus, "Mother Earth," 94, 97.

110. Carolyn Williams, "Introduction," in *The Cambridge Companion to English Melodrama*, ed. Carolyn Williams (Cambridge: Cambridge University Press, 2018), 2.

111. Williams, "Introduction."

112. Mancus, "Mother Earth," 95.

113. Author's interview with Peter Espiritu, Brussels, Belgium, 25 June 2015.

114. Williams, Introduction," 2.

115. Juliet John, *Dickens's Villains: Melodrama, Character, Popular Culture* (Oxford: Oxford University Press, 2001), 31.

116. Karen McNamara and Chris Gibson, "'We Do Not Want to Leave Our Land': Pacific Ambassadors at the United Nations Resist the Category of 'Climate Refugee,'" *Geoforum* 40 (2009): 480.

117. Kempf and Hermann, "Uncertain Futures," 195.

118. Hereniko et al., *Moana: The Rising of the Sea*, program, Bergen International Festival, 2015, 19–21.

119. Carteret Islanders from Papua New Guinea, for instance, who face climate-induced relocation, have formed the association Tulele Peisa, "sailing the waves on our own," which posits Islanders as strong and self-reliant, not refugees dependent on charity for survival (Farbotko and Lazrus, "First Climate Refugees," 383–84).

120. McNamara and Gibson, "We Do Not Want to Leave," 476.

121. McNamara and Gibson, "We Do Not Want to Leave," 479. See also Jane McAdam and Maryanne Loughry, "We Aren't Refugees," in *Climate Change and Displacement Reader*, ed. Scott Leckie, Ezekiel Simperingham, and Jordan Bakker (New York: Earthscan, 2012), 379–82.

122. Hereniko et al., *Moana: The Rising of the Sea*, program, Bergen International Festival, 2015, 22. These remarks recall former Kiribati president Anote Tong's relocation program, Migration with Dignity.

123. Michael Balfour, "Preface," in *Refugee Performance: Practical Encounters*, ed. Michael Balfour (Bristol, UK: Intellect, 2013), xx.

124. See, for instance, S. E. Wilmer, *Performing Statelessness in Europe* (Cham, Switzerland: Palgrave Macmillan, 2018); and Alison Jeffers, *Refugees, Theatre and Crisis: Performing Global Identities* (New York: Palgrave Macmillan, 2012).

125. Hedda Ransan-Cooper, Carol Farbotko, Karen E. McNamara, Fanny Thornton, and Emilie Chevalier, "Being(s) Framed: The Means and Ends of Framing Environmental Migrants," *Global Environmental Change* 35 (2015): 110.

126. Wilmer, *Performing Statelessness in Europe*, 193.

127. Kempf, "Sea of Environmental Refugees," 195.

128. Kempf, "Sea of Environmental Refugees," 200.

129. Wolfgang Kempf, "The Rainbow's Power: Climate Change Sea Level Rise, and Reconfigurations of the Noah Story in Oceania," in *Pacific Voices: Local Governments and Climate Change*, ed. Ropate Qalo (Suva, Fiji: USP Press, 2014),

83. See also Wolfgang Kempf, "Climate Change, Christian Religion and Songs: Revisiting the Noah Story in the Central Pacific," in *Environmental Transformations and Cultural Responses: Ontologies, Discourses, and Practices in Oceania*, ed. Eveline Dürr and Arno Pascht (New York: Palgrave Macmillan, 2017), 19–48.

130. This discussion of *Birds with Skymirrors* is drawn from my live experience of the Australian premiere performance at Carriageworks, Sydney, 3 May 2013, as well as from the audience talkback with Ponifasio after the show and my Zoom conversation with Ponifasio on 11 March 2021.

131. Creative New Zealand, "UNESCO Announces Lemi Ponifasio for International Dance Day," 12 April 2016, http://www.creativenz.govt.nz/news/unesco-announces-lemi-ponifasio-for-international-dance-day

132. Tim Douglas, "Choreographer Lemi Ponifasio Explores Flight and Shade with MAU Dance Group," *The Australian*, 20 April 2013; Victor Swoboda, "Ponifasio Warms to His Kiribati Dance Work," *Montreal Gazette*, 24 May 2013.

133. Francesca Horsley, "The Dance of Life," *DANZ Quarterly* 10 (January 2008): 5.

134. Balme, *Pacific Performances*, 213.

135. Dee Jefferson, "Consciousness Aerobics with a Samoan Choreographer," *Timeout* [Sydney] 5 May 2013.

136. Lisa Taouma, "Gettin' Jiggy with It: The Evolving of Pasifika Dance in New Zealand," in Mallon and Pereira, *Pacific Art Niu Sila*, 139–40.

137. Horsley, "The Dance of Life," 4.

138. Fabienne Cabado, "Interview with Lemi Ponifasio," trans. Neil Kroetsch, in Lemi Ponifasio and MAU, *Press Kit: Birds with Skymirrors*, 7th ed., 22 May–8 June (Montreal: Festival Transamériques, 2013), 4.

139. Ian Bell, "Dancing into the Darkness," *Herald Scotland*, 12 August 2010.

140. MAU performances engage profound and serious subjects, such as the social and environmental impact of colonization in *Paradise* (2003); motifs of loss, mourning, and renewal in *Requiem* (2006); state power, refugees, and human rights in *Tempest: Without a Body* (2007); the mutable and transformative character of the city in *Le Savali* (2011); and panoptical surveillance in *The Crimson House* (2014). See http://www.mau.co.nz

141. *Birds with Skymirrors*, by Lemi Ponifasio and MAU, performance program, Australian premiere, Carriageworks, Sydney, 1–4 May 2013, n.p.

142. Kyle Powys Whyte, "Indigenous Climate Change Studies: Indigenizing Futures, Decolonizing the Anthropocene," *English Language Notes* 55, nos. 1–2 (Spring–Fall 2017): 156.

143. Whyte, "Indigenous Climate Change Studies," 160. See also DeLoughrey, *Allegories of the Anthropocene*, 7.

144. Kyle Powys Whyte, "Indigenous Science (Fiction) for the Anthropocene: Ancestral Dystopias and Fantasies of Climate Change Crises," *Environment and Planning E: Nature and Space* 1, nos. 1–2 (2018): 255.

145. Whyte, "Indigenous Science (Fiction)," 225, 228–29.

146. DeLoughrey, *Allegories of the Anthropocene*, 2.

147. Lemi Ponifasio, *Lagi Moana*, installation, performance, Venice Biennale, Fifty-Sixth International Art Exhibition, Giardino delle Vergini (Arsenale), Venice, May–November 2015, exhibition notes by Lemi Ponifasio and Albert Refiti.

148. Ponifasio and Refiti, exhibition notes.

149. Ponifasio and Refiti, exhibition notes. See also Anna Schneider, "Lemi Ponifasio," in Venice Biennale, *All the World's Futures: Biennale Arte 2015 Short Guide* (Venice: Marsilio Editori, 2015), 320–21.

150. Audience talkback with Lemi Ponifasio, Carriageworks, Sydney, 3 May 2013.

151. Rāwiri Taonui, "Whakapapa—Genealogy," in *Te Ara: The Encyclopedia of New Zealand*, 1 July 2015, http://www.TeAra.govt.nz/en/whakapapa-genealogy

152. A *karanga* is an exchange of calls that begins a *pōwhiri* (formal welcome ceremony), and is carried out by women as the visiting group moves on to the *marae* (the open space in front of a Māori meeting house).

153. To stare wildly, usually for emphasis when performing a challenge, dance, or song.

154. Rapid fluttering of the hands found in Māori *kapa haka* performance. The movement is variously understood to symbolize the life force within our bodies and/or in the natural world.

155. Māori performing arts, expressed through a variety of song and dance genres.

156. "I-Kiribati Dancers Part of a New Zealand Pacific Performing Group Touring Europe," *Kiribati Independent*, 31 August 2011.

157. See the video here: "Kiribati—the Song of the Frigate," http://www.you tube.com/watch?v=xOcMLWVNIms

158. The Deepwater Horizon oil spill was the largest accidental marine oil spill in the history of the petroleum industry.

159. Samoan male tattoo, covering the lower torso, thighs, and buttocks.

160. In its conventional Māori usage, a *poi* is a small ball tethered to a string that is swung in a variety of patterns during a performance, usually involving group choreography with song and dance accompaniment.

161. Schneider, "Lemi Ponifasio," 320.

162. *Birds with Skymirrors*, performance program.

163. Elizabeth Ashley, "*Birds with Skymirrors*—MAU," review, *Dance Informa* [Sydney], 1 May 2013.

164. Natasha Gauthier, "Seeking Truth through Dance: Samoan Choreographer Inspired by Raw Reality of Pacific Islands," *Ottawa Citizen*, 13 May 2013.

165. Audience talkback with Lemi Ponifasio, Carriageworks, Sydney, 3 May 2013.

166. Francesca Horsley, "*Birds with Skymirrors*: Lemi Ponifasio, MAU," review, *DANZ Quarterly* 27 (April–June 2012): 22.

167. Hermann and Kempf, "Prophecy from the Past," 28–29.

168. Hermann and Kempf, "Prophecy from the Past," 31.

169. Tony Whincup and Joan Whincup, *Akekeia! Traditional Dance in Kiribati* (Wellington: Susan Barrie, 2001), 119.

170. Tamango, quoted in "I-Kiribati Dancers," *Kiribati Independent*.

171. Enzo Di Martino, *The History of the Venice Biennale, 1895–2005* (Venice: Papiro Arte, 2005), 7–9, 86. More recently, in addition to the Art Biennale, similar institutions have been established at Venice in architecture, cinema, dance, music, and theater.

172. Di Martino, *History of Venice Biennale*, 117, 149, 105.

173. Paolo Baratta, "The Visitor as a Partner," in *May You Live in Interesting Times: Biennale Arte 2019 Short Guide*, La Biennale di Venezia (Venice: SIAE, 2019), 34.

174. See Bernard Lagan, "Australia Urged to Prepare for Influx of People Displaced by Climate Change," *The Guardian*, 16 April 2013, https://www.theguar dian.com/environment/2013/apr/16/australia-climate-change-refugee-status; and "Kiribati Buys a Piece of Fiji," press release, *Climate Change: Republic of Kiribati*, 30 May 2014, http://www.climate.gov.ki/2014/05/30/kiribati-buys-a-pie ce-of-fiji/

175. *Sinking Islands, Unsinkable Art* (E kai maunanako te aba, te rikia e tei n nene n aki kona ni bua), Kiribati National Pavilion at the Fifty-Seventh Venice Biennale Arte, 2017, viewed 1–2 July 2017; *Pacific Time—Time Flies* (Ana tai te Betebeke—E biribiri te tai), Kiribati National Pavilion at the Fifty-Eighth Venice Biennale Arte, 2019, viewed 30 June 2019.

176. Institute Ergo Sum: Institute for Contemporary Art and Culture, "About: Visual Artist Daniela Danica Tepes," 6 May 2019: http://institute-ergosum.org /onepage/visual-artist-daniela-danica-tepes/

177. Baratta, "Visitor as a Partner," 35.

178. Katja Kwastek, *Aesthetics of Interaction in Digital Art* (Cambridge, MA: MIT Press, 2013), xvii, 194.

179. Peter Eckersall, Helena Grehan, and Edward Scheer, *New Media Dramaturgy: Performance, Media and New-Materialism* (London: Palgrave Macmillan, 2017), 14.

180. Eckersall, Grehan, and Scheer, *New Media Dramaturgy*, 2, 14.

181. Kwastek, *Aesthetics of Interaction*, 162.

182. Kwastek, *Aesthetics of Interaction*, 160.

183. Although Claire Bishop distinguishes between "interactivity" as a one-to-one relationship and "participatory art" as the involvement of many people and social relations (her focus is the latter), her skepticism about the utopian claims of participatory engagement is well taken here, especially her call for us to think about the "*quality* of relationships" fostered by such works. See "Antagonism and Relational Aesthetics," *October*, Fall 2004, 65; also, *Artificial Hells: Participatory Art and the Politics of Spectatorship* (London: Verso, 2012), 1.

184. Jesper Juul, *A Casual Revolution: Reinventing Video Games and Their Players* (Cambridge, MA: MIT Press, 2010).

185. Kiri Miller, "Gaming the System: Gender Performance in *Dance Central*," *New Media and Society* 17, no. 6 (2015): 944.

186. Bob Rehak, "Playing at Being: Psychoanalysis and the Avatar," in *The Video Game Theory Reader*, ed. Mark J. P. Wolf and Bernard Perron (New York: Routledge, 2003), 103.

187. Rehak, "Playing at Being," 106.

188. Paul Manning, "Can the Avatar Speak?," review essay, *Journal of Linguistic Anthropology* 19, no. 2 (2009): 310–25; Gayatri Chakravorty Spivak, "Can the Subaltern Speak?," in *Marxism and the Interpretation of Culture*, ed. Cary Nelson and Lawrence Grossberg (Urbana: University of Illinois Press, 1988), 271–313.

189. Kiri Miller, *Playing Along: Digital Games, YouTube, and Virtual Performance* (Oxford: Oxford University Press, 2012), 4.

190. Jennifer Parker-Starbuck, *Cyborg Theatre: Corporeal/Technological Intersections in Multimedia Performance* (Houndmills, UK: Palgrave Macmillan, 2011), 143.

191. Parker-Starbuck, *Cyborg Theatre*, 145.

192. Parker-Starbuck, *Cyborg Theatre*, 191.

193. Kwastek, *Aesthetics of Interaction*, 39.

194. Microsoft, *World Premiere Kinect Experience*, imagined by Cirque du Soleil, Electronic Entertainment Expo, Galen Center, Los Angeles, 13 June 2010, available on YouTube in three parts: Part 1: https://www.youtube.com/watch?v=vS2_3cBjQIU; Part 2: https://www.youtube.com/watch?v=xWRO7UiDtx4; Part 3: https://www.youtube.com/watch?v=idZuBjAa_cc

195. Gina Bloom, *Gaming the Stage: Playable Media and the Rise of English Commercial Theater* (Ann Arbor: University of Michigan Press, 2018), 179–80.

196. See, for example, Colin Milburn, *Mondo Nano: Fun and Games in the World of Digital Matter* (Durham, NC: Duke University Press, 2015), especially the chapter "Tempest in a Teapot."

197. Gina Bloom, Sawyer Kemp, Nicholas Toothman, and Evan Buswell, "'A Whole Theater of Others': Amateur Acting and Immersive Spectatorship in the Digital Shakespeare Game *Play the Knave*," *Shakespeare Quarterly* 67, no. 4 (2016): 417.

198. Alison Gazzard, "Standing in the Way of Control: Relationships between Gestural Interfaces and Game Spaces," in *Ctrl-Alt-Play: Essays on Control in Video Gaming*, ed. Matthew Wysocki (Jefferson, NC: McFarland, 2013), 131.

199. Daniel Paul O'Brien, "Postphenomenological Performance: Bodily Extensions in Interactive Art," *International Journal of Performance Arts and Digital Media* 13, no. 2 (2017): 134.

200. Parker-Starbuck, *Cyborg Theatre*, 144.

201. Stephanie Boluk and Patrick LeMieux, *Metagaming: Playing, Competing, Spectating, Cheating, Trading, Making, and Breaking Videogames* (Minneapolis: University of Minnesota Press, 2017), 21.

202. Boluk and LeMieux, *Metagaming*, 3–4. In this vein, see also Kishonna L. Gray and David J. Leonard, eds., *Woke Gaming: Digital Challenges to Oppression and Social Injustice* (Seattle: University of Washington Press, 2018).

203. Taukelina Finikaso, "Preface," in *Crossing the Tide: The Tuvalu Pavilion for the 56th International Art Exhibition—la Biennale di Venezia*, exhibition catalog, Tuvalu Pavilion, 2015, 1.

204. Author's conversation with Vincent Huang, 18 May 2020.

205. See Jian Yang, *The Pacific Islands in China's Grand Strategy: Small States, Big Games* (New York: Palgrave Macmillan, 2011), esp. chap. 4, "The Taipei-Beijing Diplomatic Rivalry," 51–73.

206. Iping Liang, "'Crossing the Tide': Global Environmental Imagination Tying Venice and Tuvalu," *Crossing the Tide*, exhibition catalog, 21.

207. Liang, "Crossing the Tide," 24.

208. Radio New Zealand, "One Million People Expected at Tuvalu's Venice Biennale Pavilion," 11 May 2015, https://www.rnz.co.nz/international/pacific

-news/273325/one-million-people-expected-at-tuvalu's-venice-biennale-pavi
lion

209. Vincent J. F. Huang, *Crossing the Tide*, 2015, water, fog, Venetian footbridges, projectors, aurora video. 600 × 1,700 × 1,600 cm.

210. Joanne Tompkins, *Theatre's Heterotopias: Performance and the Cultural
Politics of Space* (Houndmills, UK: Palgrave Macmillan, 2014), 1.

211. Tompkins, *Theatre's Heterotopias*, 25, 68.

212. Tompkins, *Theatre's Heterotopias*, 7, 29.

213. Tompkins, *Theatre's Heterotopias*, 69.

214. Tompkins, *Theatre's Heterotopias*, 34.

215. Tompkins, *Theatre's Heterotopias*, 40.

216. Ursula K. Heise, *Sense of Place and Sense of Planet: The Environmental Imagination of the Global* (Oxford: Oxford University Press, 2008), 59.

217. Heise, *Sense of Place*, 61.

CHAPTER 4

1. GAFA Arts Collective, "About Us," https://www.gafasamoa.com/about
-us, accessed 5 November 2018.

2. Theda Lehmann, "My Family Called Samoa," blog post, 16 October
2017, https://www.gafasamoa.com/single-post/2017/10/16/My-family-called
-Samoa. According to Lehmann, the issue of inviting a foreign delegation to
represent Samoa's interests at FestPac was subject to considerable debate in the
Samoan parliament.

3. See Caroline Sinavaiana, "Comic Theater in Samoa," in *Clowning as Critical Practice: Performance Humor in the South Pacific*, ed. W. E. Mitchell (Pittsburgh: University of Pittsburgh Press, 1992), 192–218.

4. Ferrari, *Transnational Chinese Theatres*, 9.

5. The first European to sight Samoa was the Dutch explorer Jacob Rog-
geveen in 1722, but he did not land.

6. Salesa, "Travel-Happy Samoa," 173, 172.

7. Salesa, "Travel-Happy Samoa," 174.

8. Salesa, "Travel-Happy Samoa," 175.

9. Sa'iliemanu Lilomaiava-Doktor, "Beyond 'Migration': Samoan Population Movement (*Malaga*) and the Geography of Social Space (*Vā*)," *Contemporary Pacific* 21, no. 1 (2009): 9–10.

10. To sort out colonial rivalry between Britain, the United States, and
Germany.

11. Samoa dropped the "Western" from its name in 1997. American Samoans disagreed with the name change, arguing that it diminished their own
identity, and they continue to refer to that country as Western Samoa. Sometimes "independent Samoa" is used as a disambiguation, as I do here.

12. Primarily agricultural exports, as well as tourism.

13. In other words, the territory is not a formal possession, has its own constitution, and is essentially self-governing, but is still under the supervisory
control of the US government.

14. Cluny Macpherson, "Transnationalism and Transformation in Samoan Society," in *Globalization and Culture Change in the Pacific Islands*, ed. Victoria S. Lockwood (Upper Saddle River, NJ: Pearson / Prentice Hall, 2004), 167.

15. John Connell, "Paradise Left? Pacific Island Voyagers in the Modern World," in Spickard, Rondilla, and Wright, *Pacific Diaspora*, 72.

16. Connell, "Paradise Left," 69.

17. Helen Lee, "Pacific Migration and Transnationalism: Historical Perspectives," in *Migration and Transnationalism: Pacific Perspectives*, ed. Helen Lee and Steve Tupai Francis (Canberra: ANU E-Press, 2009), 10–12.

18. Salesa, "Travel-Happy Samoa," 184.

19. Lee, "Pacific Migration and Transnationalism," 9–11.

20. Craig R. Janes, "From Village to City: Samoan Migration to California," in Spickard, Rondilla, and Wright, *Pacific Diaspora*, 119–20; Lee, "Pacific Migration and Transnationalism," 11.

21. Lee, "Pacific Migration and Transnationalism," 12.

22. Spickard, Rondilla, and Wright, *Pacific Diaspora*, 133.

23. Macpherson, "Transnationalism and Transformation," 170.

24. Macpherson, "Transnationalism and Transformation," 171.

25. Camille Nakhid, "The Concept and Circumstances of Pacific Migration and Transnationalism," in Lee and Francis, *Migration and Transnationalism*, 215.

26. Nakhid, "Concept and Circumstances," 218.

27. Paul Lyons, *American Pacificism: Oceania in the U.S. Imagination* (New York: Routledge, 2006), 199.

28. *Oxford English Dictionary*, online edition, www.oed.com, accessed 8 November 2018.

29. Migration Policy Institute, "Global Remittances Guide," https://www.migrationpolicy.org/programs/data-hub/global-remittances-guide, accessed 31 July 2020. The full range of remittances, including those that flow through informal channels, would total a much larger number. These flows, however, declined markedly in 2020 due to the coronavirus pandemic.

30. Paul Shankman, "Samoan Journeys: Migration, Remittances, and Traditional Gift Exchange," in *Change and Continuity in the Pacific: Revisiting the Region*, ed. John Connell and Helen Lee (New York: Routledge, 2018), 91.

31. Shankman, "Samoan Journeys," 94–95.

32. Peggy Levitt, "Social Remittances: Migration-Driven Local-Level Forms of Cultural Diffusion," *International Migration Review* 32, no. 4 (Winter 1998): 929. See also Levitt, *Transnational Villagers* (Berkeley: University of California Press, 2001).

33. Peggy Levitt and Deepak Lamba-Nieves, "Social Remittances Revisited," *Journal of Ethnic and Migration Studies* 37 (January 2011), 19.

34. Levitt, "Social Remittances," 926.

35. Levitt, "Social Remittances," 936.

36. Some scholars use the term "socio-cultural remittances" to indicate how remittances frequently cross the boundaries of the social and the cultural.

37. Juan Flores, *The Diaspora Strikes Back: Caribeño Tales of Learning and Turning* (New York: Routledge, 2009), 44–45.

38. Aside from a small selection of articles on dance, the only other applica-

tion of social or cultural remittances to theater practice that I have come across (and that predates citations of my own published research) is Camilla Stevens's article, "'Home Is Where Theatre Is': Performing Dominican Transnationalism," *Latin American Theatre Review*, Fall 2010, 29–48. An updated version appears in Stevens's book *Aquí and Allá: Transnational Dominican Theater and Performance* (Pittsburgh: University of Pittsburgh Press, 2019).

39. Pauliina Järvinen-Alenius, Pirkko Pitkänen, and Anna Virkama, "Transformative Impact of Social Remittances in Transnational Settings," in *Transnationalisation and Institutional Transformations*, collected working papers from the TRANS-NET Project (No 87.), ed. Thomas Faist, Pirkko Pitkänen, Jürgen Gerdes, and Eveline Reisenauer (Bielefeld: University of Bielefeld, Center on Migration, Citizenship and Development, 2010), 194.

40. Järvinen-Alenius, Pitkänen, and Virkama, "Transformative Impact," 195.

41. Sa'iliemanu Lilomaiava-Doktor, "Samoan Transnationalism: Cultivating 'Home' and 'Reach,'" in Lee and Francis, *Migration and Transnationalism*, 68.

42. Lee, "Pacific Migration," 17.

43. Helen Lee, "Generational Change: The Children of Tongan Migrants and Their Ties to the Homeland," in *Tonga and the Tongans: Heritage and Identity*, ed. E. Wood-Ellem (Melbourne: Tonga Research Association, 2007), 213.

44. Lee, "Generational Change," 213.

45. Lee, "Pacific Migration," 17.

46. For a summary overview, see Maruška Svašek, "Emotions and Human Mobility: Key Concerns," in *Emotions and Human Mobility: Ethnographies of Movement*, ed. Maruška Svašek (New York: Routledge, 2012), 1–16. See also Amanda Wise and Selvaraj Velayutham, "Transnational Affect and Emotion in Migration Research," *International Journal of Sociology* 47 (2017): 116–30. In a different context, Diane Wolf has proposed the notion of "emotional transnationalism" to describe how children of immigrants "live a kind of transnational life at the level of emotions, even if it is based in one geographical place" (285), in terms of how they "manage and inhabit multiple cultural and ideological zones" (285), often in tension. See Diane L. Wolf, "There's No Place Like 'Home': Emotional Transnationalism and the Struggles of Second-Generation Filipinos," in *The Changing Face of Home: The Transnational Lives of the Second Generation*, ed. Peggy Levitt and Mary C. Waters (New York: Russell Sage Foundation, 2002), 255–94.

47. Jenny Burman, *Transnational Yearnings: Tourism, Migration, and the Diasporic City* (Vancouver: UBC Press, 2010), 89.

48. Burman, *Transnational Yearnings*, 90.

49. Burman, *Transnational Yearnings*, 90.

50. Burman, *Transnational Yearnings*, 90.

51. Burman, *Transnational Yearnings*, 10.

52. Stevens, "Home Is Where Theatre Is," 30.

53. Stevens, "Home Is Where Theatre Is, 31.

54. Lilomaiava-Doktor, "Beyond Migration," 18.

55. Tēvita O. Ka'ili, *Marking Indigeneity: The Tongan Art of Sociospatial Relations* (Tucson: University of Arizona Press, 2017), 26. Also refer to 'Ōkusitino

Māhina, "Tā, Vā, and Moana: Temporality, Spatiality, and Indigeneity," *Pacific Studies* 33, nos. 2–3 (2010): 168–202.

56. Wendt, "Afterword," 402.

57. Lilomaiava-Doktor, "Beyond Migration," 18.

58. Ka'ili, *Marking Indigeneity*, 36–37.

59. Albert L. Refiti, "Mavae and Tofiga: Spatial Exposition of Samoan Cosmogony and Architecture" (PhD diss, Auckland University of Technology, 2014), 16.

60. Lilomaiava-Doktor, "Beyond Migration," 21.

61. I'uogafa Tuagalu, "Heuristics of the Vā," *AlterNative* 4, no. 1 (2008): 118.

62. Refiti, "Mavae and Tofiga," 14, 16, 22.

63. Levitt, "Social Remittances," 928.

64. Ka'ili, *Marking Indigeneity*, 27.

65. Carol Brown and Moana Nepia, "*Te Kore* and the Encounter of Performance," in *Collaboration in Performance Practice: Premises, Workings and Failures*, ed. Noyale Colin and Stefanie Sachsenmaier (Houndmills, UK: Palgrave, 2016), 202, 204.

66. Rosanna Raymond aka Sistar S'Pacific, "A Body of VA'rt," *Te Kaharoa*, special issue, "Ka Haka—Empowering Performance: Māori and Indigenous Performance Studies Symposium," 9 (2016): 20.

67. Raymond, "A Body of VA'rt," 21. For example, treasured ancestral objects held in overseas museums.

68. Ka'ili, *Marking Indigeneity*, 28.

69. Caroline Sinavaiana Gabbard, "Samoan Literature and the Wheel of Time: Cartographies of the Vā," *Symplokē* 26, nos. 1–2 (2018): 37.

70. Gabbard, "Samoan Literature," 45, 47.

71. Barbara Burns McGrath, "Seattle *Fa'a Sāmoa*," *Contemporary Pacific* 14, no. 2 (Fall 2002): 309.

72. "Seattle *Fa'a Sāmoa*," 309.

73. "Seattle *Fa'a Sāmoa*," 309.

74. April K. Henderson, "The I and the We: Individuality, Collectivity, and Samoan Artistic Responses to Cultural Change," *Contemporary Pacific* 28, no. 2 (2016): 316–45.

75. Cluny Macpherson and La'avasa Macpherson, "Kinship and Transnationalism," in Lee and Francis, *Migration and Transnationalism*, 87, my emphasis.

76. Quotations are taken from Tusiata Avia, *Wild Dogs under My Skirt*, solo performance, Musgrove Theatre, Auckland, New Zealand, 9–10 March 2007: https://www.youtube.com/watch?v=Se1tBljcU-w. To assist readers, page references, where relevant, are taken from Avia's published collection of poetry, *Wild Dogs under My Skirt* (Wellington: Victoria University Press, 2004). The analysis is also based on my live viewing of the ensemble performance, directed by Anapela Polata'ivao, for the Auckland Arts Festival, Q Theatre, 9 March 2019.

77. Literally the Samoan word for "pea soup," the first canned food to be introduced to the Pacific Islands. *Pisupo* is a generic term for many kinds of canned foods eaten in Samoa, including corned beef.

78. Richard Bedford, Elsie Ho, Vasantha Krishnan, and Bev Hong, "The Neighborhood Effect: The Pacific in Aotearoa and Australia," *Asian and Pacific Migration Journal* 16, no. 2 (2007): 256.

79. These opportunities have shifted with New Zealand's social attitudes and economic needs. Pacific Islanders have also been subject to a high degree of discrimination, including being targeted as migrant "overstayers" in the police's infamous "dawn raids" of the 1970s.

80. See Arts Council of New Zealand Toi Aotearoa (Creative New Zealand), 2016, *Statement of Intent Tauākī Whakamaunga Utu 2016–2021*, accessed 1 March 2019, http://www.creativenz.govt.nz/assets/paperclip/publication_documents /documents/519/original/statement_of_intent_2016_-_2021_web_final.pdf?147 5618202

81. Warrington and O'Donnell, *Floating Islanders*.

82. In Samoa, a *fa'afafine* (lit. "in the manner of a woman") is a biological male whose gendered behaviors are feminine, or who inhabits the spirit of more than one gender. While the term is also used broadly to describe those who are LGBTQI in the Western context, the ways in which *fa'afafine* identity and social roles are understood and expressed are varied and complex. See, for instance, Penelope Schoeffel, "Representing *Fa'afafine*: Sex, Socialization, and Gender Identity in Samoa," in *Gender on the Edge: Transgender, Gay, and Other Pacific Islanders*, ed. Niko Besnier and Kalissa Alexeyeff (Honolulu: University of Hawai'i Press, 2014), 73–90.

83. Literally "half caste," but without the derogatory connotations of the English term.

84. Stevens, "Home Is Where Theatre Is," 32.

85. Macpherson, "Transnationalism and Transformation," 175, 178.

86. A suburb of South Auckland with a high proportion of Pacific Islander residents.

87. Avia, *Wild Dogs*, 46.

88. See "Full Text: Helen Clark's Apology to Samoa," *NZ Herald*, 4 June 2002, https://www.nzherald.co.nz/nz/news/article.cfm?c_id=1&objectid=204 4857. For a good historical account of this period, see Mālama Meleiseā, *The Making of Modern Samoa: Traditional Authority and Colonial Administration in the History of Western Samoa* (Suva, Fiji: Institute of Pacific Studies, University of the South Pacific, 1987), esp. chaps. 5 and 6.

89. Avia, *Wild Dogs*, 47. Umu refers to an earth oven, ground oven, cooking pit.

90. Avia, *Wild Dogs*, 47.

91. White people.

92. Avia, *Wild Dogs*, 25.

93. Avia, *Wild Dogs*, 25.

94. Avia, *Wild Dogs*, 41.

95. "Who Are Those Women?," *Tales from Pasifika*, blog post, 18 February 2014, https://talesfrompasifika.com/tag/teine-sa/

96. Avia, *Wild Dogs*, 65.

97. Lana Lopesi, "The Power of Mangy Dogs," n.p., performance program. *Wild Dogs under My Skirt* by Tusiata Avia, directed by Anapela Polata'ivao, Silo

Theatre, copresentation with the Auckland Arts Festival | Te Ahurei Toi o Tāmaki Makaurau and Victor Rodger—FCC, Q Theatre (Rangatira), Auckland, 7–11 March 2019.

98. Wendt, "Afterword," 403.

99. Wendt, "Afterword," 403.

100. Juniper Ellis, *Tattooing the World: Pacific Designs in Print and Skin* (New York: Columbia University Press, 2008), 21, 22.

101. Ellis, *Tattooing the World*, 32–33.

102. Ellis, *Tattooing the World*, 25.

103. In this case, the change was significant. As the story goes, having learned *tatau* in Fiji, Ta'emā and Tilafaigā swam back to Samoa, singing that the women should be tattooed and not the men. On their way, however, due to the cold and the stress of the journey (in one version, the sisters are distracted by spying a clam on the ocean floor and diving down to get it), the words of their song were reversed: they now sang that men, not women, should be tattooed. Although there are male and female tattoos in Samoa, the men's *tatau* is the more pronounced design. See Robert D. Craig, *Handbook of Polynesian Mythology* (Santa Barbara: ABC-CLIO, 2004), 246–47.

104. Ellis, *Tattooing the World*, 33.

105. Warrington and O'Donnell, *Floating Islanders*, 182.

106. Nicholas Wright, "The Task of the Tusitala: Tusiata Avia's *Wild Dogs under My Skirt*," *Journal of Commonwealth Literature* 46, no. 2 (2011): 232.

107. Ellis, *Tattooing the World*, 169.

108. Avia, *Wild Dogs*, 66.

109. The Musgrave Studio at the University of Auckland is an intimate black-box theater with fixed seating for 104; Rangatira is Q Theatre's main performance space with a flexible setup that can accommodate up to 450 people.

110. Avia, *Wild Dogs*, 32.

111. I am using this term in Erika Fischer-Lichte's sense of the continually operating feedback loop occasioned in performance by the ongoing interactions of performers and spectators, which, through the synergy between the actor's embodiment and the spectator's imagination, might lead to new understandings and insights. See Erika Fischer-Lichte, *The Transformative Power of Performance: A New Aesthetics*, trans. Saskya Iris Jain (New York: Routledge, 2008).

112. Nicola Baker, "New Zealand and Australia in Pacific Regionalism," in *The New Pacific Diplomacy*, ed. Greg Fry and Sandra Tarte (Canberra: ANU Press, 2015), 141.

113. Philippa Mein Smith, Peter Hempenstall, and Shaun Goldfinch, *Remaking the Tasman World* (Christchurch, NZ: Canterbury University Press, 2008), 62–65.

114. Suvendrini Perera, *Australia and the Insular Imagination: Beaches, Borders, Boats, and Bodies* (New York: Palgrave Macmillan, 2009), 39.

115. Perera, *Australia*, 120.

116. Davey, "We're Not Australian"; Perera, *Australia*, 57, 120.

117. Author's interview with Leah Shelton, Brisbane, Australia, 22 June 2016.

118. "Company Profile: Polytoxic," ArtsHub, 12 December 2007, http://www

.artshub.com.au/au/news-article/news/performing-arts/company-profile-polyt oxic-168865

119. Phil Brown, "Crossing Cultures: Efeso Fa'anana Puts a New Spin on Post-colonial Island Life," *Brisbane News*, 22 February 2006, 21.

120. Refiti, "Mavae and Tofiga," 5.

121. Refiti, "Mavae and Tofiga," 13.

122. Kirsten McGavin, "Being 'Nesian': Pacific Islander Identity in Australia," *Contemporary Pacific* 26, no. 1 (2014): 126–27, 142, 147.

123. For further immersion, consult—if you dare—Sven A. Kirsten, *The Book of Tiki: The Cult of Polynesian Pop in Fifties America* (New York: Taschen, 2000).

124. On the effacement of Pacific Islander representation within tiki aesthetics, see Daniel McMullin, "Tiki Kitsch, American Appropriation, and the Disappearance of the Pacific Islander Body," *LUX: A Journal of Transdisciplinary Writing and Research from Claremont Graduate University* 2, no. 1 (2013), Article 21: 1–6. Available at http://scholarship.claremont.edu/lux/vol2/iss1/21

125. Analysis based on my viewing of the live performance of *Teuila Postcards*, Cremorne Theatre, QPAC, Brisbane, 25 June 2009; as well as a video-recording of the 2006 show, courtesy of Polytoxic.

126. Fa'anana quoted in Brown, "Crossing Cultures," 21.

127. Author's interview with Leah Shelton, Brisbane, 22 June 2016.

128. *South Pacific*, dir. Joshua Logan, Twentieth Century Fox, 1958; *Blue Hawaii*, dir. Norman Taurog, Paramount Pictures, 1961.

129. Margaret Mead, *Coming of Age in Samoa: A Psychological Study of Primitive Youth for Western Civilisation* (New York: William Morrow, 1928).

130. Katrin Sieg, *Ethnic Drag: Performing Race, Nation, Sexuality in West Germany* (Ann Arbor: University of Michigan Press, 2002), 222.

131. Mary Ann Hunter, "Unpacking South Pacific Fantasies," *Realtime* 72 (April–May 2006), 35.

132. Foreigners, white people; plural of *Pālagi*.

133. Perera, *Australia*, 132.

134. McMullin, "Tiki Kitsch," 4.

135. Sieg, *Ethnic Drag*, 222.

136. Kalissa Alexeyeff, "Re-purposing Paradise: Tourism, Image and Affect," in *Touring Pacific Cultures*, ed. Kalissa Alexeyeff and John Taylor (Canberra: Australian National University Press, 2016), 407.

137. Alexeyeff, "Re-purposing Paradise," 404.

138. Alexeyeff, "Re-purposing Paradise," 403.

139. Alexeyeff, "Re-purposing Paradise," 414.

140. Alexeyeff, "Re-purposing Paradise," 416, 419.

141. Alexeyeff, "Re-purposing Paradise," 406.

142. See Fry, "Framing the Islands."

143. It is important to acknowledge the work of Paul Rae on this emerging topic, including his recent symposium, "Performing Island Australia," Australian Centre and the School of Culture and Communication, University of Melbourne, Australia, 28 November 2018.

144. Peter J. Hempenstall, *Pacific Islanders under German Rule: A Study in the*

Meaning of Colonial Resistance (Canberra: Australian National University Press, 1978), 17.

145. See Harmut Berghoff, Frank Biess, and Ulrike Strasser, eds., *Explorations and Entanglements: Germans in Pacific Worlds from the Early Modern Period to World War I* (New York: Berghahn, 2019).

146. Hempenstall, *Pacific Islanders*, 22–23.

147. Christopher Balme, chap. 5, "Kindred Spirits: Spectacles of Samoa in Wilhelminian Germany," in *Pacific Performances*, 123.

148. Peter Hempenstall, "Germany's Pacific Pearl," in *From Samoa with Love? Samoan Travellers in Germany 1895–1911: Retracing the Footsteps*, ed. Hilke Thode-Arora (Munich: Hirmer, 2014), 27.

149. Balme, *Pacific Performances*, 126.

150. Hempenstall, *Pacific Islanders*, 53.

151. Hempenstall, "Germany's Pacific Pearl," 41.

152. Avia's piece is in development with The Conch (New Zealand) and Carriageworks (Sydney), Rosanna Raymond, *Acti.VA.tion*, 2014, https://vimeo.com/110965423; Yuki Kihara, *Culture for Sale*, 2012, https://vimeo.com/40031800; Jochen Roller and Yuki Kihara, *Them and Us*, 2015, https://vimeo.com/154989326; Yuki Kihara, *Der Papālagi* (The White Man), 2016, Milford Galleries, Dunedin, New Zealand, presented in association with the Auckland Arts Festival, 24 February–31 March 2017, viewed at St Paul St Gallery Three, Auckland, 23 March 2017.

153. "About Michel Tuffery," http://micheltuffery.co.nz/about-michel-tuffery/, accessed 1 February 2019.

154. Emma Bugden, "Creating Conversations: The Work of Michel Tuffery," in Anne Loxley, Emma Bugden, Peter Johnson, and Megan Monte, *Michel Tuffery: Transforma* (Sydney: Museum of Contemporary Art Australia, 2015), 4.

155. Bugden, "Creating Conversations," 4–5.

156. Te Rangihiroa / Peter Buck reads these combs as a mix of traditional and modern aesthetics and technologies: the general shape of the comb and the intaglio carving come within the sphere of Samoan craftsmanship, but the perforated work suggests that the carved wooden comb was a modern development rendered possible by steel tools (*Samoan Material Culture*, 627).

157. Michel Tuffery, "My *Siamani-Samoa* Series," interview by Hilke Thode-Arora, in Thode-Arora, *From Samoa with Love*, 213–14; Andrew Baker, *Michel Tuffery: Siamani Samoa* (Brisbane: Andrew Baker Art Dealer, 2012), 10.

158. Tuffery, "My *Siamani-Samoa* Series," 214.

159. Author's interview with Michel Tuffery, Skype, 28 August 2016.

160. Tuffery, interview.

161. Tuffery, interview.

162. Michel Tuffery, *Siamani Samoa*, performance, Apia, Samoa, 17–22 September 2011.

163. Tuffery, "My *Siamani-Samoa* Series," 217.

164. Baker, *Michel Tuffery*, 14.

165. Author's interview with Tuffery.

166. Edgar A. Porter and Terence Wesley-Smith, "Oceania Matters," in *China*

in Oceania: Reshaping the Pacific?, ed. Edgar A. Porter and Terence Wesley-Smith (New York: Berghahn Books, 2010), 21, 22.

167. Iati Iati, "China in the Pacific: Alternative Perspectives," in *China and the Pacific: The View from Oceania*, ed. Michael Powles (Wellington: Victoria University Press, 2016), 128; A. S. Noa Siaosi, "Catching the Dragon's Tail: The Impact of the Chinese in Samoa" (MA thesis, University of Canterbury, New Zealand, 2010), 78–81.

168. Michel Tuffery, interview on Radio New Zealand, 22 November 2011, https://www.radionz.co.nz/collections/nzfa/audio/2503151/michel-tuffery

169. A *taupou* is the virginal daughter of a high chief in a village and takes the role of a ceremonial hostess at social events.

170. Selected footage from the Apia presentation of *Siamani Samoa* can be viewed in six parts on YouTube, starting here: https://www.youtube.com/watch?v=-90MZ4lJBKA, accessed August 26, 2020.

171. Refiti, "Mavae and Tofiga," 6–7.

172. Refiti, "Mavae and Tofiga," 76.

173. Refiti, "Mavae and Tofiga," 90.

174. Refiti, "Mavae and Tofiga," 36.

175. Refiti, "Mavae and Tofiga," 99.

176. Refiti, "Mavae and Tofiga," 51.

177. Refiti, "Mavae and Tofiga," 53.

178. Refiti, "Mavae and Tofiga," 110.

179. Michel Tuffery and the Royal Samoa Police Band, *Siamani Samoa*, Carriageworks, Sydney, 18 July 2015.

180. Refiti, "Mavae and Tofiga," 222.

181. Refiti, "Mavae and Tofiga," 195.

182. Refiti, "Mavae and Tofiga," 231.

183. Refiti, "Mavae and Tofiga," 24.

184. Refiti, "Mavae and Tofiga," 127.

185. Refiti, "Mavae and Tofiga," 193.

186. Refiti, "Mavae and Tofiga," 231.

187. A drink made from the root of the *Piper methysticum* mixed with water.

188. Michel Tuffery and the Royal Samoa Police Band, *Siamani Samoa*, program, Carriageworks, Sydney, 16–18 July 2015.

189. Author's interview with Tuffery.

190. For an excellent account of this era, see Joseph Kennedy, *The Tropical Frontier: America's South Sea Colony* (Mangilao: Micronesian Area Research Center, University of Guam, 2009).

191. Stephen R. Koletty, "The Samoan Archipelago in Urban America," in *Geographical Identities of Ethnic America: Race, Space, and Place*, ed. Kate A. Berry and Martha L. Henderson (Reno: University of Nevada Press, 2002), 132.

192. Janes, "From Village to City," 120.

193. Here and throughout, biographical and professional information about Taulapapa is drawn from three interviews with the artist via Skype and Zoom, 19 August 2013, 30 August 2013, and 18 June 2020.

194. Taulapapa, interview, 19 August 2013.

195. Taulapapa, interview.

196. Taulapapa, interview.

197. Dan Taulapapa McMullin, *Pink Heaven*, typescript, 2000. Courtesy of the playwright. All page references are to this document, 14.

198. Kezia Page, *Transnational Negotiations in Caribbean Diasporic Literature: Remitting the Text* (New York: Routledge, 2011), 9.

199. Page, *Transnational Negotiations*, 82.

200. This trope is not, of course, confined to the Pacific. See, for instance, Sharae Deckard, *Paradise Discourse, Imperialism, and Globalization: Exploiting Eden* (New York: Routledge, 2010).

201. Lyons, *American Pacificism*, 124.

202. Taulapapa, *Pink Heaven*, 1.

203. Taulapapa, *Pink Heaven*, 1.

204. Taulapapa, *Pink Heaven*, 26.

205. Taulapapa, *Pink Heaven*, 2.

206. Taulapapa, *Pink Heaven*, 11.

207. Taulapapa, *Pink Heaven*, 3.

208. Taulapapa, *Pink Heaven*, 11.

209. Taulapapa, *Pink Heaven*, 21.

210. A ceremonial presentation and gift exchange that accompanies major life events like weddings, graduations, funerals, etc.

211. Taulapapa, *Pink Heaven*, 51.

212. Taulapapa, *Pink Heaven*, 2.

213. Literally, "two blood"; Taulapapa's preferred term instead of *afakasi*.

214. Taulapapa, *Pink Heaven*, 34.

215. Taulapapa, *Pink Heaven*, 48.

216. Taulapapa, *Pink Heaven*, 60–61.

217. Taulapapa, interview, 30 August 2013.

218. Rod Edmond, *Representing the South Pacific: Colonial Discourse from Cook to Gauguin* (Cambridge: Cambridge University Press, 1997), 196.

219. Edmond, *Representing the South Pacific*, 200.

220. Edmond, *Representing the South Pacific*, 205.

221. Taulapapa, *Pink Heaven*, 42.

222. This episode is based on Taulapapa's experience of many *fa'afafine* of his acquaintance who faced pressure to polarize by living either as transgender women or as gay men after migrating to the United States. Interview, 30 August 2013. This situation is also true in other sites like New Zealand: see Johanna Schmidt, *Migrating Genders: Westernisation, Migration, and Samoan Fa'afafine* (Farnham, UK: Ashgate, 2010).

223. Taulapapa, *Pink Heaven*, 38–39.

224. Taulapapa, *Pink Heaven*, 40.

225. Taulapapa, *Pink Heaven*, 47.

226. Taulapapa, *Pink Heaven*, 41.

227. Taulapapa, *Pink Heaven*, 49.

228. Maja Horn, "Queer Caribbean Homecomings: The Collaborative Art Exhibits of Nelson Ricart-Guerrero and Christian Vauzelle," *GLQ* 14, nos. 2–3 (2008): 363–64.

229. Horn, "Queer Caribbean Homecomings," 363.

230. Horn, "Queer Caribbean Homecomings," 363.

231. Horn, "Queer Caribbean Homecomings," 376.

232. Taulapapa, interview, 30 August 2013.

233. Dan Taulapapa McMullin, "Over My Queer Samoan Body," blog post, 7 July 2016, from *Poetry* magazine: https://www.poetryfoundation.org/harriet/20 16/07/pm-over-my-queer-samoan-body/

234. Sinavaiana Gabbard, "Samoan Literature," 45, 47.

235. I have written elsewhere about this aspect of Kneubuhl's oeuvre in "'The Ancestors That We Carry On Our Backs': Restaging Hawai'i's History in the Plays of Victoria Nalani Kneubuhl." *The Contemporary Pacific* 23, no. 1 (January 2011): 73–104 and chapter 4 of *Remaking Pacific Pasts*.

236. See W. S. Maugham, *A Writer's Notebook* (Toronto: Heinemann, 1949), 105–6; and "Rain" in *The Trembling of a Leaf* (London: Heinemann, 1935), 234–95.

237. Daniel Akiyama, interview with Victoria Nalani Kneubuhl, Kumu Kahua March Happenings Newsletter, 26 March 2011, n.p.

238. Victoria Nalani Kneubuhl, *The Holiday of Rain*, dir. Harry Wong III, performance program, Kumu Kahua Theatre, Honolulu, 24 March–23 April 2011.

239. Akiyama interview.

240. A Sadie Thompson Inn does in fact exist in Pago Pago, and is reputed to be the place where Sadie hung her red light.

241. All page references in this section are to *The Holiday of Rain*, Draft 4, unpublished typescript, 2010. Courtesy of Victoria Kneubuhl, 5. My analysis is also based on my viewing of the live performance at Kumu Kahua Theatre on 22 April 2011.

242. Balme, *Pacific Performances*, 146–47.

243. Balme, *Pacific Performances*, 157, 160–63.

244. One could of course say the same thing about Aotearoa New Zealand, but the difference in this context is that New Zealand has its own modern history of sovereign status and neocolonial power—as exercised in Samoa—which is not the case with Hawai'i.

245. Kneubuhl, *The Holiday of Rain*, 11.

246. Kneubuhl, *The Holiday of Rain*, 13.

247. Kneubuhl, *The Holiday of Rain*, 13.

248. Kneubuhl, *The Holiday of Rain*, 30.

249. Kneubuhl, *The Holiday of Rain*, 23.

250. Kneubuhl, *The Holiday of Rain*, 51.

251. Kneubuhl, *The Holiday of Rain*, 76.

252. Kneubuhl, *The Holiday of Rain*, 35.

253. Kneubuhl, *The Holiday of Rain*, 25.

254. Rob Wilson, *Be Always Converting, Be Always Converted: An American Poetics* (Cambridge, MA: Harvard University Press, 2009), 75.

255. Wilson, *Be Always Converting*, 80.

256. Wilson, *Be Always Converting*, 79.

257. Wilson, *Be Always Converting*, 80.

258. Wilson, *Be Always Converting*, 80, 120–21.

259. Kneubuhl, *The Holiday of Rain*, 74.

260. Fepulea'i Micah Van der Ryn, "Return Migration to American Samoa," *Pacific Studies* 35, nos. 1–2 (April–August 2012): 255.

261. Macpherson and Macpherson, "Kinship and Transnationalism," 87.

262. See Immanuel Wallerstein, *Capitalist Agriculture and Origins of the European World-Economy in the Sixteenth Century*, vol. 1 of *The Modern World System* (New York: Academic Press, 1974).

263. Van der Ryn, "Return Migration," 256–57.

CHAPTER 5

1. James Nokise, Te Kahu Rolleston, and Jahra "Rager" Wasasala, "Combination of Three Pieces in an Urbanesian Political Presentation," New Zealand delegation, University of Guam Fine Arts Theatre, for the Twelfth Festival of Pacific Arts, Guam, 31 May 2016.

2. Readers may recall that Larry Thomas's Fijian urban drama *The Visitors* was programmed at FestPac in 2008 but failed to reflect desired notions of Pacific identity (chapter 2). In the Urbanesian case, this group presentation of identity was accepted as part of that "Pacificness."

3. David O'Donnell, ed., *Urbanesia: Four Pasifika Plays* (Wellington: Playmarket, 2012); Urbanesia Festival, Auckland, New Zealand: www.urbanesia.org .nz

4. The scholars now working in the field of urban performance studies are too numerous to list individually here, as are the many essays and monographs on the broad subject. But key questions for the development of the subfield have been laid out in a number of texts and collections, including Jen Harvie, *Theatre & the City* (2009); D. J. Hopkins, Shelley Orr, and Kim Solga, eds., *Performance and the City* (2009); D. J. Hopkins and Kim Solga, eds., *Performance and the Global City* (2013); Nicolas Whybrow, ed., *Performance and the Contemporary City: An Interdisciplinary Reader* (2010); and Nicolas Whybrow, ed., *Performing Cities* (2014), all published by Palgrave Macmillan.

5. Whybrow, "Introduction," in *Performance and the Contemporary City*, 12.

6. D. J. Hopkins and Kim Solga, "Introduction: Borders, Performance, and the Global Urban Condition," in *Performance and the Global City*, 11.

7. This term is Henri Lefebvre's, and usefully fuses the notion of *citizen* with that of *denizen* and *inhabitant* to describe membership of a community of urban dwellers that is not circumscribed by national citizenship. See Henri Lefebvre, *Writings on Cities*, ed. and trans. Eleonore Kofman and Elizabeth Lebas (Oxford: Blackwell, 1996), 34.

8. John Connell and John Lea, *Urbanisation and the Island Pacific: Towards Sustainable Development* (New York: Routledge, 2002), 1.

9. Connell and Lea, *Urbanisation*, 15.

10. Connell and Lea, *Urbanisation*, 28.

11. Connell and Lea, *Urbanisation*, 26.

12. Connell and Lea, *Urbanisation*, 33.

13. Connell and Lea, *Urbanisation*, 35.

14. Paul Jones and Asian Development Bank, *The Emergence of Pacific Urban Villages: Urbanization Trends in the Pacific Islands* (Mandaluyong City, Metro Manila, Philippines: Asian Development Bank, 2016).

15. Fulimalo Pereira, "Arts Specific: Pacific Peoples and New Zealand's Arts," in *Tangata o le Moana: New Zealand and the People of the Pacific*, ed. Sean Mallon, Kolokesa Māhina-Tuai, and Damon Salesa (Wellington: Te Papa Press, 2012), 326.

16. Manuhuia Barcham, "The Challenge of Urban Maori: Reconciling Conceptions of Indigeneity and Social Change," *Asia Pacific Viewpoint* 39, no. 3 (December 1998): 303–14. See also Natacha Gagné, *Being Māori in the City: Indigenous Everyday Life in Auckland* (Toronto: University of Toronto Press, 2013).

17. Pereira, "Arts Specific," 326.

18. Sean Mallon and Pandora Fulimalo Pereira, "Pacific Art Niu Sila: Introduction," in Mallon and Pereira, *Pacific Art Niu Sila*, 7.

19. Raymond, quoted in Caroline Vercoe and Robert Leonard, "Pacific Sisters: Doing It for Themselves," *Art Asia Pacific*, no. 14 (1997): para. 10, http://robertleonard.org/pacific-sisters-doing-it-for-themselves/

20. Te Papa Tongarewa, Museum of New Zealand, "21st Sentry Cyber Sister by Pacific Sisters," 2007, https://collections.tepapa.govt.nz/topic/1547, accessed 26 September 2019.

21. Mallon and Pereira, "Pacific Art Niu Sila," 9–10.

22. Pereira, "Arts Specific," 319. See also, inter alia, Robbie Shilliam, *The Black Pacific: Anti-colonial Struggles and Oceanic Connections* (London: Bloomsbury, 2015); and April K. Henderson, "Dancing between Islands: Hip Hop and the Samoan Diaspora," in *The Vinyl Ain't Final: Hip Hop and the Globalization of Black Popular Culture*, ed. Dipannita Basu and Sidney J. Lemelle (London: Pluto, 2006), 180–99.

23. Jakki Leota-Ete, Shigeyuki Kihara, and Rosanna Raymond, "Body Beautiful: New Zealand Fashion—Pacific Style," in Mallon and Pereira, *Pacific Art Niu Sila*, 100.

24. Author's conversation with Courtney Sina Meredith, Zoom, 19 January 2021.

25. O'Donnell, *Urbanesia*, 261.

26. O'Donnell, *Urbanesia*, 265.

27. All page references to *Rushing Dolls* are from the version published in O'Donnell, *Urbanesia*, 266.

28. Meredith, *Rushing Dolls*, 274.

29. In Lefebvre's sense, rather than Foucault's; that is, liminal social spaces that hold the possibility, through collective action, to create something different in urban daily life.

30. Karangahape Road, one of the main streets in Auckland's central business district and one of the city's cultural centers.

31. Meredith, *Rushing Dolls*, 268. Tagging is an act of hand-style graffiti writing; a dairy is like a convenience store or corner store. South Auckland is not an official place-name, but often refers to an urban area of Auckland with lower incomes than other parts of the city, and with a young, largely Māori/Pasifika demographic.

32. Meredith, *Rushing Dolls*, 293.

33. Meredith, *Rushing Dolls*, 296.

34. Meredith, *Rushing Dolls*, 307.

35. Richard L. Florida, *Cities and the Creative Class* (New York: Routledge, 2005), 34.

36. Florida, *Cities*, 1.

37. Makerita Urale, *Frangipani Perfume*, in *Mapaki/Frangipani Perfume*, by Dianna Fuemana and Makerita Urale (Wellington: Play Press, 2004), 1–35.

38. Meredith, *Rushing Dolls*, 279.

39. Meredith, *Rushing Dolls*, 279.

40. Meredith, *Rushing Dolls*, 294.

41. Meredith, *Rushing Dolls*, 296.

42. Henri Lefebvre, "The Right to the City," in *Writings on Cities*, 158.

43. Lefebvre, "Introduction" to *Space and Politics*, in *Writings on Cities*, 194–95.

44. Lefebvre, "Introduction," 195.

45. Mark Purcell, "Excavating Lefebvre: The Right to the City and Its Urban Politics of the Inhabitant," *GeoJournal* 58 (2002): 103.

46. Purcell, "Excavating Lefebvre," 102.

47. Purcell, "Excavating Lefebvre," 99, 101.

48. Lefebvre, "Right to the City," 158.

49. See, for instance, David Harvey, *Rebel Cities: From the Right to the City to the Urban Revolution* (London: Verso, 2013).

50. Meredith, *Rushing Dolls*, 311.

51. Meredith, *Rushing Dolls*, 312.

52. José Esteban Muñoz, "Preface: Fragment from the *Sense of Brown* Manuscript," *GLQ* 24, no. 4 (2018): 395–97.

53. David O'Donnell, "Foreword" to Mīria George, *and what remains* (Wellington: Tawata Press, 2007), viii. All subsequent page references to the play are from this published edition.

54. Adam Goodall, "A Woman, Leaving: An Oral History of *and what remains*," *Pantograph Punch*, 17 July 2016: https://www.pantograph-punch.com/posts/a-woman-leaving-an-oral-history-and-what-remains

55. That is, Overseas Experience, an aspirational rite of passage for many young New Zealanders.

56. Max Hirsh, *Airport Urbanism: Infrastructure and Mobility in Asia* (Minneapolis: University of Minnesota Press, 2016), 7.

57. Stephen Graham and Simon Marvin, *Splintering Urbanism: Networked Infrastructures, Technological Mobilities and the Urban Condition* (New York: Routledge, 2001), 122.

58. Manuel Castells, *The Rise of the Network Society*, 2nd ed. (Malden, MA: John Wiley & Sons, 2010), xliv.

59. Graham and Marvin, *Splintering Urbanism*, 122.

60. Graham and Marvin, *Splintering Urbanism*, 122.

61. Graham and Marvin, *Splintering Urbanism*, 122.

62. See Gillian Fuller and Ross Harley, *Aviopolis: A Book about Airports* (London: Black Dog, 2004).

63. John D. Kasarda and Greg Lindsay, *Aerotropolis: The Way We'll Live Next* (New York: Farrar, Straus and Giroux, 2011); see also John Kasarda, *The Rise of the Aerotropolis* (Washington, DC: Urban Land Institute, 2000).

64. Hirsh, *Airport Urbanism*, 5, 11.

65. Hirsh, *Airport Urbanism*, 12.

66. Marc Augé, *Non-places: Introduction to an Anthropology of Supermodernity*, trans. John Howe (London: Verso, 1995), 34.

67. Augé, *Non-places*, 52, 101.

68. Augé, *Non-places*, 77–78.

69. Augé, *Non-places*, 103, 104.

70. Augé, *Non-places*, 107, 79.

71. Augé, *Non-places*, 94.

72. Christopher Schaberg, *The Textual Life of Airports: Reading the Culture of Flight* (London: Continuum, 2011), 1.

73. Schaberg, *The Textual Life of Airports*, 36.

74. Henri Lefebvre, "The Social Text," in *Henri Lefebvre: Key Writings*, ed. Stuart Elden, Elizabeth Lebas, and Eleonore Kofman (New York: Continuum, 2003), 91.

75. Schaberg, *Textual Life of Airports*, 36.

76. Schaberg, *Textual Life of Airports*, 89.

77. Brendan Hokowhitu, "Producing Indigeneity," in *Indigenous in the City*, ed. Evelyn Peters and Chris Andersen (Vancouver: UBC Press, 2013), 360.

78. An affluent suburb of Auckland.

79. "Nationhood," address by Don Brash, leader of the National Party to the Orewa Rotary Club, 27 January 2004: http://www.scoop.co.nz/stories/PA0401/S00220.htm

80. Brash, "Nationhood."

81. George, *and what remains*, 32.

82. Hokowhitu, "Producing Indigeneity," 371.

83. George, *and what remains*, 27.

84. George, *and what remains*, 35.

85. George, *and what remains*, 47.

86. George, *and what remains*, 20.

87. Don Brash, "National's Immigration Plan: A Responsible Middle Course," speech in Wanganui near the beginning of the general election campaign outlining National Party immigration policy, 9 August 2005: http://www.donbrash.com/national-party/nationals-immigration-plan-a-responsible-middle-course/

88. Te Punga Somerville, *Once Were Pacific*, 207, 208.

89. George, *and what remains*, 36.

90. George, *and what remains*, 27.

91. George, *and what remains*, 61.

92. George, *and what remains*, 76.

93. George, *and what remains*, 77.

94. Hokowhitu, "Producing Indigeneity," 354.

95. George, *and what remains*, 5.

96. Auckland Art Gallery Toi o Tāmaki, "Home AKL," art exhibition, 7 July

2012–22 October 2012: https://www.aucklandartgallery.com/whats-on/exhibiti on/home-akl, accessed 8 October 2019.

97. Anthony Byrt, *This Model World: Travels to the Edge of Contemporary Art* (Auckland: Auckland University Press, 2016), 43.

98. Byrt, *This Model World*, 43–45.

99. Byrt, *This Model World*, 45.

100. Byrt, *This Model World*, 45.

101. Byrt, *This Model World*, 51.

102. See John Vea, "The Emic Avenue: Art through *Talanoa*" (master's thesis, Auckland University of Technology, 2015).

103. Ioana Gordon-Smith, "Planting Objects, Yielding Stories," blog post, 26 October 2015, https://ioanagordonsmith.com/2015/10/26/planting-objects-yield ing-stories/

104. Vea adds the English plural to "taros," and I have followed his usage throughout.

105. Scott Hamilton, "Planting Plaster: John Vea and the Art of Migrant Labor," *EyeContact*, 14 January 2014, http://eyecontactsite.com/2014/01/planti ng-plaster-john-vea-and-the-art-of-migrant-l

106. Author's conversation with John Vea, Skype, 11 November 2019.

107. HEPT was created by Vea and two fellow art school students at the Auckland University of Technology to provide support and encouragement for Māori and Pasifika art students, who had high attrition rates. The initiative eventually extended to all the art schools in Auckland, emphasizing alternative ways of learning that drew upon Indigenous perspectives in contrast to Western pedagogies (author's conversation with Vea).

108. Auckland Council, "Waterfront Plan | Te Mahere mō te Taha Moana," 2019, https://www.aucklandcouncil.govt.nz/plans-projects-policies-reports-byl aws/our-plans-strategies/place-based-plans/Pages/waterfront-plan.aspx, accessed 14 October 2019; Panuku Development Auckland, "Wynyard Quarter," 2019, https://www.panuku.co.nz/wynyard-quarter, accessed 14 October 2019. See also https://www.wynyard-quarter.co.nz

109. John Vea, funding statement, *Cultivate*, 2015: https://www.boosted.org .nz/projects/cultivate

110. Gordon-Smith, "Planting Objects, Yielding Stories."

111. Pradeep C. Deo, Anand P. Tyagi, Mary Taylor, Douglas K. Becker, and Robert M. Harding, "Improving Taro (*Colocasia esculenta var. esculenta*) Production Using Biotechnological Approaches," *South Pacific Journal of Natural Science* 27 (2009): 6.

112. Inno Onwueme, *Taro Cultivation in Asia and the Pacific* (Bangkok: Food and Agriculture Organization of the United Nations, Regional Office for Asia and the Pacific, 1999), v, 3.

113. Juliana Flinn, *Mary, the Devil, and Taro: Catholicism and Women's Work in a Micronesian Society* (Honolulu: University of Hawai'i Press, 2010), 67.

114. Benjamin D. Jones, Thegn N. Ladefoged, and Gregory Asner, "Tracing the Resilience and Revitalisation of Historic Taro Production in Waipi'o Valley, Hawai'i," *Journal of the Polynesian Society* 124, no. 1 (2015): 83, 87.

115. Onwueme, *Taro Cultivation*, 3.

116. Deo et al., "Improving Taro," 8, 7.

117. See Cabranes-Grant, *From Scenarios to Networks*, 5, 13.

118. John Vea and HEPT Collective, *Cultivate*, Papakura Art Gallery, Auckland, 2013. Analysis based on a video-recording of the performance, courtesy of the artist.

119. The song tells of two sets of footsteps on the beach that have now become one. A version of the song is also sung from the perspective of a man whose female lover is going away (sometimes in a migrant context).

120. Author's conversation with John Vea.

121. Gordon-Smith, "Planting Objects, Yielding Stories"; see also Ioana Gordon-Smith, "Visible Traces," blog post, 1 October 2013, https://ioanagordon smith.com/2013/10/01/visible-traces/

122. Author's conversation with John Vea.

123. Luke Willis Thompson in conversation with Polly Staple, Chisenhale Gallery, London, 24 June 2017, https://vimeo.com/225657347

124. Luke Willis Thompson, *Luke Willis Thompson*, exhibition, curated by Stephen Cleland, Adam Art Gallery | Te Pātaka Toi, Wellington, 21 February–15 April 2018. I am grateful to Stephen Cleland for his conversation with me on 11 August 2020.

125. Annie Armstrong, "'Black Pain Is Not for Profit': Collective Protests Luke Willis Thompson's Turner Prize Nomination at Tate Britain," *ARTnews*, 25 September 2018, http://www.artnews.com/2018/09/25/black-pain-not-profit-col lective-protests-luke-willis-thompsons-turner-prize-nomination-tate-britain/

126. Tina Campt, "Adjacency: Luke Willis Thompson's Poethics of Care," *Flash Art* 327 (September–October 2019), https://flash---art.com/article/adjacen cy-luke-willis-thompsons-poethics-of-care/

127. Campt, "Adjacency."

128. Campt, "Adjacency."

129. See Shilliam, *Black Pacific*; and Taketani, *Black Pacific Narrative*.

130. Shilliam, *Black Pacific*, 174.

131. Taketani, *Black Pacific Narrative*, 12.

132. Jodi Kim, "Militarization," in Lee, *Routledge Companion*, 154.

133. Kim, "Militarization," 155.

134. Kim, "Militarization," 164.

135. Exhibition notes, Thompson, *Luke Willis Thompson*.

136. Stephen Cleland, "Embodied Timelines," in *The Time of the Now: Collected Papers and Interviews from the 2018 Circuit Symposium and Artist Week* (Auckland, 2018), https://www.circuit.org.nz/sites/default/files/2019.03.01_ti me_of_the_now_final_0.pdf, 44.

137. Torika Bolatagici, "Export Quality: Representing Fijian Bodies and the Economy of War," *Asia Pacific Viewpoint* 52, no. 1 (2011): 9.

138. Bolatagici, "Export Quality," 9.

139. Cleland, "Embodied Timelines," 45.

140. Brigitte Weingart, "'That Screen Magnetism': Warhol's Glamour," *October* 132 (Spring 2010): 49.

141. Noa Steimatsky, *The Face on Film* (New York: Oxford University Press, 2017), 181.

142. Harvey Young, *Embodying Black Experience: Stillness, Critical Memory, and the Black Body* (Ann Arbor: University of Michigan Press, 2010), 27.

143. Stephen Graham, "When Life Itself Is War: On the Urbanization of Military and Security Doctrine," *International Journal of Urban and Regional Research* 36, no. 1 (2012): 137.

144. Jaclyn M. D'Esposito, "Are Officers Equipped to Protect and Serve Their Communities? An Examination into the Militarization of America's Police and Police Legitimacy," *Notre Dame Journal of Law, Ethics & Public Policy* 30 (2016): 407–8.

145. Kashif Jerome Powell, "The Time to Break (Silence): Disavowing the Affects of Militarization and Death through the Performance of Black Experience," in *Performance in a Militarized Culture*, ed. Sara Brady and Lindsey Mantoan (New York: Routledge, 2018), 319.

146. Steimatsky, *The Face on Film*, 223.

147. Callie Angell, *Andy Warhol Screen Tests: The Films of Andy Warhol Catalogue Raisonné*, vol. 1 (New York: Abrams, in association with the Whitney Museum of American Art, New York, 2006), 14.

148. Steimatsky, *The Face on Film*, 9.

149. Amelia Jones, *Self/Image: Technology, Representation and the Contemporary Subject* (New York: Routledge, 2006), xvii, 23.

150. Judith Butler, *Precarious Life: The Powers of Mourning and Violence* (New York: Verso, 2004), 132.

151. Butler, *Precarious Life*, 137.

152. Butler, *Precarious Life*, 135.

153. Butler, *Precarious Life*, 140.

154. Butler, *Precarious Life*, 144.

155. Butler, *Precarious Life*, 145.

156. Alex Quicho, "Luke Willis Thompson *Autoportrait* at Chisenhale," *ArtReview*, 4 September 2017, https://artreview.com/reviews/online_review_aug_2017_luke_willis_thompson/

157. Black Lives Matter, "About—Black Lives Matter," https://blacklivesmatter.com/about/, accessed 16 November 2019.

158. Powell, "Time to Break (Silence)," 325–26.

159. Greg Dvorak, *Coral and Concrete: Remembering Kwajalein Atoll between Japan, America, and the Marshall Islands* (Honolulu: University of Hawai'i Press, 2018), 7. Dvorak's penetrating cross-cultural history, which insightfully connects Asia, the United States, and the Pacific Islands, is well worth a patient, considered read.

160. Connell and Lea, *Urbanisation*, 39.

161. Connell and Lea, *Urbanisation*, 39.

162. Dvorak, *Coral and Concrete*, 8.

163. Dvorak, *Coral and Concrete*, 8, 9.

164. Quoted in Stewart Firth, *Nuclear Playground* (Honolulu: University of Hawai'i Press, 1987), 66.

165. Sasha Davis, *The Empires' Edge: Militarization, Resistance, and Transcending Hegemony in the Pacific* (Athens: University of Georgia Press, 2015), 40.

166. Robert Barclay, *Meḷaḷ: A Novel of the Pacific* (Honolulu: University of Hawai'i Press, 2002), 3–4.

167. Barclay, *Meḷaḷ*, 9.

168. Hirsh, *Airport Urbanism*, viii.

169. Keith L. Camacho and Laurel A. Monnig, "Uncomfortable Fatigues: Chamorro Soldiers, Gendered Identities, and the Question of Decolonization in Guam," in *Militarized Currents: Toward a Decolonized Future in Asia and the Pacific*, ed. Setsu Shigematsu and Keith L. Camacho (Minneapolis: University of Minnesota Press, 2010), 153.

170. Camacho and Monnig, "Uncomfortable Fatigues," 153.

171. Setsu Shigematsu and Keith L. Camacho, "Introduction: Militarized Currents, Decolonizing Futures," in Shigematsu and Camacho, *Militarized Currents*, xxvi.

172. Victor Bascara, Keith L. Camacho, and Elizabeth DeLoughrey, "Gender and Sexual Politics of Pacific Island Militarisation: A Call for Critical Militarisation Studies," *Intersections: Gender and Sexuality in Asia and the Pacific* 37 (March 2015): para. 2, http://intersections.anu.edu.au/issue37/bascara_camacho_delou ghrey.html

173. Davis, *Empires' Edge*, 2.

174. Bascara, Camacho, and DeLoughrey, "Gender and Sexual Politics," para. 1.

175. Bascara, Camacho, and DeLoughrey, "Gender and Sexual Politics," para. 16.

176. Bascara, Camacho, and DeLoughrey, "Gender and Sexual Politics," para. 1.

177. Mike Allen, "America's First Pacific President," *Politico*, 13 November 2009, https://www.politico.com/story/2009/11/americas-first-pacific-president -029511

178. Bascara, Camacho, and DeLoughrey, "Gender and Sexual Politics," paras. 2 and 5.

179. Davis, *Empires' Edge*, 5, 6.

180. Walden Bello, "From American Lake to a People's Pacific in the Twenty-First Century," in Shigematsu and Camacho, *Militarized Currents*, 311.

181. Brian Ireland, *The US Military in Hawai'i: Colonialism, Memory and Resistance* (Houndmills, UK: Palgrave, 2011), xiii–xiv. By way of example: I grew up in the South Island of New Zealand just down the road from a US Air Force base at Christchurch Airport, which provides military support for the United States' Antarctic Program.

182. Shigematsu and Camacho, *Militarized Currents*, xxi.

183. Bello, "American Lake," 312.

184. Davis, *Empires' Edge*, 38.

185. Antonio Benítez-Rojo, *The Repeating Island: The Caribbean and the Postmodern Perspective*, 2nd ed., trans. James E. Maraniss (Durham, NC: Duke University Press, 1996), 9.

186. Davis, *Empires' Edge*, 70.

187. B. A. Harmon, W. D. Goran, and R. S. Harmon, "Military Installations

and Cities in the Twenty-First Century: Towards Sustainable Military Installations and Adaptable Cities," in *Sustainable Cities and Military Installations*, ed. Igor Linkov, NATO Science for Peace and Security Series—C: Environmental Security (Dordrecht: Springer, 2014), 22.

188. Harmon, Goran, and Harmon, "Military Installations and Cities," 22.

189. Harmon, Goran, and Harmon, "Military Installations and Cities," 25. A theatrical glimpse of this Baseworld occurs in the Shakespearean adaptation *Moore – A Pacific Island Othello* (2020) by Native Hawaiian playwright, filmmaker, and former US Marine Kepano (Stephen) Richter. Set within the US Marine Corps, the play addresses issues of race and American imperialism in the Pacific in the late Trump years as its characters are deployed across military sites from the US mainland to Hawaiʻi, Okinawa, and Korea. See https://global shakespeares.mit.edu/moore-taft-mattos-justina-2020/#video=moore-taft-matt os-justina-2020

190. C. T. Perez, "Inside Out," in *Indigenous Literatures from Micronesia*, ed. Evelyn Flores and Emelihter Kihleng (Honolulu: University of Hawaiʻi Press, 2019), 81.

191. Perez, "Inside Out," 81.

192. Perez, "Inside Out," 83.

193. Air force base on Guam.

194. Jan Furukawa, "Local," in Flores and Kihleng, *Indigenous Literatures from Micronesia*, 79.

195. Furukawa, "Local," 79.

196. Furukawa, "Local," 80.

197. Davis, *Empires' Edge*, 18–19.

198. Giorgio Agamben, *Homo Sacer: Sovereign Power and Bare Life*, trans. Daniel Heller-Roazen (Stanford: Stanford University Press, 1998).

199. Firth, *Nuclear Playground*, 1–2.

200. Nic Maclellan, *Grappling with the Bomb: Britain's Pacific H-Bomb Tests* (Canberra: Australia National University Press, 2017), xv.

201. See Elizabeth DeLoughrey, "The Myth of Isolates: Ecosystem Ecologies in the Nuclear Pacific," *Cultural Geographies* 20, no. 2 (2013): 167–84.

202. Firth, *Nuclear Playground*, 34.

203. Firth, *Nuclear Playground*, 8.

204. Maclellan, *Grappling with the Bomb*, 6.

205. Maclellan, *Grappling with the Bomb*, 7.

206. Maclellan, *Grappling with the Bomb*, 12.

207. Hugh Gusterson, *Nuclear Rites: A Weapons Laboratory at the End of the Cold War* (Berkeley: University of California Press, 1996), 104.

208. Gusterson, *Nuclear Rites*, 104.

209. Gusterson, *Nuclear Rites*, 109.

210. Gusterson, *Nuclear Rites*, 154.

211. DeLoughrey, *Allegories of the Anthropocene*, 171–72. The very process of testing, with its drive for feedback for ever greater effectiveness, might usefully be connected to Jon McKenzie's concept of "techno-performance"; see *Perform or Else: From Discipline to Performance* (London: Routledge, 2001).

212. On metaphors, see discussions in Gusterson, *Nuclear Rites*; DeLoughrey, *Allegories of the Anthropocene*; and Michelle Keown, "War and Redemption: Militarism, Religion and Anti-colonialism in Pacific Literature," in *Anglo-American Imperialism and the Pacific: Discourses of Encounter*, ed. Michelle Keown, Andrew Taylor, and Mandy Treagus (New York: Routledge, 2018). On the semantics of the bikini, see Teresia Teaiwa, "Bikinis and Other S/pacific N/oceans," *Contemporary Pacific* 6, no. 1 (1994): 87–109.

213. Tracy C. Davis, *Stages of Emergency: Cold War Nuclear Civil Defense* (Durham, NC: Duke University Press, 2007), 1, 2.

214. Firth, *Nuclear Playground*, xi.

215. For a balanced historical account, consult Keith M. Parsons and Robert A. Zaballa, *Bombing the Marshall Islands: A Cold War Tragedy* (Cambridge: Cambridge University Press, 2017).

216. The version of Kathy Jetñil-Kijiner's "History Project" quoted here is from *Indigenous Literatures from Micronesia*, ed. Evelyn Flores and Emelihter Kihleng (Honolulu: University of Hawai'i Press, 2019), 114. The performance can be viewed here: https://www.youtube.com/watch?v=DIIrrPyK0eU

217. Jetñil-Kijiner, "History Project," 112–13.

218. Jetñil-Kijiner, "History Project," 115.

219. Jetñil-Kijiner, "History Project," 113.

220. Jetñil-Kijiner, "History Project," 115.

221. Jetñil-Kijiner, "History Project," 115.

222. Herbs, *Light of the Pacific*, musical album, Warrior Records, 1983.

223. Matsuda, *Pacific Worlds*, 321.

224. For a capillary analysis of these events and their contexts, see Malcolm Templeton, *Standing Upright Here: New Zealand in the Nuclear Age, 1945–1990* (Wellington: Victoria University Press, 2006).

225. See Roy H. Smith, *The Nuclear Free and Independent Pacific Movement after Moruroa* (London: I. B. Tauris, 1997).

226. Matsuda, *Pacific Worlds*, 319, 323.

227. For one useful survey, see Michelle Keown, "Waves of Destruction: Nuclear Imperialism and Anti-nuclear Protest in the Indigenous Literatures of the Pacific," *Journal of Postcolonial Writing* 54, no. 5 (2018): 585–600.

228. Angelique Chrisafis, "French Nuclear Tests 'Showered Vast Area of Polynesia with Radioactivity,'" *The Guardian*, 3 July 2013, https://www.theguardian.com/world/2013/jul/03/french-nuclear-tests-polynesia-declassified

229. Teresia Teaiwa, "Reading Paul Gauguin's *Noa Noa* with Epeli Hau'ofa's *Kisses in the Nederends*: Militourism, Feminism, and the 'Polynesian' Body," in Wilson and Hereniko, *Inside Out*, 251.

230. Analysis based on my live viewing of *Les Champignons de Paris*, dir. François Bourcier, Le Petit Théâtre, La Maison de la Culture, Pape'ete, Tahiti, 19 and 20 October 2019.

231. Emilie Génaédig and Compagnies du Caméléon, *Les Champignons de Paris—au nom de la paix: Pièce de théâtre sur les essais nucléaires français*, trans. Emma Faua-Tufariua, *Te mau tuputupuā a Paris—no te hau nei ā: Ha'uti teata i ni'a i te mau tāmatamatara'a 'atomi a Farāni* (Pape'ete: Editions Haere Pō, 2017). All

page references to the play are from the French text in this published edition, translations mine.

232. Achille Mbembe, *Necropolitics*, trans. Steven Corcoran (Durham, NC: Duke University Press, 2019), 19.

233. Mbembe, *Necropolitics*, 80.

234. Miriam Kahn, *Tahiti beyond the Postcard: Power, Place, and Everyday Life* (Seattle: University of Washington Press, 2011), 72.

235. The term "slow violence" is taken from Rob Nixon, in his sense of "a violence that occurs gradually and out of sight, a violence of delayed destruction that is dispersed across time and space, an attritional violence that is typically not viewed as violence at all" (2). In Rob Nixon, *Slow Violence and the Environmentalism of the Poor* (Cambridge, MA: Harvard University Press, 2011).

236. Keown, "War and Redemption," 43.

237. Génaédig, *Les Champignons de Paris*, 21.

238. Mbembe, *Necropolitics*, 77.

239. Mbembe, *Necropolitics*, 92.

240. This 1966 fallout, in fact, spread over much of the South Pacific, including the Tuamotu and Society Islands, the Cook Islands, Samoa, Fiji, and Kiribati.

241. Génaédig, *Les Champignons de Paris*, 30.

242. Mbembe, *Necropolitics*, 77.

243. Génaédig, *Les Champignons de Paris*, 31.

244. Génaédig, *Les Champignons de Paris*, 41.

245. Génaédig, *Les Champignons de Paris*, 42.

246. Kahn, *Tahiti beyond the Postcard*, 43–45, 70, 73–75; Bengt Danielsson and Marie-Thérèse Danielsson, *Poisoned Reign: French Nuclear Colonialism in the Pacific*, 2nd ed. (Ringwood, VIC: Penguin, 1986), 83–86.

247. Danielsson and Danielsson, *Poisoned Reign*, 11.

248. Génaédig, *Les Champignons de Paris*, 48.

249. Génaédig, *Les Champignons de Paris*, 48.

250. Pacific Testing Center, the organization responsible for the nuclear testing program.

251. Génaédig, *Les Champignons de Paris*, 32.

252. Génaédig, *Les Champignons de Paris*, 33.

253. French (mis)spelling of Moruroa.

254. Génaédig, *Les Champignons de Paris*, 34.

255. Génaédig, *Les Champignons de Paris*, 59–60.

256. Génaédig, *Les Champignons de Paris*, 60.

257. Génaédig, *Les Champignons de Paris*, 74.

258. See Pieter de Vries and Han Seur, *Moruroa and Us: Polynesians' Experiences during Thirty Years of Nuclear Testing in the French Pacific* (Lyon: Centre de Documentation et de Recherche sur la Paix et les Conflits, 1997).

259. Génaédig, *Les Champignons de Paris*, 72.

260. Génaédig, *Les Champignons de Paris*, 74.

CHAPTER 6

1. Simon Winchester, *Pacific: Silicon Chips and Surfboards, Coral Reefs and Atom Bombs, Brutal Dictators, Fading Empires, and the Coming Collision of the World's Superpowers* (New York: Harper, 2015), 22.

2. Winchester, *Pacific*, 17, 3, 22.

3. Chris Ballard, "Pacific Futurities," in *Pacific Futures Past and Present*, ed. Warwick Anderson, Miranda Johnson, and Barbara Brookes (Honolulu: University of Hawai'i Press, 2018), 280.

4. Ballard, "Pacific Futurities," 280.

5. Hoskins and Nguyen, *Transpacific Studies*, 7.

6. Suzuki, "Transpacific," 352.

7. California is first mentioned as an island in a Spanish romance of the early 1500s. The concept became firmly embedded on European maps and persisted—despite substantial evidence to the contrary—until the eighteenth century. Eventually, Spanish king Ferdinand VI outlawed the practice by royal decree in 1747, stating simply: "California is not an island." For a historical overview, refer to Dora Beale Polk, *The Island of California: A History of the Myth* (Lincoln: University of Nebraska Press, 1995).

8. Diaz, "To P," 189.

9. See, for instance, Jon McKenzie, "Is Performance Studies Imperialist?," *TDR* 50, no. 4 (T192) (Winter 2006): 5–8; Janelle Reinelt, "Is Performance Studies Imperialist? Part 2," *TDR* 51, no. 3 (T195) (Fall 2007): 7–16; D. Raznovich, Richard Schechner, Eugenio Barba, Kusuhara Tomoko, Takahashi Yuichiro, William Huizhu Sun, Diana Taylor, and Guillermo Gómez-Peña, "Is Performance Studies Imperialist? Part 3: A Forum," *TDR* 51, no. 4 (T196) (Winter 2007): 7–23; Jon McKenzie, Heike Roms, and C. J. W.-L. Wee, "Introduction: Contesting Performance in an Age of Globalization," in *Contesting Performance: Global Sites of Research*, ed. Jon McKenzie, Heike Roms, and C. J. W.-L. Wee (Houndmills, UK: Palgrave Macmillan, 2010), 1–22; selected essays in Harding and Rosenthal, *Rise of Performance Studies* (2011); and conference debates held at Performance Studies (small i) international. For a particularly clear-eyed critique from beyond the American academy, see Nien Yuan Cheng, "Globalisation, Transgression, and the Call to Performance Studies," *About Performance* 14–15 (2017): 261–84. See also Stephanie Nohelani Teves, "The Theorist and the Theorized: Indigenous Critiques of Performance Studies," *TDR* 62, no. 4 (T240) (Winter 2018): 131–40; and Sharon Mazer's essay, "Uneasy Reckonings: A Response to 'The Theorist and the Theorized: Indigenous Critiques of Performance Studies' by Stephanie Nohelani Teves (*TDR* 62.4 T240)," *TDR* 63, no. 2 (T242) (Summer 2019): 195–99.

10. Diana Taylor in Raznovich et al., "Is Performance Studies Imperialist? Part 3," 22.

11. Charlotte McIvor and Justine Nakase, "Annotated Bibliography," in *The Methuen Drama Handbook of Interculturalism and Performance* (London: Methuen, 2020), 239.

12. McIvor and Nakase, "Annotated Bibliography," 240.

13. D. Soyini Madison, "'That Was My Occupation': Oral Narrative, Performance, and Black Feminist Thought," *Text and Performance Quarterly* 13, no. 3 (July 1993): 213.

14. Madison, "That Was My Occupation," 215, 216.

15. On this point, see Dwight Conquergood, "Of Caravans and Carnivals: Performance Studies in Motion," in *Cultural Struggles: Performance, Ethnography, Praxis*, ed. E. Patrick Johnson (Ann Arbor: University of Michigan Press, 2013), 26–31.

16. Conquergood, "Of Caravans and Carnivals," 26.

17. Wakeham, "Beyond Comparison," 125.

18. Teresia Teaiwa, "AmneSia," in *Terenesia: Amplified Poetry and Songs by Teresia Teaiwa and Sia Figiel*, Hawaii Dub Machine, 2000, CD.

Index